The Court and Public Policy

The Court
and
Public Policy

by Robert H. Birkby

CQ Press

a division of

Congressional Quarterly Inc.
1414 22nd Street N.W., Washington, D.C. 20037

Printed in the United States of America

Library of Congress Cataloging in Publication Data

Birkby, Robert H., 1930-
    The Court and public policy

    Bibliography: p.
    1. Civil rights—United States—Cases.
2. Public policy (Law)—United States—Cases.
3. United States.   Supreme Court.   I. Title
KF4748.B57   1983   342.73'085'02643   82-22014
ISBN 0-87187-248-X   347.3028502643

To My Family

Preface

This casebook is the outgrowth of a frustration that often arises in teaching a standard undergraduate course in constitutional law. The necessity for breadth of coverage precludes the attainment of significant depth in any one issue area, an appreciation for or awareness of subtle changes in the Supreme Court's interpretation, and an understanding of the reaction of other policymakers to the Court's decisions. While I remain convinced that the usual case law course is the base on which all other undergraduate public law courses must be built, it seemed to me that a collection of cases and materials such as this one could solve the above problems and be a useful supplement to the standard fare or, alternatively, could be a second step in a student's exploration of this "subfield" of political science.

The work of the Supreme Court as a whole could not be treated in this way without utilizing multiple volumes. The issue areas included here are merely representative of Court policymaking and interaction with other participants in the political process. In choosing the issues to be included two criteria were applied. The issue had to be of contemporary importance, and it had to illustrate some facet of the Court's involvement in policymaking. Other issues could have been chosen under the same criteria, but the areas of reapportionment, equal protection, capital punishment, free press, and abortion seemed to create a viable combination.

The reader will find there are no final answers offered to the questions raised by these materials and will note that in many instances the participants' future actions will have to be watched to see how the argument is resolved. One of the fascinating things about being a Supreme Court watcher is that any day's news can upset all earlier notions about the current state of the law.

In editing the decisions, I have been painfully aware of the loss caused by dropping part of the argument presented by the justices. Nevertheless, some paragraphs and even pages had to be omitted for reasons of space; every effort was made to distill the essential points and to avoid distorting the development of the Court's position or analysis. Omitted materials are indicated by the traditional ellipses.

A number of people have contributed to whatever merits this casebook may have. The members of the Court have done most of the work by writing the decisions. My colleagues J. Leiper Freeman, George J. Graham, Jr., Michael C. Nelson, Richard A. Pride, and Benjamin Walter have patiently endured monologues on the subject. Department Chairman William C. Havard has been supportive in a number of ways. Mildred W. Tyler and Elizabeth R. McKee have typed and retyped and have remained pleasant about it. At Congressional Quarterly, Susan Sullivan and Mary McNeil have encouraged me, made consistently helpful suggestions, and saved me from a number of embarrassing errors. Finally, and probably most importantly, two groups of students—one freshman seminar and one upper-level class—have cheerfully permitted me to try out these materials and this approach on them. Of course, errors of both omission and commission are solely my responsibility.

Robert H. Birkby

Table of Contents

The Court and Public Policy

INTRODUCTION: JUDGES AS POLICYMAKERS

"Do judges make law?" "Hell, yes! Made some myself," was the exchange between a law student and a New England jurist. The judge's response states the primary theme of this casebook: Courts do make law—public policy—and the judges know it. This should cause no surprise. It's not a new revelation despite judicial efforts to be modest about it. Nor is this state of affairs peculiar to the United States although it may exist to a greater extent here than in most other countries. Courts in any political system participate to some degree in the policymaking process because it is their job. Any judge faced with a choice between two or more interpretations and applications of a legislative act, executive order, or constitutional provision must choose among them because the controversy must be decided. And when the judge chooses, his or her interpretation becomes policy for the specific litigants. If the interpretation is accepted by other judges, the judge has made policy for all jurisdictions in which that view prevails. Chief Justice Charles Evans Hughes once said that the "Constitution is what the judges say it is," but he could have broadened that to include all law. And law, of course, is one expression of public policy.

This power of the courts to make policy is inherent in the judicial function. Courts have not usurped the power from some other part of government; it is theirs of necessity. The only way to oust the courts from their participation in policymaking would be for other policymakers (especially legislatures) to express their wishes in language specific enough to avoid ambiguity and broad enough to cover every conceivable contingency. But such a state of legislative exactness and prescience never was and never will be.

This is not to assert that the courts are indistinguishable from other makers of policy or that they can ever replace them. The courts can and must be differentiated from both legislative and executive policymakers because it is from those differences that they draw both their strengths and weaknesses. There are at least ten characteristics in this process of differentiation; some are fairly obvious while others require some explication.[1]

1. *The courts have no "self-starter."* This phrase, coined by Justice Robert H. Jackson, simply means that judges have to wait for problems to be brought to them; they do not, despite occasional appearances to the contrary, have a roving commission to go out and cure whatever ills they consider worth eradicating. If there is no controversy, there is no litigation. If there is no litigation, there is no judicial policymaking even though a judge might wish to make law in the issue area. On the other hand, a legislature or executive can identify and define a problem, devise a solution for it, and adopt the solution without any request from an outside source. Legislatures and executives may take the initiative; courts may not.

2. *The courts decide on specific issues shaped both by the demands made by the litigants and the technical rules of the judicial process.* Lawsuits are normally presented to the courts in specific, concrete, and particularized form. The judge is forced to take that particular set of facts and a specific plea for relief and make a rule that will resolve the immediate problem. That rule may or may not be applicable to other situations. Sometimes the facts are so idiosyncratic that the decision is pertinent only to the litigants of the moment. Other times the facts are sufficiently unusual for later litigants to assert that a different or contrary decision is warranted by them. A legislature, on the other hand, starts with rules of general application that are broad enough to cover a wide spectrum of similar but not identical facts. The reasoning and policymaking processes are different; the former is inductive and the latter deductive.

The rules of the judicial process and the demands of the litigants determine the manner in which the problem is presented to the judge. Anyone may seek action from a legislature or administrative agency, but the person seeking to invoke the power of the courts must have "standing to sue,"* must present a "case or controversy," † must show direct legal injury for which there is an available remedy, and must have exhausted state or administrative remedies before a judge will listen to the complaint. These requirements shape the issue presented for resolution. School desegregation, for example, was presented to the courts as a question of whether a given set of facts constituted a state's denial of equal protection of the laws as guaranteed in the Constitution. But the same issue could have been argued before a school board or state legislature as providing quality education for all children in the community or as the social utility of desegregation or integration. The way an issue is presented may have a

---

*The plaintiff has "standing to sue" only when asserting a personal right or claim rather than claims of other persons or of the general public.

†A "case or controversy" is a real dispute in which rights or claims are in conflict. Hypothetical or abstract arguments do not present a case or controversy.

profound effect on the solution adopted by the policymaker. A judge is presented with a specific person or persons seeking action on certain facts that have been adjusted to meet the rules of the judicial process.

3. *The judge must make a decision.* In practically all instances, judges do not have the legislative luxury of deciding not to decide. The facts may be too peculiar, the litigant the wrong person, the timing wrong for the acceptance of policy, and the state of the law too fluid for a good decision. But having started, the judge must move on to a conclusion and an order. In some instances the judge may find that the issue has been mooted by the passage of time or that a "political question" is presented. He may avoid a decision, but this will not happen too often.* The U.S. Supreme Court has greater discretionary control over its caseload than has just been suggested, but even there, after the case has been accepted and argued, a conclusion must be reached. In addition, as in other areas, a decision not to decide is a policy choice because it leaves the status quo intact.

4. *The judge is confined by the doctrine of stare decisis.*† What has been decided in previous and similar cases must be the starting point for the judge and in a majority of instances will be the end result as well. Adherence to precedent in the common law system gives to the law a degree of certainty which, along with adaptability, is one of its prime requirements. However, American courts have not been slaves to precedent; they have shown a willingness to overrule prior decisions when their usefulness has passed and society has changed. In contrast, the legislative process encourages consideration of departures from the settled way of doing things.

5. *The judge is often confined by statutory or constitutional language.* In other words, the judge usually is not confronted with a blank slate. He or she generally will be constrained not only by precedent but by constitutional requirements that may not be ignored, and by legislative action which ought not to be. The legislature may have foreclosed several solutions to the problem presented by the litigation. Or it may have declared a preferred method of dealing with the problem. In either event, the judge must shape decisions within the imposed constraints or run the risk of conflict with the legislature or executive. Legislators, of course, are equally restrained by

---

*Passage of time may so alter the relationship of the parties to each other that there is no longer an issue for the courts to resolve. It will then be dismissed for mootness. The political question is defined by the Court in *Baker* v. *Carr* (p. 53). A political question is one given to another branch of the government by the Constitution; it is a separation of powers limitation on the exercise of judicial power.
†"Stare decisis" means "let the decision stand." The phrase is a reminder that a judge should follow precedent rather than depart from it.

constitutional provisions as construed by the Supreme Court, but their earlier pronouncements on an issue may be repealed or ignored. The legislature is much freer than the courts to declare that the game henceforth will be played according to new rules.

6. *The judge may not have access to a broad range of facts bearing on the issue.* The rules of evidence may restrict the judge's view of the problem, the number of available solutions, and the nature and weight of the arguments for and against each possible choice. Subjective opinions, perfectly acceptable in the legislative chamber, usually are not germane in the courtroom. Only since the development of the "Brandeis Brief"* have medical, economic, and social opinions become acceptable to the courts even though they have long had their place in legislative committee reports. There is still some doubt about the propriety of judicial use of such information. One of the most persistent criticisms of the 1954 school desegregation decision (*Brown* v. *Board of Education of Topeka*, p. 104) has been its reliance on psychological and sociological evidence which many argue is not as conclusive as data developed by the natural sciences. Antitrust cases are sometimes decided without judges hearing the most detailed and sophisticated economic analysis. This is done because of some lingering doubt that such testimony is appropriate for the judicial forum. By contrast, legislatures have no compunctions about gathering every piece of information that might have a bearing on proposed statutes.

7. *Judges and lawyers tend to be generalists rather than specialists.* Legal education is a general education with little opportunity for the development of narrow expertise. Some practicing lawyers have the chance to specialize as they develop professionally, but attorneys who ascend to the bench are expected and even required to remain generalists. A judge of a court of general jurisdiction (and this is the overwhelming majority of state court judges and all but a handful of federal court judges) must be able to shift from property to tax to contract to criminal to bankruptcy law all in the course of a day or a week. Even with nights and weekends for study it would be unreasonable to expect judges to become instant experts in each field presented to them for decision. This influences the ability and willingness of judges to consider highly technical data and arguments. Justice Oliver Wendell Holmes made the point well in his colorful style: "Judges commonly are elderly men and are more likely to hate at sight any analysis to which they are not accustomed, and which disturbs repose of mind, than to fall in love with novelties."[2]

---

*This written argument to an appellate court presenting nonlegal data was first used by Louis D. Brandeis in *Muller* v. *Oregon*, 208 U.S. 412 (1908). A novel approach to litigation at the time, it has since become standard procedure.

The important contrast here is with the tendency of legislators to specialize in one or two areas and to rely on colleagues for advice and cues in all other subject areas of legislative activity. Ironically, no student of the legislative process expects a legislator to be a generalist even though he is a member of an elected body that deals with the widest possible range of policy issues. At the same time, every student of the judicial process expects judges to be generalists capable of shifting fields as rapidly as the changing of cases being presented to them. The jurisdiction of most courts is structured to reinforce this expectation. In the United States even collegial courts have failed to display the trend toward individual specialization that has become characteristic of legislators, although Chief Justice William Howard Taft had a tendency to think of his colleagues as being experts in some fields. (He often gave opinion-writing chores to Harlan F. Stone in patent and copyright, James C. McReynolds in admiralty, and Willis VanDevanter in Indian claims, for example, and interestingly enough, those so singled out complained about it.)

The net effect of this lack of judicial specialization is that the more technical and intricate issues perhaps are not heard with the same degree of understanding in the courts as in the legislature and executive branch agencies. To compensate for this inadequacy, judges usually pay considerable respect to the decisions of "expert" agencies such as the regulatory commissions.

8. *The judge must consider remedies in a piecemeal fashion.* This repeats, from a different angle, a point already made about the form in which controversies are presented to the courts. The problems are specific and therefore the remedies must be specific and tailored to the controversy before the court. For example, in *Lochner v. New York,* 198 U.S. 45 (1905), the Supreme Court told the State of New York that it could not regulate the number of hours worked by bakers. We are not sure from that decision what the fate of legislation affecting the hours of labor in other occupations would be, although we might be able to make a good guess. The Court does not even make clear what additional evidence might be required to make a compelling case for regulating hours worked by bakers. A legal adviser could only advise a legislature to try to build a better case and then let the courts decide. The judicial decree is not well suited to the enunciation of broad, generally applicable remedies because so much of the stuff of litigation is fact and situation specific. Legislative actions, by their very nature, have a general applicability and breadth that a judge's order does not have. A legislator may have reason to believe that one action will put an issue to rest for a period of time; a judge knows that one decision will spawn more litigation as individuals and groups try to find out whether they

are within or out of its scope. In short, judicial policy tends to be even more incremental than legislative policy.

9. *The judge has no means for systematically following up on his or her orders.* Typically a court issues a decree or order and assumes that everyone affected by it will do what they are supposed to do. However, unless they retain jurisdiction in the case and require further action by the parties, judges must rely on the litigants to come back with complaints of noncompliance before there can be official awareness of that fact. Follow-up is even more difficult for an appellate court which usually remands a case to the trial court for implementation of the decision. Under those circumstances, one of the parties has to complain to the trial court about implementation and be rebuffed before the appellate court knows that there is difficulty. Still worse is the situation when a court hands down a rule in a specific case with an intent to have it generally applied. Others not party to the original litigation can continue to ignore the ruling until a lawsuit is filed against them asserting the applicability of the precedent. The school prayer decision (*School District of Abington Township v. Schempp,* 374 U.S. 203, 1963), for example, banned the use of prayer and Bible reading as a religious exercise in public schools in Baltimore, Maryland, and Abington Township, Pennsylvania. In fact, the Court meant the decision to have general application and intended for school boards across the country to note and comply with the decision. But the only way a court could become aware of a continuation of the banned practice in another jurisdiction would be for new litigation to be introduced. The contrast with the legislature is clear: statutes are of general applicability rather than addressed to specific parties; they almost always mandate some enforcement activity by the executive branch. It is the responsibility of legislative committees, either through oversight or appropriation hearings, to be sure that enforcement is taking place and producing the desired result. Courts simply do not have the same oversight capability or authority.

10. *Judges in a democratic system appear to feel constrained by the nonrepresentative nature of the judiciary.* Judges, even when elected, as some state judges are, do not have the same quality of representativeness that legislators have. This removal from the mainstream of democratically chosen officials makes judges aware that their policymaking position is not as firmly rooted in the "will of the people" as is the legislators'; no judge could ever claim to have a "mandate." The effect of this constraint is difficult to evaluate. Some judges become timid in the face of it; others become defiant, but most become sensitive to the limits of their authority and often express that sensitivity by phrases such as "deference to legislative judgment." A presumed advantage of the nonrepresentative

nature of the courts is their insulation from the vagaries and hasty shifts of public opinion and from the pressures of "special interests." But they are vulnerable to attack by majoritarians. The legislature is a better reflector of public opinion while the courts offer an opportunity for a "sober second thought."

These ten characteristics of judicial policymaking power are generally applicable to courts in any country, and each characteristic operates in obvious ways to constrain that power. The constraints on any collegial decisionmaking body are generally applicable to the Supreme Court. A majority of strong-minded and strong-willed judges must agree upon a result and, unlike a legislature, they must then agree upon a decision explaining why that result is the only one consistent with the law, good judgment, and common sense. That explanation is not always forthcoming. When it is not, the value of the decision as a guide for the future and as a means of influencing behavior is limited. Plurality opinions may settle the immediate controversy, but nothing is as convincing as a unanimous decision with only one opinion for the Court. There is more in these observations than first meets the eye. When courts are making policy at the cutting edge of the law and therefore in controversial areas, their opinions are intended more to affect general behavior and to chart a course of development than to resolve a particular dispute. But that is also the time when judges are likely to be divided among themselves on the meaning of the law and, therefore, they produce conflicting directions for other policymakers to digest. The death penalty cases contained herein are a good illustration of what can happen to doctrinal development when the Court is badly divided over policy objectives. Inevitably, the conflicting signals from the justices produce anger, frustration, and confusion among the other actors in the process and generate defiance and further litigation in an effort to elicit better guidance.

As if the foregoing were not enough to give a judge bad dreams, the American systems of checks and balances and federalism have introduced further constraints on court policymaking. Most of these are familiar to students of American government and only need to be mentioned. The president appoints federal judges with the advice and consent of the Senate and may in that way affect policy outcomes; compatability with the president's views is the prime criterion in appointments. The president also may instruct his lawyers in the Justice Department to bring certain types of cases, to refrain from bringing others, and to intervene in some in which the United States is not a party to the litigation. This is an effort to ensure that the courts are aware of the policy preferences of the president's administration. The extent to which these signals from the executive branch are heeded is unclear, but knowing what the president wants is more of a constraint than is being uncertain of his desires. And, of course, the courts are dependent on the executive branch for the enforcement of their orders. Andrew Jackson probably never actually said "John Marshall has made his decision, now let him enforce it," but he or any other president could have thrown down the gauntlet. More subtly, the rest of the executive branch can in a variety of ways alter judicial decisions; both presidents and the courts are, to a degree, at the mercy of the bureaucracy. Bureaucrats "alter" presidential and judicial decisions as they apply, interpret, and enforce them.

Congress is not without its own checks on the courts as some of the materials that follow will show. It is difficult to use the extreme power of amending the Constitution, but it has been done to overturn judicial interpretations. Many more times a simple statute is enough to clarify congressional intent and "correct" the judiciary, as was the case with the Hyde Amendment cutting off federal funding of nontherapeutic abortions for indigents. Congress may tinker with the appellate jurisdiction of the Supreme Court and with the original jurisdiction of the entire federal judiciary, although to what extent has never been tested. It may be difficult for Congress to find the time and the votes to do anything about a judicially announced policy, but it can be done when the members or their constituents are sufficiently aroused.

The Court also pays considerable deference to the position of the states and the concept of them as "laboratories for experimentation." For example, the states have used a variety of methods to ensure that criminal defendants are not unduly disadvantaged by the use of improperly seized evidence. In 1963, the Supreme Court concluded that this experimentation had been unsuccessful and imposed a uniform rule for dealing with this problem. (*Mapp v. Ohio,* 367 U.S. 643, 1963)

The very idea of a federal system requires that the states be left free to make their own decisions in some areas, and state governors, legislatures, and courts have their own ways of showing their displeasure with hyperactivity by the federal courts, including the legislative requests for calling a constitutional convention.

From all of the foregoing, it may be hard to resist Yale law professor Alexander Bickel's conclusion that the judiciary is "the least dangerous branch." Even so, the courts are with regularity accused of usurping power from some other branch of government or of deciding cases contrary to the desires of the people. Discounting the hyperbole characteristic of political rhetoric, there is no doubt that from time to time courts have thrust themselves onto center stage despite limitations that argue for no more than a supporting role. To define with precision the proper role of the courts may be impossible and certainly is beyond the intention of this collection of cases. It is hoped, however, that the activity of the courts in the policy areas presented here will illustrate the judicial role with both its strengths and limitations.

Regardless of the policy area under consideration, some questions must be asked in order to evaluate judicial policymaking. The list that follows is merely suggestive, not exhaustive, and is presented to provide a beginning for individual analysis and evaluation. The first questions address the adequacy of the court's power and reasoning in announcing the policy. Is the judicial power properly invoked? Is there a firm constitutional or statutory base supporting the decision? Is the development of the argument from premise to conclusion sound, logical, and convincing? Does the decision have to overturn the precedents or statutes to find support, and, if so, were they good solid ones or ones that time and circumstances had weakened? In short, has the judicial power been brought to bear in a reasonable, responsible, and persuasive manner?

A second set of questions is broadly interinstitutional. Is the court moving ahead of, in concert with, or contrary to the other policymaking organs of government? None of those relations is necessarily bad, but the answer may give rise to still other questions about the wisdom of the policy adopted. The same set of questions must be asked of the relation between the policy announced by the court and public opinion: Is the court following, anticipating, or bucking contemporary attitudes? And whose attitudes? Justice Benjamin N. Cardozo put the relation of the judge to public opinion ambiguously: "My own notion is that he would be under a duty to conform to the accepted standards of the community, the *mores* of the times. This does not mean, however, that a judge is powerless to raise the level of prevailing conduct." [3]

A third group of questions is perhaps more susceptible to objective answers. These concern the effectiveness of the decision. Is what the court requires clear and unambiguous? Do the persons who must implement the decision have at their disposal adequate means for carrying it out? Here we must include political means in addition to personnel, money, and material, which takes us back to the first two sets of questions. A subset of this group of questions is one that must be asked when there is opposition to the court's announced policy. What is the motivation for the opposition? What is the political basis for it? How effective is it? What do the opponents present as a policy alternative? Did the court consider that alternative and reject it? Why? And how does the court react to the opposition?

Finally, a set of questions that are often implicit but should be brought out into the open. What are the social, moral, and economic issues addressed by the policy? What are the social, moral, and economic consequences of implementing the policy? Decisions announced by any policymaker must be subjected to more than political and legal analysis.

There are no unarguable answers to any of these questions, which may be one reason why the lawyers will always be with us. However, these questions should serve as a reminder that while judges make policy, they do so within certain limits and under several constraints. Judicial policymaking is not as simple as Justice Owen J. Roberts modestly asserted: "[T]he judicial branch of the Government has only one duty,—to lay the article of the Constitution which is invoked beside the statute which is challenged and to decide whether the latter squares with the former." [4] Nor is it an act of unfettered free will. Justice Oliver Wendell Holmes summed it up: "I recognize without hesitation that judges do and must legislate, but they can do so only interstitially; they are confined from molar to molecular motions." [5]

NOTES

1. Donald L. Horowitz in *The Courts and Social Policy* identifies several but not all of these.
2. "Law in Science and Science in Law," 12 *Harvard Law Review* 443, 1899.
3. *The Nature of the Judicial Process* (New Haven: Yale University Press, 1921), p. 108.
4. *United States v. Butler,* 297 U.S. 1 (1936), at 62.
5. Dissenting in *Southern Pacific Co. v. Jensen.* 244 U.S. 205 (1917), at 200.

SELECTED BIBLIOGRAPHY

Abraham, Henry J. *Freedom and the Court.* 4th ed. New York: Oxford University Press, 1982.

Bickel, Alexander M. *The Least Dangerous Branch.* Indianapolis: Bobbs-Merrill, 1962.

Cardozo, Benjamin N. *The Nature of the Judicial Process.* New Haven: Yale University Press, 1921.

Ely, John Hart. *Democracy and Distrust.* Cambridge: Harvard University Press, 1980.

Frank, Jerome. *Courts on Trial.* Princeton: Princeton University Press, 1949.

Friedman, Lawrence M., and Scheiber, Harry N., eds. *American Law and the Constitutional Order.* Cambridge: Harvard University Press, 1978.

Horowitz, Donald L. *The Courts and Social Policy.* Washington: Brookings Institution, 1977.

Mason, Alpheus Thomas. *The Supreme Court from Taft to Burger.* 3rd ed. Baton Rouge: Louisiana State University Press, 1979.

Swindler, William F. *Court and Constitution in the Twentieth Century.* 3 vols. Indianapolis: Bobbs-Merrill, 1969, 1970, 1974.

Wasby, Stephen L. *The Impact of the United States Supreme Court.* Homewood, Ill.: Dorsey Press, 1970.

I

The Establishment of Judicial Power

Even though all courts make policy to one degree or another, American courts have a means of policymaking at their disposal that the courts of most other countries do not have: judicial review—the power to declare legislative and executive acts invalid under the Constitution. Alexis de Tocqueville explained in 1832:

> . . . an American judge can pronounce a decision only when litigation has arisen, he is conversant only with special cases, and he cannot act until the cause has been duly brought before the court. His position is therefore exactly the same as that of the magistrates of other nations; and yet he is invested with immense political power. How does this come about? If the sphere of his authority and his means of action are the same as those of other judges, where does he derive a power which they do not possess? The cause of this difference lies in the simple fact that the Americans have acknowledged the right of judges to found their decision on the *Constitution* rather than on the laws. In other words, they have permitted them not to apply such laws as may appear to them to be unconstitutional.[1]

Tocqueville was correct about the effect of judicial review, but from what source do the courts in America claim this authority? Not even the most ardent supporter of judicial review would claim that it is anywhere conferred by the Constitution itself; there is no language in the document that directly speaks to this issue. The Constitution, however, is declared to be a form of "higher law" in Article VI, Section 2, The Supremacy Clause: "This Constitution, and the Laws of the United States which shall be made in pursuance thereof . . . shall be the supreme Law of the Land. . ." The Constitution's superiority to state laws is unmistakable and its supremacy over laws of the United States *not* "made in pursuance" of its commands is fairly clear. But the Constitution does not say which government agency is

11

to interpret the higher law.

The question of whether or not the Framers of the Constitution intended judicial review has been debated endlessly. Some conclude that judicial review was definitely intended but was taken for granted, and others just as firmly believe that the Philadelphia Convention adjourned without resolving the question. In fact, the evidence is merely suggestive, thus allowing each investigator to support his or her own conclusion. Such evidence of intent should be mentioned, even though the ultimate resolution of the debate lies in the fact that most Americans most of the time accept the courts' power to declare acts of the other branches of the government invalid.

The American colonists knew that England's Sir Edward Coke, Chief Justice of the Court of Common Pleas, had told James I in 1609 that "when an Act of Parliament is against common right and reason, the common law will control it and adjudge such act to be void." [2] The King and the Chief Justice did not put this assertion to the ultimate test, but an American could have easily substituted "Constitution" for "common law" in Coke's dictum. And it should be remembered that Coke's legal writings were the leading authority in the American colonies despite subsequent changes in English law prior to 1776. On this side of the Atlantic, James Otis had advanced the idea of judicial review in his argument in the Writs of Assistance Cases (1761) and in his 1764 pamphlet "The Rights of the British Colonies Asserted and Proved." In the 1761 case he put the argument forcefully: "An Act against the Constitution is void; an Act against Equity is void; and if an Act of Parliament should be made in the very words of this petition, it would be void. The Executive Courts must pass such Acts into disuse." One last colonial straw in the wind needs to be noted. The Privy Council in England had the authority to annul an act of a colonial legislature as contrary to the laws, customs, or policy of England. This is admittedly *administrative* rather than *judicial* review and there are few indications that the power was used, but it does embody the concept of testing legislative acts for their conformity with an external standard.

Some of the most controversial evidence in this chain of inference is found in eight state judicial pronouncements between the Declaration of Independence and the opening of the Constitutional Convention. In these eight cases, state courts claimed the power to declare acts of their own state legislatures invalid. The affected legislatures are not on record as opposing the claimed power, but there is considerable doubt about the accuracy of the case reports. Indeed, in several of them the assertion is merely *obiter dicta** because the issue was not squarely presented to the

---

*Obiter dicta (or just dicta) is language in a judicial opinion that is not required to support the conclusion reached. It is not binding as precedent on later courts.

court. In short, the state court decisions are shaky evidence and add little weight to the argument that the Framers were familiar with the exercise of the power and intended to endow the federal courts with it.

In the Constitutional Convention, several delegates made unchallenged assertions that judges have the power of judicial review. Madison reported that Luther Martin of Maryland opposed associating Supreme Court judges with the executive in the exercise of the veto power because "as to the constitutionality of laws, that point will come before the judges in their official character. In this character they have a negative on the laws. Join them with the executive . . . and they will have a double negative." No one spoke up to tell Martin that he was wrong, and another delegate, James Wilson, thought that the "double negative" would be a good thing. "Laws may be unjust, may be unwise, may be dangerous, may be destructive; and yet not be so unconstitutional as to justify the judges in refusing to give them effect." He therefore wanted judges to participate in the veto to provide an even broader scope to the judicial power; delegate George Mason of Virginia agreed. However, Elbridge Gerry of Massachusetts joined Martin in opposition because he had doubts "whether the Judiciary ought to form a part of it, as they will have a sufficient check against encroachments on their own department by their exposition of the laws, which involved a power of deciding on their constitutionality." He then added: "In some states the Judges had actually set aside laws as being against the [state] Constitution. This was done, too, with general approbation." Finally, John Dickinson of Pennsylvania observed that "he thought no such power ought to exist. He was at the same time at a loss what expedient to substitute." Since Dickinson was not addressing a specific proposal to give the courts the power, his use of the word "ought" should be understood to refer to an accepted principle of which he was not sure he approved.[3]

Other remarks in the convention, in the public debates on the proposed Constitution, and in the state ratifying conventions could lead one to conclude that judicial review was assumed by many to be an inherent power of the courts. One American statesman who observed the Constitution-making process from Paris also appeared to accept the existence of judicial review. Writing to Madison about the lack of a Bill of Rights in the Constitution, Thomas Jefferson said: "In the arguments in favor of a declaration of rights, you omit one which has great weight with me, the legal check which it puts into the hands of the judiciary."[4]

A variety of interpretations can be drawn from these individual testimonials. In most instances the speakers were not directly addressing the powers of the courts. Therefore, what could be interpreted as acceptance of judicial review could equally well have been a passing and not well-thought out comment. The context of the remarks could also explain why no one challenged the assumptions—it was not germane to the subject under discussion. Then, too, one should note that Madison's notes of the convention debates were just that—notes—and not a verbatim transcript. In short, those who want confirmation that the Framers intended for the courts to have the power of judicial review can find some strong inferential evidence. Those who believe to the contrary can qualify the evidence out of existence and confirm their negative position.

One simple fact remains. In 1803 John Marshall announced for a unanimous court that the judiciary had the power to declare an act of Congress unconstitutional, and he made that assertion stick. Whether *Marbury* v. *Madison* (p. 27) was a political coup or a plain statement of what everyone assumed to be the proper outcome may be largely irrelevant. The courts have continued to exercise the power Marshall claimed for them and have survived political attacks with that power intact.

Marbury was not the only occasion where Marshall had to assert the power of the courts. In *Fletcher* v. *Peck,* 6 Cr. 87 (1810), he successfully invalidated an act of a state legislature, and in *Cohens* v. *Virginia* (p. 34) he included state court decisions within his Court's purview. Finally he used *McCulloch* v. *Maryland,* 4 Wheat. 316 (1819), not only to validate the establishment of the Bank of the United States but, more importantly, to express in clear terms his view of the nature of the Union, the powers of the national government within that Union, and the powers of the Court within the national government. John Marshall's decisions are the basis on which the power of the judiciary has been built. They also are the foundation for the policymaking role played by the courts in subsequent years. Without Marshall's foundation, American courts would still be policymakers, but of a lesser sort. With his foundation they come closer to (some would say surpass) the role played by the other branches of government.

Whether the court should or should not be limited in its power to make policy has, perhaps, been debated at even greater length than whether or not the courts have the power to make policy at all. Again, there has been no resolution of the issues, despite many instances of judicial-legislative conflict over the proper policy to be adopted in a particular area. Several of these are illustrated in the chapters that follow. It is skeptical but true that critics of court policymaking often are saying that they do not like the policy, rather than arguing that the courts should not make policy at all. Had the courts' policy decisions conformed with those of the critic, his or her criticism would have been changed to approbation.

NOTES

1. Phillips Bradley, trans., *Democracy in America* (Vintage, 1960), Vol. I, p. 104.
2. *Dr. Bonham's Case.* Quoted in Catherine D. Bowen, *The Lion and the Throne* (Boston: Little, Brown & Co., 1956), p. 315.
3. These comments are drawn from Max Farrand, ed., *The Records of the Federal Convention* (New Haven: Yale University Press, 1937), 4 vols.
4. Thomas Jefferson to James Madison, March 15, 1789. Julian P. Boyd, ed., *The Papers of Thomas Jefferson* (Princeton: Princeton University Press, 1950), XIV, p. 659.

SELECTED BIBLIOGRAPHY

Beard, Charles A. *The Supreme Court and the Constitution.* New York: Macmillan, 1914.

Corwin, Edward S. *The Doctrine of Judicial Review.* Princeton: Princeton University Press, 1914.

Cox, Archibald. *The Role of the Supreme Court in American Government.* New York: Oxford University Press, 1976.

Dewey, Donald O. *Marshall versus Jefferson: The Political Background of Marbury v. Madison.* New York: Knopf, 1970.

Farrand, Max, ed. *The Records of the Federal Convention.* 4 vols. New Haven: Yale University Press, 1937.

Gunther, Gerald. *John Marshall's Defense of McCulloch v. Maryland.* Stanford: Stanford University Press, 1969.

Hamilton, Alexander et al. *The Federalist.*

Haines, Charles Grove. *The American Doctrine of Judicial Supremacy.* New York: Russell and Russell, 1959.

_____. *The Role of the Supreme Court in American Government and Politics: 1795-1835.* Berkeley: University of California Press, 1944.

_____. *The Role of the Supreme Court in American Government and Politics: 1835-1864.* Berkeley: University of California Press, 1957.

Haskins, George L. and Johnson, Herbert A. *Foundations of Power: John Marshall, 1801-1815.* New York: Macmillan, 1981.

Jackson, Robert H. *The Struggle for Judicial Supremacy.* New York: Vintage Books, 1941.

Lusky, Louis. *By What Right?: A Commentary on the Supreme Court's Power to Revise the Constitution.* Charlottesville, Va.: The Michie Co., 1975.

Neely, Richard. *How Courts Govern America.* New Haven: Yale University Press, 1981.

Storing, Herbert, ed. *The Complete Anti-Federalist.* 7 vols. Chicago: University of Chicago Press, 1981.

Warren, Charles. *The Supreme Court in United States History.* 2 vols. Boston: Little, Brown & Co., 1926.

The Federalist is a series of 85 newspaper essays published anonymously in New York to explain the proposed Constitution and to argue for its ratification. Actually written by John Jay, Alexander Hamilton, and James Madison, The Federalist is the most systematic, although not unbiased, explication of what the Constitution's supporters believed to be the meaning of the document. The excerpts from Nos. 10 and 51 that follow reveal Madison's perception of the pluralist nature of American society. No. 78 is Hamilton's explanation of the role the judiciary would play in that society.

The Federalist No. 10

Among the numerous advantages promised by a well constructed Union, none deserves to be more accurately developed than its tendency to break and control the violence of faction. . . .

. . .

Complaints are everywhere heard from our most considerate and virtuous citizens, equally the friends of public and private faith, and of public and personal liberty, that our governments are too unstable, that the public good is disregarded in the conflicts of rival parties, and that measures are too often decided, not according to the rules of justice and the rights of the minor party, but by the superior force of an interested and overbearing majority. . . .

. . .

By a faction, I understand a number of citizens, whether amounting to a majority or minority of the whole, who are united and actuated by some common impulse of passion, or of interest, adverse to the rights of other citizens, or to the permanent and aggregate interests of the community.

There are two methods of curing the mischiefs of faction: the one, by removing its causes; the other, by controlling its effects.

There are again two methods of removing the causes of faction: the one, by destroying the liberty which is essential to its existence; the other, by giving to every citizen the same opinions, the same passions, and the same interests.

It could never be more truly said than of the first remedy, that it was worse than the disease. Liberty is to faction what air is to fire, an aliment without which it instantly expires. But it could not be less folly to abolish liberty, which is essential to political life, because it nourishes faction, than it would be to wish the annihilation of air, which is essential to animal life, because it imparts to fire its destructive agency.

The second expedient is as impracticable as the first would be unwise. As long as the reason of man continues fallible, and he is at liberty to exercise it, different opinions will be formed. As long as the connection subsists between his reason and his self-love, his opinions and his passions will have a reciprocal influence on each other; and the former will be objects to which the latter will attach themselves. The diversity in the faculties of men, from which the rights of property originate, is not less an insuperable obstacle to a uniformity of interests. . . .

. . .

The latent causes of faction are thus sown in the nature of man; and we see them everywhere brought into different degrees of activity, according to the different circumstances of civil society. A zeal for different opinions concerning religion, concerning government, and many other points, as well of speculation as of practice; an attachment to different leaders ambitiously contending for pre-eminence and power; or to persons of other descriptions whose fortunes have been interesting to the human passions, have, in turn, divided mankind into parties, inflamed them with mutual animosity, and rendered them much more disposed to vex and oppress each other than to co-operate for their common good. So strong is this propensity of mankind to fall into mutual animosities, that where no substantial occasion presents itself, the most frivolous and fanciful distinctions have been sufficient to kindle their unfriendly passions and excite their most violent conflicts. But the most common and durable source of factions has been the various and unequal distribution of property. Those who hold and those who are without property have ever formed distinct interests in society. Those who are creditors, and those who are debtors, fall under a like discrimination. A landed interest, a manufacturing interest, a mercantile interest, a moneyed interest, with many lesser interests, grow up of necessity in civilized nations, and divide them into different classes, actuated by different sentiments and views. The regulation of these various and interfering interests forms the principal task of modern legislation, and involves the spirit of party and faction in the necessary and ordinary operations of the government. . . .

. . .

The inference to which we are brought is, that the *causes* of faction cannot be removed, and that relief is only to be sought in the means of controlling its *effects*.

If a faction consists of less than a majority, relief is supplied by the republican principle, which enables the majority to defeat its sinister views by regular vote. It may clog the administration, it may convulse the society; but it will be unable to execute and mask its violence under the forms of the Constitution. When a majority is included in a faction, the form of popular government, on the other hand, enables it to sacrifice to its ruling passion or interest both the public good and the rights of other citizens. To secure the public good and private rights against the danger of such a faction, and at the same time to preserve the spirit and the form of popular government, is then the great object to which our inquiries are directed. . . .

. . .

By what means is this object attainable? Evidently by one of two only. Either the existence of the same passion or interest in a majority at the same time must be prevented, or the majority, having such coexistent passion or interest, must be rendered, by their number and local situation, unable to concert and carry into effect schemes of oppression. If the impulse and the opportunity be suffered to coincide, we will know that neither moral nor religious motives can be relied on as an adequate control. . . .

. . .

From this view of the subject it may be concluded that a pure democracy, by which I mean a society consisting of a small number of citizens, who assemble and administer the government in person, can admit of no cure for the mischiefs of faction. A common passion or interest will, in almost every case, be felt by a majority of the whole; a communication and concert result from the form of government itself; and there is nothing to check the inducements to sacrifice the weaker party or an obnoxious individual. . . .

.   .   .

A republic, by which I mean a government in which the scheme of representation takes place, opens a different prospect, and promises the cure for which we are seeking. Let us examine the points in which it varies from pure democracy, and we shall comprehend both the nature of the cure and the efficacy which it must derive from the Union.

The two great points of difference between a democracy and a republic are: first, the delegation of the government, in the latter, to a small number of citizens elected by the rest; secondly, the greater number of citizens, and greater sphere of country, over which the latter may be extended.

The effect of the first difference is, on the one hand, to refine and enlarge the public views, by passing them through the medium of a chosen body of citizens, whose wisdom may best discern the true interest of their country, and whose patriotism and love of justice will be least likely to sacrifice it to temporary or partial considerations. . . .

.   .   .

The question resulting is, whether small or extensive republics are more favorable to the election of proper guardians of the public weal; and it is clearly decided in favor of the latter by two obvious considerations:

In the first place, it is to be remarked that, however small the republic may be, the representatives must be raised to a certain number, in order to guard against the cabals of a few; and that, however large it may be, they must be limited to a certain number, in order to guard against the confusion of a multitude. Hence, the number of representatives in the two cases not being in proportion to that of the two constituents, and being proportionally greater in the small republic, it follows that, if the proportion of fit characters be not less in the large than in the small republic, the former will present a greater option, and consequently a greater probability of a fit choice.

In the next place, as each representative will be chosen by a greater number of citizens in the large than in the small republic, it will be more difficult for unworthy candidates to practise with success the vicious arts by which elections are too often carried; and the suffrages of the people being more free, will be more likely to centre in men who possess the most attractive merit and the most diffusive and established characters. . . .

. . .

The other point of difference is, the greater number of citizens and extent of territory which may be brought within the compass of republican than of democratic government; and it is this circumstance principally which renders factious combinations less to be dreaded in the former than in the latter. The smaller the society, the fewer probably will be the distinct parties and interests composing it; the fewer the distinct parties and interests, the more frequently will a majority be found of the same party; and the smaller the number of individuals composing a majority, and the smaller the compass within which they are placed, the more easily will they concert and execute their plans of oppression. Extend the sphere, and you take in a greater variety of parties and interests; you make it less probable that a majority of the whole will have a common motive to invade the rights of other citizens; or if such a common motive exists, it will be more difficult for all who feel it to discover their own strength, and to act in unison with each other. . . .

. . .

The influence of factious leaders may kindle a flame within their particular States, but will be unable to spread a general conflagration through the other States. A religious sect may degenerate into a political faction in a part of the Confederacy; but the variety of sects dispersed over the entire face of it must secure the national councils against any danger from that source. A rage for paper money, for an abolition of debts, for an equal division of property, or for any other improper or wicked project, will be less apt to pervade the whole body of the Union than a particular member of it; in the same proportion as such a malady is more likely to taint a particular county or district, than an entire State.

In the extent and proper structure of the Union, therefore, we behold a republican remedy for the diseases most incident to republican government. And according to the degree of pleasure and pride we feel in being republicans, ought to be our zeal in cherishing the spirit and supporting the character of Federalists.

The Federalist No. 51

. . .

[T]he great security against a gradual concentration of the several powers in the same department, consists in giving to those who administer each department the necessary constitutional means and personal motives to resist encroachments of the others. The provision for defence must in this, as in all other cases, be made commensurate to the danger of attack. Ambition must be made to counteract ambition. The interest of the man must be connected with the constitutional rights of the place. It may be a reflection on human nature, that such devices should be necessary to control the abuses of government. But what is government itself, but the greatest of all reflections on human nature? If men were angels, no government would be necessary. If angels were to govern men, neither external nor internal controls on government would be necessary. In framing a government, which is to be administered by men over men, the great difficulty lies in this: you must first enable the government to control the governed; and in the next place oblige it to control itself. A dependence on the people is, no doubt, the primary control on the government; but experience has taught mankind the necessity of auxiliary precautions.

This policy of supplying, by opposite and rival interests, the defect of better motives, might be traced through the whole system of human affairs, private as well as public. We see it particularly displayed in all the subordinate distributions of power, where the constant aim is to divide and arrange the several offices in such a manner as that each may be a check on the other. . . .

. . .

But it is not possible to give to each department an equal power of self-defence. In republican government, the legislative authority necessarily predominates. The remedy for this inconveniency is to divide the legislature into different branches; and to render them, by different modes of election and different principles of action, as little connected with each other as the nature of their common functions and their common dependence on the society will admit. It may even be necessary to guard against dangerous encroachments by still further precautions....

. . .

There are, moreover, two considerations particularly applicable to the federal system of America, which place that system in a very interesting point of view.

First. In a single republic, all the power surrendered by the people is submitted to the administration of a single government; and the usurpations are guarded against by a division of the government into distinct and separate departments. In the compound republic of America, the power surrendered by the people is first divided between two distinct governments, and then the portion allotted to each subdivided among distinct and separate departments. Hence a double security arises to the rights of the people. The different governments will control each other, at the same time that each will be controlled by itself.

Second. It is of great importance in a republic not only to guard the society against the oppression of its rulers, but to guard one part of the society against the injustice of the other part. Different interests necessarily exist in different classes of citizens. If a majority be united by a common interest, the rights of the minority will be insecure. There are but two methods of providing against this evil: the one by creating a will in the community independent of the majority—that is, of the society itself; the other, by comprehending in the society so many separate descriptions of citizens as will render an unjust combination of a majority of the whole very improbable, if not impracticable... The second method will be exemplified in the federal republic of the United States. Whilst all authority in it will be derived from and dependent on the society, the society itself will be broken into so many parts, interests and classes of citizens, that the rights of individuals, or of the minority, will be in little danger from interested combinations of the majority. In a free government the security for civil rights must be the same as that for religious rights. It consists in the one case in the multiplicity of interests, and in the other in the multiplicity of sects. The degree of security in both cases will depend on the number of interests and sects; and this may be presumed to depend on the extent of country and number of people comprehended under the same government... In the extended republic of the United States, and among the great variety of interests, parties, and sects which it embraces, a coalition of a majority of the whole society could seldom take place on any other principles than those of justice and the general good; whilst there being thus less danger to a minor from the will of a major party, there must be less pretext, also, to provide for the security of the former, by introducing into the government a will not dependent on the latter, or, in other words, a will independent of the society itself. It is no less certain than it is important, notwithstanding the contrary opinions which have been entertained, that the larger the society, provided it lie within a practical sphere, the more duly capable it will be of self-government....

The Federalist No. 78

We proceed now to an examination of the judiciary department of the proposed government....

.   .   .

According to the plan of the convention, all judges who may be appointed by the United States are to hold their offices *during good behavior;* which is conformable to the most approved of the State constitutions, ... The standard of good behavior for the continuance in office of the judicial magistracy, is certainly one of the most valuable of the modern improvements in the practice of government. In a monarchy it is an excellent barrier to the despotism of the prince; in a republic it is a no less excellent barrier to the encroachments and oppressions of the representative body. And it is the best expedient which can be devised in any government, to secure a steady, upright, and impartial administration of the laws.

Whoever attentively considers the different departments of power must perceive, that, in a government in which they are separated from each other, the judiciary, from the nature of its functions, will always be the least dangerous to the political rights of the Constitution; because it will be least in a capacity to annoy or injure them. The Executive not only dispenses the honors, but holds the sword of the community. The legislature not only commands the purse, but prescribes the rules by which the duties and rights of every citizen are to be regulated. The judiciary, on the contrary, has no influence over either the sword or the purse; no direction either of the strength or of the wealth of the society; and can take no active resolution whatever. It may truly be said to have neither FORCE nor WILL, but merely judgment; and must ultimately depend upon the aid of the executive arm even for the efficacy of its judgments.

This simple view of the matter suggests several important consequences. It proves incontestably, that the judiciary is beyond comparison the weakest of the three departments of power; that it can never attack with success either of the other two; and that all possible care is requisite to enable it to defend itself against their attacks. It equally proves, that though individual oppression may now and then proceed from the courts of justice, the general liberty of the people can never be endangered from that quarter; I mean so long as the judiciary remains truly distinct from both the legislature and the Executive. . . And it proves, in the last place, that as liberty can have nothing to fear from the judiciary alone, but would have every thing to fear from its union with either of the other departments; that as all the effects of such a union must ensue from a dependence of the former on the latter, notwithstanding a nominal and apparent separation; that as, from the natural feebleness of the judiciary, it is in continual jeopardy of being overpowered, awed, or influenced by its coordinate branches; and that as nothing can contribute so much to its firmness and independence as permanency in office, this quality may therefore be justly regarded as an indispensable ingredient in its constitution, and, in a great measure, as the citadel of the public justice and the public security.

The complete independence of the courts of justice is peculiarly essential in a limited Constitution. By a limited Constitution, I understand one which contains certain specified exceptions to the legislative authority; such, for instance, as that it shall pass no bills of attainder, no *ex-post-facto* laws, and the like. Limitations of this kind can be preserved in practice no other way than through the medium of courts of justice, whose duty it must be to declare all acts contrary to the manifest tenor of the Constitution void. Without this, all the reservations of particular rights or privileges would amount to nothing.

Some perplexity respecting the rights of the courts to pronounce legislative acts void, because contrary to the constitution, has arisen from an imagination that the doctrine would imply a superiority of the judiciary to the legislative power. It is urged that the authority which can declare the acts of another void, must necessarily be superior to the one whose acts may be declared void. As this doctrine is of great importance in all the American constitutions, a brief discussion of the ground on which it rests cannot be unacceptable.

There is no position which depends on clearer principles, than that every act of a delegated authority, contrary to the tenor of the commission under which it is exercised, is void. No legislative act, therefore, contrary to the Constitution, can be valid. To deny this, would be to affirm, that the deputy is greater than his principal; that the servant is above his master; that the representatives of the people are superior to the people themselves; that men acting by virtue of powers, may do not only what their powers do not authorize, but what they forbid.

If it be said that the legislative body are themselves the constitutional judges of their own powers, and that the construction they put upon them is conclusive upon the other departments, it may be answered, that this cannot be the natural presumption, where it is not to be collected from any particular provisions in the Constitution. It is not otherwise to be supposed, that the Constitution could intend to enable the representatives of the people to substitute their *will* to that of their constituents. It is far more rational to suppose, that the courts were designed to be an intermediate body between the people and the legislature, in order, among other things, to keep the latter within the limits assigned to their authority. The interpretation of the laws is the proper and peculiar province of the courts. A constitution is, in fact, and must be regarded by the judges, as a fundamental law. It therefore belongs to them to ascertain its meaning, as well as the meaning of any particular act proceeding from the legislative body. If there should happen to be an irreconcilable variance between the two, that which has the superior obligation and validity ought, of course, to be preferred; or, in other words, the Constitution ought to be preferred to the statute, the intention of the people to the intention of their agents.

Nor does this conclusion by any means suppose a superiority of the judicial to the legislative power. It only supposes that the power of the people is superior to both; and that where the will of the legislature, declared in its statutes, stands in opposition to that of the people, declared in the Constitution, the judges ought to be governed by the latter rather than the former. They ought to regulate their decisions by the fundamental laws, rather than by those which are not fundamental. . . .

.   .   .

It can be of no weight to say that the courts, on the pretence of a repugnancy, may substitute their own pleasure to the constitutional intentions of the legislature. This might as well happen in the case of two contradictory statutes; or it might as well happen in every adjudication upon any single statute. The courts must declare the sense of the law; and if they should be disposed to exercise WILL instead of JUDGMENT, the consequence would equally be the substitution of their pleasure to that of the legislative body. The observation, if it prove any thing, would prove that there ought to be no judges distinct from that body.

If, then, the courts of justice are to be considered as the bulwarks of a limited Constitution against legislative encroachments, this consideration will afford a strong argument for the permanent tenure of judicial offices, since nothing will contribute so much as this to that independent spirit in the judges which must be essential to the faithful performance of so arduous a duty.

This independence of the judges is equally requisite to guard the Constitution and the rights of individuals from the effects of those ill humors, which the arts of designing men, or the influence of particular conjunctures, sometimes disseminate among the people themselves, and which, though they speedily give place to better information, and more deliberate reflection, have a tendency, in the meantime, to occasion dangerous innovations in the government, and serious oppressions of the minor party in the community. Though I trust the friends of the proposed Constitution will never concur with its enemies, in questioning that fundamental principle of republican government, which admits the right of the people to alter or abolish the established Constitution, whenever they find it inconsistent with their happiness, yet it is not to be inferred from this principle, that the representatives of the people, whenever a momentary inclination happens to lay hold of a majority of their constituents, incompatible with the provisions in the existing Constitution, would, on that account, be justifiable in a violation of those provisions; or that the courts would be under a greater obligation to connive at infractions in this shape, than when they had proceeded wholly from the cabals of the representative body. Until the people have, by some solemn and authoritative act, annulled or changed the established form, it is binding upon themselves collectively, as well as individually; and no presumption, or even knowledge, of their sentiments, can warrant their representatives in a departure from it, prior to such an act. But it is easy to see, that it would require an uncommon portion of fortitude in the judges to do their duty as faithful guardians of the Constitution, where legislative invasions of it had been instigated by the major voice of the community.

But it is not with a view to infractions of the Constitution only, that the independence of the judges may be an essential safeguard against the effects of occasional ill humors in the society. These sometimes extend no farther than to the injury of the private rights of particular classes of citizens, by unjust and partial laws. Here also the firmness of the judicial magistracy is of vast importance in mitigating the severity and confining the operation of such laws. It not only serves to moderate the immediate mischiefs of those which may have been passed but it operates as a check upon the legislative body in passing them; who, perceiving that obstacles to the success of iniquitous intention are to be expected from the scruples of the courts, are in a manner compelled, by the very motives of the injustice they meditate, to qualify their attempts. This is a circumstance calculated to have more influence upon the character of our governments, than but few may be aware of. . . .

Marbury v. Madison

1 Cranch 137, 2 L ed 60 (1803)

Near the end of President Adams' term in office, he nominated Marbury and three others to be justices of the peace in the District of Columbia. The nominations were approved by the Senate and the commissions were signed by both the president and the secretary of state as required by law. However, Secretary of State John Marshall failed to deliver the commissions to Marbury and the other appointees. Secretary of State James Madison was instructed by President Jefferson to refuse to deliver the commissions on the assumption that delivery was required to complete the appointment process. Marbury and friends ignored the lower federal courts and filed an original suit in the Supreme Court for a writ of mandamus.

.   .   .

[T]he following opinion of the Court was delivered by the *Chief Justice*. [Marshall]

Opinion of the Court.

At the last term on the affidavits then read and filed with the clerk, a rule was granted in this case, requiring the secretary of state to show cause why a mandamus should not issue, directing him to deliver to William Marbury his commission as a justice of the peace for the county of Washington, in the District of Columbia.

No cause has been shown, and the present motion is for a mandamus. The peculiar delicacy of this case, the novelty of some of its circumstances, and the real difficulty attending the points which occur in it, require a complete exposition of the principles on which the opinion to be given by the court is founded.

These principles have been, on the side of the applicant very ably argued at the bar. In rendering the opinion of the court, there will be some departure in form, though not in substance, from the points stated in that argument.

In the order in which the court has viewed this subject, the following questions have been considered and decided.

1st. Has the applicant a right to the commission he demands?

2d. If he has a right, and that right has been violated, do the laws of his country afford him a remedy?

3d. If they do afford him a remedy, is it a mandamus issuing from this court? . . .

[The Court finds that as the appointment was complete, Marbury has a right to the commission and that the law affords a remedy.]

.   .   .

It remains to be inquired whether,

He is entitled to the remedy for which he applies. This depends on,

1st. The nature of the writ applied for; and,

2d. The power of this court. . . .

.   .   .

This, then, is a plain case for a mandamus, either to deliver the commission, or a copy of it from the record; and it only remains to be inquired,

Whether it can issue from this court.

The act to establish the judicial courts of the United States authorizes the Supreme Court "to issue writs of mandamus in cases warranted by the principles and usages of law, to any courts appointed, or persons holding office, under the authority of the United States.". . .

.   .   .

The constitution vests the whole judicial power of the United States in one Supreme Court, and such inferior courts as congress shall, from time to time, ordain and establish. This power is expressly extended to all cases arising under the laws of the United States; and, consequently, in some form, may be exercised over the present case; because the right claimed is given by a law of the United States.

In the distribution of this power it is declared that "the Supreme Court shall have original jurisdiction in all cases affecting ambassadors, other public ministers and consuls, and those in which a state shall be a party. In all other cases, the Supreme Court shall have appellate jurisdiction.". . .

.   .   .

If it had been intended to leave it in the discretion of the legislature to apportion the judicial power between the supreme and inferior courts according to the will of that body, it would certainly have been useless to have proceded further than to have defined the judicial power, and the tribunals in which it should be vested. The subsequent part of the section is mere surplusage, is entirely without meaning, if such is to be the construction. If congress remains at liberty to give this court appellate jurisdiction, where the constitution has declared their jurisdiction shall be original; and original jurisdiction where the constitution has declared it shall be appellate; the distribution of jurisdiction, made in the constitution, is form without substance. . . .

.   .   .

When an instrument organizing fundamentally a judicial system, divides it into one supreme, and so many inferior courts as the legislature may ordain and establish; then enumerates its powers, and proceeds so far to distribute them, as to define the jurisdiction of the Supreme Court by declaring the cases in which it shall take original jurisdiction, and that in

29

others it shall take appellate jurisdiction; the plain import of the words seems to be, that in one class of cases its jurisdiction is original, and not appellate; in the other it is appellate, and not original. If any other construction would render the clause inoperative, that is an additional reason for rejecting such other construction, and for adhering to their obvious meaning.

To enable this court, then, to issue a mandamus, it must be shown to be an exercise of appellate jurisdiction, or to be necessary to enable them to exercise appellate jurisdiction. . . .

.   .   .

It is the essential criterion of appellate jurisdiction, that it revises and corrects the proceedings in a cause already instituted, and does not create that cause. Although, therefore, a mandamus may be directed to courts, yet to issue such a writ to an officer for the delivery of a paper, is in effect the same as to sustain an original action for that paper, and, therefore, seems not to belong to appellate but to original jurisdiction. Neither is it necessary in such a case as this, to enable the court to exercise its appellate jurisdiction.

The authority, therefore, given to the Supreme Court, by the act establishing the judicial courts of the United States, to issue writs of mandamus to public officers, appears not to be warranted by the constitution; and it becomes necessary to inquire whether a jurisdiction so conferred can be exercised.

The question, whether an act, repugnant to the constitution, can become the law of the land, is a question deeply interesting to the United States; but, happily, not of an intricacy proportioned to its interest. It seems only necessary to recognize certain principles, supposed to have been long and well established, to decide it.

That the people have an original right to establish, for their future government, such principles, as, in their opinion, shall most conduce to their own happiness is the basis on which the whole American fabric has been erected. The exercise of this original right is a very great exertion; nor can it, nor ought it, to be frequently repeated. The principles, therefore, so established, are deemed fundamental. And as the authority from which they proceed is supreme, and can seldom act, they are designed to be permanent.

This original and supreme will organizes the government, and assigns to different departments their respective powers. It may either stop here, or establish certain limits not to be transcended by those departments.

The government of the United States is of the latter description. The powers of the legislature are defined and limited; and that those limits may not be mistaken, or forgotten, the constitution is written. To what purpose are powers limited, and to what purpose is that limitation committed to writing, if these limits may, at any time, be passed by those intended to be restrained? The distinction between a government with limited and unlimited powers is abolished, if those limits do not confine the persons on whom they are imposed, and if acts prohibited and acts allowed, are of equal obligation. It is a proposition too plain to be contested, that the constitution controls any legislative act repugnant to it; or, that the legislature may alter the constitution by an ordinary act.

Between these alternatives there is no middle ground. The constitution is either a superior paramount law, unchangeable by ordinary means, or it is on a level with ordinary legislative acts, and, like other acts, is alterable when the legislature shall please to alter it.

If the former part of the alternative be true, then a legislative act contrary to the constitution is not law: if the latter part be true, then written constitutions are absurd attempts, on the part of the people, to limit a power in its own nature illimitable.

Certainly all those who have framed written constitutions contemplate them as forming the fundamental and paramount law of the nation, and, consequently, the theory of every such government must be, that an act of the legislature, repugnant to the constitution, is void.

This theory is essentially attached to a written constitution, and, is consequently, to be considered, by this court, as one of the fundamental principles of our society. It is not therefore to be lost sight of in the further consideration of this subject.

If an act of the legislature, repugnant to the constitution, is void, does it, notwithstanding its invalidity, bind the courts, and oblige them to give it effect? Or, in other words, though it be not law, does it constitute a rule as operative as if it was a law? This would be to overthrow in fact what was established in theory; and would seem, at first view, an absurdity too gross to be insisted on. It shall, however, receive a more attentive consideration.

It is emphatically the province and duty of the judicial department to say what the law is. Those who apply the rule to particular cases, must of necessity expound and interpret that rule. If two laws conflict with each other, the courts must decide on the operation of each.

So if a law be in opposition to the constitution; if both the law and the constitution apply to a particular case, so that the court must either decide that case conformably to the law, disregarding the constitution; or conformably to the constitution, disregarding the law; the court must determine which of these conflicting rules governs the case. This is of the very essence of judicial duty.

If, then, the courts are to regard the constitution, and the constitution is superior to any ordinary act of the legislature, the constitution, and not such ordinary act, must govern the case to which they both apply.

Those, then, who controvert the principle that the constitution is to be considered, in court, as a paramount law, are reduced to the necessity of maintaining that courts must close their eyes on the constitution, and see only the law.

This doctrine would subvert the very foundation of all written constitutions. It would declare that an act which, according to the principles and theory of our government, is entirely void, is yet, in practice, completely obligatory. It would declare that if the legislature shall do what is expressly forbidden, such act, notwithstanding the express prohibition, is in reality effectual. It would be given to the legislature a practical and real omnipotence, with the same breath which professes to restrict their powers within narrow limits. It is prescribing limits, and declaring that those limits may be passed at pleasure.

That it thus reduces to nothing what we have deemed the greatest improvement on political institutions, a written constitution, would of itself be sufficient, in America, where written constitutions have been viewed with so much reverence, for rejecting the construction. But the peculiar expressions of the constitution of the United States furnish additional arguments in favour of its rejection.

The judicial power of the United States is extended to all cases arising under the constitution.

Could it be the intention of those who gave this power, to say that in using it the constitution should not be looked into? That a case arising under the constitution should be decided without examining the instrument under which it arises?

This is too extravagant to be maintained.

In some cases, then, the constitution must be looked into by the judges. And if they can open it at all, what part of it are they forbidden to read or to obey?

There are many other parts of the constitution which serve to illustrate this subject.

It is declared that "no tax or duty shall be laid on articles exported from any state." Suppose a duty on the export of cotton, of tobacco, or of flour; and a suit instituted to recover it. Ought judgment to be rendered in such a case? Ought the judges to close their eyes on the constitution, and only see the law?

The constitution declares "that no bill of attainder or ex post facto law shall be passed."

If, however, such a bill should be passed, and a person should be prosecuted under it; must the court condemn to death those victims whom the constitution endeavors to preserve?

"No person," says the constitution, "shall be convicted of treason unless on the testimony of two witnesses to the same overt act, or on confession in open court."

Here the language of the constitution is addressed especially to the courts. It prescribes, directly for them, a rule of evidence not to be departed from. If the legislature should change that rule, and declare one witness, or a confession out of court, sufficient for conviction, must the constitutional principle yield to the legislative act?

From these, and many other selections which might be made, it is apparent, that the framers of the constitution contemplated that instrument as a rule for the government of courts, as well as of the legislature.

Why otherwise does it direct the judges to take an oath to support it? This oath certainly applies in an especial manner, to their conduct in their official character. How immoral to impose it on them, if they were to be used as the instruments, and the knowing instruments, for violating what they swear to support!

The oath of office, too, imposed by the legislature, is completely demonstrative of the legislative opinion on this subject. It is in these words: "I do solemnly swear that I will administer justice without respect to persons, and do equal right to the poor and to the rich; and that I will faithfully and impartially discharge all the duties incumbent on me as ____, according to the best of my abilities and understanding agreeably to the constitution and laws of the United States."

33

Why does a judge swear to discharge his duties agreeably to the constitution of the United States, if that constitution forms no rule for his government? if it is closed upon him, and cannot be inspected by him?

If such be the real state of things, this is worse than solemn mockery. To prescribe, or to take this oath, becomes equally a crime.

It is also not entirely unworthy of observation, that in declaring what shall be the supreme law of the land, the constitution itself is first mentioned; and not the laws of the United States generally, but those only which shall be made in pursuance of the constitution, have that rank.

Thus, the particular phraseology of the constitution of the United States confirms and strengthens the principle, supposed to be essential to all written constitutions, that a law repugnant to the constitution is void; and that courts, as well as other departments, are bound by that instrument.

The rule must be discharged.

. . .

Marshall used *Cohens* v. *Virginia*, 6 Wheat. 264 (1821), to successfully assert the Court's power to review decisions of state courts by using a broad definition of *federal* jurisdiction: "A case in law or equity consists of the right of the one party, as well as of the other, and may truly be said to arise under the constitution or a law of the United States, whenever its correct decision depends on the construction of either." Federal courts and, ultimately, the Supreme Court have a broad scope of authority under this federal question jurisdiction and that authority is broadened even more by the breadth of power Marshall was willing to grant to Congress under the Constitution. "Let the end be legitimate, let it be within the scope of the constitution, and all means which are appropriate, which are plainly adapted to that end, which are not prohibited, but consistent with the letter and spirit of the constitution, are constitutional." (*McCulloch* v. *Maryland,* 4 Wheat. 316, 1819, at 421) With these assertions of an expansive view of both national power and of judicial power, John Marshall set the stage for the courts to become policymakers in the large sense referred to by Tocqueville.

Eakin v. Raub

12 Sergeant and Rawle (Pennsylvania Supreme Court) 330 (1825)

The facts and majority opinion in this case from the Pennsylvania Supreme Court are unimportant for present purposes. At issue was the power of the state court to declare an act of the state legislature invalid. Justice John B. Gibson's dissent from the acceptance of that power is the best response to Marshall's assertion of the power in *Marbury*. In 1845, Gibson withdrew his opposition to the exercise of judicial review because the legislature had by silence "sanctioned the pretensions of the court to deal freely with the acts of the legislature, and from experience of the necessity of the case." *Norris* v. *Clymen*, 2 Pa. St. 281 (1845).

. . .

Gibson, J., dissenting.

I am aware, that a right to declare all unconstitutional acts void . . . is generally held as a professional dogma; but I apprehend, rather as a matter of faith than of reason. I admit, that I once embraced the same doctrine, but without examination, and I shall, therefore, state the arguments that impelled me to abandon it, with great respect for those by whom it is still maintained. But I may premise, that it is not a little remarkable that although the right in question has all along been claimed by the judiciary, no judge has ventured to discuss it, except Chief Justice Marshall and if the argument of a jurist so distinguished for the strength of his ratiocinative powers be found inconclusive, it may fairly be set down to the weakness of the position which he attempts to defend; . . .

I begin, then, by observing, that in this country, the powers of the judiciary are divisible into those that are POLITICAL, and those that are purely CIVIL. Every power by which one organ of the government is enabled to control another, or to exert an influence over its acts, is a political power. The political powers of the judiciary are *extraordinary* and *adventitious;* such, for instance, as are derived from certain peculiar provisions in the constitution of the *United States,* of which hereafter: and they are derived, by direct grant from the common fountain of all political power. On the other hand, its civil, are its *ordinary* and *appropriate* powers; being part of its essence, and existing independently of any supposed grant in the constitution. But where the government exists by virtue of a *written* constitution, the judiciary does not necessarily derive from that circumstance, any other than its ordinary and appropriate powers. Our judiciary is constructed on the principles of the common law, which enters so essentially into the composition of our social institutions as to be inseparable from them, and to be, in fact, the basis of the whole scheme of our civil and political liberty. In adopting any organ or instrument of the common law, we take it with just such powers and capacities as were incident to it, at the common law, except where these are expressly, or by necessary implication, abridged or enlarged in the act of adoption; and that such act is a written instrument, cannot vary its consequences or construction. . . Now, what are the powers of the judiciary, at the common law? They are those that necessarily arise out of its immediate business; and they are, therefore, commensurate only with the judicial execution of the municipal law, or, in other words, with the administration of distributive justice, without extending to any of a political cast whatever.

With us, although the legislature be the depository of only so much of the sovereignty as the people have thought fit to impart, it is, nevertheless, sovereign within the limit of its powers, and may relatively claim the same pre-eminence here, that it may claim elsewhere. It will be conceded, then, that the ordinary and essential powers of the judiciary do not extend to the annulling of an act of the legislature.

The constitution of *Pennsylvania* contains no express grant of political powers to the judiciary. But to establish a grant by implication, the constitution is said to be a law of superior obligation; and consequently, that if it were to come into collision with an act of the legislature, the latter would have to give way; this is conceded. But it is a fallacy, to suppose, that they can come into collision *before the judiciary.* What is a constitution? It is an act of extraordinary legislation, by which the people establish the structure and mechanism of their government; and in which they prescribe fundamental rules to regulate the motion of the several parts. What is a statute? It is an act of ordinary legislation, by the appropriate organ of the government; the provisions of which are to be executed by the executive or judiciary, or by officers subordinate to them. The constitution, then, contains no practical rules for the administration of *distributive justice,* with which alone the judiciary has to do; these being furnished in acts of ordinary legislation, by that organ of the government, which, in this respect, is exclusively the representative of the people; and it is generally true, that the provisions of a constitution are to be carried into effect immediately by the legislature, and only mediately, if at all, by the judiciary. In what respect is the constitution of *Pennsylvania* inconsistent with this principle? Only, perhaps, in one particular provision, to regulate the style of process, and establish an appropriate form of conclusion in criminal prosecutions: in this alone, the constitution furnishes a rule for the judiciary, and this the legislature cannot alter, because it cannot alter the constitution. In all other cases, if the act of assembly supposed to be unconstitutional, were laid out of the question, there would remain no rule to determine the point in controversy in the cause, but the statute or common law, as it existed before the act of assembly was passed; and the constitution and act of assembly, therefore, do not furnish conflicting rules *applicable to the point before the court;* nor is it at all necessary, that the one or the other of them should give way.

The constitution and the *right* of the legislature to pass the act, may be in collision; but is that a legitimate subject for judicial determination? If it be, the judiciary must be a peculiar organ, to revise the proceedings of the legislature, and to correct its mistakes; and in what part of the constitution are we to look for this proud preeminence? Viewing the matter in the opposite direction, what would be thought of an act of assembly in which it should be declared that the supreme court had, in a particular case, put a wrong construction on the constitution of the *United States,* and that the judgment should therefore be reversed? It would, doubtless, be thought a usurpation of judicial power. But it is by no means clear, that to declare a law void, which has been enacted according to the forms prescribed in the constitution, is not a usurpation of legislative power. . . It is the business of the judiciary, to interpret the laws, not scan the authority of the lawgiver; and without the latter, it cannot take cognizance of a collision between a law and the constitution. So that to affirm that the judiciary has a right to judge of the existence of such collision, is to take for granted the very thing to be proved; and that a very cogent argument may be made in this way, I am not disposed to deny; . . .

But it has been said to be emphatically the business of the judiciary, to ascertain and pronounce what the law is; and that this necessarily involves a consideration of the constitution. It does so: but how far? If the judiciary will inquire into anything beside the form of enactment, where shall it stop? There must be some point of limitation to such an inquiry; for no one will pretend, that a judge would be justifiable in calling for the election returns, or scrutinizing the qualifications of those who composed the legislature.

.   .   .

[L]et it be supposed that the power to declare a law unconstitutional has been exercised. What is to be done? The legislature must acquiesce, although it may think the construction of the judiciary wrong. But why must it acquiesce? Only because it is bound to pay that respect to every other organ of the government, which it has a right to exact from each of them in turn. This is the argument. But it will not be pretended, that the legislature has not, at least, an equal right with the judiciary to put a construction on the constitution; nor that either of them is infallible; nor that either ought to be required to surrender its judgment to the other. Suppose, then, they differ in opinion as to the constitutionality of a particular law; if the organ whose business it first is to decide on the subject, is not to have its judgment treated with respect, what shall prevent it from securing the preponderance of its opinion by the strong arm of power? . . .

.   .   .

But, in theory, all the organs of the government are of equal capacity; or, if not equal, each must be supposed to have superior capacity only for those things which peculiarly belong to it; and as legislation peculiarly involves the consideration of those limitations which are put on the law-making power, and the interpretation of the laws when made, involves only the construction of the laws themselves, it follows, that the construction of the constitution, in this particular, belongs to the legislature, which ought, therefore, to be taken to have superior capacity to judge of the constitutionality of its own acts. But suppose all to be of equal capacity, in every respect, why should one exercise a controlling power over the rest? That the judiciary is of superior rank, has never been pretended, although it has been said to be co-ordinate. It is not easy, however, to comprehend how the power which gives law to all the rest, can be of no more than equal rank with one which receives it, and is answerable to the former for the observance of its statutes. Legislation is essentially an act of sovereign power; but the execution of the laws by instruments that are governed by prescribed rules, and exercise no power of volition, is essentially otherwise. . . It may be said, the power of the legislature, also, is limited by prescribed rules: it is so. But it is, nevertheless, the power of the people, and sovereign as far as it extends. It cannot be said, that the judiciary is co-ordinate, merely because it is established by the constitution; if that were sufficient sheriffs, registers of wills and recorders of deeds would be so too. Within the pale of their authority, the acts of these officers will have the power of the people for their support; but no one will pretend, they are of equal dignity with the acts of the legislature. Inequality of rank arises not from the manner in which the organ has been constituted, but from its essence and the nature of its functions; and the legislative organ is superior to every other, inasmuch as the power to will and to command, is essentially superior to the power to act and to obey. . . .

.   .   .

Every one knows how seldom men think exactly alike on ordinary subjects; and a government constructed on the principle of assent by all its parts, would be inadequate to the most simple operations. The notion of a complication of counter-checks has been carried to an extent in theory, of which the framers of the constitution never dreamt. When the entire sovereignty was separated into its elementary parts, and distributed to the appropriate branches, all things incident to the exercise of its powers were committed to each branch exclusively. The negative which each part of the legislature may exercise, in regard to the acts of the other, was thought sufficient to prevent material infractions of the restraints which were put on the power of the whole; for, had it been intended to interpose the judiciary as an additional barrier, the matter would surely not have been left in doubt. The judges would not have been left to stand on the insecure and ever-shifting ground of public opinion, as to constructive power; they would have been placed on the impregnable ground of an express grant; they would not have been compelled to resort to the debates in the convention, or the opinion that was generally entertained at the time. A constitution, or a statute, is supposed to contain the whole will of the body from which it emanated; and I would just as soon resort to the debates in the legislature, for the construction of an act of assembly, as to the debates in the convention, for the construction of the constitution.

39

The power is said to be restricted to cases that are free from doubt or difficulty. But the abstract existence of a power cannot depend on the clearness or obscurity of the case in which it is to be exercised; for that is a consideration that cannot present itself, before the question of the existence of the power shall have been determined; and if its existence be conceded, no considerations of policy, arising from the obscurity of the particular case, ought to influence the exercise of it. . . . To say, therefore, that the power is to be exercised but in perfectly clear cases, is to betray a doubt of the propriety of exercising it at all. Were the same caution used in judging of the existence of the power, that is inculcated as to the exercise of it, the profession would, perhaps, arrive at a different conclusion. The grant of a power so extraordinary, ought to appear so plain, that he who should run might read. . . .

But the judges are sworn to support the constitution, and are they not bound by it as the law of the land? In some respects they are. In the very few cases in which the judiciary, and not the legislature, is the immediate organ to execute its provisions, they are bound by it, in preference to any act of assembly to the contrary; in such cases, the constitution is a rule to the courts. But what I have in view in this inquiry is, the supposed right of the judiciary, to interfere, in cases where the constitution is to be carried into effect through the instrumentality of the legislature, and where that organ must necessarily first decide on the constitutionality of its own act. The oath to support the constitution is not peculiar to the judges, but is taken indiscriminately by every officer of the government, and is designed rather as a test of the political principles of the man, than to bind the officer in the discharge of his duty: otherwise, it were difficult to determine, what operation it is to have in the case of a recorder of deeds, for instance, who, in the execution of his office, has nothing to do with the constitution. But granting it to relate to the official conduct of the judge, as well as every other officer, and not to his political principles, still, it must be understood in reference to supporting the constitution, *only as far as that may be involved in his official duty;* and consequently, if his official duty does not comprehend an inquiry into the authority of the legislature, neither does his oath. . . .

But do not the judges do a *positive* act in violation of the constitution, when they give effect to an unconstitutional law? Not if the law has been passed according to the forms established in the constitution. The fallacy of the question is, in supposing that the judiciary adopts the acts of the legislature as its own; whereas, the enactment of a law and the interpretation of it are not concurrent acts, and as the judiciary is not required to concur in the enactment, neither is it in the breach of the constitution which may be the consequence of the enactment; the fault is imputable to the legislature, and on it the responsibility exclusively rests. . . .

. . .

But it has been said, that this construction would deprive the citizen of the advantages which are peculiar to a written constitution, by at once declaring the power of the legislature, in practice, to be illimitable. . . But there is no magic or inherent power in parchment and ink, to command respect, and protect principles from violation. In the business of government, a recurrence to first principles answers the end of an observation at sea, with a view to correct the dead-reckoning; and for this purpose, a written constitution is an instrument of inestimable value. It is of inestimable value also, in rendering its principles familiar to the mass of the people; for, after all, there is no effectual guard against legislative usurpation, but public opinion, the force of which, in this country, is inconceivably great. . . Once let public opinion be so corrupt, as to sanction every misconstruction of the constitution, and abuse of power, which the temptation of the moment may dictate, and the party which may happen to be predominant, will laugh at the puny efforts of a dependent power to arrest it in its course.

For these reasons, I am of opinion, that it rests with the people, in whom full and absolute sovereign power resides, to correct abuses in legislation, by instructing their representatives to repeal the obnoxious act. What is wanting to plenary power in the government, is reserved by the people, for their own immediate use; and to redress an infringment of their rights in this respect, would seem to be an accessory of the power thus reserved. It might, perhaps, have been better to vest the power in the judiciary; as it might be expected, that its habits of deliberation, and the aid derived from the arguments of counsel, would more frequently lead to accurate conclusions. On the other hand, the judiciary is not infalliable; and an error by it would admit of no remedy but a more distinct expression of the public will, through the extraordinary medium of a convention; whereas, an error by the legislature admits of a remedy by an exertion of the same will, in the ordinary exercise of the right of suffrage—a mode better calculated to attain the end, without popular excitement. It may be said, the people would probably not notice an error of their representatives. But they would as probably do so, as notice an error of the judiciary; and beside, it is a *postulate* in the theory of our government, and the very basis of the superstructure, that the people are wise, virtuous, and competent to manage their own affairs; and if they are not so, in fact, still, every question of this sort must be determined according to the principles of the constitution, as it came from the hands of its framers, and the existence of a defect which was not foreseen, would not justify those who administer the government, in applying a corrective in practice, which can be provided only by a convention. . . .

. . .

But in regard to an act of assembly, which is found to be in collision with the constitution, laws or treaties of the *United States,* I take the duty of the judiciary to be exactly the reverse. By becoming parties to the federal constitution, the states have agreed to several limitations of their individual sovereignty, to enforce which, it was thought to be absolutely necessary, to prevent them from giving effect to laws in violation of those limitations, through the instrumentality of their own judges. Accordingly, it is declared in the sixth article and second section of the federal constitution, that "this constitution, and the laws of the *United States* which shall be made in pursuance thereof, and all treaties made, or which shall be made under the authority of the *United States,* shall be the *supreme* law of the land; and the *judges* in every *state* shall be BOUND thereby; anything in the *laws* or *constitution* of any *state* to the contrary notwithstanding."

This is an express grant of a political power, and it is conclusive, to show that no law of inferior obligation, as every state law must necessarily be, can be executed at the expense of the constitution, laws or treaties of the *United States.* It may be said, these are to furnish a rule only when there is no state provision on the subject. But in that view, they could, with no propriety, be called supreme; for supremacy is a relative term, and cannot be predicated of a thing which exists separately and alone: and this law, which is called supreme, would change its character and become subordinate, as soon as it should be found in conflict with a state law. But the judges are to be bound by the federal constitution and laws, notwithstanding anything in the constitution or laws of the particular state *to the contrary.* If, then, a state were to declare the laws of the *United*

States not to be obligatory on her judges, such an act would unquestionably be void; for it will not be pretended, that any member of the union can dispense with the obligation of the federal constitution; and if it cannot be done directly, and by a general declaratory law, neither can it indirectly, and by by-laws dispensing with it in particular cases.

II

Reapportionment

The courts have made policy affecting many aspects of American life, but they usually have done so with apologies to the legislative branch—the primary policymaker, supposedly, in the American system of government. When, after some hesitation, the courts entered the "political thicket" of legislative apportionment, they penetrated to the heart of the policymaking process. Apportionment decisions concern who makes policy and, more importantly, what political theory underlies that policymaking. The principles determining just who or what a representative represents go a long way toward explaining the policy that emerges. The Court decisions in this chapter, then, presuppose a particular political philosophy and are not just explications of the meaning of "equal protection of the laws."

Two contradictory philosophies are at war in these cases: majority rule versus minority rights and, with a slightly different connotation, numbers versus interests. American political institutions and practices, despite a generally dominant position accorded majority rule, are an unreconciled blend of these two themes. In the American experience, the two benchmarks of majoritarian philosophy were the rallying cry of the Revolution: "No taxation without representation" and Thomas Jefferson's statement in the Declaration of Independence that governments derive "their just powers from the consent of the governed." These twin concepts, one that calls for advancing the views and protecting the interests of constituents (representation), and the other that requires a broad-based participation by the citizenry in the selection of legislators (consent), have been the foundation of the majority theory of American political institutions. Both concepts have loomed large in American political thought and constitutional law. Consent, in the form of the expansion of the right to vote, has accounted for four amendments to the Constitution (the Fifteenth, Nineteenth, Twenty-fourth, and Twenty-sixth) and untold hours of legislative debate. In general terms, that right has been expanded slowly (almost totally by legislative action) from belonging exclusively to the adult, male, white, property-owner voter at the time of the adoption of the Declaration to belonging to the eighteen and older (without reference to gender, race, or economic status) voter of the present. At the same time that legislative action was broadening the base of the electorate, courts were busy ensuring that those formally eligible could actually vote. The courts struck down "grandfather clauses," white primaries, the discriminatory use of literacy tests, and the poll tax to ensure this right.

The proper basis of representation has been as persistent an issue as consent. In his *Notes on Virginia* (1782), Thomas Jefferson complained about the disproportionate share of seats held by the Tidewater region in the Virginia legislature. Whether or not to base representation in the House of Representatives on people or on property divided the Constitutional Convention, leading delegate James Wilson of Pennsylvania to ask: "Can we forget for whom we are forming a Government? Is it for men, or for the imaginary beings called States?" He had answered his own questions earlier when he said that his first premise was "that all authority was derived from the people, equal numbers of people ought to have an equal number of representatives, and different numbers of people different numbers of representatives." The "Connecticut Compromise"* made it possible for Wilson's view to prevail in developing the composition of the House of Representatives, and for the Framers to ensure continuation of Wilson's principle by requiring a decennial census followed by reapportionment of the House. In this way the people would be assured that the popularly chosen house of Congress would be, and would remain, responsive to them. Most states adopted the same rule for at least one house of their bicameral legislature. This principle also is reflected in the Seventeenth Amendment which says that those eligible to vote for national senators shall be those eligible to vote for the larger, more population-based, house of the state legislature. Likewise, those eligible to vote for presidential electors—a qualification determined by the states—generally have been those permitted to vote for members of the population-based house of the state legislature. This might give the impression that a continuing feature of American political institutions has been the idea of a broad base of eligible participants in the selection process, and the responsiveness of those institutions to the participants' desires.

---

*Proposed by delegate William Samuel Johnson of Connecticut, this compromise resulted in representation of population in the U.S. House of Representatives and of states in the U.S. Senate.

But there is another side to the coin; the struggle to make the equality-majority rule concept the operative one would not have been required had there been no opposition. In American political development, majority rule has been as much feared as praised. Madison's *Federalist* No. X (p. 16) and Hamilton's *Federalist* No. IX attempt to explain how to control the majority so that the rights of the minority are not trampled upon. Jefferson reminded us in his first inaugural address that "though the will of the majority is in all cases to prevail, that will to be rightful must be reasonable. . . The minority possess their equal rights which equal law must protect, and to violate would be oppression." The entire system of checks and balances and separation of powers, including judicial review, is designed and intended to prevent pure (or mere) majority rule. Every extension of the right to vote has been opposed on the grounds that the group about to be given the vote (property-less males, blacks, women, 18-20 year olds) would alter policy outcomes, usually to the disadvantage of defenders of the status quo. The U.S. Senate is a constant reminder that the Constitutional Convention was concerned not only with numerical equality, but also with protection of numerical minorities, protection of states, and protection of property. And many state legislatures have been apportioned to give to certain interests or geographic regions a legislative influence greater than that provided by numbers alone. To a degree, Americans have followed a principle enunciated by Daniel Webster in the 1820 Massachusetts Constitutional Convention: "The true principle of free and popular government would seem to be so to construct it as to give to all, or at least a very great majority, an interest in its preservation. To found it, as other things are founded, on men's interest . . . not always to be measured by mere numbers." Or as Judge Abel P. Upshur put it a few years later in a Virginia Constitutional Convention, "There are two kinds of majority. There is a majority in interest, as well as a majority in number." [1] In short, majority rule has never been totally accepted in our institutional arrangements because of a fear that the majority would not be sufficiently sensitive to, and protective of, the rights and interests of the minority. The Court was asked to resolve this conflict between numbers and interests in the apportionment cases.

The U.S. House of Representatives has been regularly reapportioned over the years to reflect the acceptance of population-based representation, and during the nineteenth century state legislatures generally adhered to the same principle. Twentieth century state legislators began to ignore their own constitutional mandates and maintain a turn-of-the-century status quo in the allocation of representatives, despite major shifts in population distribution within each state. As a result, state legislative districts, which had had more or less the same population in 1901, became widely variable

47

in size by 1960 while still retaining equal numbers of representatives. In Florida, for example, the smallest district in 1961 had a population of 2,868 while the largest was 311,682; yet each district sent one legislator to Tallahassee. This phenomenon is called malapportionment. The effect of increasing population without a corresponding increase in the number of representatives is often referred to by the Court as "dilution of the vote."

Efforts to convince state legislators to reapportion were not overly successful. Incumbents feared a loss of their electoral base, rural legislators feared domination of the policy process by urban representatives and voters, and each political party feared that the other would be the beneficiary of any redistricting. As is so often the case in the American system, aggrieved persons finally turned to the courts for relief, but their first major attempt met with defeat in Colegrove v. Green, 328 U.S. 549 (1946). The Court that decided the case was shorthanded; Chief Justice Harlan F. Stone had died and his successor had not yet been named, and Justice Robert H. Jackson was in Nuremberg as the American prosecutor in the Nazi war crimes trials.

The resulting seven-man Court produced three opinions, two majorities, and may have settled one thing. Colegrove had relied on the guaranty clause of the Constitution (Article IV, Section 4), in which the United States guarantees each state a republican form of government, as the basis of his claim for reapportionment of the congressional districts in Illinois. Justice Felix Frankfurter's prevailing opinion held that claims under that clause presented a political question which could not or should not be decided by the Court. "In effect," declared Frankfurter for himself, Justice Harold Burton, and Justice Stanley Reed, "this is an appeal to the federal courts to reconstruct the electoral process of Illinois. . ." [2] But all the courts could possibly have done was to declare the existing districting invalid, leaving the candidates for all congressional seats to run at large. The cure would have been worse than the problem. Furthermore, "Nothing is clearer than that this controversy concerns matters that bring courts into immediate and active relations with party contests. From the determination of such issues this Court has traditionally held aloof. It is hostile to a democratic system to involve the judiciary in the politics of the people. And it is not less pernicious if such judicial intervention in an essentially political contest be dressed up in the abstract phrases of the law." [3]

Even though Colegrove dealt with congressional districting, the language of the prevailing opinion was broad enough to encompass state legislative apportionment as well. The three dissenters (Justices Hugo L. Black, William O. Douglas, and Frank Murphy) agreed on the nature of the guaranty clause claim but found the equal protection clause of the

Fourteenth Amendment an alternative ground to use to decide the case in Colegrove's favor. Justice Wiley Rutledge, with the deciding vote, agreed that there were grounds for relief but found "a want of equity"* in Colegrove's claim and joined Frankfurter in denying it. Later litigants learned their lesson and stopped relying on the guaranty clause, shifting instead to the equal protection clause of the Fourteenth Amendment.

In *Baker* v. *Carr* (p. 53), the Court accepted the new argument. It now appeared that a claim based on the equal protection clause did not present a political question even if it *might* do so if premised on the guaranty clause. The Court developed its argument fairly rapidly after *Baker*. "One person-one vote" became the constitutional talisman; it was applied to both houses of state legislatures, exceptions based on analogies drawn from the U.S. Senate were rebuffed, and the "one person-one vote" principle was extended to governing bodies in local units of government. In a two-year period the Court opted for numbers and majority rule rather than interests and minority rights as a guiding principle of representation.

The effects of state legislative reapportionment have been mixed. Some incumbents were ousted or forced to campaign more strenuously than before. The minority party gained strength in some state legislatures but not enough to control both houses. The urban-suburban areas gained in representation, but without having the effect of completely restructuring the policy output of the legislature. One effect of the change was measurable and fairly dramatic in some states. The "electoral percentage" is the percentage of the population theoretically required to elect a majority of the members of one or both houses of the legislature; an electoral system based on perfect population equality of districts would require 51 percent of the population to elect 51 percent of the legislature. Some of the more striking before and after electoral percentages are presented in Table 2.1. By this electoral percentage measure, at least, the Court's reapportionment requirement of one person-one vote has been approached fairly well.

Other consequences of these decisions are not so clear, but one is notable: it triggered a major legislative reaction. Beginning in 1964 and continuing through 1967, various members of Congress attempted to reverse or modify the Supreme Court's apportionment rulings. Although none of these efforts was successful, it may be useful to look at the tactics chosen by the legislators. One was the introduction of legislation stripping the Court of its appellate jurisdiction in the area of state legislative apportionment. Article III, Section 2, subjects the Court's appellate jurisdiction to this type of statutory control which, unlike an amendment, requires

---

*A lack of fairness in the ultimate result if the claim were granted.

Table 2.1 Selected Electoral Percentages Before and After Reapportionment

State	Before	After	Legislative Chamber
Arizona	12.8	49.1	Senate
California	10.7	48.9	Senate
Connecticut	11.9	43.8	House
Kansas	19.4	48.7	House
Nevada	8.0	49.7	Senate
New Jersey	19.0	47.0	Senate
Vermont	11.6	48.7	House

SOURCE: Congressional Quarterly, *Representation and Apportionment* (Washington, D.C.: Congressional Quarterly Service, 1966), pp. 68-69.

only a simple majority vote in each house and approval by the president. In this instance, the effort was unsuccessful in the Senate but subsequently passed the House in 1964.

Senator Everett Dirksen, R-Ill., the Senate minority leader from 1959 to 1969, introduced proposed amendments to the Constitution (p. 90). Amendments do not run the risk of judicial invalidation as does a jurisdiction-curbing statute, and joint resolutions presenting amendments for ratification do not require the approval of the president. However, they do require support from two-thirds of each house of Congress and from three-fourths of the states. Senator Dirksen's efforts gained approval of a majority of the Senate, but each fell short of the two-thirds required. At the same time, Dirksen had tried to buy time for his first amending effort by attaching a rider to a foreign aid bill to delay all court proceedings for two to four years. This movement was also defeated.

The third tactic employed began as early as 1963 when state legislators first realized the implications of *Baker* v. *Carr.* That year, legislators began a drive to bring into operation a device never used before for amending the Constitution—petitions from two-thirds of the states—which could result in the calling of a convention. Many unresolved questions about this amending process remained, but they were never put to the test because the petition drive peaked in 1967 with 32 states, two short of the 34 needed, calling for the convention. One might suspect that state interest in having a convention declined with the increases in the number of states which reapportioned either voluntarily or under court order. The new legislators would be unlikely to undo the changes that were responsible for putting them in office.

The burst of activity following *Baker* v. *Carr* has not settled the whole reapportionment issue. With continuing shifts in population, reapportionment is an ongoing necessity if the principle of one-person, one-vote is to be maintained. Yet the groups benefitting from the actions examined here undoubtedly will be reluctant to give up what they have gained should future censuses warrant it. At some future date more litigation, and more requests for a policy decision saying the majoritarian side of the issue is the correct one, will be presented to the courts. *Baker* and its progeny will make it easier for a court to continue to apply the equality principle, but because judges are sufficiently inventive, such a continuation is not foreordained. A majority that ignores Jefferson's admonition to be reasonable could find the courts less friendly than they were in this group of cases.

The Court's entry into this major policymaking area was, from the justices' point of view, successful. They got what they wanted and did not suffer severe legislative reprisals; they were able to press on with the development of the line of decisions despite some unrest in Congress. But the reasons for their success are not so clear. Politically, the Court had some support. House members from urban areas, and senators dependent on those areas for the margin of victory at the polls, had to support the idea of one-person, one-vote. State legislators from urban areas had long been agitating for reapportionment and could be counted on to do everything in their power to protect the gains the Court had made for them. And, of course, the voters in the districts gaining strength by reapportionment offered generalized support to the Court.

Psychologically, the Court had a couple of things in its favor. Several of the state legislatures were caught in a violation of their own state constitutions; *Baker* v. *Carr* makes the point that Tennessee legislators had not obeyed the state constitution for 50 years. It was difficult for them to react indignantly under those circumstances. The second psychological advantage is impossible to measure. These decisions came just as Congress and the Court were jointly developing the means of ensuring equality for racial minorities within the system, and it might have been contradictory for legislators to reject one-person, one-vote at the same time they were supporting the Civil Rights Act of 1964 and the Voting Rights Act of 1965. In addition, equality is an appealing idea in the abstract and policymakers might not have wanted to challenge it for fear of being labelled undemocratic.

The courts did two things that may have softened the reaction to these decisions. The Supreme Court noted that absolute equality was not a

51

requirement and accepted some variation in district size under this doctrine. And the lower courts gave the states ample opportunity to devise their own districting plans to meet the requirement, rather than starting by imposing judicially crafted plans on them. The combined influence of all these factors gave the Court the opportunity to make its own policy decisions, and get them in place, without unduly suffering from the reactions of other policymakers in the political process.

NOTES

1. A. T. Mason, *Free Government in the Making* (New York: Oxford University Press, 1965), pp. 414, 431.
2. *Colegrove* v. *Green,* 328 U.S. 549 (1946), at 552.
3. Ibid., pp. 553-554.

SELECTED BIBLIOGRAPHY

Baker, Gordon E. *The Reapportionment Revolution: Representation, Political Power, and the Supreme Court.* New York: Random House, 1966.
Congressional Quarterly. *Representation and Reapportionment.* Washington: Congressional Quarterly Service, 1966.
Cortner, Richard C. *The Apportionment Cases.* Knoxville: University of Tennessee Press, 1970.
David, Paul T. and Eisenberg, Ralph. *Devaluation of the Urban and Suburban Vote.* Charlottesville: Bureau of Public Administration, University of Virginia, 1961.
Dixon, Robert, Jr. *Democratic Representation in Law and Politics.* New York: Oxford University Press, 1969.
Hanson, Roger and Crew, Robert E. Jr. "The Policy Impact of Reapportionment," 8 *Law and Society Review* 69 (1973).
Hanson, Royce. *The Political Thicket.* Englewood Cliffs: Prentice Hall, 1966.
Lee, Calvin B. T. *One Man One Vote.* New York: Scribner's, 1965.
McCloskey, Robert G. "Foreword: The Reapportionment Cases," 75 *Harvard Law Review* 54 (1962).
McKay, Robert B. *Reapportionment.* New York: Twentieth Century Fund, 1965.
Niemi, Richard G. and Deegan, John Jr. "A Theory of Political Redistricting," 72 *American Political Science Review* 1304 (1978).
Schubert, Glendon A., ed. *Reapportionment.* New York: Scribner's, 1965.
Walter, Benjamin; Wirt, Frederick M.; Rabinovitz, Francine F.; and Hensler, Deborah R. *On the City's Rim: Suburban Politics and Policy.* Lexington, Mass.: D. C. Heath, 1972.

Baker v. Carr

369 U.S. 186, 7 L ed 2d 663, 82 S Ct 691 (1962)

Qualified Tennessee voters challenged the apportionment of seats in the state legislature. They asserted that the general assembly had not been reapportioned since 1901 and that, even then, districting had not conformed with the state constitutional requirement of approximate population equality of districts. They further asserted that the disparities in district size deprived them of equal protection of the laws contrary to the Fourteenth Amendment. The plaintiffs were able to show that the largest Senate district had a population of 237,905 while the smallest was only 39,727. In the House, the range was from 79,301 to 3,454. Less than one-third of the population could elect a majority of each legislative chamber. A three-judge district court dismissed the suit believing that it lacked jurisdiction and that the complaint failed to state a claim upon which courts could grant relief. The Supreme Court noted probable jurisdiction on direct appeal.

. . .

Mr. Justice Brennan delivered the opinion of the Court.

This civil action was brought under 42 USC §§ 1983 and 1988 to redress the alleged deprivation of federal constitutional rights. The complaint, alleging that by means of a 1901 statute of Tennessee apportioning the members of the General Assembly among the State's 95 counties, "these plaintiffs and others similarly situated, are denied the equal protection of the laws accorded them by the Fourteenth Amendment to the Constitution of the United States by virtue of the debasement of their votes," was dismissed by a three-judge court. . . The court held that it lacked jurisdiction of the subject matter and also that no claim was stated upon which relief could be granted. We noted probable jurisdiction of the appeal. We hold that the dismissal was error, and remand the cause to the District Court for trial and further proceedings consistent with this opinion. . . .

. . .

Tennessee's standard for allocating legislative representation among her counties is the total number of qualified voters resident in the respective counties, subject only to minor qualifications. Decennial reapportionment in compliance with the constitutional scheme was effected by the General Assembly each decade from 1871 to 1901... In 1901 the General Assembly abandoned separate enumeration in favor of reliance upon the Federal Census and passed the Apportionment Act here in controversy. In the more than 60 years since that action, all proposals in both Houses of the General Assembly for reapportionment have failed to pass.

Between 1901 and 1961, Tennessee has experienced substantial growth and redistribution of her population. In 1901 the population was 2,020,616, of whom 487,380 were eligible to vote. The 1960 Federal Census reports the State's population at 3,567,089, of whom 2,092,891 are eligible to vote. The relative standings of the counties in terms of qualified voters have changed significantly. It is primarily the continued application of the 1901 Apportionment Act to this shifted and enlarged voting population which gives rise to the present controversy.

Indeed, the complaint alleges that the 1901 statute, even as of the time of its passage, "made no apportionment of Representatives and Senators in accordance with the constitutional formula . . . , but instead arbitrarily and capriciously apportioned representatives in the Senate and House without reference . . . to any logical or reasonable formula whatever." It is further alleged that "because of the population changes since 1900, and the failure of the Legislature to reapportion itself since 1901," the 1901 statute became "unconstitutional and obsolete." Appellants also argue that, because of the composition of the legislature effected by the 1901 Apportionment Act, redress in the form of a state constitutional amendment to change the entire mechanism for reapportioning, or any other change short of that, is difficult or impossible. . . .

. . .

I.

The dismissal order [by the District Court] recited that the court sustained the appellees' grounds "(1) that the Court lacks jurisdiction of the subject matter, and (2) that the complaint fails to state a claim upon which relief can be granted. . . ."

. . .

We treat the first ground of dismissal as "lack of jurisdiction of the subject matter." The second we consider to result in a failure to state a justiciable cause of action. . . .

. . .

[W]e hold today only (a) that the court possessed jurisdiction of the subject matter; (b) that a justiciable cause of action is stated upon which appellants would be entitled to appropriate relief; and (c) because appellees raise the issue before this Court, that the appellants have standing to challenge the Tennessee apportionment statutes. Beyond noting that we have no cause at this stage to doubt the District Court will be able to fashion relief if violations of constitutional rights are found, it is improper now to consider what remedy would be most appropriate if appellants prevail at the trial.

II.

Jurisdiction of the Subject Matter.

The District Court was uncertain whether our cases withholding federal judicial relief rested upon a lack of federal jurisdiction or upon the inappropriateness of the subject matter for judicial consideration—what we have designated "nonjusticiability." The distinction between the two grounds is significant. In the instance of nonjusticiability, consideration of the cause is not wholly and immediately foreclosed; rather, the Court's inquiry necessarily proceeds to the point of deciding whether the duty asserted can be judicially identified and its breach judicially determined, and whether protection for the right asserted can be judicially molded. In the instance of lack of jurisdiction the cause either does not "arise under" the Federal Constitution, laws or treaties (or fall within one of the other enumerated categories of Art 3 § 2), or is not a "case or controversy" within the meaning of that section; or the cause is not one described by any jurisdictional statute. Our conclusion that this cause presents no nonjusticiable "political question" settles the only possible doubt that it is a case or controversy. Under the present heading of "Jurisdiction of the

Subject Matter" we hold only that the matter set forth in the complaint does arise under the Constitution. . . .

. . .

Since the District Court obviously and correctly did not deem the asserted federal constitutional claim unsubstantial and frivolous, it should not have dismissed the complaint for want of jurisdiction of the subject matter. And of course no further consideration of the merits of the claim is relevant to a determination of the court's jurisdiction of the subject matter. . . .

. . .

IV.

Justiciability.

In holding that the subject matter of this suit was not justiciable, the District Court relied on Colegrove v Green. . . We understand the District Court to have read the cited cases as compelling the conclusion that since the appellants sought to have a legislative apportionment held unconstitutional, their suit presented a "political question" and was therefore nonjusticiable. We hold that this challenge to an apportionment presents no nonjusticiable "political question." The cited cases do not hold the contrary.

Of course the mere fact that the suit seeks protection of a political right does not mean it presents a political question. Such an objection "is little more than a play upon words." Rather, it is argued that apportionment cases, whatever the actual wording of the complaint, can involve no federal constitutional right except one resting on the guaranty of a republican form of government, and that complaints based on that clause have been held to present political questions which are nonjusticiable.

We hold that the claim pleaded here neither rests upon nor implicates the Guaranty Clause and that its justiciability is therefore not foreclosed by our decisions of cases involving that clause. The District Court misinterpreted Colegrove v Green and other decisions of this Court on which it relied. Appellants' claim that they are being denied equal protection is justiciable, and if "discrimination is sufficiently shown, the right to relief under the equal protection clause is not diminished by the fact that the discrimination relates to political rights.". . .

. . .

The nonjusticiability of a political question is primarily a function of the separation of powers. Much confusion results from the capacity of the "political question" label to obscure the need for case-by-case inquiry. Deciding whether a matter has in any measure been committed by the Constitution to another branch of government, or whether the action of that branch exceeds whatever authority has been committed, is itself a delicate exercise in constitutional interpretation, and is a responsibility of this Court as ultimate interpreter of the Constitution. To demonstrate this requires no less than to analyze representative cases and to infer from them the analytical threads that make up the political question doctrine. . . .

. . .

[The opinion proceeds to an examination of all the prior decisions of the Court dealing with the political question doctrine.]

. . .

It is apparent that several formulations which vary slightly according to the settings in which the questions arise may describe a political question, although each has one or more elements which identify it as essentially a function of the separation of powers. Prominent on the surface of any case held to involve a political question is found a textually demonstrable constitutional commitment of the issue to a coordinate political department; or a lack of judicially discoverable and manageable standards for resolving it; or the impossibility of deciding without an initial policy determination of a kind clearly for nonjudicial discretion; or the impossibility of a court's undertaking independent resolution without expressing lack of the respect due coordinate branches of government; or an unusual need for unquestioning adherence to a political decision already made; or the potentiality of embarrassment from multifarious pronouncements by various departments on one question.

Unless one of these formulations is inextricable from the case at bar, there should be no dismissal for nonjusticiability on the ground of a political question's presence. The doctrine of which we treat is one of "political questions," not one of "political cases." The courts cannot reject as "no law suit" a bona fide controversy as to whether some action denominated "political" exceeds constitutional authority. . . .

. . .

We come, finally, to the ultimate inquiry whether our precedents as to what constitutes a nonjusticiable "political question" bring the case before us under the umbrella of that doctrine. A natural beginning is to note whether any of the common characteristics which we have been able to identify and label descriptively are present. We find none: The question here is the consistency of state action with the Federal Constitution. We have no question decided, or to be decided, by a political branch of government coequal with this Court. Nor do we risk embarrassment of our government abroad, or grave disturbance at home if we take issue with Tennessee as to the constitutionality of her action here challenged. Nor need the appellants, in order to succeed in this action, ask the Court to enter upon policy determinations for which judicially manageable standards are lacking. Judicial standards under the Equal Protection Clause are well developed and familiar, and it has been open to courts since the enactment of the Fourteenth Amendment to determine, if on the particular facts they must, that a discrimination reflects *no* policy, but simply arbitrary and capricious action.

This case does, in one sense, involve the allocation of political power within a State, and the appellants might conceivably have added a claim under the Guaranty Clause. . . . [A]ny reliance on that clause would be futile. But because any reliance on the Guaranty Clause could not have succeeded it does not follow that appellants may not be heard on the equal protection claim which in fact they tender. True, it must be clear that the Fourteenth Amendment claim is not so enmeshed with those political question elements which render Guaranty Clause claims nonjusticiable as actually to present a political question itself. But we have found that not to be the case here. . . .

. . .

We conclude that the complaint's allegations of a denial of equal protection present a justiciable constitutional cause of action upon which appellants are entitled to a trial and a decision. The right asserted is within the reach of judicial protection under the Fourteenth Amendment.

The judgment of the District Court is reversed and the cause is remanded for further proceedings consistent with this opinion.

Reversed and remanded.

. . .

Mr. Justice Whittaker did not participate in the decision of this case.

. . .

Mr. Justice Douglas, concurring.

While I join the opinion of the Court and, like the Court, do not reach the merits, a word of explanation is necessary. I put to one side the problems of "political" questions involving the distribution of power between this Court, the Congress, and the Chief Executive. We have here a phase of the recurring problem of the relation of the federal courts to state agencies. More particularly, the question is the extent to which a State may weight one person's vote more heavily than it does another's.

So far as voting rights are concerned, there are large gaps in the Constitution. Yet the right to vote is inherent in the republican form of government envisaged by Article 4 § 4 of the Constitution. The House— and now the Senate—are chosen by the people. The time, manner, and place of elections of Senators and Representatives are left to the States (Article 1 § 4, cl 1; Amendment 17) subject to the regulatory power of Congress. A "republican form" of government is guaranteed each State by Article 4 § 4, and each is likewise promised protection against invasion. Ibid. That the States may specify the qualifications for voters is implicit in Article 1 § 2, Clause 1, which provides that the House of Representatives shall be chosen by the people and that "the Electors (voters) in each State shall have the Qualifications requisite for Electors (voters) of the most numerous Branch of the State Legislature." The same provision, contained in the Seventeenth Amendment, governs the election of Senators. Within limits those qualifications may be fixed by state law. [T]hose who vote for members of Congress do not "owe their right to vote to the State law in any sense which makes the exercise of the right to depend exclusively on the law of the State." The power of Congress to prescribe the qualifications for voters and thus override state law is not in issue here. It is, however, clear that by reason of the commands of the Constitution there are several qualifications that a State may not require.

Race, color, or previous condition of servitude is an impermissible standard by reason of the Fifteenth Amendment. . . .

. . .

Sex is another impermissible standard by reason of the Nineteenth Amendment.

There is a third barrier to a State's freedom in prescribing qualifications of voters and that is the Equal Protection Clause of the Fourteenth Amendment, the provision invoked here. And so the question is, may a State weight the vote of one county or one district more heavily than it weights the vote in another? . . .

It is said that any decision in cases of this kind is beyond the competence of the courts. Some make the same point as regards the problem of equal protection in cases involving racial segregation. Yet the legality of claims and conduct is a traditional subject for judicial determination. . . .

.   .   .

The justiciability of the present claims being established, any relief accorded can be fashioned in the light of well-known principles of equity.

.   .   .

Mr. Justice Clark, concurring.

One emerging from the rash of opinions with their accompanying clashing of views may well find himself suffering a mental blindness. The Court holds that the appellants have alleged a cause of action. However, it refuses to award relief here—although the facts are undisputed—and fails to give the District Court any guidance whatever. One dissenting opinion, bursting with words that go through so much and conclude with so little, contemns the majority action as "a massive repudiation of the experience of our whole past." Another describes the complaint as merely asserting conclusory allegations that Tennessee's apportionment is "incorrect," "arbitrary," "obsolete," and "unconstitutional." I believe it can be shown that this case is distinguishable from earlier cases dealing with the distribution of political power by a State, that a patent violation of the Equal Protection Clause of the United States Constitution has been shown, and that an appropriate remedy may be formulated. . . .

.   .   .

II.

The controlling facts cannot be disputed. It appears from the record that 37% of the voters of Tennessee elect 20 of the 33 Senators while 40%

of the voters elect 63 of the 99 members of the House. But this might not on its face be an "invidious discrimination," for a "statutory discrimination will not be set aside if any state of facts reasonably may be conceived to justify it."

It is true that the apportionment policy incorporated in Tennessee's Constitution, i.e., state-wide numerical equality of representation with certain minor qualifications, is a rational one. On a county-by-county comparison a districting plan based thereon naturally will have disparities in representation due to the qualifications. But this to my mind does not raise constitutional problems, for the overall policy is reasonable. However, the root of the trouble is not in Tennessee's Constitution, for admittedly its policy has not been followed. The discrimination lies in the action of Tennessee's Assembly in allocating legislative seats to counties or districts created by it. Try as one may, Tennessee's apportionment just cannot be made to fit the pattern cut by its Constitution. This was the finding of the District Court. The policy of the Constitution referred to by the dissenters, therefore, is of no relevance here. We must examine what the Assembly has done. . . . Tennessee's apportionment is a crazy quilt without rational basis. . . .

. . .

The truth is that—although this case has been here for two years and has had over six hours' argument (three times the ordinary case) and has been most carefully considered over and over again by us in Conference and individually—no one, not even the State nor the dissenters, has come up with any rational basis for Tennessee's apportionment statute.

No one . . . contends that mathematical equality among voters is required by the Equal Protection Clause. But certainly there must be some rational design to a State's districting. The discrimination here does not fit any pattern—as I have said, it is but a crazy quilt. My Brother Harlan contends that other proposed apportionment plans contain disparities. Instead of chasing those rabbits he should first pause long enough to meet appellants' proof of discrimination by showing that in fact the present plan follows a rational policy. Not being able to do this, he merely counters with such generalities as "classic legislative judgment," no "significant discrepancy," and "de minimis departures." I submit that even a casual glance at the present apportionment picture shows these conclusions to be entirely fanciful. If present representation has a policy at all, it is to maintain the status quo of invidious discrimination at any cost. Like the District Court, I conclude that appellants have met the burden of showing "Tennessee is guilty of a clear violation of the state constitution and of the [federal] rights of the plaintiffs. . . ."

III.

Although I find the Tennessee apportionment statute offends the Equal Protection Clause, I would not consider intervention by this Court into so delicate a field if there were any other relief available to the people of Tennessee. But the majority of the people of Tennessee have no "practical opportunities for exerting their political weight at the polls" to correct the existing "invidious discrimination." Tennessee has no initiative and referendum. I have searched diligently for other "practical opportunities" present under the law. I find none other than through the federal courts. The majority of the voters have been caught up in a legislative strait jacket. Tennessee has an "informed, civically militant electorate" and "an aroused popular conscience," but it does not sear "the conscience of the people's representatives." This is because the legislative policy has riveted the present seats in the Assembly to their respective constituencies, and by the votes of their incumbents a reapportionment of any kind is prevented. The people have been rebuffed at the hands of the Assembly; they have tried the constitutional convention route, but since the call must originate in the Assembly it, too, has been fruitless. They have tried Tennessee courts with the same result, and Governors have fought the tide only to flounder. It is said that there is recourse in Congress and perhaps that may be, but from a practical standpoint this is without substance. To date Congress has never undertaken such a task in any State. We therefore must conclude that the people of Tennessee are stymied and without judicial intervention will be saddled with the present discrimination in the affairs of their state government.

IV.

Finally, we must consider if there are any appropriate modes of effective judicial relief. The federal courts are of course not forums for political debate, nor should they resolve themselves into state constitutional conventions or legislative assemblies. Nor should their jurisdiction be exercised in the hope that such a declaration, as is made today may have the direct effect of bringing on legislative action and relieving the courts of the problem of fashioning relief. To my mind this would be nothing less than blackjacking the Assembly into reapportioning the State. If judicial competence were lacking to fashion an effective decree, I would dismiss this appeal. However, like the Solicitor General of the United States, I see no such difficulty in the position of this case. One plan might be to start with the existing assembly districts, consolidate some of them, and award the seats thus released to those counties suffering the most egregious discrimination. Other possibilities are present and might be more effective. But the plan here suggested would at least release the strangle hold now on the Assembly and permit it to redistrict itself. . . .

. . .

[The Court's] decision today supports the proposition for which our forebears fought and many died, namely, that to be fully conformable to the principle of right, the form of government must be representative. That is the keystone upon which our government was founded and lacking which no republic can survive. It is well for this Court to practice self-restraint and discipline in constitutional adjudication, but never in its history have those principles received sanction where the national rights of so many have been so clearly infringed for so long a time. National respect for the courts is more enhanced through the forthright enforcement of those rights rather than by rendering them nugatory through the interposition of subterfuges. In my view the ultimate decision today is in the greatest tradition of this Court.

. . .

Mr. Justice Stewart, concurring.

The separate writings of my dissenting and concurring Brothers stray so far from the subject of today's decision as to convey, I think, a distressingly inaccurate impression of what the Court decides. For that reason, I think it appropriate, in joining the opinion of the Court, to emphasize in a few words what the opinion does and does not say.

The Court today decides three things and no more: "(a) that the court possessed jurisdiction of the subject matter; (b) that a justiciable cause of action is stated upon which appellants would be entitled to appropriate relief; and (c) ... that the appellants have standing to challenge the Tennessee apportionment statutes."

The complaint in this case asserts that Tennessee's system of apportionment is utterly arbitrary—without any possible justification in rationality. The District Court did not reach the merits of that claim, and this Court quite properly expresses no view on the subject... The Court does not say or imply that there is anything in the Federal Constitution "to prevent a State, acting not irrationally, from choosing any electoral legislative structure it thinks best suited to the interests, temper, and customs of its people." ... [T]he Court most assuredly does not decide the question, "may a State weight the vote of one county or one district more heavily than it weights the vote in another?"...

. . .

My Brother Clark has made a convincing prima facie showing that Tennessee's system of apportionment is in fact utterly arbitrary—without any possible justification in rationality. My Brother Harlan has, with imagination and ingenuity, hypothesized possibly rational bases for Tennessee's system. But the merits of this case are not before us now. The defendants have not yet had an opportunity to be heard in defense of the State's system of apportionment; indeed, they have not yet even filed an answer to the complaint. As in other cases, the proper place for the trial is in the trial court, not here.

. . .

Mr. Justice Frankfurter, whom Mr. Justice Harlan joins, dissenting.

The Court today reverses a uniform course of decision established by a dozen cases, including one by which the very claim now sustained was unanimously rejected only five years ago. The impressive body of rulings thus cast aside reflected the equally uniform course of our political history regarding the relationship between population and legislative representation—a wholly different matter from denial of the franchise to individuals because of race, color, religion or sex. Such a massive repudiation of the experience of our whole past in asserting destructively novel judicial power demands a detailed analysis of the role of this Court in our constitutional scheme. Disregard of inherent limits in the effective exercise of the Court's "judicial Power" not only presages the futility of judicial intervention in the essentially political conflict of forces by which the relation between population and representation has time out of mind been and now is determined. It may well impair the Court's position as the ultimate organ of "the supreme Law of the Land" in that vast range of legal problems, often strongly entangled in popular feeling, on which this Court must pronounce. The Court's authority—possessed of neither the purse nor the sword—ultimately rests on sustained public confidence in its moral sanction. Such feeling must be nourished by the Court's complete detachment, in fact and in appearance, from political entanglements and by abstention from injecting itself into the clash of political forces in political settlements.

A hypothetical claim resting on abstract assumptions is now for the first time made the basis for affording illusory relief for a particular evil even though it foreshadows deeper and more pervasive difficulties in consequence. The claim is hypothetical and the assumptions are abstract because the Court does not vouchsafe the lower courts—state and federal—guidelines for formulating specific, definite, wholly unprecedented remedies for the inevitable litigations that today's unbrageous disposition is bound to stimulate in connection with politically motivated reapportionments in so many States. In such a setting, to promulgate jurisdiction in the abstract is meaningless. It is as devoid of reality as "a brooding omnipresence in the sky," for it conveys no intimation what relief, if any, a District Court is capable of affording that would not invite legislatures to play ducks and drakes with the judiciary. For this Court to direct the District Court to enforce a claim to which the Court has over the years consistently found itself required to deny legal enforcement and at the same time to find it necessary to withhold any guidance to the lower court how to enforce this turnabout, new legal claim, manifests an odd—indeed an esoteric—conception of judicial propriety... Even assuming the indispensable intellectual disinterestedness on the part of judges in such matters, they do not have accepted legal standards or criteria or even reliable analogies to draw upon for making judicial judgments. To charge courts with the task of accommodating the incommensurable factors of policy that underlie these mathematical puzzles is to attribute, however flatteringly, omnicompetence to judges. The Framers of the Constitution persistently rejected a proposal that embodied this assumption and Thomas Jefferson never entertained it. . . .

. . .

In effect, today's decision empowers the courts of the country to devise what should constitute the proper composition of the legislature of the fifty States. If state courts should for one reason or another find themselves unable to discharge this task, the duty of doing so is put on the federal courts or on this Court, if State views do not satisfy this Court's notion of what is proper districting.

We were soothingly told at the bar of this Court that we need not worry about the kind of remedy a court could effectively fashion once the abstract constitutional right to have courts pass on a state-wide system of electoral districting is recognized as a matter of judicial rhetoric, because legislatures would heed the Court's admonition. This is not only a euphoric hope. It implies a sorry confession of judicial impotence in place of a frank acknowledgment that there is not under our Constitution a judicial remedy for every political mischief, for every undesirable exercise of legislative power. The Framers carefully and with deliberate forethought refused so to enthrone the judiciary. In this situation, as in others of like nature, appeal for relief does not belong here. Appeal must be to an informed, civically militant electorate. In a democratic society like ours, relief must come through an aroused popular conscience that sears the conscience of the people's representatives. In any event there is nothing judicially more unseemly nor more self-defeating than for this Court to make in terrorem pronouncements, to indulge in merely empty rhetoric, sounding a word of promise to the ear, sure to be disappointing to the hope. . . .

. . .

From its earliest opinions this Court has consistently recognized a class of controversies which do not lend themselves to judicial standards and judicial remedies. To classify the various instances as "political questions" is rather a form of stating this conclusion than revealing of analysis. . . .

. . .

A controlling factor in such cases is that, decision respecting these kinds of complex matters of policy being traditionally committed not to courts but to the political agencies of government for determination by criteria of political expediency, there exists no standard ascertainable by settled judicial experience or process by reference to which a political decision affecting the question at issue between the parties can be judged. Where the question arises in the course of a litigation involving primarily the adjudication of other issues between the litigants, the Court accepts as a basis for adjudication the political departments' decision of it. But where its determination is the sole function to be served by the exercise of the judicial power, the Court will not entertain the action. . . .

. . .

The Court has been particularly unwilling to intervene in matters concerning the structure and organization of the political institutions of the States. The abstention from judicial entry into such areas has been greater even than that which marks the Court's ordinary approach to issues of state power challenged under broad federal guarantees. "We should be very reluctant to decide that we had jurisdiction in such a case, and thus in an action of this nature to supervise and review the political administration of a state government by its own officials and through its own courts. The jurisdiction of this court would only exist in case there had been . . . such a plain and substantial departure from the fundamental principles upon which our government is based that it could with truth and propriety be said that if the judgment were suffered to remain, the party aggrieved would be deprived of his life, liberty or property in violation of the provisions of the Federal Constitution.". . .

. . .

The Court has refused to exercise its jurisdiction to pass on "abstract questions of political power, of sovereignty, of government." The "political question" doctrine, in this aspect reflects the policies underlying the requirement of "standing": that the litigant who would challenge official action must claim infringement of an interest particular and personal to himself, as distinguished from a cause of dissatisfaction with the general frame and functioning of government—a complaint that the political institutions are awry. What renders cases of this kind non-justiciable is not necessarily the nature of the parties to them, for the Court has resolved other issues between similar parties; nor is it the nature of the legal questions involved, for the same type of question has been adjudicated when presented in other forms of controversy. The crux of the matter is that courts are not fit instruments of decision where what is essentially at stake is the composition of those large contests of policy traditionally fought out in non-judicial forums, by which governments and the actions of governments are made and unmade. . . .

.   .   .

The influence of these converging considerations—the caution not to undertake decision where standards meet for judicial judgment are lacking, the reluctance to interfere with matters of state government in the absence of an unquestionable and effectively enforceable mandate, the unwillingness to make courts arbiters of the broad issues of political organization historically committed to other institutions and for whose adjustment the judicial process is ill-adapted—has been decisive of the settled line of cases, reaching back more than a century, . . .

.   .   .

At first blush, this charge of discrimination based on legislative underrepresentation is given the appearance of a more private, less impersonal claim, than the assertion that the frame of government is askew. Appellants appear as representatives of a class that is prejudiced as a class, in contradiction to the polity in its entirety. However, the discrimination relied on is the deprivation of what appellants conceive to be their proportionate share of political influence. This, of course, is the practical effect of any allocation of power within the institutions of government. Hardly any distribution of political authority that could be assailed as rendering government nonrepublican would fail similarly to operate to the prejudice of some groups, and to the advantage of others, within the body politic. It would be ingenuous not to see, or consciously blind to deny, that the real battle over the initiative and referendum, or over a delegation of power to local rather than state-wide authority, is the battle between forces whose influence is disparate among the various organs of government to whom power may be given. No shift of power but works a corresponding shift in political influence among the groups composing a society.

What, then, is this question of legislative apportionment? Appellants invoke the right to vote and to have their votes counted. But they are permitted to vote and their votes are counted. They go to the polls, they cast their ballots, they send their representatives to the state councils. Their complaint is simply that the representatives are not sufficiently numerous or powerful—in short, that Tennessee has adopted a basis of representation with which they are dissatisfied. Talk of "debasement" or "dilution" is circular talk. One cannot speak of "debasement" or "dilution" of the value of a vote until there is first defined a standard of reference as to what a vote should be worth. What is actually asked of the Court in this case is to choose among competing bases of representation—ultimately, really, among competing theories of political philosophy—in order to establish an appropriate frame of government for the State of Tennessee and thereby for all the States of the Union.

In such a matter, abstract analogies which ignore the facts of history deal in unrealities; they betray reason. This is not a case in which a State has, through a device however oblique and sophisticated, denied Negroes or Jews or redheaded persons a vote, or given them only a third or a sixth of a vote. What Tennessee illustrates is an old and still widespread method of representation—representation by local geographical division, only in part respective of population—in preference to others, others, forsooth, more appealing. Appellants contest this choice and seek to make this Court the arbiter of the disagreement. They would make the Equal Protection Clause the charter of adjudication, asserting that the equality which it guarantees comports, if not the assurance of equal weight to every voter's vote, at least the basic conception that representation ought to be proportionate to population, a standard by reference to which the reasonableness of apportionment plans may be judged. . . .

. . .

The notion that representation proportioned to the geographic spread of population is so universally accepted as a necessary element of equality between man and man that it must be taken to be the standard of a political equality preserved by the Fourteenth Amendment—that it is, in appellants' words "the basic principle of representative government"—is, to put it bluntly, not true. However desirable and however desired by some among the great political thinkers and framers of our government, it has never been generally practiced, today or in the past. It was not the English system, it was not the colonial system, it was not the system chosen for the national government by the Constitution, it was not the system exclusively or even predominantly practiced by the States at the time of adoption of the Fourteenth Amendment, it is not predominantly practiced by the States today. Unless judges, the judges of this Court, are to make their private views of political wisdom the measure of the Constitution—views which in all honesty cannot but give the appearance, if not reflect the reality, of involvement with the business of partisan politics so inescapably a part of apportionment controversies—the Fourteenth Amendment, "itself a historical product," provides no guide for judicial oversight of the representation problem. . . .

. . .

The stark fact is that if among the numerous widely varying principles and practices that control state legislative apportionment today there is any generally prevailing feature, that feature is geographic inequality in relation to the population standard. . . These figures show more than individual variations from a generally accepted standard of electoral equality. They show that there is not—as there has never been—a standard by which the place of equality as a factor in apportionment can be measured. . . .

. . .

Apportionment, by its character, is a subject of extraordinary complexity, involving—even after the fundamental theoretical issues concerning what is to be represented in a representative legislature have been fought out or compromised—considerations of geography, demography, electoral convenience, economic and social cohesions or divergencies among particular local groups, communications, the practical effects of political institutions like the lobby and the city machine, ancient traditions and ties of settled usage, respect for proven incumbents of long experience and senior status, mathematical mechanics, censuses compiling relevant data, and a host of others. Legislative responses throughout the country to the reapportionment demands of the 1960 Census have glaringly confirmed that these are not factors that lend themselves to evaluations of a nature that are the staple of judicial determinations or for which judges are equipped to adjudicate by legal training or experience or native wit. And this is the more so true because in every strand of this complicated, intricate web of values meet the contending forces of partisan politics. The practical significance of apportionment is that the next election results may differ because of it. Apportionment battles are overwhelmingly party or intra-party contests. It will add a virulent source of friction and tension in federal-state relations to embroil the federal judiciary in them. . . .

. . .

Dissenting opinion of Mr. Justice Harlan, whom Mr. Justice Frankfurter joins.

The dissenting opinion of Mr. Justice Frankfurter, in which I join, demonstrates the abrupt departure the majority makes from judicial history by putting the federal courts into this area of state concerns—an area which, in this instance, the Tennessee state courts themselves have refused to enter.

It does not detract from his opinion to say that the panorama of judicial history it unfolds, though evincing a steadfast underlying principle of keeping the federal courts out of these domains, has a tendency, because of variants in expression, to becloud analysis in a given case. With due respect to the majority, I think that has happened here.

Once one cuts through the thicket of discussion devoted to "jurisdiction," "standing," "justiciability" and "political question," there emerges a straightforward issue which, in my view, is determinative of this case. Does the complaint disclose a violation of a federal constitutional right, in other words, a claim over which a United States District Court would have jurisdiction? . . .

. . .

In the last analysis, what lies at the core of this controversy is a difference of opinion as to the function of representative government. It is surely beyond argument that those who have the responsibility for devising a system of representation may permissibly consider that factors other than bare numbers should be taken into account. The existence of the United States Senate is proof enough of that. To consider that we may ignore the Tennessee Legislature's judgment in this instance because that body was the product of an asymmetrical electoral apportionment would in effect be to assume the very conclusion here disputed. Hence we must accept the present form of the Tennessee Legislature as the embodiment of the State's choice, or, more realistically, its compromise, between competing political philosophies. The federal courts have not been empowered by the Equal Protection Clause to judge whether this resolution of the State's internal political conflict is desirable or undesirable, wise or unwise. . . .

. . .

In short, there is nothing in the Federal Constitution to prevent a State, acting not irrationally, from choosing any electoral legislative structure it thinks best suited to the interests, temper, and customs of its people. . . . A State's choice to distribute electoral strength among geographical units, rather than according to a census of population, is certainly no less a rational decision of policy than would be its choice to levy a tax on property rather than a tax on income. Both are legislative judgments entitled to equal respect from this Court. . . .

.   .   .

Courts are unable to decide when it is that an apportionment originally valid becomes void because the factors entering into such a decision are basically matters appropriate only for legislative judgment. And so long as there exists a possible rational legislative policy for retaining an existing apportionment, such a legislative decision cannot be said to breach the bulwark against arbitrariness and caprice that the Fourteenth Amendment affords. . . .

.   .   .

From a reading of the majority and concurring opinions one will not find it difficult to catch the premises that underlie this decision. The fact that the appellants have been unable to obtain political redress of their asserted grievances appears to be regarded as a matter which should lead the Court to stretch to find some basis for judicial intervention. While the Equal Protection Clause is invoked, the opinion for the Court notably eschews explaining how, consonant with past decisions, the undisputed facts in this case can be considered to show a violation of that constitutional provision. The majority seems to have accepted the argument, pressed at the bar, that if this Court merely asserts authority in this field, Tennessee and other "malapportioning" States will quickly respond with appropriate political action, so that this Court need not be greatly concerned about the federal courts becoming further involved in these matters. At the same time the majority has wholly failed to reckon with what the future may hold in store if this optimistic prediction is not fulfilled. Thus, what the Court is doing reflects more an adventure in judicial experimentation than a solid piece of constitutional adjudication. . . .

.   .   .

Those observers of the Court who see it primarily as the last refuge for the correction of all inequality or injustice, no matter what its nature or source, will no doubt applaud this decision and its break with the past. Those who consider that continuing national respect for the Court's authority depends in large measure upon its wise exercise of self-restraint and discipline in constitutional adjudication, will view the decision with deep concern.

I would affirm.

. . .

In *Gray v. Sanders,* 372 U.S. 368 (1963), the Court invalidated the Georgia county unit system used in statewide primary elections as a dilution of the votes of citizens because of where they live. Speaking for the majority, Justice Douglas said: "The conception of political equality from the Declaration of Independence, to Lincoln's Gettysburg Address, to the Fifteenth, Seventeenth, and Nineteenth Amendments means only one thing—one person, one vote." And in *Wesberry v. Sanders,* 376 U.S. 1 (1964), that principle of "one person, one vote" was applied to require that congressional districts within a state be substantially equal in population.

Reynolds v. Sims

377 U.S. 533, 12 L ed 2d 506, 84 S Ct 1362 (1964)

Urban Alabamians challenged the existing apportionment of the legislature, a proposed reapportioning constitutional amendment, and a "stand-by" statutory scheme to be used if the amendment failed. None of the three approached population equality of districts and the variances in the upper house were particularly large. A three-judge court used part of the proposed amendment and part of the "stand-by" statute to fashion a temporary apportionment in the hope that a new and somewhat redistricted legislature could then finish the task. The Court accepted the case on direct appeal.

Mr. Chief Justice Warren delivered the opinion of the Court.

Involved in these cases are an appeal and two cross-appeals from a decision of the Federal District Court for the Middle District of Alabama holding invalid, under the Equal Protection Clause of the Federal Constitution, the existing and two legislatively proposed plans for the apportionment of seats in the two houses of the Alabama Legislature, and ordering into effect a temporary reapportionment plan comprised of parts of the proposed but judicially disapproved measures. . . .

.   .   .

Undeniably the Constitution of the United States protects the right of all qualified citizens to vote, in state as well as in federal elections. A consistent line of decisions by this Court in cases involving attempts to deny or restrict the right of suffrage has made this indelibly clear. It has been repeatedly recognized that all qualified voters have a constitutionally protected right to vote and to have their votes counted, . . . The right to vote can neither be denied outright, nor can it be destroyed by alteration of ballots, nor diluted by ballot-box stuffing. . . Racially based gerrymandering, and the conducting of white primaries, both of which result in denying to some citizens their right to vote, have been held to be constitutionally impermissible. And history has seen a continuing expansion of the scope of the right of suffrage in this country. The right to vote freely for the candidate of one's choice is of the essence of a democratic society, and any restrictions on that right strike at the heart of representative government. And the right of suffrage can be denied by a debasement or dilution of the weight of a citizen's vote just as effectively as by wholly prohibiting the free exercise of the franchise.

In Baker v Carr, 369 US 186, we held that a claim asserted under the Equal Protection Clause challenging the constitutionality of a State's apportionment of seats in its legislature, on the ground that the right to vote of certain citizens was effectively impaired since debased and diluted in effect, presented a justiciable controversy subject to adjudication by federal courts. The spate of similar cases filed and decided by lower courts since our decision in Baker amply shows that the problem of state legislative malapportionment is one that is perceived to exist in a large number of the States. . . .

.   .   .

A predominant consideration in determining whether a State's legislative apportionment scheme constitutes an invidious discrimination violative of rights asserted under the Equal Protection Clause is that the rights allegedly impaired are individual and personal in nature. While the result of a court decision in a state legislative apportionment controversy may be to require the restructuring of the geographical distribution of seats in a state legislature, the judicial focus must be concentrated upon ascertaining whether there has been any discrimination against certain of the State's citizens which constitutes an impermissible impairment of their constitutionally protected right to vote. . . Undoubtedly, the right of suffrage is a fundamental matter in a free and democratic society. Especially since the right to exercise the franchise in a free and unimpaired manner is preservative of other basic civil and political rights, any alleged infringement of the right of citizens to vote must be carefully and meticulously scrutinized. . . .

. . .

Legislators represent people, not trees or acres. Legislators are elected by voters, not farms or cities or economic interests. As long as ours is a representative form of government, and our legislatures are those instruments of government elected directly by and directly representative of the people, the right to elect legislators in a free and unimpaired fashion is a bedrock of our political system. It could hardly be gainsaid that a constitutional claim had been asserted by an allegation that certain otherwise qualified voters had been entirely prohibited from voting for members of their state legislature. And, if a State should provide that the votes of citizens in one part of the State should be given two times, or five times, or 10 times the weight of votes of citizens in another part of the State, it could hardly be contended that the right to vote of those residing in the disfavored areas had not been effectively diluted. It would appear extraordinary to suggest that a state could be constitutionally permitted to enact a law providing that certain of the state's voters could vote two, five, or 10 times for their legislative representatives, while voters living elsewhere could vote only once. And it is inconceivable that a state law to the effect that, in counting votes for legislators, the votes of citizens in one part of the State would be multiplied by two, five, or 10, while the votes of persons in another area would be counted only at face value, could be constitutionally sustainable. Of course, the effect of state legislative districting

75

schemes which give the same number of representatives to unequal number of constituents is identical. Overweighting and overvaluation of the votes of those living here has the certain effect of dilution and undervaluation of the votes of those living there. The resulting discrimination against those individual voters living in disfavored areas is easily demonstrable mathematically. Their right to vote is simply not the same right to vote as that of those living in a favored part of the State. Two, five, or 10 of them must vote before the effect of their voting is equivalent to that of their favored neighbor. Weighting the votes of citizens differently, by any method or means, merely because of where they happen to reside, hardly seems justifiable. One must be ever aware that the Constitution forbids "sophisticated as well as simple-minded modes of discrimination.". . .

. . .

[R]epresentative government is in essence self-government through the medium of elected representatives of the people, and each and every citizen has an inalienable right to full and effective participation in the political processes of his State's legislative bodies. Most citizens can achieve this participation only as qualified voters through the election of legislators to represent them. Full and effective participation by all citizens in state government requires, therefore, that each citizen have an equally effective voice in the election of members of his state legislature. Modern and viable state government needs, and the Constitution demands, no less.

Logically, in a society ostensibly grounded on representative government, it would seem reasonable that a majority of the people of a State could elect a majority of that State's legislators. To conclude differently, and to sanction minority control of state legislative bodies, would appear to deny majority rights in a way that far surpasses any possible denial of minority rights that might otherwise be thought to result. Since legislatures are responsible for enacting laws by which all citizens are to be governed, they should be bodies which are collectively responsive to the popular will. And the concept of equal protection has been traditionally viewed as requiring the uniform treatment of persons standing in the same relation to the governmental action questioned or challenged. With respect to the allocation of legislative representation, all voters, as citizens of a State, stand in the same relation regardless of where they live. Any suggested criteria for the differentiation of citizens are insufficient to justify any discrimination, as to the weight of their votes, unless relevant to the permissible purposes of legislative apportionment. Since the achieving of fair and effective representation for all citizens is concededly the basic aim of legislative apportionment, we conclude that the Equal Protection Clause guarantees the opportunity for equal participation by all voters in the election of state legislators. Diluting the weight of votes because of place of residence impairs basic constitutional rights under the Fourteenth Amendment just as much as invidious discriminations based upon factors such as race, or economic status. Our constitutional system amply provides for the protection of minorities by means other than giving them majority control of state legislatures. And the democratic ideals of equality and majority rule, which have served this Nation so well in the past, are hardly of any less significance for the present and the future.

We are told that the matter of apportioning representation in a state legislature is a complex and many-faceted one. We are advised that States can rationally consider factors other than population in apportioning legislative representation. We are admonished not to restrict the power of the States to impose differing views as to political philosophy on their citizens. We are cautioned about the dangers of entering into political thickets and mathematical quagmires. Our answer is this: a denial of constitutionally protected rights demands judicial protection; our oath and our office require no less of us. . . .

· · ·

To the extent that a citizen's right to vote is debased, he is that much less a citizen. The fact that an individual lives here or there is not a legitimate reason for overweighting or diluting the efficacy of his vote. The complexions of societies and civilizations change, often with amazing rapidity. A nation once primarily rural in character becomes predominantly urban. Representation schemes once fair and equitable become archaic and outdated. But the basic principle of representative government remains, and must remain, unchanged—the weight of a citizen's vote cannot be made to depend on where he lives. Population is, of necessity, the starting point for consideration and the controlling criterion for judgment in legislative apportionment controversies. A citizen, a qualified voter, is no more nor no less so because he lives in the city or on the farm. This is the clear and strong command of our Constitution's Equal Protection Clause. This is an essential part of the concept of a government of laws and not men. This is at the heart of Lincoln's vision of "government of the people, by the people, [and] for the people." The Equal Protection Clause demands no less than substantially equal state legislative representation for all citizens, of all places as well as of all races.

We hold that, as a basic constitutional standard, the Equal Protection Clause requires that the seats in both houses of a bicameral state legislature must be apportioned on a population basis. Simply stated, an individual's right to vote for state legislators is unconstitutionally impaired when its weight is in a substantial fashion diluted when compared with votes of citizens living in other parts of the State. Since, under neither the existing apportionment provisions nor under either of the proposed plans was either of the houses of the Alabama Legislature apportioned on a population basis, the District Court correctly held that all three of these schemes were constitutionally invalid. . . .

.   .   .

Legislative apportionment in Alabama is signally illustrative and symptomatic of the seriousness of this problem in a number of the States. At the time this litigation was commenced, there had been no reapportionment of seats in the Alabama Legislature for over 60 years. Legislative inaction, coupled with the unavailability of any political or judicial remedy, had resulted, with the passage of years, in the perpetuated scheme becoming little more than an irrational anachronism. Consistent failure by the Alabama Legislature to comply with state constitutional requirements as to the frequency of reapportionment and the bases of legislative representation resulted in a minority strangle hold on the State Legislature. Inequality of representation in one house added to the inequality in the other. . . .

.   .   .

Much has been written since our decision in Baker v Carr about the applicability of the so-called federal analogy to state legislative apportionment arrangements. After considering the matter, the court below concluded that no conceivable analogy could be drawn between the federal scheme and the apportionment of seats in the Alabama Legislature under the proposed constitutional amendment. We agree with the District Court, and find the federal analogy inapposite and irrelevant to state legislative districting schemes. Attempted reliance on the federal analogy appears often to be little more than an after-the-fact rationalization offered in defense of maladjusted state apportionment arrangements. The original constitutions of 36 of our States provided that representation in both houses of the state legislatures would be based completely, or predominantly, on population. And the Founding Fathers clearly had no intention of establishing a pattern or model for the apportionment of seats in state legislatures when the system of representation in the Federal Congress was adopted. . . .

· · ·

The system of representation in the two Houses of the Federal Congress is one ingrained in our Constitution, as part of the law of the land. It is one conceived out of compromise and concession indispensable to the establishment of our federal republic. Arising from unique historical circumstances, it is based on the consideration that in establishing our type of federalism a group of formerly independent States bound themselves together under one national government. Admittedly, the original 13 States surrendered some of their sovereignty in agreeing to join together "to form a more perfect Union." But at the heart of our constitutional system remains the concept of separate and distinct governmental entities which have delegated some, but not all, of their formerly held powers to the single national government. The fact that almost three-fourths of our present States were never in fact independently sovereign does not detract from our view that the so-called federal analogy is inapplicable as a sustaining precedent for state legislative apportionments. The developing history and growth of our republic cannot cloud the fact that, at the time of the inception of the system of representation in the Federal Congress, a compromise between the larger and smaller States on this matter averted a deadlock in the constitutional convention which had threatened to abort the birth of our Nation. . . .

· · ·

Political subdivisions of States—counties, cities, or whatever—never were and never have been considered as sovereign entities. Rather, they have been traditionally regarded as subordinate governmental instrumentalities created by the State to assist in the carrying out of state governmental functions... The relationship of the States to the Federal Government could hardly be less analogous....

. . .

Since we find the so-called federal analogy inapposite to a consideration of the constitutional validity of state legislative apportionment schemes, we necessarily hold that the Equal Protection Clause requires both houses of a state legislature to be apportioned on a population basis. The right of a citizen to equal representation and to have his vote weighted equally with those of all other citizens in the election of members of one house of a bicameral state legislature would amount to little if States could effectively submerge the equal-population principle in the apportionment of seats in the other house. If such a scheme were permissible, an individual citizen's ability to exercise an effective voice in the only instrument of state government directly representative of the people might be almost as effectively thwarted as if neither house were apportioned on a population basis. Deadlock between the two bodies might result in compromise and concession on some issues. But in all too many cases the more probable result would be frustration of the majority will through minority veto in the house not apportioned on a population basis, stemming directly from the failure to accord adequate overall legislative representation to all of the State's citizens on a nondiscriminatory basis. In summary, we can perceive no constitutional difference, with respect to the geographical distribution of state legislative representation, between the two houses of a bicameral state legislature.

We do not believe that the concept of bicameralism is rendered anachronistic and meaningless when the predominant basis of representation in the two state legislative bodies is required to be the same—population. A prime reason for bicameralism, modernly considered, is to insure mature and deliberate consideration of, and to prevent precipitate action on, proposed legislative measures. Simply because the controlling criterion for apportioning representation is required to be the same in both houses does not mean that there will be no differences in the composition and complexion of the two bodies. Different constituencies can be represented in the two houses. One body could be composed of single-member districts while the other could have at least some multimember districts. The length of terms of the legislators in the separate bodies could differ. The numerical size of the two bodies could be made to differ, even significantly, and the geographical size of districts from which legislators are elected could also be made to differ. And apportionment in one house could be arranged so as to balance off minor inequities in the representation of certain areas in the other house. In summary, these and other factors could be, and are presently in many States, utilized to engender differing complexions and collective attitudes in the two bodies of a state legislature, although both are apportioned substantially on a population basis.

By holding that as a federal constitutional requisite both houses of a state legislature must be apportioned on a population basis, we mean that the Equal Protection Clause requires that a State make an honest and good faith effort to construct districts, in both houses of its legislature, as nearly of equal population as is practicable. We realize that it is a practical impossibility to arrange legislative districts so that each one has an identical number of residents, or citizens, or voters. Mathematical exactness or precision is hardly a workable constitutional requirement. . . .

. . .

[I]t may be feasible to use political subdivision lines to a greater extent in establishing state legislative districts than in congressional districting while still affording adequate representation to all parts of the State. To do so would be constitutionally valid, so long as the resulting apportionment was one based substantially on population and the equal-population principle was not diluted in any significant way. Somewhat more flexibility may therefore be constitutionally permissible with respect to state legislative apportionment than in congressional districting. Lower courts can and assuredly will work out more concrete and specific standards for evaluating state legislative apportionment schemes in the context of actual litigation. For the present, we deem it expedient not to attempt to spell out any precise constitutional tests. What is marginally permissible in one state may be unsatisfactory in another, depending on the particular circumstances of the case. Developing a body of doctrine on a case-by-case basis appears to us to provide the most satisfactory means of arriving at detailed constitutional requirements in the area of state legislative apportionment. Thus, we proceed to state here only a few rather general considerations which appear to us to be relevant.

A State may legitimately desire to maintain the integrity of various political subdivisions, insofar as possible, and provide for compact districts of contiguous territory in designing a legislative apportionment scheme. Valid considerations may underlie such aims. Indiscriminate districting, without any regard for political subdivision or natural or historical boundary lines, may be little more than an open invitation to partisan gerrymandering. Single-member districts may be the rule in one State, while another State might desire to achieve some flexibility by creating multimember or floterial districts. Whatever the means of accomplishment, the overriding objective must be substantial equality of population among the various districts, so that the vote of any citizen is approximately equal in weight to that of any other citizen in the State.

History indicates, however, that many States have deviated, to a greater or lesser degree, from the equal-population principle in the apportionment of seats in at least one house of their legislatures. So long as the divergences from a strict population standard are based on legitimate considerations incident to the effectuation of a rational state policy, some deviations from the equal-population principle are constitutionally permissible with respect to the apportionment of seats in either or both of the two houses of a bicameral state legislature. But neither history alone, nor economic or other sorts of group interests, are permissible factors in attempting to justify disparities from population-based representation. Citizens, not history or economic interests, cast votes. Considerations of area alone provide an insufficient justification for deviations from the equal-population principle. Again, people, not land or trees or pastures, vote. Modern developments and improvements in transportation and communications make rather hollow, in the mid-1960's, most claims that deviations from population-based representation can validly be based solely on geographical considerations. Arguments for allowing such deviations in order to insure effective representation for sparsely settled areas and to prevent legislative districts from becoming so large that the availability of access of citizens to their representatives is impaired are today, for the most part, unconvincing. . . .

. . .

That the Equal Protection Clause requires that both houses of a state legislature be apportioned on a population basis does not mean that States cannot adopt some reasonable plan for periodic revision of their apportionment schemes. Decennial reapportionment appears to be a rational approach to readjustment of legislative representation in order to take into account population shifts and growth. Reallocation of legislative seats every 10 years coincides with the prescribed practice in 41 of the States, often honored more in the breach than the observance, however. . . Limitations on the frequency of reapportionment are justified by the need for stability and continuity in the organization of the legislative system, although undoubtedly reapportioning no more frequently than every 10 years leads to some imbalance in the population of districts toward the end of the decennial period and also to the development of resistance to change on the part of some incumbent legislators. In substance, we do not regard the Equal Protection Clause as requiring daily, monthly, annual or biennial reapportionment, so long as a State has a reasonably conceived plan for periodic readjustment of legislative representation. While we do not intend to indicate that decennial reapportionment is a constitutional requisite, compliance with such an approach would clearly meet the minimal requirements for maintaining a reasonably current scheme of legislative representation. And we do not mean to intimate that more frequent reapportionment would not be constitutionally permissible or practicably desirable. But if reapportionment were accomplished with less frequency, it would assuredly be constitutionally suspect. . . .

. . .

[W]e affirm the judgment below and remand the cases for further proceedings consistent with the views stated in this opinion.

It is so ordered.

. . .

Mr. Justice Clark, concurring in the affirmance.

. . .

It seems to me that all that the Court need say in this case is that each plan considered by the trial court is "a crazy quilt," clearly revealing invidious discrimination in each house of the Legislature and therefore violative of the Equal Protection Clause. . . .

. . .

I, therefore, do not reach the question of the so-called "federal analogy." But in my view, if one house of the State Legislature meets the population standard, representation in the other house might include some

departure from it so as to take into account, on a rational basis, other factors in order to afford some representation to the various elements of the
State.

. . .

Mr. Justice Stewart.

In this case all of the parties have agreed with the District Court's
finding that legislative inaction for some 60 years in the face of growth and
shifts in population has converted Alabama's legislative apportionment
plan enacted in 1901 into one completely lacking in rationality. . . .

. . .

I also agree with the Court that it was proper for the District Court,
in framing a remedy, to adhere as closely as practicable to the apportionments approved by the representatives of the people of Alabama, and to
afford the State of Alabama full opportunity, consistent with the requirements of the Federal Constitution, to devise its own system of legislative
apportionment.

. . .

Mr. Justice Harlan, dissenting.

. . .

Today's holding is that the Equal Protection Clause of the Fourteenth·
Amendment requires every State to structure its legislature so that all the
members of each house represent substantially the same number of people;
other factors may be given play only to the extent that they do not
significantly encroach on this basic "population" principle. Whatever may
be thought of this holding as a piece of political ideology—and even on
that score the political history and practices of this country from its earliest
beginnings leave wide room for debate—I think it demonstrable that the
Fourteenth Amendment does not impose this political tenet on the States
or authorize this Court to do so. . . .

. . .

Stripped of aphorisms, the Court's argument boils down to the
assertion that petitioners' right to vote has been invidiously "debased" or
"diluted" by systems of apportionment which entitle them to vote for

fewer legislators than other voters, an assertation which is tied to the Equal Protection Clause only by the constitutionally frail tautology that "equal" means "equal."

Had the Court paused to probe more deeply into the matter, it would have found that the Equal Protection Clause was never intended to inhibit the States in choosing any democratic method they pleased for the apportionment of their legislatures. This is shown by the language of the Fourteenth Amendment taken as a whole, by the understanding of those who proposed and ratified it, and by the political practices of the States at the time the Amendment was adopted. It is confirmed by numerous state and congressional actions since the adoption of the Fourteenth Amendment, and by the common understanding of the Amendment as evidenced by subsequent constitutional amendments and decisions of this Court before Baker v Carr ... made an abrupt break with the past in 1962.

The failure of the Court to consider any of these matters cannot be excused or explained by any concept of "developing" constitutionalism. It is meaningless to speak of constitutional "development" when both the language and history of the controlling provisions of the Constitution are wholly ignored. Since it can, I think, be shown beyond doubt that state legislative apportionments, as such, are wholly free of constitutional limitations, save such as may be imposed by the Republican Form of Government Clause (Const, Art IV, § 4), the Court's action now bringing them within the purview of the Fourteenth Amendment amounts to nothing less than an exercise of the amending power by this Court. . . .

.   .   .

The Court relies exclusively on that portion of § 1 of the Fourteenth Amendment which provides that no State shall "deny to any person within its jurisdiction the equal protection of the laws," and disregards entirely the significance of § 2, which reads:

"Representatives shall be apportioned among the several States according to their respective numbers counting the whole number of persons in each State, excluding Indians not taxed. *But when the right to vote at any election for* the choice of electors for President and Vice President of the United States, Representatives in Congress, *the executive and Judicial officers of a State, or the members of the Legislature thereof, is denied* to any of the male inhabitants of such State, being twenty-one years of age, and citizens of the United States, *or in any way abridged,* except for participation in rebellion, or other crime, the basis of representation therein shall be reduced in the proportion which the number of such male citizens shall bear to the whole number of male citizens twenty-one years of age in such State." (Emphasis added.)

The Amendment is a single text. It was introduced and discussed as such in the Reconstruction Committee, which reported it to the Congress. It was discussed as a unit in Congress and proposed as a unit to the States, which ratified it as a unit. A proposal to split up the Amendment and submit each section to the States as a separate amendment was rejected by the Senate. Whatever one might take to be the application to these cases of the Equal Protection Clause if it stood alone, I am unable to understand the Court's utter disregard of the second section which expressly recognizes the States' power to deny "or in any way" abridge the right of their inhabitants to vote for "the members of the [State] Legislature," and its express provision of a remedy for such denial or abridgment. The comprehensive scope of the second section and its particular reference to the state legislatures precludes the suggestion that the first section was intended to have the result reached by the Court today. If indeed the words of the Fourteenth Amendment speak for themselves, as the majority's disregard of history seems to imply, they speak as clearly as may be against the construction which the majority puts on them. . . .

. . .

The Court's elaboration of its new "constitutional" doctrine indicates how far—and how unwisely—it has strayed from the appropriate bounds of its authority. The consequence of today's decision is that in all but the handful of States which may already satisfy the new requirements the local District Court or, it may be, the state courts, are given blanket authority and the constitutional duty to supervise apportionment of the State Legislatures. It is difficult to imagine a more intolerable and inappropriate interference by the judiciary with the independent legislatures of the States. . . .

. . .

Records such as these in the cases decided today are sure to be duplicated in most of the other States if they have not already. They present a jarring picture of courts threatening to take action in an area which they have no business entering, inevitably on the basis of political judgments which they are incompetent to make. They show legislatures of the States meeting in haste and deliberating and deciding in haste to avoid the threat of judicial interference. So far as I can tell, the Court's only response to this unseemly state of affairs is ponderous insistence that "a denial of constitutionally protected rights demands judicial protection,". . . . By thus refusing to recognize the bearing which a potential for conflict of this kind may have on the question whether the claimed rights are in fact constitutionally entitled to judicial protection, the Court assumes, rather than supports, its conclusion.

It should by now be obvious that these cases do not mark the end of reapportionment problems in the courts. Predictions once made that the courts would never have to face the problem of actually working out an apportionment have proved false. This Court, however, continues to avoid the consequences of its decisions, simply assuring us that the lower courts "can and . . . will work out more concrete and specific standards," Deeming it "expedient" not to spell out "precise constitutional tests," the Court contents itself with stating "only a few rather general considerations."

Generalities cannot obscure the cold truth that cases of this type are not amenable to the development of judicial standards. No set of standards can guide a court which has to decide how many legislative districts a State shall have, or what the shape of the districts shall be, or where to draw a particular district line. No judicially manageable standard can determine whether a State should have single-member districts or multimember districts or some combination of both. No such standard can control the balance between keeping up with population shifts and having stable districts. In all these respects, the courts will be called upon to make particular decisions with respect to which a principle of equally populated districts will be of no assistance whatsoever. Quite obviously, there are limitless possibilities for districting consistent with such a principle. Nor can these problems be avoided by judicial reliance on legislative judgments so far as possible. Reshaping or combining one or two districts, or modifying just a few district lines, is no less a matter of choosing among many possible solutions, with varying political consequences, than reapportionment broadside. . . .

•   •   •

With these cases the Court approaches the end of the third round set in motion by the complaint filed in Baker v Carr. What is done today deepens my conviction that judicial entry into this realm is profoundly ill-advised and constitutionally impermissible. As I have said before, I believe that the vitality of our political system, on which in the last analysis all else depends, is weakened by reliance on the judiciary for political reform; in time a complacent body politic may result.

These decisions also cut deeply into the fabric of our federalism. What must follow from them may eventually appear to be the product of State Legislatures. Nevertheless, no thinking person can fail to recognize that the aftermath of these cases, however desirable it may be thought in itself, will have been achieved at the cost of a radical alteration in the relationship between the States and the Federal Government, more particularly the Federal Judiciary. Only one who has an overbearing impatience with the federal system and its political processes will believe that that cost was not too high or was inevitable.

Finally, these decisions give support to a current mistaken view of the Constitution and the constitutional function of this Court. This view, in a nutshell, is that every major social ill in this county can find its cure in some constitutional "principle," and that this Court should "take the lead" in promoting reform when other branches of government fail to act. The Constitution is not a panacea for every blot upon the public welfare, nor should this Court, ordained as a judicial body, be thought of as a general haven for reform movements. The Constitution is an instrument of government, fundamental to which is the premise that in a diffusion of governmental authority lies the greatest promise that this Nation will realize liberty for all its citizens. This Court, limited in function in accordance with that premise, does not serve its high purpose when it exceeds its authority, even to satisfy justified impatience with the slow workings of the political process. For when, in the name of constitutional interpretation, the Court *adds* something to the Constitution that was deliberately excluded from it, the Court in reality substitutes its view of what should be so for the amending process.

. . .

Lucas v. Forty-Fourth General Assembly of Colorado, 377 U.S. 713 (1964), was decided at the same time as Reynolds. Colorado voters had adopted by referendum an apportionment of the General Assembly that did not embody the population equality principle. The District Court dismissed challenges to the apportionment on the ground that it had been adopted by the voters themselves.

In a six to three decision the Supreme Court reversed because of excessive departures from one-person, one-vote. Recognizing that Colorado voters have the initiative available to them and have used it on numerous occasions, the majority nonetheless stated "we find no significance in the fact that a non-judicial, political remedy may be available for the effectuation of asserted rights to equal representation in a state legislature. . . An individual's constitutionally protected right to cast an equally weighted vote cannot be denied even by a vote of a majority of a state's electorate. . ." (p. 736) The initiated proposal not only won a majority of the total vote but also carried in every one of the State's 63 counties.

Justice Stewart's dissent advanced an alternative to the majority's "draconian pronouncement." "I think that the Equal Protection Clause demands but two basic attributes of any plan of state legislative apportionment. First, it demands that, in light of the state's own characteristics and needs, the plan must be a rational one. Secondly, it demands that the plan must be such as not to permit the systematic frustration of the will of a majority of the electorate of the state." (377 U.S. 713, at 753-754)

House Bill 11926, 88th Congress, 2nd Session (Tuck Bill)

The Supreme Court shall not have the right to review the action of a Federal court or a State court of last resort concerning any action taken upon a petition or complaint seeking to apportion or reapportion any legislature of any State of the Union or any branch thereof.

The district courts shall not have any jurisdiction to entertain any petition or complaint seeking to apportion or reapportion the legislature of any State of the Union or any branch thereof.

.   .   .

Senator Everett Dirksen (R., Ill.) tried twice to get a constitutional amendment on reapportionment through the Senate.

Senate Joint Resolution 2, 89th Congress, 1st Session

That the following article is proposed as an amendment to the Constitution of the United States, which shall be valid to all intents and purposes as part of the Constitution when ratified by the legislatures of three-fourths of the several states within seven years from the date of its submission by the Congress:

Section 1. The People of a state may apportion one house of a bicameral legislature using population, geography, and political subdivisions as factors giving each factor such weight as they deem appropriate, or giving reasonable weight to the same factors in apportioning a unicameral legislature, if in either case such plan of apportionment has been submitted to a vote of the people in accordance with law and with the provisions of this Constitution and has been approved by a majority of those voting on that issue. When a plan of apportionment based on factors of population, geography, and political subdivisions is submitted to a vote of the people under this Section there shall also be submitted, at the same election, an alternative plan of apportionment based upon substantial equality of population.

Section 2. Any plan of apportionment which has been approved under this article shall be resubmitted to a vote of the people, or, another plan may be submitted under the provisions of Section 1, at the November general election held two years following each year in which there is commenced any enumeration provided for in Section 2 of Article I, and upon approval by a majority of those voting thereon, such plan of apportionment shall continue in effect until changed in accordance with law and with the provisions of this Constitution.

.   .   .

The Senate voted 57-39 in favor of this proposal on August 4, 1965. This was seven votes short of the two-thirds majority required for a constitutional amendment to pass.

Senate Joint Resolution 103, 89th Congress, 2nd Session

That the following article is proposed as an amendment to the Constitution of the United States, which shall be valid to all intents and purposes as part of the Constitution when ratified by the legislatures of three-fourths of the several states within seven years of its submission to the states by the Congress, provided that each such legislature shall include one house apportioned on the basis of substantial equality of population in accordance with the most recent enumeration provided for in Section 2 of Article I:

Section 1. The legislature of each state shall be apportioned by the people of that state at each general election for Representatives to the Congress held next following the year in which there is commenced each enumeration provided for in Section 2 of Article I. In the case of a bicameral legislature, the members of one house shall be apportioned among the people on the basis of their numbers and the members of the other house may be apportioned among the people on the basis of population, geography, and political subdivisions in order to insure effective representation in the state's legislature of the various groups and interests making up the electorate. In the case of a unicameral legislature, the house may be apportioned among the people on the basis of substantial equality of population with such weight given to geography and political subdivisions as will insure effective representation in the state's legislature of the various groups and interests making up the electorate.

Section 2. A plan of apportionment shall become effective only after it has been submitted to a vote of the people of the state and approved by a majority of those voting on that issue at a statewide election held in accordance with law and the provisions of this Constitution. If submitted by a bicameral legislature the plan of apportionment shall have been approved prior to such election by both houses, one of which shall be apportioned on the basis of substantial equality of population; if otherwise submitted it shall have been found by the courts prior to such election to be consistent with the provisions of this Constitution, including this Article. In addition to any other plans of apportionment which may be submitted at such election, there shall be submitted to a vote of the people an alternative plan of apportionment based solely on substantial equality of population. The plan of apportionment approved by a majority of those voting on that issue shall be promptly placed in effect.

On April 20, 1966, the Senate voted 55-38 on this version, again falling seven votes short of the two-thirds majority.

Senate Joint Memorial 1 (Idaho)

A typical state call for a constitutional convention is this one from Idaho, presented to Congress January 27, 1965 [111 *Congressional Record* 1402]

To the Honorable Senate and House of Representatives of the United States in Congress assembled:

We your memorialists, the members of the Senate and the House of Representatives of the Legislature of the State of Idaho, assembled in the 38th session thereof, do respectfully represent that:

Whereas the Constitution of the United States should not prohibit any State which has a bicameral legislature from apportioning the members of one house of such legislature on factors other than population, provided that the plan of such apportionment shall have been submitted to and approved by a vote of the electorate of that State; and

Whereas the Constitution of the United States should not restrict or limit a State in its determination of how membership of governing bodies of its subordinate units should be apportioned; and

Whereas in proposing an article as an amendment to the Constitution of the United States implementing the above freedom from prohibition, restriction or limitation of apportionment, the article, as proposed, should be inoperative unless it shall have been ratified as an amendment to the Constitution by the legislatures of three-fourths of the several States within seven years from the date of its submission to the States by Congress.

Now therefore, we your memorialists respectfully make application to the Congress of the United States to call a convention for the purpose of proposing an article as an amendment to the Constitution of the United States, to read as follows:

"ARTICLE—

"Section 1. Nothing in this Constitution shall prohibit any State which has a bicameral legislature from apportioning the numbers of one house of such legislature on factors other than population, provided that the plan of such apportionment shall have been submitted to and approved by a vote of the electorate of that State.

"Sec. 2. Nothing in this Constitution shall restrict or limit a State in its determination of how membership of governing bodies of its subordinate units shall be apportioned.

"Sec. 3. This article shall be inoperative unless it shall have been ratified as an amendment to the Constitution by the legislatures of three-fourths of the several States within 7 years from the date of its submission to the States by Congress."

Now, therefore, be it resolved, That if Congress shall have proposed an amendment to the Constitution identical with that contained in this memorial prior to June 1, 1965, this application for a convention shall no longer be of any force or effect; Be it further

Resolved, That the secretary of state of the State of Idaho be, and he is hereby authorized and directed to forward certified copies of this memorial to the Secretary of the Senate of the United States, the Clerk of the House of Representatives of the United States and to each Member of the U.S. Congress from this State, as being an application of the Legislature of the State of Idaho, pursuant to Article V of the Constitution of the United States.

. . .

Avery v. *Midland County,* 390 U.S. 474 (1968), and *Hadley* v. *Junior College District,* 397 U.S. 50 (1970), applied the one-person, one-vote requirement to substate governmental units. Justice White stated in *Avery* the general principle: ". . . the Constitution permits no substantial variation from equal population in drawing districts for units of local government having general governmental powers over the entire geographic area served by the body." (p. 485) *Hadley* rephrased and broadened this requirement: "We therefore hold today that as a general rule, whenever state or local government decides to select persons by popular election to perform governmental functions, the Equal Protection Clause of the Fourteenth Amendment requires that each qualified voter must be given an equal opportunity to participate in that election, and when members of an elected body are chosen from separate districts, each district must be established on a basis that will ensure, as far as is practicable, that equal numbers of voters can vote for proportionally equal numbers of officials." (p. 56) Justices Harlan, Fortas, and Stewart dissented in *Avery* while Harlan, Stewart, and Chief Justice Burger dissented in *Hadley.*

The general principle from these two cases was used in *Hill* v. *Stone,* 421 U.S. 289 (1975), to hold that limiting the vote in local bond elections to property owners violated equal protection rights of nonproperty owners. But in three other cases the general rule of *Avery* and *Hadley* was modified (*Salyer Land Co.* v. *Tulare Lake Basin Water Storage District,* 410 U.S. 719, 1973; *Associated Enterprises* v. *Toltec Watershed Improvement District,* 410 U.S. 743, 1973; *Ball* v. *James,* 451 U.S. 355, 1981). In all three instances the litigation involved the limiting of voting for water district directors to land owners and weighting those votes according to either the assessed value of the land or the acreage owned. The Court upheld these arrangements on the ground that such special purpose units of government have a disproportionate effect on those within their jurisdiction, making weighted voting schemes a rational recognition of that effect. The cost of and benefits from these districts are closely related to the value and quantity of land owned so that weighted voting reflects the degree of interest in the operation of the unit of government.

III

Equal Protection of the Laws

The equal protection clause of the Fourteenth Amendment is deceptively clear: "No State . . . shall deny to any person within its jurisdiction the equal protection of the laws." In spite of this apparent clarity, the Court has had difficulty deciding just exactly what Congress had in mind when it wrote the amendment. In 1873, the justices opted for a restrictive interpretation. Speaking through Justice Samuel F. Miller in *The Slaughterhouse Cases,* 16 Wall. 36 (1873), they declared that "the existence of laws in the states where the newly emancipated negroes resided, which discriminated with gross injustice against them as a class, was the evil to be remedied by this clause. . . . We doubt very much whether any action of a state not directed by way of discrimination against the negroes as a class, or on account of their race, will ever be held to come within the purview of this provision." [1] This narrow interpretation of the equal protection clause was especially persuasive as it was handed down by judges who had been active in public life at the time the amendment was adopted; the judges thought they were providing a contemporary explanation of the intent of the writers of the provision.

Even so, the Court found itself forced to explain the clause further. A decade later in the *Civil Rights Cases* of 1883, 109 U.S. 3 (1883), the Court said that the clause applied only to actions taken by the state; purely private discrimination could not be regulated by legislation enforcing the clause. It went on to explain in *Yick Wo* v. *Hopkins,* 118 U.S. 356 (1886), that state action includes discriminatory administration of a law that appears fair on its face value. In other decisions, the Court has found state action present in state court enforcement of a discriminatory private contract (*Shelly* v. *Kraemer,* 334 U.S. 1, 1948), a speech by a police chief calling for continued separation of the races in public places (*Bell* v. *Maryland,* 378 U.S. 226, 1964), and discrimination by a private business leasing its premises from a public authority (*Burton* v. *Wilmington Parking Authority,* 365 U.S. 715, 1961). Only Justice William O. Douglas has contended that the mere issuance of a license by the state to a private business makes the clause applicable to that business (*Moose Lodge* v. *Irvis,* 407 U.S. 173, 1972). What constitutes state action is usually clear but remains, at the margin, a question of judgment for the courts.

The state action concept has been blurred by several subsequent decisions of the Court where congressional statutes were applied. In *Heart of Atlanta Motel* v. *United States,* 379 U.S. 241 (1964), the Court upheld as a valid exercise of the commerce power Title II of the Civil Rights Acts of 1964, which forbids discrimination by owners and operators of places of public accommodation. And in *Jones* v. *Alfred H. Mayer Co.,* 392 U.S. 409 (1968), the Court upheld an 1866 statute barring private discrimination in the sale of real property. (The Civil Rights Act of 1968 reinforced and expanded the scope of the right declared in the 1866 statute.) Thus, Congress was able to use the commerce power to forbid some forms of private discrimination. The state action limitation has been modified to permit an individual to complain in the courts about an act of private discrimination when a statute specifically defines a cause of action fitting the case.

Yick Wo v. *Hopkins* not only expanded the definition of state action, but it also established a new understanding of the variety of persons protected by the clause: "These provisions are universal in their application, to all persons within the territorial jurisdiction, without regard to any differences of race, of color, or of nationality." [2] The *Slaughterhouse* restriction of the Amendment's applicability to a limited set of conditions and persons was modified, and the equal protection clause was infused with the potential for a broader application than Justice Miller (who silently acquiesced in *Yick Wo*) had given it.

Two additional features of equal protection emerged when business tried to use the clause to escape state regulation. The requirement was not that all persons (including, of course, corporations) be treated in exactly the same way, but rather that all persons *similarly situated* be treated equally. In other words, the legislature may classify persons into groups and treat those groups differently as long as each person within the group is treated the same. The issue for the courts then becomes the legitimacy of the legislature's classification or, to put it another way, whether the differentiating characteristics outlined by the legislature are proper ones. Up until 1942 all that the Court required on this point was a reasonable relation between the classificatory scheme and the result to be achieved by the legislation. As Justice Willis Van Devanter explained:

The rules by which [an equal protection] contention must be tested, as is shown by repeated decisions of this court, are these: 1. The equal protection clause of the 14th Amendment does not take from the state the power to classify in the adoption of police laws, but admits of the exercise of a wide scope of discretion in that regard, and avoids what is done only when it is without any reasonable basis, and therefore is purely arbitrary. 2. A classification having some reasonable basis does not offend against that clause merely because it is not made with mathematical nicety, or because in practice it results in some inequality. 3. When the classification in such a law is called into question, if any state of facts reasonably can be conceived that would sustain it, the existence of that state of facts at the time the law was enacted must be assumed. 4. One who assails the classification in such a law must carry the burden of showing that it does not rest upon any reasonable basis, but is essentially arbitrary. [3]

While the Court found some statutes invalid using this test, the main thrust of the decisions was to uphold challenged legislation, leaving the equal protection clause an anemic tool for judicial policymaking. As late as 1927, Justice Oliver Wendell Holmes scornfully referred to it as "the usual last resort of constitutional arguments." [4]

It was not until 1942 that a member of the Court suggested a way to broaden equal protection to require more of legislatures than the absence of arbitrariness. In *Skinner* v. *Oklahoma,* 316 U.S. 535 (1942), Justice Douglas argued that some classifications are "suspect" and hence must be subjected to "strict scrutiny" by the courts. [5] This suggestion bore fruit, and by the 1960s the justices had developed the so-called "two-tier" test for use in all equal protection cases. A statute would be examined only for reasonableness unless a suspect classification or a fundamental right were involved; in such a case, strict scrutiny would be given to the purpose of the classification. The state would be forced to demonstrate a compelling interest in the end it was seeking, and the burden of proof would be shifted from the challenger of the statute to its defender. In general terms, the legislature is said to have used a suspect classification if the defined class possesses "an immutable characteristic determined solely by the accident of birth" or is "saddled with such disabilities, or subjected to such a history of purposeful unequal treatment, or relegated to such a position of political powerlessness as to command extraordinary protection from the majoritarian political process." [6]

In practice, race, national origin, and alienage have been recognized as suspect classifications by the Court; the status of gender, age, illegitimacy, and indigency is still unclear. Fundamental rights have been defined as those rights explicitly mentioned in the Constitution plus the "right to privacy." Having added privacy to the class of fundamental rights, some members of the Court have wanted to similarly elevate the "rights" of education and travel.

This lack of clarity is one of the problems of the two-tier test: What classifications are suspect and which rights are so fundamental that their use subjects a statute to more stringent testing? Some justices consider both groups as closed classes, while others consider them open categories. A twilight zone between the two tiers has developed, and it is occupied by categories such as gender and wealth. These categories are too suspect to have the rational basis test applied, yet not suspect enough to call for strict scrutiny. (See *Frontiero* v. *Richardson,* p. 195 and *San Antonio Independent School District* v. *Rodriguiez,* p. 200.) Similarly, some rights, such as education, are not fundamental because they are not mentioned in the Constitution, but they are clearly important enough to merit heightened concern. Just how the Court will resolve this problem remains to be seen, but it is certain that disagreement will continue among the justices for some time to come. [7]

Not only do the justices decide the degree of justification the state must offer to support using a particular classification, but they also must consider the remedy to apply if a deprivation of equal protection is found. The school desegregation and affirmative action decisions included in this chapter are the best illustrations of this search for a remedy. The events leading up to these decisions need only a brief mention. The doctrine of *Plessy* v. *Ferguson,* 163 U.S. 357 (1896), approving separate facilities for blacks and whites as long as they were equal, was quickly accepted and applied in the area of public education (*Cumming* v. *Board of Education,* 175 U.S. 528, 1899; *Gong Lum* v. *Rice,* 275 U.S. 78, 1927). Separate but equal was maintained until 1954, despite hints from the justices in 1948 and 1950 that their opinions were going to change. *Brown* v. *Board of Education* (p. 104) changed that doctrine by flatly stating that "separate educational facilities are inherently unequal," but the decision gave no guidance to school boards and state legislatures on how to implement the ruling. A year later the Court added to the confusion by issuing an order demanding that state mandated segregated school systems be dismantled "with all deliberate speed." [8]

The initial reaction to *Brown* v. *Board of Education* was delay, foot-dragging, and downright defiance of the 1954 decision. Some school districts closed all of their public schools and paid student tuition at private segregated schools from public funds; others adopted elaborate "freedom of choice" or voluntary transfer plans to preserve the status quo. Practically all school boards begged for more time to plan the transition, and some federal judges sympathized more with their local communities than with the Supreme Court. This pattern of obstruction and delay prompted the Court's uncompromising 1968 demand: "Such delays are no longer tolerable. . . . The burden on a school board today is to come forward with a plan that promises realistically to work, and promises realistically to work *now*." [9] A year later the demand was even more unequivocal: " [A] ll deliberate speed for desegregation is no longer constitutionally permissible. . . . Every school district is to terminate dual school systems at once." [10]

Up to this point, the Court had been dealing with an easily answerable question: Does the state or locality formally require segregation of the races in public schools? If the answer were "yes" the first remedy would be obvious—repeal or invalidate the segregation laws. By 1970, a new question had come into sharp focus: How can it be shown that separate but equal does not prevail when the laws have been repealed or voided or never have been adopted in the first place? For some, the easy answer to that question was to look at the racial composition of each school in the district and require that it approximate the racial mix within the general population.

Swann v. *Charlotte-Mecklenberg Board of Education* (p. 111) introduced the school bus as a tool of judicial policy implementation and marked the shift in Court policymaking from desegregation to integration. This shift to a result-oriented examination of each district posed a number of questions for the justices to answer in subsequent cases. Once a dual system has been dismantled, does the school board have a continuing obligation to enforce integration? To what extent are schools supposed to reflect the racial composition of the community? Must attendance zones be redrawn every few years to reflect changes in the population of the community? To what extent should courts try to equalize the burden of busing, and should they consider the degree of public resistance that will emerge in response to their orders? Is busing across school district lines ever permissible and, if so, is it wise? Can or should anything be done about "white flight" from public to private schools? The nature of these questions and others leads to the most important question of all: Once dual systems are eliminated, are the remaining issues judicial or legislative in nature?

The answer to these questions may lie in the answer to an earlier question. In the absence of an explicitly segregative statute or ordinance, should the courts look at the *effect* of what has been done or only at the *intent* with which it has been done? Analyzing effect only would lead to the invalidation of any actions having a disproportionate impact on a specific group. For example, if a single school in a school district contained a larger proportion of a minority group in its student body than the proportion of the same minority group in the population at large, this would be proof of discriminatory purpose if a pure effects test were used. A search for segregative *intent*, on the other hand, requires a demonstration that the decisionmakers (school board, legislature, etc.) desired the result and took actions to bring it about. Proving intent may place an intolerable burden on the challengers of a policy, and can lead the courts in a number of directions as they try to determine the motivation of the decisionmaker. *Keyes* and *Milliken* illustrate the Court's discomfort with either approach in its pure form, although the justices show a clear preference to deal with intent.

In two nonschool decisions the Court attempted to clarify its position. In *Washington* v. *Davis,* 426 U.S. 229 (1976), and *Arlington Heights* v. *Metropolitan Housing Development Corp.,* 429 U.S. 252 (1977), the Court flatly stated that "our cases have not embraced the proposition that a law or other official act, without regard to whether it reflects a racially discriminatory purpose, is unconstitutional *solely* because it has a racially disproportionate impact. . . Disproportionate impact is not irrelevant, but it is not the sole touchstone of an invidious racial discrimination forbidden by the Constitution." [11] The Court insists that "proof of racially discriminatory intent or purpose is required to show violation." [12] Even this leaves a problem: policymakers are rarely candid about improper motives; so how can malign purpose or intent be shown? Impact, Justice Lewis Powell tells us, is a starting point and may result in "a clear pattern, unexplainable on grounds other than race," in which case intent can be inferred. "But such cases are rare." Failing a clear pattern, judges must look at the historical background of the decision, the details of the events leading up to it, and the presence or absence of procedural regularity in reaching or implementing a policy. [13] From this information a conclusion about intent can be drawn. Even though these two decisions were handed down after *Keyes* and *Milliken,* they helped explain the search for some indication of segregative intent in those two cases, and they signalled all litigants that more than disproportionate impact must be presented by challengers of governmental decisions.

In the affirmative action cases (*Bakke, Weber,* and *Fullilove,* p. 169), the Court searched for another sort of remedy. The school desegregation cases involved mostly court-originated remedies dealing with a captive group (because of mandatory school attendance laws) and were "prospective in operation"; in other words, the Court was concerned with what would happen after those cases were decided. The affirmative action decisions are retrospective in order to cure the effects of past discrimination. They also differ from the school desegregation decisions in that their policies were initiated elsewhere in the system. The Court's role here was to give or to withhold approval of the means of correcting discrimination chosen by someone not in the judicial system. The Constitutional issue was the same as before, but the policy objective being attacked was different, as was the identity of the complainants. White Caucasians like Alan Bakke and Brian Weber were invoking the principle of equal protection to combat what they considered to be "reverse discrimination." The division among the justices in *Bakke* indicated the difficulties these cases presented when their focus changed from outlawing segregation to enforcing integration. The gender-based discrimination cases present the same pattern, even though the Court has refused to declare gender a suspect classification; *Frontiero* (p. 195) declared the discrimination to be bad; *Gunther* (p. 224) is an exploration for a remedy. In neither instance has a final conclusion been reached, nor have the questions presented to the courts become easier to answer.

These decisions were not made by courts working in a vacuum. In June 1956, 101 of the 128 members of Congress representing 11 southern states signed the Southern Manifesto condemning the *Brown* decision.

> Though there has been no constitutional amendment or act of Congress changing this established legal principle [separate but equal] almost a century old, the Supreme Court of the United States, with no legal basis for such action, undertook to exercise their naked judicial power and substituted their personal political and social ideas for the established law of the land.
>
> This unwarranted exercise of power by the Court, contrary to the Constitution, is creating chaos and confusion in the States principally affected. It is destroying the amicable relations between the white and Negro races that have been created through 90 years of patient effort by the good people of both races. It has planted hatred and suspicion where there has been heretofore friendship and understanding. . . .
>
> Even though we constitute a minority in the present Congress, we have full faith that a majority of the American people believe in the dual system of government which has enabled us to achieve our greatness and will in time demand that the reserved rights of the States and of the people be made secure against judicial usurpation.
>
> We pledge ourselves to use all lawful means to bring about a reversal of this decision which is contrary to the Constitution and to prevent the use of force in its implementation.

The signers of the Manifesto remained in the minority as Congress painfully passed the Civil Rights Acts of 1958, 1960, and 1964, and the Voting Rights Act of 1965. These laws recognized the demise of the separate but equal doctrine and unmistakably placed the support of Congress and the president behind the Court's efforts to undo the effects of *Plessy*. The decision in *Swann*, however, upset this cooperative state of affairs. President Richard M. Nixon proposed in 1972 that Congress adopt legislation halting judicially ordered busing as a remedy in school desegregation cases. (Message of President, March 17, 1972, and H.R. 13916, 92nd Congress, 2nd Session p. 159) The moratorium proposal was unsuccessful, but the Equal Educational Opportunity Act of 1974 (p. 165) dampened the Court's enthusiasm for using the school bus as a tool of desegregation. And S. 951 (p. 167), passed by the Senate on March 2, 1982, was a later attempt by the legislature to slow the courts in this field.

As long as the justices confined their use of the equal protection clause to the protection of blacks from discriminatory activity by the states, the problems presented to the Court were relatively straightforward. If state action singled out blacks as a group for the purpose of imposing a burden or depriving them of a benefit, the equal protection clause would be violated. However, limits of the scope of judicial policymaking were illustrated—if not demonstated—by some of the school integration cases. Courts have taken over school districts with the federal district judge in charge, they have become demographers, and they increasingly have become the targets of legislative hostility.

These decisions illustrate a constant dilemma for judicial policymakers. There is some reason to believe that the two *Brown* decisions were acceptable to a majority of the general public; opposition to the decisions was largely confined to a single region of the country. Therefore, the Court had legislative and executive support because most other decisionmakers, and most of the public, did not perceive that they could be affected by the new policy. When busing was used to remedy violations, when integration rather than desegregation became the goal, and when *Keyes* and *Millikin* extended the policy to the North and West, political and popular support for the Court's position began to erode. Thus, when the Court's policy position evolves over time to affect a sufficiently large number of persons, reaction from the public is inevitable. The justices, to some extent, must evaluate the degree of risk in this possibility and decide whether to stop short of the reaction point (if they can accurately identify it) and settle for less than total implementation of the policy, or to press forward and hope to weather the resultant storm.

There is yet another way to assess these decisions. Are there limits to what the courts can accomplish, and how can judges identify those limits? The courts can tell persons or governments when they are doing something that they ought not to do, but they also should wait for legislatures to frame the rules that impose affirmative responsibilities on the people. It also is worth considering that courts ought not decide cases in which equally plausible social theories are in conflict. The choice between a neighborhood school and an integrated school may not be a proper subject for judicial choice, even when that choice is dressed in the robes of a constitutional command.

NOTES

1. *The Slaughterhouse Cases,* 16 Wall. 36 (1873), at 81.
2. *Yick Wo* v. *Hopkins,* 118 U.S. 356, (1886), at 369.
3. *Lindsley* v. *Natural Carbonic Gas Co.,* 220 U.S. 61 (1911), at 78-79.
4. *Buck* v. *Bell,* 274 U.S. 200 (1927), at 208.
5. *Skinner* v. *Oklahoma,* 316 U.S. 535 (1942), at 541.
6. *Johnson* v. *Robison,* 415 U.S. 361 (1974), at 375, n.14.
7. A variant on this theme can be found in the abortion decisions in Chapter VI, p. 381.
8. *Brown* v. *Board of Education,* 349 U.S. 294 (1955).
9. *Green* v. *New Kent County School Board,* 391 U.S. 430 (1968), at 439.
10. *Alexander* v. *Holmes County Board of Education,* 396 U.S. 19 (1969), at 20.
11. *Washington,* p. 239.
12. *Arlington Heights,* p. 265.
13. *Arlington Heights,* pp. 266-268, passim.

SELECTED BIBLIOGRAPHY

Babcock, Barbara et al. *Sex Discrimination and the Law: Causes and Remedies.* Boston: Little Brown, 1975.

Boles, Janet K. *The Politics of the Equal Rights Amendment.* New York: Longman, 1979.

Cary, Eve and Peratis, Kathleen W. *Woman and the Law.* Skokie, Ill.: National Textbook Co., 1977.

Davidson, Kenneth B. et al. *Sex-Based Discrimination: Text, Cases and Materials.* St. Paul, Minn.: West., 1975.

Gross, Barry R. *Discrimination in Reverse: Is Turnabout Fair Play?* New York: New York University Press, 1978.

Harris, Robert J. *The Quest for Equality.* Baton Rouge: Louisiana State University Press, 1960.

Kluger, Richard. *Simple Justice.* New York: Knopf, 1976.

Miller, Loren. *The Petitioners.* Cleveland: World, 1967.

O'Connor, Karen. *Women's Organizations' Use of the Courts.* Lexington, Mass.: Lexington Books, 1980.

Orfield, Gary. *Must We Bus?* Washington: Brookings, 1978.

Peltason, Jack W. *Fifty-Eight Lonely Men.* New York: Harcourt, Brace and World, 1961.

Sindler, Allen P. *Bakke, DeFunis, and Minority Admissions.* New York: Longman, 1978.

Tussman, Joseph and tenBroek, Jacobus. "The Equal Protection of the Laws," 37 *California Law Review* 341 (1949).

Wilkinson, J. Harvie. *From Brown to Bakke.* New York: Oxford University Press, 1979.

Wolf, Eleanor P. *Trial and Error: The Detroit School Segregation Case.* Detroit: Wayne State University Press, 1981.

Brown v. Board of Education of Topeka

347 U.S. 483, 98 L ed 873, 74 S Ct. 686 (1954)

The facts are contained in the opinion.

. . .

Mr. Chief Justice Warren delivered the opinion of the Court.

These cases come to us from the States of Kansas, South Carolina, Virginia, and Delaware. They are premised on different facts and different local conditions, but a common legal question justifies their consideration together in this consolidated opinion.

In each of the cases, minors of the Negro race, through their legal representatives, seek the aid of the courts in obtaining admission to the public schools of their community on a nonsegregated basis. In each instance, they had been denied admission to schools attended by white children under laws requiring or permitting segregation according to race. This segregation was alleged to deprive the plaintiffs of the equal protection of the laws under the Fourteenth Amendment. In each of the cases other than the Delaware case, a three-judge federal district court denied relief to the plaintiffs on the so-called "separate but equal" doctrine announced by this Court in Plessy v. Ferguson, 163 US 537. Under that doctrine, equality of treatment is accorded when the races are provided substantially equal facilities, even though these facilities be separate. In the Delaware case, the Supreme Court of Delaware adhered to that doctrine, but ordered that the plaintiffs be admitted to the white schools because of their superiority to the Negro schools.

The plaintiffs contend that segregated public schools are not "equal" and cannot be made "equal," and that hence they are deprived of the equal protection of the laws. Because of the obvious importance of the question presented, the Court took jurisdiction. Argument was heard in the 1952 Term, and reargument was heard this Term on certain questions propounded by the Court.

Reargument was largely devoted to the circumstances surrounding the adoption of the Fourteenth Amendment in 1868. It covered exhaustively consideration of the Amendment in Congress, ratification by the states, then existing practices in racial segregation, and the views of proponents and opponents of the Amendment. This discussion and our own investigation convince us that, although these sources cast some light, it is not enough to resolve the problem with which we are faced. At best, they are inconclusive. The most avid proponents of the post-War Amendments undoubtedly intended them to remove all legal distinctions among "all persons born or naturalized in the United States." Their opponents, just as certainly, were antagonistic to both the letter and the spirit of the Amendments and wished them to have the most limited effect. What others in Congress and the state legislatures had in mind cannot be determined with any degree of certainty.

An additional reason for the inconclusive nature of the Amendment's history, with respect to segregated schools, is the status of public education at that time. In the South, the movement toward free common schools, supported by general taxation, had not yet taken hold. Education of white children was largely in the hands of private groups. Education of Negroes was almost nonexistent, and practically all of the race were illiterate. In fact, any education of Negroes was forbidden by law in some states. Today, in contrast, many Negroes have achieved outstanding success in the arts and sciences as well as in the business and professional world. It is true that public school education at the time of the Amendment had advanced further in the North, but the effect of the Amendment on Northern States was generally ignored in the congressional debates. Even in the North, the conditions of public education did not approximate those existing today. The curriculum was usually rudimentary; ungraded schools were common in rural areas; the school term was but three months a year in many states; and compulsory school attendance was virtually unknown. As a consequence, it is not surprising that there should be so little in the history of the Fourteenth Amendment relating to its intended effect on public education. . . .

．　　．　　．

The doctrine of "separate but equal" did not make its appearance in this Court until 1896 in the case of Plessy v. Ferguson, involving not education but transportation. American courts have since labored with the doctrine for over half a century. In this Court, there have been six cases involving the "separate but equal" doctrine in the field of public education. In Cumming v. County Board of Education and Gong Lum v. Rice, the validity of the doctrine itself was not challenged. In more recent cases, all on the graduate school level, inequality was found in that specific benefits enjoyed by white students were denied to Negro students of the same educational qualifications. Missouri ex rel. Gaines v. Canada, Sipuel v. University of Oklahoma, Sweatt v. Painter, McLaurin v. Oklahoma State Regents. In none of these cases was it necessary to reexamine the doctrine to grant relief to the Negro plaintiff. And in Sweatt v. Painter, the Court expressly reserved decision on the question whether Plessy v. Ferguson should be held inapplicable to public education.

In the instant cases, that question is directly presented. Here, unlike Sweatt v. Painter, there are findings below that the Negro and white schools involved have been equalized, or are being equalized, with respect to buildings, curricula, qualifications and salaries of teachers, and other "tangible" factors. Our decision, therefore, cannot turn on merely a comparison of these tangible factors in the Negro and white schools involved in each of the cases. We must look instead to the effect of segregation itself on public education.

In approaching this problem, we cannot turn the clock back to 1868 when the Amendment was adopted, or even to 1896 when Plessy v. Ferguson was written. We must consider public education in the light of its full development and its present place in American life throughout the Nation. Only in this way can it be determined if segregation in public schools deprives these plaintiffs of the equal protection of the laws.

Today, education is perhaps the most important function of state and local governments. Compulsory school attendance laws and the great expenditures for education both demonstrate our recognition of the importance of education to our democratic society. It is required in the performance of our most basic public responsibilities, even service in the armed forces. It is the very foundation of good citizenship. Today it is a principal instrument in awakening the child to cultural values, in preparing him for later professional training, and in helping him to adjust normally to his environment. In these days, it is doubtful that any child may reasonably be expected to succeed in life if he is denied the opportunity of an education. Such an opportunity, where the state has undertaken to provide it, is a right which must be made available to all on equal terms.

We come then to the question presented: Does segregation of children in public schools solely on the basis of race, even though the physical facilities and other "tangible" factors may be equal, deprive the children of the minority group of equal educational opportunities? We believe that it does.

In Sweatt v. Painter, in finding that a segregated law school for Negroes could not provide them equal educational opportunities, this Court relied in large part on "those qualities which are incapable of objective measurement but which make for greatness in a law school.". . . Such considerations apply with added force to children in grade and high schools. To separate them from others of similar age and qualifications solely because of their race generates a feeling of inferiority as to their status in the community that may affect their hearts and minds in a way unlikely ever to be undone. The effect of this separation on their educational opportunities was well stated by a finding in the Kansas case by a court which nevertheless felt compelled to rule against the Negro plaintiffs:

"Segregation of white and colored children in public schools has a detrimental effect upon the colored children. The impact is greater when it has the sanction of the law; for the policy of separating the races is usually interpreted as denoting the inferiority of the negro group. A sense of inferiority affects the motivation of a child to learn. Segregation with the sanction of law, therefore, has a tendency to [retard] the educational and mental development of Negro children and to deprive them of some of the benefits they would receive in a racial[ly] integrated school system."

Whatever may have been the extent of psychological knowledge at the time of Plessy v. Ferguson, this finding is amply supported by modern authority. Any language in Plessy v. Ferguson contrary to this finding is rejected.

We conclude that in the field of public education the doctrine of "separate but equal" has no place. Separate educational facilities are inherently unequal. Therefore, we hold that the plaintiffs and others similarly situated for whom the actions have been brought are, by reason of the segregation complained of, deprived of the equal protection of the laws guaranteed by the Fourteenth Amendment. This disposition makes unnecessary any discussion whether such segregation also violates the Due Process Clause of the Fourteenth Amendment.

Because these are class actions, because of the wide applicability of this decision, and because of the great variety of local conditions, the formulation of decrees in these cases presents problems of considerable complexity. On reargument, the consideration of appropriate relief was necessarily subordinated to the primary question—the constitutionality of segregation in public education. We have now announced that such segregation is a denial of the equal protection of the laws. In order that we may have the full assistance of the parties in formulating decrees, the cases will be restored to the docket, and the parties are requested to present further argument. . . .

· · ·

Bolling v. Sharpe

We have this day held that the Equal Protection Clause of the Fourteenth Amendment prohibits the states from maintaining racially segregated public schools. The legal problem in the District of Columbia is somewhat different, however. The Fifth Amendment, which is applicable in the District of Columbia, does not contain an equal protection clause as does the Fourteenth Amendment which applies only to the states. But the concepts of equal protection and due process, both stemming from our American ideal of fairness, are not mutually exclusive. The "equal protection of the laws" is a more explicit safeguard of prohibited unfairness than "due process of law," and, therefore, we do not imply that the two are always interchangeable phrases. But, as this Court has recognized, discrimination may be so unjustifiable as to be violative of due process.

Classifications based solely upon race must be scrutinized with particular care, since they are contrary to our traditions and hence constitutionally suspect. . . .

· · ·

Although the Court has not assumed to define "liberty" with any great precision, that term is not confined to mere freedom from bodily restraint. Liberty under law extends to the full range of conduct which the individual is free to pursue, and it cannot be restricted except for a proper governmental objective. Segregation in public education is not reasonably related to any proper governmental objective, and thus it imposes on Negro children of the District of Columbia a burden that constitutes an arbitrary deprivation of their liberty in violation of the Due Process Clause.

In view of our decision that the Constitution prohibits the states from maintaining racially segregated public schools, it would be unthinkable that the same Constitution would impose a lesser duty on the Federal Government. We hold that racial segregation in the public schools of the District of Columbia is a denial of the due process of law guaranteed by the Fifth Amendment to the Constitution.

Brown v. Board of Education of Topeka

349 U.S. 294, 99 L ed 1083, 75 S Ct 753 (1955)

After deciding in Brown I that racial discrimination in public education is unconstitutional, the Supreme Court set the cases for further argument on the question of the relief to be granted by the courts.

. . .

Mr. Chief Justice Warren delivered the opinion of the Court.

These cases were decided on May 17, 1954. The opinions of that date, declaring the fundamental principle that racial discrimination in public education is unconstitutional, are incorporated herein by reference. All provisions of federal, state, or local law requiring or permitting such discrimination must yield to this principle. There remains for consideration the manner in which relief is to be accorded.

Because these cases arose under different local conditions and their disposition will involve a variety of local problems, we requested further argument on the question of relief. In view of the nationwide importance of the decision, we invited the Attorney General of the United States and the Attorneys General of all states requiring or permitting racial discrimination in public education to present their views on that question. The parties, the United States, and the States of Florida, North Carolina,

Arkansas, Oklahoma, Maryland, and Texas filed briefs and participated in the oral argument. . . .

. . .

Full implementation of these constitutional principles may require solution of varied local school problems. School authorities have the primary responsibility for elucidating, assessing, and solving these problems; courts will have to consider whether the action of school authorities constitutes good faith implementation of the governing constitutional principles. Because of their proximity to local conditions and the possible need for further hearings, the courts which originally heard these cases can best perform this judicial appraisal. Accordingly, we believe it appropriate to remand the cases to those courts.

In fashioning and effectuating the decrees, the courts will be guided by equitable principles. Traditionally, equity has been characterized by a practical flexibility in shaping its remedies and by a facility for adjusting and reconciling public and private needs. These cases call for the exercise of these traditional attributes of equity power. At stake is the personal interest of the plaintiffs in admission to public schools as soon as practicable on a nondiscriminatory basis. To effectuate this interest may call for elimination of a variety of obstacles in making the transition to school systems operated in accordance with the constitutional principles set forth in our May 17, 1954, decision. Courts of equity may properly take into account the public interest in the elimination of such obstacles in a systematic and effective manner. But it should go without saying that the vitality of these constitutional principles cannot be allowed to yield simply because of disagreement with them.

While giving weight to these public and private considerations, the courts will require that the defendants make a prompt and reasonable start toward full compliance with our May 17, 1954, ruling. Once such a start has been made, the courts may find that additional time is necessary to carry out the ruling in an effective manner. The burden rests upon the defendants to establish that such time is necessary in the public interest and is consistent with good faith compliance at the earliest practicable date. To that end, the courts may consider problems related to administration, arising from the physical condition of the school plant, the school transportation system, personnel, revision of school districts and attendance areas into compact units to achieve a system of determining admission to the public schools on a nonracial basis, and revision of local laws and regulations which may be necessary in solving the foregoing problems. They will also consider the adequacy of any plans the defendants may propose to meet these problems and to effectuate a transition to a racially nondiscriminatory school system. During this period of transition, the courts will retain jurisdiction of these cases.

The judgments below, except that in the Delaware case, are accordingly reversed and the cases are remanded to the District Courts to take such proceedings and enter such orders and decrees consistent with this opinion as are necessary and proper to admit to public schools on a racially nondiscriminatory basis with all deliberate speed the parties to these cases. The judgment in the Delaware case—ordering the immediate admission of the plaintiffs to schools previously attended only by white children—is affirmed on the basis of the principles stated in our May 17, 1954, opinion, but the case is remanded to the Supreme Court of Delaware for such further proceedings as that Court may deem necessary in light of this opinion.

It is so ordered.

Swann v. Charlotte-Mecklenburg Board of Education

402 U.S. 1, 28 L Ed 2d 554, 91 S Ct 1267 (1971)

Suit was brought in 1965 to force respondent school board to abandon a racially segregated dual school system. After several years the system remained largely segregated, and the District Court ordered a) reassignment of faculty to result in approximately the same black-white ratio in each school, b) new attendance zones, pairing and clustering of schools accompanied by increased busing of students so that each high school would be 17 to 36 percent black, each junior high school nine to 33 percent black, and each elementary school nine to 38 percent. The Court of Appeals affirmed those parts of the order concerning faculty reassignments and secondary school rezoning and busing. That court vacated the part of the order dealing with elementary schools on the ground that the amount of additional busing would be unduly extensive. On remand the district court requested that the board adopt a new plan for the elementary schools, the board failed to do so, and the court reinstituted its original plan.

. . .

Mr. Chief Justice Burger delivered the opinion of the Court.

We granted certiorari in this case to review important issues as to the duties of school authorities and the scope of powers of federal courts under this Court's mandates to eliminate racially separate public schools established and maintained by state action.

This case and those argued with it arose in states having a long history of maintaining two sets of schools in a single school system deliberately operated to carry out a governmental policy to separate pupils in schools solely on the basis of race. That was what Brown v Board of Education was all about. These cases present us with the problem of defining in more precise terms than heretofore the scope of the duty of school authorities and district courts in implementing Brown I and the mandate to eliminate dual systems and establish unitary systems at once. Meanwhile district courts and courts of appeals have struggled in hundreds of cases with a multitude and variety of problems under this Court's general directive. Understandably, in an area of evolving remedies, those courts had to improvise and experiment without detailed or specific guidelines. This Court, in Brown I, appropriately dealt with the large constitutional principles; other federal courts had to grapple with the flinty, intractable realities of day-to-day implementation of those constitutional commands. Their efforts, of necessity, embraced a process of "trial and error," and our effort to formulate guidelines must take into account their experience. . . .

. . .

Nearly 17 years ago this Court held, in explicit terms, that state-imposed segregation by race in public schools denies equal protection of the laws. At no time has the Court deviated in the slightest degree from that holding or its constitutional underpinnings. None of the parties before us challenges the Court's decision of May 17, 1954, that "in the field of public education the doctrine of 'separate but equal' has no place. . . .

112

. . .

None of the parties before us questions the Court's 1955 holding in Brown II, that "[s]chool authorities have the primary responsibility for elucidating, assessing, and solving these problems; courts will have to consider whether the action of school authorities constitutes good faith implementation of the governing constitutional principles. . . ."

. . .

By the time the Court considered Green v County School Board in 1968, very little progress had been made in many areas where dual school systems had historically been maintained by operation of state laws. In Green, the Court was confronted with a record of a freedom-of-choice program that the District Court had found to operate in fact to preserve a dual system more than a decade after Brown II. While acknowledging that a freedom-of-choice concept could be a valid remedial measure in some circumstances, its failure to be effective in Green required that, "The burden on a school board today is to come forward with a plan that promises realistically to work . . . *now* . . . until it is clear that state-imposed segregation has been completely removed.". . .

. . .

The problems encountered by the district courts and courts of appeals make plain that we should now try to amplify guidelines, however incomplete and imperfect, for the assistance of school authorities and courts. The failure of local authorities to meet their constitutional obligations aggravated the massive problem of converting from the state-enforced discrimination of racially separate school systems. This process has been rendered more difficult by changes since 1954 in the structure and patterns of communities, the growth of student population, movement of families, and other changes, some of which had marked impact on school planning, sometimes neutralizing or negating remedial action before it was fully implemented. Rural areas accustomed for half a century to the consolidated school systems implemented by bus transportation could make adjustments more readily than metropolitan areas with dense and shifting population, numerous schools, congested and complex traffic patterns.

The objective today remains to eliminate from the public schools all vestiges of state-imposed segregation. . . .

113

. . .

If school authorities fail in their affirmative obligations under these holdings, judicial authority may be invoked. Once a right and a violation have been shown, the scope of a district court's equitable powers to remedy past wrongs is broad, for breadth and flexibility are inherent in equitable remedies....

. . .

The task is to correct, by a balancing of the individual and collective interests, the condition that offends the Constitution.

In seeking to define even in broad and general terms how far this remedial power extends it is important to remember that judicial powers may be exercised only on the basis of a constitutional violation. Remedial judicial authority does not put judges automatically in the shoes of school authorities whose powers are plenary. Judicial authority enters only when local authority defaults.

School authorities are traditionally charged with broad power to formulate and implement educational policy and might well conclude, for example, that in order to prepare students to live in a pluralistic society each school should have a prescribed ratio of Negro to white students reflecting the proportion for the district as a whole. To do this as an educational policy is within the broad discretionary powers of school authorities; absent a finding of a constitutional violation, however, that would not be within the authority of a federal court. As with any equity case, the nature of the violation determines the scope of the remedy. In default by the school authorities of their obligation to proffer acceptable remedies, a district court has broad power to fashion a remedy that will assure a unitary school system....

. . .

We turn now to the problem of defining with more particularity the responsibilities of school authorities in desegregating a state-enforced dual school system in light of the Equal Protection Clause. Although the several related cases before us are primarily concerned with problems of student assignment, it may be helpful to begin with a brief discussion of other aspects of the process.

In Green, we pointed out that existing policy and practice with regard to faculty, staff, transportation, extracurricular activities, and facilities were among the most important indicia of a segregated system. Independent of student assignment, where it is possible to identify a "white school" or a "Negro school" simply by reference to the racial composition of teachers and staff, the quality of school buildings and equipment, or the organization of sports activities, a prima facie case of violation or substantive constitutional rights under the Equal Protection Clause is shown.

When a system has been dual in these respects, the first remedial responsibility of school authorities is to eliminate invidious racial distinctions. With respect to such matters as transportation, supporting personnel, and extracurricular activities, no more than this may be necessary. Similar corrective action must be taken with regard to the maintenance of buildings and the distribution of equipment. In these areas, normal administrative practice should produce schools of like quality, facilities, and staffs. Something more must be said, however, as to faculty assignment and new school construction. . . .

.   .   .

[T]he . . . school board has argued that the Constitution requires that teachers be assigned on a "color blind" basis. It also argues that the Constitution prohibits district courts from using their equity power to order assignment of teachers to achieve a particular degree of faculty desegregation. We reject that contention. . . .

.   .   .

The construction of new schools and the closing of old ones is one of the most important functions of local school authorities and also one of the most complex. They must decide questions of location and capacity in light of population growth, finances, land values, site availability, through an almost endless list of factors to be considered. The result of this will be a decision which, when combined with one technique or another of student assignment, will determine the racial composition of the student body in each school in the system. Over the long run, the consequences of the choices will be far reaching. People gravitate toward school facilities, just as schools are located in response to the needs of people. The location of schools may thus influence the patterns of residential development of a metropolitan area and have important impact on composition of inner city neighborhoods.

In the past, choices in this respect have been used as a potent weapon for creating or maintaining a state-segregated school system. In addition to the classic pattern of building schools specifically intended for Negro or white students, school authorities have sometimes, since Brown, closed schools which appeared likely to become racially mixed through changes in neighborhood residential patterns. This was sometimes accompanied by building new schools in the areas of white suburban expansion farthest from Negro population centers in order to maintain the separation of the races with a minimum departure from the formal principles of "neighborhood zoning." Such a policy does more than simply influence the short-run composition of the student body of a new school. It may well promote segregated residential patterns which, when combined with "neighborhood zoning," further lock the school system into the mold of separation of the races. Upon a proper showing a district court may consider this in fashioning a remedy. . . .

. . .

The central issue in this case is that of student assignment, and there are essentially four problem areas: . . .
(1) *Racial Balances or Racial Quotas.* . . .
We are concerned in these cases with the elimination of the discrimination inherent in the dual school systems, not with myriad factors of human existence which can cause discrimination in a multitude of ways on racial, religious, or ethnic grounds. The target of the cases from Brown I to the present was the dual school system. The elimination of racial discrimination in public schools is a large task and one that should not be retarded by efforts to achieve broader purposes lying beyond the jurisdiction of school authorities. One vehicle can carry only a limited amount of baggage. It would not serve the important objective of Brown I to seek to use school desegregation cases for purposes beyond their scope, although desegregation of schools ultimately will have impact on other forms of discrimination. . . .

. . .

In this case it is urged that the District Court has imposed a racial balance requirement of 71%-29% on individual schools. The fact that no such objective was actually achieved—and would appear to be impossible—tends to blunt that claim, yet in the opinion and order of the District

Court of December 1, 1969, we find that court directing: "that efforts should be made to reach a 71-29 ratio in the various schools so that there will be no basis for contending that one school is racially different from the others. . . ."

.   .   .

If we were to read the holding of the District Court to require, as a matter of substantive constitutional right, any particular degree of racial balance or mixing, that approach would be disapproved and we would be obliged to reverse. The constitutional command to desegregate schools does not mean that every school in every community must always reflect the racial composition of the school system as a whole. . . .

.   .   .

We see therefore that the use made of mathematical ratios was no more than a starting point in the process of shaping a remedy, rather than an inflexible requirement. From that starting point the District Court proceeded to frame a decree that was within its discretionary powers, an equitable remedy for the particular circumstances. As we said in Green, a school authority's remedial plan or a district court's remedial decree is to be judged by its effectiveness. Awareness of the racial composition of the whole school system is likely to be a useful starting point in shaping a remedy to correct past constitutional violations. In sum, the very limited use made of mathematical ratios was within the equitable remedial discretion of the District Court.

(2) *One-Race Schools.*

The record in this case reveals the familiar phenomenon that in metropolitan areas minority groups are often found concentrated in one part of the city. In some circumstances certain schools may remain all or largely of one race until new schools can be provided or neighborhood patterns change. Schools all or predominately of one race in a district of mixed population will require close scrutiny to determine that school assignments are not part of state-enforced segregation.

In light of the above, it should be clear that the existence of some small number of one-race, or virtually one-race, schools within a district is not in and of itself the mark of a system which still practices segregation by law. The district judge or school authorities should make every effort to achieve the greatest possible degree of actual desegregation and will thus necessarily be concerned with the elimination of one-race schools. No per se rule can adequately embrace all the difficulties of reconciling the competing interests involved; but in a system with a history of segregation the need for remedial criteria of sufficient specificity to assure a school authority's compliance with its constitutional duty warrants a presumption against schools that are substantially disproportionate in their racial composition. Where the school authority's proposed plan for conversion from a dual to a unitary system contemplates the continued existence of some schools that are all or predominately of one race, they have the burden of showing that such school assignments are genuinely nondiscriminatory. The court should scrutinize such schools, and the burden upon the school authorities will be to satisfy the court that their racial composition is not the result of present or past discriminatory action on their part. . . .

. . .

(3) *Remedial Altering of Attendance Zones.*

The maps submitted in these cases graphically demonstrate that one of the principal tools employed by school planners and by courts to break up the dual school system has been a frank—and sometimes drastic—gerrymandering of school districts and attendance zones. An additional step was pairing, "clustering," or "grouping" of schools with attendance assignments made deliberately to accomplish the transfer of Negro students out of formerly segregated Negro schools and transfer of white students to formerly all-Negro schools. More often than not, these zones are neither compact nor contiguous; indeed they may be on opposite ends of the city. As an interim corrective measure, this cannot be said to be beyond the broad remedial powers of a court.

Absent a constitutional violation there would be no basis for judicially ordering assignment of students on a racial basis. All things being equal, it might well be desirable to assign pupils to schools nearest their homes. But all things are not equal in a system that has been deliberately constructed and maintained to enforce racial segregation. The remedy for such segregation may be administratively awkward, inconvenient and even bizarre in some situations and may impose burdens on some; but all awkwardness and inconvenience cannot be avoided in the interim period when remedial adjustments are being made to eliminate the dual school systems.

No fixed or even substantially fixed guidelines can be established as to how far a court can go, but it must be recognized that there are limits. . . .

. . .

When school authorities present a district court with a "loaded game board," affirmative action in the form of remedial altering of attendance zones is proper to achieve truly nondiscriminatory assignments. In short, an assignment plan is not acceptable simply because it appears to be neutral. . . .

. . .

We hold that the pairing and grouping of non-contiguous school zones is a permissible tool and such action is to be considered in light of the objectives sought. Judicial steps in shaping such zones going beyond combinations of contiguous areas should be examined in light of what is said in subdivisions (1), (2), and (3) of this opinion concerning the objectives to be sought. Maps do not tell the whole story since non-contiguous school zones may be more accessible to each other in terms of the critical travel time, because of traffic patterns and good highways, than schools geographically closer together. Conditions in different localities will vary so widely that no rigid rules can be laid down to govern all situations.

(4) *Transportation of Students.*

The scope of permissible transportation of students as an implement of a remedial decree has never been defined by this Court and by the very nature of the problem it cannot be defined with precision. No rigid guidelines as to student transportation can be given for application to the infinite variety of problems presented in thousands of situations. Bus transportation has been an integral part of the public education system for years, and was perhaps the single most important factor in the transition from the one-room schoolhouse to the consolidated school. Eighteen million of the nation's public school children, approximately 39%, were transported to their schools by bus in 1969-1970 in all parts of the country.

The importance of bus transportation as a normal and accepted tool of educational policy is readily discernible in this and the companion case. The Charlotte school authorities did not purport to assign students on the basis of geographically drawn zones until 1965 and then they allowed

119

almost unlimited transfer privileges. The District Court's conclusion that assignment of children to the school nearest their home serving their grade would not produce an effective dismantling of the dual system is supported by the record. . . .

The decree provided that the buses used to implement the plan would operate on direct routes. Students would be picked up at schools near their homes and transported to the schools they were to attend. The trips for elementary school pupils average about seven miles and the District Court found that they would take "not over 35 minutes at the most." This system compares favorably with the transportation plan previously operated in Charlotte under which each day 23,600 students on all grade levels were transported an average of 15 miles one way for an average trip requiring over an hour. In these circumstances, we find no basis for holding that the local school authorities may not be required to employ bus transportation as one tool of school desegregation. Desegregation plans cannot be limited to the walk-in school.

An objection to transportation of students may have validity when the time or distance of travel is so great as to risk either the health of the children or significantly impinge on the educational process. District courts must weigh the soundness of any transportation plan in light of what is said in subdivisions (1), (2), and (3) above. It hardly needs stating that the limits on time of travel will vary with many factors, but probably with none more than the age of the students. The reconciliation of competing values in a desegregation case is, of course, a difficult task with many sensitive facets but fundamentally no more so than remedial measures courts of equity have traditionally employed. . . .

.   .   .

At some point, these school authorities and others like them should have achieved full compliance with this Court's decision in Brown I. The systems will then be "unitary" in the sense required by our decisions in Green and Alexander.

It does not follow that the communities served by such systems will remain demographically stable, for in a growing, mobile society, few will do so. Neither school authorities nor district courts are constitutionally required to make year-by-year adjustments of the racial composition of student bodies once the affirmative duty to desegregate has been accomplished and racial discrimination through official action is eliminated from the system. This does not mean that federal courts are without power to deal with future problems; but in the absence of a showing that either the school authorities or some other agency of the State has deliberately attempted to fix or alter demographic patterns to affect the racial composition of the schools, further intervention by a district court should not be necessary.

For the reasons herein set forth, the judgment of the Court of Appeals is affirmed as to those parts in which it affirmed the judgment of the District Court. The order of the District Court dated August 7, 1970, is also affirmed.

Keyes v. School District No. 1

413 U.S. 189, 37 L Ed 548, 93 S. Ct 2686 (1973)

The district court found that for a decade the school board had engaged in deliberately segregative actions in one part (Park Hill) of the entire district which is coterminous with the city and county of Denver, Colorado. It also found that petitioners had failed to make out a case that the core city schools were intentionally segregated but agreed that it was shown that the core city schools were inferior to the predominantly white schools in other areas of the city. On these findings the district court ordered desegregation of Park Hill schools and substantial upgrading but not complete desegregation of the core city schools. The court of appeals affirmed as to the Park Hill schools but reversed as to the core city schools on the grounds that *de jure* segregation had not been proven. The U.S. Supreme Court granted certiorari to review the reversal of that part of the district court's order applying to the schools in the core city.

. . .

Mr. Justice Brennan delivered the opinion of the Court.

This school desegregation case concerns the Denver, Colorado, school system. That system has never been operated under a constitutional or statutory provision that mandated or permitted racial segregation in public education. Rather, the gravamen of this action, brought in June 1969 in the District Court for the District of Colorado by parents of Denver school children, is that respondent School Board alone, by use of various techniques such as the manipulation of student attendance zones, school site selection and a neighborhood school policy, created or maintained racially or ethnically (or both racially and ethnically) segregated schools throughout the school district, entitling petitioners to a decree directing desegregation of the entire school district. . . .

· · ·

The District Court found that by the construction of a new, relatively small elementary school, Barrett, in the middle of the Negro community west of Park Hill, by the gerrymandering of student attendance zones, by the use of so-called "optional zones," and by the excessive use of mobile classroom units, among other things, the respondent School Board had engaged over almost a decade after 1960 in an unconstitutional policy of deliberate racial segregation with respect to the Park Hill schools. The court therefore ordered the Board to desegregate those schools. . . .

· · ·

Segregation in Denver schools is not limited, however, to the schools in the Park Hill area, and not satisfied with their success in obtaining relief for Park Hill, petitioners pressed their prayer that the District Court order desegregation of all segregated schools in the city of Denver, particularly the heavily segregated schools in the core city area. But that court concluded that its finding of a purposeful and systematic program of racial segregation affecting thousands of students in the Park Hill area did not, in itself, impose on the School Board an affirmative duty to eliminate segregation throughout the school district. Instead, the court fractionated the district and held that petitioners must make a fresh showing of de jure segregation in each area of the city for which they seek relief. Moreover, the District Court held that its finding of intentional segregation in Park Hill was not in any sense material to the question of segregative intent in other areas of the city. . . .

· · ·

Nevertheless, the District Court went on to hold that the proofs established that the segregated core city schools were educationally inferior to the predominantly "white" or "Anglo" schools in other parts of the district—that is, "separate facilities ... unequal in the quality of education provided." Thus, the court held that respondent School Board constitutionally "must at a minimum ... offer an equal educational opportunity," and, therefore, although all-out desegregation "could not be decreed, ... the only feasible and constitutionally acceptable program— the only program which furnishes anything approaching substantial equality—is a system of desegregation and integration which provides compensatory education in an integrated environment.". . . .

* * *

Before turning to the primary question we decide today, a word must be said about the District Court's method of defining a "segregated" school. Denver is a tri-ethnic, as distinguished from a bi-racial, community. The overall racial and ethnic composition of the Denver public schools is 66% Anglo, 14% Negro and 20% Hispano. The District Court, in assessing the question of de jure segregation in the core city schools, preliminarily resolved that Negroes and Hispanos should not be placed in the same category to establish the segregated character of a school. Later, in determining the schools that were likely to produce an inferior educational opportunity, the court concluded that a school would be considered inferior only if it had "a concentration of either Negro or Hispano students in the general area of 70 to 75 percent.". . . The District Court used those figures to signify educationally inferior schools, and there is no suggestion in the record that those same figures were or would be used to define a "segregated" school in the de jure context. What is or is not a segregated school will necessarily depend on the facts of each particular case. In addition to the racial and ethnic composition of a school's student body, other factors such as the racial and ethnic composition of faculty and staff and the community and administration attitudes toward the school must be taken into consideration. . . .

* * *

We conclude, however, that the District Court erred in separating Negroes and Hispanos for purposes of defining a "segregated" school. We have held that Hispanos constitute an identifiable class for purposes of the Fourteenth Amendment. Indeed, the District Court recognized this in classifying predominantly Hispano schools as "segregated" schools in their own right. But there is also much evidence that in the Southwest Hispanos

123

and Negroes have a great many things in common. The United States Commission on Civil Rights has recently published two Reports on Hispano education in the Southwest. Focusing on students in the States of Arizona, California, Colorado, New Mexico, and Texas, the Commission concluded that Hispanos suffer from the same educational inequities as Negroes and American Indians. . . In that circumstance, we think petitioners are entitled to have schools with a combined predominance of Negroes and Hispanos included in the category of "segregated" schools. . .

[T]he only other question that requires our decision at this time is . . . whether the District Court and the Court of Appeals applied an incorrect legal standard in addressing petitioners' contention that respondent School Board engaged in an unconstitutional policy of deliberate segregation in the core city schools. Our conclusion is that those courts did not apply the correct standard in addressing that contention.

Petitioners apparently concede for the purposes of this case that in the case of a school system like Denver's, where no statutory dual system has ever existed, plaintiffs must prove not only that segregated schooling exists but also that it was brought about or maintained by intentional state action. Petitioners proved that for almost a decade after 1960 respondent School Board had engaged in an unconstitutional policy of deliberate racial segregation in the Park Hill schools. . . This finding did not relate to an insubstantial or trivial fragment of the school system. On the contrary, respondent School Board was found guilty of following a deliberate segregation policy at schools attended, in 1969, by 37.69% of Denver's total Negro school population, including one-fourth of the Negro elementary pupils, over two-thirds of the Negro junior high pupils, and over two-fifths of the Negro high school pupils. In addition, there was uncontroverted evidence that teachers and staff had for years been assigned on a minority teacher-to-minority school basis throughout the school system. Respondent argues, however, that a finding of state-imposed segregation as to a substantial portion of the school system can be viewed in isolation from the rest of the district, and that even if state-imposed segregation does exist in a substantial part of the Denver school system, it does not follow that the District Court could predicate on that fact a finding that the entire school system is a dual system. We do not agree. We have never suggested that plaintiffs in school desegregation cases must bear the burden of proving the elements of de jure segregation as to each and every school or each and every student within the school system. Rather, we have held that where plaintiffs prove that a current condition of segregated schooling exists within a school district where a dual system was compelled or authorized by statute at the time of our decision in Brown v Board of Education, the State automatically assumes an affirmative duty "to effectuate a transition to a racially nondiscriminatory school system," that is, to eliminate from the public schools within their school system "all vestiges of state-imposed segregation."

This is not a case, however, where a statutory dual system has ever existed. Nevertheless, where plaintiffs prove that the school authorities have carried out a systematic program of segregation affecting a substantial portion of the students, schools, teachers and facilities within the school system, it is only common sense to conclude that there exists a predicate for a finding of the existence of a dual school system. Several considerations support this conclusion. First, it is obvious that a practice of concentrating Negroes in certain schools by structuring attendance zones or designating "feeder" schools on the basis of race has the reciprocal effect of keeping other nearby schools predominantly white. Similarly, the practice of building a school—such as the Barrett Elementary School in this case—to a certain size and in a certain location, "with conscious knowledge that it would be a segregated school," has a substantial reciprocal effect on the racial composition of other nearby schools. So also, the use of mobile classrooms, the drafting of student transfer policies, the transportation of students, and the assignment of faculty and staff, on racially identifiable bases, have the clear effect of earmarking schools according to their racial composition, and this, in turn, together with the elements of student assignment and school construction, may have a profound reciprocal effect on the racial composition of residential neighborhoods within a metropolitan area, thereby causing further racial concentration within the schools. . . .

.   .   .

In short, common sense dictates the conclusion that racially inspired school board actions have an impact beyond the particular schools that are the subjects of those actions. This is not to say, of course, that there can never be a case in which the geographical structure of or the natural boundaries within a school district may have the effect of dividing the district into separate, identifiable and unrelated units. . . In the absence of such a determination, proof of state-imposed segregation in a substantial portion of the district will suffice to support a finding by the trial court of the existence of a dual system. Of course, where that finding is made, as in cases involving statutory dual systems, the school authorities have an affirmative duty "to effectuate a transition to a racially nondiscriminatory school system."

On remand, therefore, the District Court should decide in the first instance whether respondent School Board's deliberate racial segregation policy with respect to the Park Hill schools constitutes the entire Denver school system a dual school system. We observe that on the record now before us there is indication that Denver is not a school district which might be divided into separate, identifiable and unrelated units. . . .

. . .

In any event, inquiry whether the District Court and the Court of Appeals applied the correct legal standards in addressing petitioners' contention of deliberate segregation in the core city schools is not at an end even if it be true that Park Hill may be separated from the rest of the Denver school district as a separate, identifiable and unrelated unit.

The District Court proceeded on the premise that the finding as to the Park Hill schools was irrelevant to the consideration of the rest of the district, and began its examination of the core city schools by requiring that petitioners prove all of the essential elements of de jure segregation—that is, stated simply, a current condition of segregation resulting from intentional state action directed specifically to the core city schools. The segregated character of the core city schools could not be and is not denied. . . .

. . .

Although petitioners had already proved the existence of intentional school segregation in the Park Hill schools, this crucial finding was totally ignored when attention turned to the core city schools. Plainly, a finding of intentional segregation as to a portion of a school system is not devoid of probative value in assessing the school authorities' intent with respect to other parts of the same school system. On the contrary, where, as here, the case involves one school board, a finding of intentional segregation on its part in one portion of a school system is highly relevant to the issue of the board's intent with respect to other segregated schools in the system. This is merely an application of the well-settled evidentiary principle that "the prior doing of other similar acts, whether clearly a part of a scheme or not, is useful as reducing the possibility that the act in question was done with innocent intent." "Evidence that similar and related offenses were committed ... tend[s] to show a consistent pattern of conduct highly relevant to the issue of intent.". . . .

* * *

Applying these principles in the special context of school desegregation cases, we hold that a finding of intentionally segregative school board actions in a meaningful portion of a school system, as in this case, creates a presumption that other segregated schooling within the system is not adventitious. It establishes, in other words, a prima facie case of unlawful segregative design on the part of school authorities, and shifts to those authorities the burden of proving that other segregated schools within the system are not also the result of intentionally segregative actions. This is true even if it is determined that different areas of the school district should be viewed independently of each other because, even in that situation, there is high probability that where school authorities have effectuated an intentionally segregative policy in a meaningful portion of the school system, similar impermissible considerations have motivated their actions in other areas of the system. We emphasize that the differentiating factor between de jure segregation and so-called de facto segregation to which we referred in Swann is *purpose* or *intent* to segregate. Where school authorities have been found to have practiced purposeful segregation in part of a school system, they may be expected to oppose system-wide desegregation, as did the respondents in this case, on the ground that their purposefully segregative actions were isolated and individual events, thus leaving plaintiffs with the burden of proving otherwise. But at that point where an intentionally segregative policy is practiced in a meaningful or significant segment of a school system, as in this case, the school authorities cannot be heard to argue that plaintiffs have proved only "isolated and individual" unlawfully segregative actions. In that circumstance, it is both fair and reasonable to require that the school authorities bear the burden of showing that their actions as to other segregated schools within the system were not also motivated by segregative intent.

This burden-shifting principle is not new or novel. There are no hard and fast standards governing the allocation of the burden of proof in every situation. . . In the context of racial segregation in public education, the courts, including this Court, have recognized a variety of situations in which "fairness" and "policy" require state authorities to bear the burden of explaining actions or conditions which appear to be racially motivated. . . Thus, be it a statutory dual system or an allegedly unitary system where a meaningful portion of the system is found to be intentionally segregated, the existence of subsequent or other segregated schooling within the same system justifies a rule imposing on the school authorities the burden of proving that this segregated schooling is not also the result of intentionally segregative acts.

In discharging that burden, it is not enough, of course, that the school authorities rely upon some allegedly logical, racially neutral explanation for their actions. Their burden is to adduce proof sufficient to support a finding that segregative intent was not among the factors that motivated their actions. The courts below attributed much significance to the fact that many of the Board's actions in the core city area antedated our decision in Brown. We reject any suggestion that remoteness in time has any relevance to the issue of intent. If the actions of school authorities were to any degree motivated by segregative intent and the segregation resulting from those actions continues to exist, the fact of remoteness in time certainly does not make those actions any less "intentional.". . .

· · ·

The respondent School Board invoked at trial its "neighborhood school policy" as explaining racial and ethnic concentrations within the core city schools, arguing that since the core city area population had long been Negro and Hispano, the concentrations were necessarily the result of residential patterns and not of purposefully segregated policies. We have no occasion to consider in this case whether a "neighborhood school policy" of itself will justify racial or ethnic concentrations in the absence of a finding that school authorities have committed acts constituting de jure segregation. It is enough that we hold that the mere assertion of such a policy is not dispositive where, as in this case, the school authorities have been found to have practiced de jure segregation in a meaningful portion of the school system by techniques that indicate that the "neighborhood school" concept has not been maintained free of manipulation. . . .

· · ·

In summary, the District Court on remand, *first*, will afford respondent School Board the opportunity to prove its contention that the Park Hill area is a separate identifiable and unrelated section of the school district that should be treated as isolated from the rest of the district. If respondent School Board fails to prove that contention, the District Court, *second*, will determine whether respondent School Board's conduct over almost a decade after 1960 in carrying out a policy of deliberate racial segregation in the Park Hill schools constitutes the entire school system a dual school system. If the District Court determines that the Denver school system is a dual school system, respondent School Board has the affirmative duty to desegregate the entire system "root and branch." If the District Court determines, however, that the Denver school system is not a dual school system by reason of the Board's actions in Park Hill, the court, *third*, will afford respondent School Board the opportunity to rebut petitioners' prima facie case of intentional segregation in the core city schools raised by the finding of intentional segregation in the Park Hill schools. There, the Board's burden is to show that its policies and practices with respect to school site location, school size, school renovations and additions, student attendance zones, student assignment and transfer options, mobile classroom units, transportation of students, assignment of faculty and staff, etc., considered together and premised on the Board's so-called "neighborhood school" concept, either were not taken in effectuation of a policy to create or maintain segregation in the core city schools, or, if unsuccessful in that effort, were not factors in causing the existing condition of segregation in these schools. . . .

·   ·   ·

[T]he case is remanded to the District Court for further proceedings consistent with this opinion.

·   ·   ·

Mr. Chief Justice Burger concurs in the result.

·   ·   ·

Mr. Justice White took no part in the decision of this case.

. . .

Mr. Justice Douglas.

While I join the opinion of the Court, I agree with my Brother Powell that there is, for the purposes of the Equal Protection Clause of the Fourteenth Amendment as applied to the school cases, no difference between de facto and de jure segregation. The school board is a state agency and the lines that it draws, the allocation it makes of students, the budgets it prepares are state action for Fourteenth Amendment purposes. . . .

I think it is time to state that there is no constitutional difference between de jure and de facto segregation, for each is the product of state actions or policies. If a "neighborhood" or "geographical" unit has been created along racial lines by reason of the play of restrictive covenants that restrict certain areas to "the elite," leaving the "undesirables" to move elsewhere, there is state action in the constitutional sense because the force of law is placed behind those covenants.

There is state action in the constitutional sense when public funds are dispersed by urban development agencies to build racial ghettoes.

Where the school district is racially mixed and the races are segregated in separate schools, where black teachers are assigned almost exclusively to black schools, where the school board closed existing schools located in fringe areas and built new schools in black areas and in distant white areas, where the school board continued the "neighborhood" school policy at the elementary level, these actions constitute state action. They are of a kind quite distinct from the classical de jure type of school segregation. Yet calling them de facto is a misnomer, as they are only more subtle types of state action that create or maintain a wholly or partially segregated school system.

When a State forces, aids, or abets, or helps create a racial "neighborhood," it is a travesty of justice to treat that neighborhood as sacrosanct in the sense that its creation is free from the taint of state action.

The Constitution and Bill of Rights have described the design of a pluralistic society. The individual has the right to seek such companions as he desires. But a State is barred from creating by one device or another ghettoes that determine the school one is compelled to attend.

. . .

Mr. Justice Powell concurring in part and dissenting in part.

. . .

This is the first school desegregation case to reach this Court which involves a major city outside the South. It comes from Denver, Colorado, a city and a State which have not operated public schools under constitutional or statutory provisions which mandated or permitted racial segregation. Nor has it been argued that any other legislative actions (such as zoning and housing laws) contributed to the segregation which is at issue. The Court has inquired only to what extent the Denver public school authorities may have contributed to the school segregation which is acknowledged to exist in Denver. . . .

. . .

The situation in Denver is generally comparable to that in other large cities across the country in which there is a substantial minority population and where desegregation has not been ordered by the federal courts. There is segregation in the schools of many of these cities fully as pervasive as that in southern cities prior to the desegregation decrees of the past decade and a half. The focus of the school desegregation problem has now shifted from the South to the country as a whole. Unwilling and footdragging as the process was in most places, substantial progress toward achieving integration has been made in southern States. No comparable progress has been made in many nonsouthern cities with large minority populations primarily because of the de facto/de jure distinction nurtured by the courts and accepted complacently by many of the same voices which denounced the evils of segregated schools in the South. But if our national concern is for those who attend such schools, rather than for perpetuating a legalism rooted in history rather than present reality, we must recognize that the evil of operating separate schools is no less in Denver than in Atlanta. . . .

. . .

The great contribution of Brown I was its holding in unmistakable terms that the Fourteenth Amendment forbids state-compelled or authorized segregation of public schools. Although some of the language was more expansive, the holding in Brown I was essentially negative: It was impermissible under the Constitution for the States, or their instrumentalities, to force children to attend segregated schools. The forbidden action was de jure, and the opinion in Brown I was construed—for some years and by many courts—as requiring only state neutrality. . . .

131

. . .

But the doctrine of Brown I, as amplified by Brown II, did not retain its original meaning. In a series of decisions extending from 1954 to 1971 the concept of state neutrality was transformed into the present constitutional doctrine requiring affirmative state action to desegregate school systems. . . .

. . .

In Swann, the Court . . . noted it was concerned only with States having "a long history" of officially imposed segregation and the duty of school authorities in those States to implement Brown I. In so doing, the Court refrained even from considering whether the evolution of constitutional doctrine from Brown I to Green/Swann undercut whatever logic once supported the de facto/de jure distinction. In imposing on metropolitan southern school districts an affirmative duty, entailing large-scale transportation of pupils, to eliminate segregation in the schools, the Court required these districts to alleviate conditions which in large part did *not* result from historic, state-imposed de jure segregation. Rather, the familiar root cause of segregated schools in *all* the biracial metropolitan areas of our country is essentially the same: one of segregated residential and migratory patterns the impact of which on the racial composition of the schools was often perpetuated and rarely ameliorated by action of public school authorities. This is a national, not a southern phenomenon. And it is largely unrelated to whether a particular State had or did not have segregatory school laws. . . .

. . .

I concur in the Court's position that the public school authorities are the responsible agency of the State, and that if the affirmative duty doctrine is sound constitutional law for Charlotte, it is equally so for Denver. I would not, however, perpetuate the de jure/de facto distinction nor would I leave to petitioners the initial tortuous effort of identifying "segregative acts" and deducing "segregatory intent." I would hold, quite simply, that where segregated public schools exist within a school district to a substantial degree, there is a prima facie case that the duly constituted public authorities . . . are sufficiently responsible to impose upon them a nationally applicable burden to demonstrate they nevertheless are operating a genuinely integrated school system. . . .

. . .

At the outset, one must try to identify the constitutional right which is being enforced... Although nowhere expressly articulated in these terms, I would now define it as the right, derived from the Equal Protection Clause, to expect that once the State has assumed responsibility for education, local school boards will operate *integrated school systems* within their respective districts. This means that school authorities, consistent with the generally accepted educational goal of attaining quality education for all pupils, must make and implement their customary decisions with a view toward enhancing integrated school opportunities. . . .

. . .

A system would be integrated in accord with constitutional standards if the responsible authorities had taken appropriate steps to (i) integrate faculties and administration; (ii) scrupulously assure equality of facilities, instruction and curricula opportunities throughout the district; (iii) utilize their authority to draw attendance zones to promote integration; and (iv) locate new schools, close old ones, and determine the size and grade categories with this same objective in mind. Where school authorities decide to undertake the transportation of students, this also must be with integrative opportunities in mind.

The foregoing prescription is not intended to be either definitive or all-inclusive, but rather an indication of the contour characteristics of an *integrated school system* in which all citizens and pupils may justifiably be confident that racial discrimination is neither practiced nor tolerated. An integrated school system does not mean—and indeed could not mean in view of the residential patterns of most of our major metropolitan areas— that *every school* must in fact be an integrated unit. A school which happens to be all or predominantly white or all or predominantly black is not a "segregated" school in an unconstitutional sense if the system itself is a genuinely integrated one.

Having school boards operate an integrated school system provides the best assurance of meeting the constitutional requirement that racial discrimination, subtle or otherwise, will find no place in the decisions of public school officials. Courts judging past school board actions with a view to their *general integrative effect* will be best able to assure an absence of such discrimination while avoiding the murky, subjective judgments inherent in the Court's search for "segregatory intent." Any test resting on so nebulous and elusive an element as a school board's segregatory "intent" provides inadequate assurance that minority children will not be shortchanged in the decisions of those entrusted with the nondiscriminatory operation of our public schools. . . .

. . .

There is thus no reason as a matter of constitutional principle to adhere to the de jure/de facto distinction in school desegregation cases. In addition, there are reasons of policy and prudent judicial administration which point strongly toward the adoption of a uniform national rule. The litigation heretofore centered in the South already is surfacing in other regions. The decision of the Court today, emphasizing as it does the elusive element of segregatory intent, will invite numerous desegregation suits in which there can be little hope of uniformity of result.

The issue in these cases will not be whether segregated education exists. This will be conceded in most of them. The litigation will focus as a consequence of the Court's decision on whether segregation has resulted in any "meaningful or significant" portion of a school system from a school board's "segregatory intent." The intractable problems involved in litigating this issue are obvious to any lawyer. The results of litigation—often arrived at subjectively by a court endeavoring to ascertain the subjective intent of school authorities with respect to action taken or not taken over many years—will be fortuitous, unpredictable and even capricious. . . .

. . .

Rather than continue to prop up a distinction no longer grounded in principle, and contributing to the consequences indicated above, we should acknowledge that whenever public school segregation exists to a substantial degree there is prima facie evidence of a constitutional violation by the responsible school board. It is true, of course, that segregated schools—wherever located—are not solely the product of the action or inaction of public school authorities. Indeed, as indicated earlier, there can be little doubt that principal causes of the pervasive school segregation found in the major urban areas of this country, whether in the North, West, or South, are the socio-economic influences which have concentrated our minority citizens in the inner cities while the more mobile white majority disperse to the suburbs. But it is also true that public school boards have continuing, detailed responsibility for the public school system within their

134

district. . . Moreover, as foreshadowed in Swann and as implicitly held today, school boards have a duty to minimize and ameliorate segregated conditions by pursuing an affirmative policy of desegregation. It is this policy which must be applied consistently on a national basis without regard to a doctrinal distinction which has outlived its time. . . .

. . .

[T]he question . . . becomes what reasonable affirmative desegregative steps district courts may require to place the school system in compliance with the constitutional standard. In short, what specifically is the nature and scope of the remedy? . . .

. . .

The controlling case is Swann, and the question which will confront and confound the District Court and Denver School Board is what indeed does Swann require. . . .

. . .

To the extent that Swann may be thought to require large-scale or long-distance transportation of students in our metropolitan school districts, I record my profound misgivings. Nothing in our Constitution commands or encourages any such court compelled disruption of public education. . . .

. . .

Where school authorities have defaulted in their duty to operate an integrated school system, district courts must insure that affirmative desegregative steps ensue. Many of these can be taken effectively without damaging state and parental interests in having children attend schools within a reasonable vicinity of home. Where desegregative steps are possible within the framework of a system of "neighborhood education," school authorities must pursue them. . . .

. . .

A *constitutional requirement* of extensive student transportation solely to achieve integration . . . promises on the one hand a greater degree of actual desegregation, while it infringes on what may fairly be regarded as other important community aspirations and personal rights. Such a requirement is further likely to divert attention and resources from the foremost goal of any school system: the best quality education for all pupils. The Equal Protection Clause does indeed command that racial discrimination not be tolerated in the decisions of public school authorities. But it does not require that school authorities undertake widespread student transportation solely for the sake of maximizing integration.

This obviously does not mean that bus transportation has no place in public school systems or is not a permissible means in the desegregative process. The transporting of school children is as old as public education, and in rural and some suburban settings it is as indispensable as the providing of books. It is presently estimated that approximately half of all American children ride buses to school for reasons unrelated to integration. At the secondary level in particular, where the schools are larger and serve a wider, more dispersed constituency than the elementary school, some form of public or privately financed transportation is often necessary. There is a significant difference, however, in transportation plans voluntarily initiated by local school boards for educational purposes and those imposed by a federal court. The former usually represent a necessary or convenient means of access to the school nearest home; the latter often require lengthy trips for no purpose other than to further integration. . . The crucial issue is when, under what circumstances, and to what extent such transportation may appropriately be ordered. The answer to this turns—as it does so often in the law—upon a sound exercise of discretion under the circumstances. . . .

.   .   .

The refusal of the Court in Swann to require racial balance in schools throughout the district or the arbitrary elimination of all "one-race schools" is grounded in a recognition that the State, parents, and children all have at stake in school desegregation decrees legitimate and recognizable interests.

The personal interest might be characterized as the desire that children attend community schools near home. . . The neighborhood school does provide greater ease of parental and student access and convenience, as well as greater economy of public administration. These are obvious and distinct advantages, but the legitimacy of the neighborhood concept rests on more basic grounds.

Neighborhood school systems, neutrally administered, reflect the deeply felt desire of citizens for a sense of community in their public education. Public schools have been a traditional source of strength to our Nation, and that strength may derive in part from the identification of many schools with the personal features of the surrounding neighborhood. Community support, interest and dedication to public schools may well run higher with a neighborhood attendance pattern: distance may encourage disinterest. Many citizens sense today a decline in the intimacy of our institutions—home, church, and school—which has caused a concomitant decline in the unity and communal spirit of our people. I pass no judgment on this viewpoint, but I do believe that this Court should be wary of compelling in the name of constitutional law what may seem to many a dissolution in the traditional, more personal fabric of their public schools. . . .

·   ·   ·

Most parents cannot afford the luxury of a private education for their children, and the dual obligation of private tuitions and public taxes. Those who may for numerous reasons seek public education for their children should not be forced to forfeit all interest or voice in the school their child attends. It would, of course, be impractical to allow the wishes of particular parents to be controlling. Yet the interest of the parent in the enhanced parent-school and parent-child communication allowed by the neighborhood unit ought not to be suppressed by force of law.

In the commendable national concern for alleviating public school segregation, courts may have overlooked the fact that the rights and interests of children affected by a desegregation program also are entitled to consideration. Any child, white or black, who is compelled to leave his neighborhood and spend significant time each day being transported to a distant school suffers an impairment of his liberty and his privacy. . . . A community may well conclude that the portion of a child's day spent on a bus might be used more creatively in a classroom, playground, or some other extracurricular school activity. Decisions such as these, affecting the quality of a child's daily life, should not lightly be held constitutionally errant. . . .

·   ·   ·

[B]roader considerations lead me to question just as seriously any remedial requirement of extensive student transportation solely to further integration. Any such requirement is certain to fall disproportionately on the school districts of our country, depending on their degree of urbanization, financial resources, and their racial composition. Some districts with little or no biracial population will experience little or no educational disruption, while others, notably in large, biracial metropolitan areas, must at considerable expense undertake extensive transportation to achieve the type of integration frequently being ordered by district courts. At a time when public education generally is suffering serious financial malnutrition, the economic burdens of such transportation can be severe, requiring both initial capital outlays and annual operating costs in the millions of dollars. And while constitutional requirements have often occasioned uneven burdens, never have they touched so sensitive a matter as wide differences in the compulsory transportation requirements for literally hundreds of thousands of school children. . . .

. . . . .

The compulsory transportation of students carries a further infirmity as a constitutional remedy. With most constitutional violations, the major burden of remedial action falls on offending state officials. Public officials who act to infringe personal rights of speech, voting, or religious exercise, for example, are obliged to cease the offending act or practice and, where necessary, institute corrective measures. It is they who bear the brunt of remedial action, though other citizens will to varying degrees feel its effects. School authorities responsible for segregation must, at the very minimum, discontinue segregatory acts. But when the obligation further extends to the transportation of students, the full burden of the affirmative remedial action is borne by children and parents who did not participate in any constitutional violation.

Finally, courts in requiring so far-reaching a remedy as student transportation solely to maximize integration, risk setting in motion unpredictable and unmanageable social consequences. No one can estimate the extent to which dismantling neighborhood education will hasten an exodus to private schools, leaving public school systems the preserve of the disadvantaged of both races. Or guess how much impetus such dismantlement gives the movement from innercity to suburb, and the further geographical separation of the races. Nor do we know to what degree this remedy may cause deterioration of community and parental support of public schools, or divert attention from the paramount goal of quality in education to a perennially devisive debate over who is to be transported where. . . .

.   .   .

There is nothing in the Constitution, its history or—until recently—in the jurisprudence of this Court that mandates the employment of forced transportation of young and teenage children to achieve a single interest, as important as this interest may be. We have strayed, quite far as I view it, from the rationale of Brown I and II, as reiterated in Swann, that courts in fashioning remedies must be "guided by equitable principles" which include the "adjusting and reconciling [of] public and private needs."

I urge a return to this rationale. This would result, as emphasized above, in no prohibition on court-ordered student transportation in furtherance of desegregation. But it would also require that the legitimate community interests in neighborhood school systems be accorded far greater respect. In the balancing of interests so appropriate to a fair and just equitable decree, transportation orders should be applied with special caution to any proposal as disruptive of family life and interests—and ultimately of education itself—as extensive transportation of elementary age children solely for desegregation purposes. As a minimum, this Court should not require school boards to engage in the unnecessary transportation away from their neighborhoods of elementary age children. It is at this age level that neighborhood education performs its most vital educational role. It is with respect to children of tender years that the greatest concern exists for their physical and psychological health. It is also here, at the elementary school, that the rights of parents and children are most sharply implicated. . . .

.   .   .

It is well to remember that the course we are running is a long one and the goal sought in the end—so often overlooked—is the best possible educational opportunity for all children. Communities deserve the freedom and the incentive to turn their attention and energies to this goal of quality education, free from protracted and debilitating battles over court-ordered student transportation. The single most disruptive element in education today is the widespread use of compulsory transportation, especially at elementary grade levels. This has risked distracting and diverting attention from basic educational ends, dividing and embittering communities, and exacerbating rather than ameliorating interracial friction and misunderstanding. It is time to return to a more balanced evaluation of the recognized interests of our society in achieving desegregation and other educational and societal interests a community may legitimately assert. This will help assure that integrated school systems will be established and maintained by rational action, will be better understood and supported by parents and children of both races, and will promote the enduring qualities of an integrated society so essential to its genuine success.

· · ·

Mr. Justice Rehnquist, dissenting.

· · ·

[I]n a school district the size of Denver's, it is quite conceivable that the school board might have engaged in the racial gerrymandering of the attendance boundary between two particular schools in order to keep one largely Negro and Hispano, and the other largely Anglo, as the District Court found to have been the fact in this case. Such action would have deprived affected minority students who were the victims of such gerrymandering of their constitutional right to equal protection of the law. But if the school board had been evenhanded in its drawing of the attendance lines for other schools in the district, minority students required to attend other schools within the district would have suffered no such deprivation. It certainly would not reflect normal English usage to describe the entire district as "segregated" on such a state of facts, and it would be a quite unprecedented application of principles of equitable relief to determine that if the gerrymandering of one attendance zone were proven, particular racial mixtures could be required by a federal district court for every school in the district. . . .

· · ·

The drastic extension of Brown which Green represented was barely, if at all, explicated in the latter opinion. To require that a genuinely "dual" system be disestablished, in the sense that the assignment to a child

140

of a particular school is not made to depend on his race, is one thing. To require that school boards affirmatively undertake to achieve racial mixing in schools where such mixing is not achieved in sufficient degree by neutrally drawn boundary lines is quite obviously something else. . . .

Milliken v. Bradley

418 U.S. 717, 41 L Ed 2d 1069, 94 S. Ct 3112 (1974)

In litigation seeking the desegregation of schools in the City of Detroit, the district court found 1) de jure segregation resulting from acts of both the board of education and state officials, 2) that a Detroit-only desegregation plan would not appreciably change the composition of the schools, and 3) that a Detroit-only plan, because of "white flight," would only increase the proportion of blacks in the city. The district court concluded that the only solution was the imposition of an interdistrict metropolitan remedy involving the city and 53 suburban school districts even though those suburban districts had not been parties to the suit nor had they been shown to have engaged in deliberate segregative acts. The court of appeals substantially affirmed but remanded with instructions to join the suburban districts as parties in the case. Certiorari was granted.

. . .

Mr. Chief Justice Burger delivered the opinion of the Court.

We granted certiorari in these consolidated cases to determine whether a federal court may impose a multi-district, areawide remedy to a single district de jure segregation problem absent any finding that the other included school districts have failed to operate unitary school systems within their districts, absent any claim or finding that the boundary lines of any affected school district were established with the purpose of fostering racial segregation in public schools, absent any finding that the included districts committed acts which effected segregation within the other districts, and absent a meaningful opportunity for the included

141

neighboring school districts to present evidence or be heard on the propriety of a multi-district remedy or on the question of constitutional violations by those neighboring districts. . . .

. . .

[W]e first note that in the District Court the complainants sought a remedy aimed at the *condition* alleged to offend the Constitution—the segregation within the Detroit City school district. The court acted on this theory of the case. . . Thereafter, however, the District Court abruptly rejected the proposed Detroit-only plans on the ground that "while it would provide a racial mix more in keeping with the Black-White proportions of the student population, [it] would accentuate the racial identifiability of the [Detroit] district as a Black school system, and would not accomplish desegregation." "[T]he racial composition of the student body is such," said the court, "that the plan's implementation would clearly make the entire Detroit public school system racially identifiable, leav[ing] many of its schools 75 to 90 percent Black." Consequently, the court reasoned, it was imperative to "look beyond the limits of the Detroit school district for a solution to the problem of segregation in the Detroit schools . . ." since "school district lines are simply matters of political convenience and may not be used to deny constitutional rights." Accordingly, the District Court proceeded to redefine the relevant area to include areas of predominantly white pupil population in order to ensure that "upon implementation, no school, grade or classroom [would be] substantially disproportionate to the overall racial composition" of the entire metropolitan area. . . .

. . .

Viewing the record as a whole, it seems clear that the District Court and the Court of Appeals shifted the primary focus from a Detroit remedy to the metropolitan area only because of their conclusion that total desegregation of Detroit would not produce the racial balance which they perceived as desirable. Both courts proceeded on an assumption that the Detroit schools could not be truly desegregated—in their view of what constituted desegregation—unless the racial composition of the student body of each school substantially reflected the racial composition of the population of the metropolitan area as a whole. The metropolitan area was then defined as Detroit plus 53 of the outlying school districts. That this was the approach the District Court expressly and frankly employed is shown by the order which expressed the court's view of the constitutional standard. . . .

. . .

Here the District Court's approach to what constituted "actual desegregation" raises the fundamental question, not presented in Swann, as to the circumstances in which a federal court may order desegregation relief that embraces more than a single school district. The court's analytical starting point was its conclusion that school district lines are no more than arbitrary lines on a map "drawn for political convenience." Boundary lines may be bridged where there has been a constitutional violation calling for inter-district relief, but, the notion that school district lines may be casually ignored or treated as a mere administrative convenience is contrary to the history of public education in our country. No single tradition in public education is more deeply rooted than local control over the operation of schools; local autonomy has long been thought essential both to the maintenance of community concern and support for public schools and to quality of the educational process. . . .

. . .

The Michigan educational structure involved in this case, in common with most States, provides for a large measure of local control and a review of the scope and character of these local powers indicates the extent to which the inter-district remedy approved by the two courts could disrupt and alter the structure of public education in Michigan. The metropolitan remedy would require, in effect, consolidation of 54 independent school districts historically administered as separate units into a vast new super school district. Entirely apart from the logistical and other serious problems attending large-scale transportation of students, the consolidation would give rise to an array of other problems in financing and operating this new school system. Some of the more obvious questions would be: What would be the status and authority of the present popularly elected school boards? Would the children of Detroit be within the jurisdiction and operating control of a school board elected by the parents and residents of other districts? What board or boards would levy taxes for school operations in these 54 districts constituting the consolidated metropolitan area? What provisions could be made for assuring

143

substantial equality in tax levies among the 54 districts, if this were deemed requisite? What provisions would be made for financing? Would the validity of long-term bonds be jeopardized unless approved by all of the component districts as well as the State? What body would determine that portion of the curricula now left to the discretion of local school boards? Who would establish attendance zones, purchase school equipment, locate and construct new schools, and indeed attend to all the myriad day-to-day decisions that are necessary to school operations affecting potentially more than three quarters of a million pupils? ...

．　．　．

[I]t is obvious from the scope of the inter-district remedy itself that absent a complete restructuring of the laws of Michigan relating to school districts the District Court will become first, a de facto "legislative authority" to resolve these complex questions, and then the "school superintendent" for the entire area. This is a task which few, if any, judges are qualified to perform and one which would deprive the people of control of schools through their elected representatives.

Of course, no state law is above the Constitution. School district lines and the present laws with respect to local control, are not sacrosanct and if they conflict with the Fourteenth Amendment federal courts have a duty to prescribe appropriate remedies. ...

．　．　．

The controlling principle consistently expounded in our holdings is that the scope of the remedy is determined by the nature and extent of the constitutional violation. Before the boundaries of separate and autonomous school districts may be set aside by consolidating the separate units for remedial purposes or by imposing a cross-district remedy, it must first be shown that there has been a constitutional violation within one district that produces a significant segregative effect in another district. Specifically it must be shown that racially discriminatory acts of the state or local school districts, or of a single school district have been a substantial cause of inter-district segregation. Thus an inter-district remedy might be in order where the racially discriminatory acts of one or more school districts caused racial segregation in an adjacent district, or where district lines have been deliberately drawn on the basis of race. In such circumstances an inter-district remedy would be appropriate to eliminate the inter-district segregation directly caused by the constitutional violation. Conversely, without an inter-district violation and inter-district effect, there is no constitutional wrong calling for an inter-district remedy.

The record before us, voluminous as it is, contains evidence of de jure segregated conditions only in the Detroit schools; indeed, that was the theory on which the litigation was initially based and on which the District Court took evidence. With no showing of significant violation by the 53 outlying school districts and no evidence of any inter-district violation or effect, the court went beyond the original theory of the case as framed by the pleadings and mandated a metropolitan area remedy. To approve the remedy ordered by the court would impose on the outlying districts, not shown to have committed any constitutional violation, a wholly impermissible remedy based on a standard not hinted at in Brown I and II or any holding of this Court. . . .

. . .

Disparate treatment of white and Negro students occurred within the Detroit school system, and not elsewhere, and on this record the remedy must be limited to that system.

The constitutional right of the Negro respondents residing in Detroit is to attend a unitary school system in that district. Unless petitioners drew the district lines in a discriminatory fashion, or arranged for white students residing in the Detroit district to attend schools in Oakland and Macomb Counties, they were under no constitutional duty to make provisions for Negro students to do so. The view of the dissenters, that the existence of a dual system *in Detroit* can be made the basis for a decree requiring cross-district transportation of pupils cannot be supported on the grounds that it represents merely the devising of a suitably flexible remedy for the violation of rights already established by our prior decisions. It can be supported only by drastic expansion of the constitutional right itself, an expansion without any support in either constitutional principle or precedent. . . .

. . .

[The Court of Appeals] held the State derivatively responsible for the Detroit Board's violations on the theory that actions of Detroit as a political subdivision of the State were attributable to the State. Accepting, arguendo, the correctness of this finding of State responsibility for the

145

segregated conditions within the city of Detroit, it does not follow that an inter-district remedy is constitutionally justified or required. With a single exception . . . there has been no showing that either the State or any of the 85 outlying districts engaged in activity that had a cross-district effect. The boundaries of the Detroit School District, which are coterminous with the boundaries of the city of Detroit, were established over a century ago by neutral legislation when the city was incorporated; there is no evidence in the record, nor is there any suggestion by the respondents, that either the original boundaries of the Detroit School District, or any other school district in Michigan, were established for the purpose of creating, maintaining or perpetuating segregation of races. There is no claim and there is no evidence hinting that petitioners and their predecessors, or the 40-odd other school districts in the tri-county area—but outside the District Court's "desegregation area"—have ever maintained or operated anything but unitary school systems. Unitary school systems have been required for more than a century by the Michigan Constitution as implemented by state law. Where the schools of only one district have been affected, there is no constitutional power in the courts to decree relief balancing the racial composition of that district's schools with those of the surrounding districts. . . .

． ． ．

We conclude that the relief ordered by the District Court and affirmed by the Court of Appeals was based upon an erroneous standard and was unsupported by record evidence that acts of the outlying districts affected the discrimination found to exist in the schools of Detroit. Accordingly, the judgment of the Court of Appeals is reversed and the case is remanded for further proceedings consistent with this opinion leading to prompt formulation of a decree directed to eliminating the segregation found to exist in Detroit city schools, a remedy which has been delayed since 1970.

． ． ．

Mr. Justice Stewart, concurring.

In joining the opinion of the Court, I think it appropriate, in view of some of the extravagant language of the dissenting opinions, to state briefly my understanding of what it is that the Court decides today. . . .

． ． ．

The courts were in error for the simple reason that the remedy they thought necessary was not commensurate with the constitutional violation found. Within a single school district whose officials have been shown to have engaged in unconstitutional racial segregation, a remedial decree that affects every individual school may be dictated by "common sense," and indeed may provide the only effective means to eliminate segregation "root and branch," and to "effectuate a transition to a racially nondiscriminatory school system." But in this case the Court of Appeals approved the concept of a remedial decree that would go beyond the boundaries of the district where the constitutional violation was found, and include schools and school children in many other school districts that have presumptively been administered in complete accord with the Constitution....

.　.　.

The formulation of an inter-district remedy was thus simply not responsive to the factual record before the District Court and was an abuse of that court's equitable powers....

.　.　.

Mr. Justice Douglas, dissenting.

.　.　.

Metropolitan treatment of metropolitan problems is commonplace. If this were a sewage problem or a water problem, or an energy problem, there can be no doubt that Michigan would stay well within federal constitutional bounds if she sought a metropolitan remedy... Here the Michigan educational system is unitary, heading up in the legislature under which is the State Board of Education. The State controls the boundaries of school districts. The State supervised school site selection. The construction was done through municipal bonds approved by several state agencies. Education in Michigan is a state project with very little completely local control, except that the schools are financed locally, not on a statewide basis....

.　.　.

Therefore as the Court of Appeals held there can be no doubt that as a matter of Michigan law the State herself has the final say as to where and how school district lines should be drawn....

. . .

Given the State's control over the educational system in Michigan, the fact that the black schools are in one district and the white schools are in another is not controlling—either constitutionally or equitably. No specific plan has yet been adopted. We are still at an interlocutory stage of a long drawn-out judicial effort at school desegregation. It is conceivable that ghettos develop on their own without any hint of state action. But since Michigan by one device or another has over the years created black school districts and white school districts, the task of equity is to provide a unitary system for the affected area where, as here, the State washes its hands of its own creations.

. . .

Mr. Justice White, with whom Mr. Justice Douglas, Mr. Justice Brennan, and Mr. Justice Marshall join, dissenting.

The District Court and the Court of Appeals found that over a long period of years those in charge of the Michigan public schools engaged in various practices calculated to effect the segregation of the Detroit school system. The Court does not question these findings, nor could it reasonably do so. Neither does it question the obligation of the federal courts to devise a feasible and effective remedy. But it promptly cripples the ability of the judiciary to perform this task, which is of fundamental importance to our constitutional system, by fashioning a strict rule that remedies in school cases must stop at the school district line unless certain other conditions are met. . . .

. . .

Regretfully, and for several reasons, I can join neither the Court's judgment nor its opinion. The core of my disagreement is that deliberate acts of segregation and their consequences will go unremedied, not because a remedy would be infeasible or unreasonable in terms of the usual criteria governing school desegregation cases, but because an effective remedy would cause what the Court considers to be undue administrative inconvenience to the State. The result is that the State of Michigan, the entity at which the Fourteenth Amendment is directed, has successfully insulated itself from its duty to provide effective desegregation remedies by vesting sufficient power over its public schools in its local school districts. If this is the case in Michigan, it will be the case in most States. . . .

. . .

This Court now reverses the Court of Appeals. It does not question the District Court's findings that *any* feasible Detroit-only plan would leave many schools 75 to 90 percent black and that the district would become progressively more black as whites left the city. Neither does the Court suggest that including the suburbs in a desegregation plan would be impractical or infeasible because of educational considerations, because of the number of children requiring transportation, or because of the length of their rides. Indeed, the Court leaves unchallenged the District Court's conclusion that a plan including the suburbs would be physically easier and more practical and feasible than a Detroit-only plan. Whereas the most promising Detroit-only plan, for example, would have entailed the purchase of 900 buses, the metropolitan plan would involve the acquisition of no more than 350 new vehicles.

Despite the fact that a metropolitan remedy, if the findings of the District Court accepted by the Court of Appeals are to be credited, would more effectively desegregate the Detroit schools, would prevent resegregation, and would be easier and more feasible from many standpoints, the Court fashions out of whole cloth an arbitrary rule that remedies for constitutional violations occurring in a single Michigan school district must stop at the school district line. Apparently, no matter how much less burdensome or more effective and efficient in many respects, such as transportation, the metropolitan plan might be, the school district line may not be crossed. Otherwise, it seems, there would be too much disruption of the Michigan scheme for managing its educational system, too much confusion and too much administrative burden.

The District Court, on the scene and familiar with local conditions, had a wholly different view. The Court of Appeals also addressed itself at length to matters of local law and to the problems that inter-district remedies might present to the State of Michigan. Its conclusion, flatly contrary to that of the Court, was that "the constitutional right to equality before the law [is not] hemmed in by the boundaries of a school district"....

. . .

I am surprised that the Court, sitting at this distance from the State of Michigan, claims better insight than the Court of Appeals and the District Court as to whether an inter-district remedy for equal protection violations practiced by the State of Michigan would involve undue difficulties for the State in the management of its public schools. . . .

. . .

I am even more mystified how the Court can ignore the legal reality that the constitutional violations, even if occurring locally, were committed by governmental entities for which the State is responsible and that it is the State that must respond to the command of the Fourteenth Amendment. An inter-district remedy for the infringements that occurred in this case is well within the confines and powers of the State, which is the governmental entity ultimately responsible for desegregating its schools. . . .

. . .

The Court draws the remedial line at the Detroit School District boundary, even though the Fourteenth Amendment is addressed to the State and even though the *State* denies equal protection of the laws when its public agencies, acting in its behalf, invidiously discriminate. The State's default is "the condition that offends the Constitution," and state officials may therefore be ordered to take the necessary measures to completely eliminate from the Detroit public schools "all vestiges of state-imposed segregation." I cannot understand, nor does the majority satisfactorily explain, why a federal court may not order an appropriate inter-district remedy, if this is necessary or more effective to accomplish this constitutionally mandated task... In this case, both the right and the State's Fourteenth Amendment violation have concededly been fully established, and there is no acceptable reason for permitting the party responsible for the constitutional violation to contain the remedial powers of the federal court within administrative boundaries over which the transgressor itself has plenary power. . . .

. . .

Until today, the permissible contours of the equitable authority of the district courts to remedy the unlawful establishment of a dual school system have been extensive, adaptable, and fully responsive to the ultimate goal of achieving "the greatest possible degree of actual desegregation." There are indeed limitations on the equity powers of the federal judiciary, but until now the Court has not accepted the proposition that effective enforcement of the Fourteenth Amendment could be limited by political or administrative boundary lines demarcated by the very State responsible for the constitutional violation and for the disestablishment of the dual system. Until now the Court has instead looked to practical considerations in effectuating a desegregation decree, such as excessive distance, transportation time and hazards to the safety of the school children involved in a proposed plan. That these broad principles have developed in the context of dual school systems compelled or authorized by state statute at the time of Brown v Board of Education does not lessen their current applicability to dual systems found to exist in other contexts, like that in Detroit, where intentional school segregation does not stem from the compulsion of state law, but from deliberate individual actions of local and state school authorities directed at a particular school system. The majority properly does not suggest that the duty to eradicate completely the resulting dual system in the latter context is any less than in the former. But its reason for incapacitating the remedial authority of the federal judiciary in the presence of school district perimeters in the latter context is not readily apparent. . . .

. . .

Nor does the Court's conclusion follow from the talismanic invocation of the desirability of local control over education. Local autonomy over school affairs, in the sense of the community's participation in the decisions affecting the education of its children is, of course, an important interest. But presently constituted school district lines do not delimit fixed and unchangeable areas of a local educational community. If restructuring is required to meet constitutional requirements, local authority may simply be redefined in terms of whatever configuration is adopted, with the parents of the children attending schools in the newly demarcated district or attendance zone continuing their participation in the policy management of the schools with which they are concerned most directly. . . .

. . .

I agree with my Brother Douglas that the Court of Appeals has acted responsibly in these cases. Regrettably, the majority's arbitrary limitation on the equitable power of federal district courts, based on the invisible borders of local school districts, is unrelated to the State's responsibility for remedying the constitutional wrongs visited upon the Negro school children of Detroit. It is oblivious to the potential benefits of metropolitan relief, to the noneducational communities of interest among neighborhoods located in and sometimes bridging different school districts, and to the considerable inter-district cooperation already existing in various educational areas. Ultimately, it is unresponsive to the goal of attaining the utmost actual desegregation consistent with restraints of practicability and thus augurs the frequent frustration of the remedial powers of the federal courts. . . .

. . .

Mr. Justice Marshall, with whom Mr. Justice Douglas, Mr. Justice Brennan, and Mr. Justice White join, dissenting.

. . .

[T]he Court today takes a giant step backwards. Notwithstanding a record showing widespread and pervasive racial segregation in the educational system provided by the State of Michigan for children in Detroit, this Court holds that the District Court was powerless to require the State to remedy its constitutional violation in any meaningful fashion. Ironically purporting to base its result on the principle that the scope of the remedy in a desegregation case should be determined by the nature and extent of the constitutional violation, the Court's answer is to provide no remedy at all for the violation proved in this case, thereby guaranteeing that Negro children in Detroit will receive the same separate and inherently unequal education in the future as they have been unconstitutionally afforded in the past.

I cannot subscribe to this emasculation of our constitutional guarantee of equal protection of the laws and must respectfully dissent. Our precedents, in my view, firmly establish that where, as here, state-imposed segregation has been demonstrated, it becomes the duty of the State to eliminate root and branch all vestiges of racial discrimination and to achieve the greatest possible degree of actual desegregation. I agree with both the District Court and the Court of Appeals that, under the facts of this case, this duty cannot be fulfilled unless the State of Michigan involves outlying metropolitan area school districts in its desegregation remedy. Furthermore, I perceive no basis either in law or in the practicalities of the situation justifying the State's interposition of school district boundaries as absolute barriers to the implementation of an effective desegregation remedy. Under established and frequently used Michigan procedures, school district lines are both flexible and permeable for a wide variety of purposes, and there is no reason why they must now stand in the way of meaningful desegregation relief.

The rights at issue in the case are too fundamental to be abridged on grounds as superficial as those relied on by the majority today. We deal here with the right of all of our children, whatever their race, to an equal start in life and to an equal opportunity to reach their full potential as citizens. Those children who have been denied that right in the past deserve better than to see fences thrown up to deny them that right in the future. Our Nation, I fear, will be ill-served by the Court's refusal to remedy separate and unequal education, for unless our children begin to learn together, there is little hope that our people will ever learn to live together. . . .

. . .

The District Court's consideration of this case began with its finding, which the majority accepts, that the State of Michigan, through its instrumentality, the Detroit Board of Education, engaged in widespread purposeful acts of racial segregation in the Detroit school district. Without belaboring the details, it is sufficient to note that the various techniques used in Detroit were typical of methods employed to segregate students by race in areas where no statutory dual system of education has existed. Exacerbating the effects of extensive residential segregation between Negroes and whites, the school board consciously drew attendance zones along lines which maximized the segregation of the races in schools as well. Optional attendance zones were created for neighborhoods undergoing racial transition so as to allow whites in these areas to escape integration. Negro students in areas with overcrowded schools were transported past or away from closer white schools with available space to more distant Negro schools. Grade structures and feeder school patterns were created and maintained in a manner which had the foreseeable and actual effect of keeping Negro and white pupils in separate schools. Schools were also constructed in locations and in sizes which ensured that they would open with predominantly one-race student bodies. In sum, the evidence adduced below showed that Negro children had been intentionally confined to an expanding core of virtually all-Negro schools immediately surrounded by a receding band of all-white schools. . . .

. . .

Having found a de jure segregated public school system in operation in the city of Detroit, the District Court turned next to consider which officials and agencies should be assigned the affirmative obligation to cure the constitutional violation. The court concluded that responsibility for the segregation in the Detroit city schools rested not only with the Detroit Board of Education, but belonged to the State of Michigan itself and the state defendants in this case—that is, the Governor of Michigan, the Attorney General, the State Board of Education, and the State Superintendent of Public Instruction. . . First, the evidence at trial showed that the State itself had taken actions contributing to the segregation within the Detroit schools. Second, since the Detroit Board of Education was an agency of the State of Michigan, its acts of racial discrimination were acts of the State for purposes of the Fourteenth Amendment. Finally, the District Court found that under Michigan law and practice, the system of education was in fact a *state* school system, characterized by relatively little local control and a large degree of centralized state regulation, with respect to both educational policy and the structure and operation of school districts. . . .

. . .

The essential foundation of inter-district relief in this case was not to correct conditions within outlying districts who themselves engaged in purposeful segregation. Instead, inter-district relief was seen as a necessary part of any meaningful effort by the State of Michigan to remedy the state-caused segregation within the city of Detroit. . . .

. . .

The focus of this case has always been the segregated system of education in the city of Detroit. The District Court determined that inter-district relief was necessary and appropriate only because it found that the condition of segregation within the Detroit school district could not be cured with a Detroit-only remedy. It is on this theory that the inter-district relief must stand or fall. Unlike the Court, I perceive my task to be to review the District Court's order for what it is, rather than to criticize it for what it manifestly is not.

As the foregoing demonstrates, the District Court's decision to expand its desegregation decree beyond the geographical limits of the city of

Detroit rested in large part on its conclusions (A) that the State of Michigan was ultimately responsible for curing the condition of segregation within the Detroit city schools, and (B) that a Detroit-only remedy would not accomplish this task. In my view, both of these conclusions are well supported by the facts of this case and by this Court's precedents. . . .

. . .

We recognized only last Term in Keyes that it was the State itself which was ultimately responsible for de jure acts of segregation committed by a local school board. A deliberate policy of segregation by the local board, we held, amounted to "state-imposed segregation." Wherever a dual school system exists, whether compelled by state statute or created by a local board's systematic program of segregation, "the *State* automatically assumes an affirmative duty 'to effectuate a transition to a racially nondiscriminatory school system' [and] to eliminate from the public schools within their school system 'all vestiges of state-imposed segregation.' "

Vesting responsibility with the State of Michigan for Detroit's segregated schools is particularly appropriate as Michigan, unlike some other States, operates a single statewide system of education rather than several separate and independent local school systems. The majority's emphasis on local governmental control and local autonomy of school districts in Michigan will come as a surprise to those with any familiarity with that State's system of education. School districts are not separate and distinct sovereign entities under Michigan law, but rather are "auxiliaries of the State," subject to its "absolute power." The courts of the State have repeatedly emphasized that education in Michigan is not a local governmental concern, but a state function. . . .

. . .

The State's control over education is reflected in the fact that, contrary to the Court's implication, there is little or no relationship between school districts and local political units. To take the 85 local school districts in the Detroit metropolitan area as examples, 17 districts lie in two counties, two in three counties. One district serves five municipalities; other suburban municipalities are fragmented into as many as six school districts. Nor is there any apparent state policy with regard to the size of school districts, as they now range from 2,000 to 285,000 students. . . .

. . .

Most significantly for present purposes, the State has wide-ranging powers to consolidate and merge school districts, even without the consent of the districts themselves or of the local citizenry. Indeed, recent years have witnessed an accelerated program of school district consolidations, mergers, and annexations, many of which were state imposed. . . .

. . .

Whatever may be the history of public education in other parts of our Nation, it simply flies in the face of reality to say, as does the majority, that in Michigan, "No single tradition in public education is more deeply rooted than local control over the operation of schools. . ." As the State's supreme court has said: "We have repeatedly emphasized that education in this State is not a local concern, but belongs to the State at large.". . .

. . .

Under our decisions, it was clearly proper for the District Court to take into account the so-called "white flight" from the city schools which would be forthcoming from any Detroit-only decree. The Court's prediction of white flight was well supported by expert testimony based on past experience in other cities undergoing desegregation relief. We ourselves took the possibility of white flight into account in evaluating the effectiveness of a desegregation plan in Wright [v. City of Emporia, 407 U.S. 451:1972] . . . where we relied on the District Court's finding that if the city of Emporia were allowed to withdraw from the existing system, leaving a system with a higher proportion of Negroes, it "may be anticipated that the proportion of whites in county schools may drop as those who can register in private academies. . ." One cannot ignore the white-flight problem, for where legally imposed segregation has been established, the District Court has the responsibility to see to it not only that the dual system is terminated at once but also that future events do not serve to perpetuate or re-establish segregation. . . .

. . .

Because of the already high and rapidly increasing percentage of Negro students in the Detroit system, as well as the prospect of white flight, a Detroit-only plan simply has no hope of achieving actual desegregation. Under such a plan white and Negro students will not go to school together. Instead, Negro children will continue to attend all-Negro schools. The very evil that Brown I was aimed at will not be cured, but will be perpetuated for the future. . . .

. . .

The continued racial identifiability of the Detroit schools under a Detroit-only remedy is not simply a reflection of their high percentage of Negro students. What is or is not a racially identifiable vestige of de jure segregation must necessarily depend on several factors. Foremost among these should be the relationship between the schools in question and the neighboring community. For these purposes the city of Detroit and its surrounding suburbs must be viewed as a single community. Detroit is closely connected to its suburbs in many ways, and the metropolitan area is viewed as a single cohesive unit by its residents. About 40% of the residents of the two suburban counties included in the desegregation plan work in Wayne County, in which Detroit is situated. Many residents of the city work in the suburbs. The three counties participate in a wide variety of cooperative governmental ventures on a metropolitan-wide basis, including a metropolitan transit system, park authority, water and sewer system, and council of governments. The Federal Government has classified the tri-county area as a Standard Metropolitan Statistical Area, indicating that it is an area of "economic and social integration.". . .

. . .

It will be of scant significance to Negro children who have for years been confined by de jure acts of segregation to a growing core of all-Negro schools surrounded by a ring of all-white schools that the new dividing line between the races is the school district boundary. . . .

. . .

The nature of a violation determines the scope of the remedy simply because the function of any remedy is to cure the violation to which it is addressed. In school segregation cases, as in other equitable causes, a remedy which effectively cures the violation is what is required. No more is necessary, but we can tolerate no less. To read this principle as barring a District Court from imposing the only effective remedy for past segregation and remitting the court to a patently ineffective alternative is, in my view, to turn a simple commonsense rule into a cruel and

157

meaningless paradox. Ironically, by ruling out an inter-district remedy, the only relief which promises to cure segregation in the Detroit public schools, the majority flouts the very principle on which it purports to rely.

Nor should it be of any significance that the suburban school districts were not shown to have themselves taken any direct action to promote segregation of the races. Given the State's broad powers over local school districts, it was well within the State's powers to require those districts surrounding the Detroit school district to participate in a metropolitan remedy. The State's duty should be no different here than in cases where it is shown that certain of a State's voting districts are malapportioned in violation of the Fourteenth Amendment. . . .

. . .

Desegregation is not and was never expected to be an easy task. Racial attitudes ingrained in our Nation's childhood and adolescence are not quickly thrown aside in its middle years. But just as the inconvenience of some cannot be allowed to stand in the way of the rights of others, so public opposition, no matter how strident, cannot be permitted to divert this Court from the enforcement of the constitutional principles at issue in this case. Today's holding, I fear, is more a reflection of a perceived public mood that we have gone far enough in enforcing the Constitution's guarantee of equal justice than it is the product of neutral principles of law. In the short run, it may seem to be the easier course to allow our great metropolitan areas to be divided up each into two cities—one white, the other black—but it is a course, I predict, our people will ultimately regret. I dissent.

. . .

On remand the district court developed a Detroit-only pupil assignment plan and ordered the use of certain compensatory and remedial programs in the Detroit schools. The cost of these programs was to be borne equally by the local school board and the state. The state sought relief from the cost sharing aspect of the order but the Supreme Court through Chief Justice Burger affirmed the lower court decision. (*Milliken* v. *Bradley*, 433 U.S. 267, 1977)

. . .

In *Pasadena City Board of Education* v. *Spangler*, 427 U.S. 424 (1976), a desegregation order in 1970 had required, among other things, that there be in the district no school "with a majority of any minority students." The board initially complied but did not redraw attendance zones annually thereafter with the result that by 1974 some schools did have a majority of minority students. When the board asked to be relieved of this requirement, the district court refused making it clear that "no majority of any minority" was a permanent requirement. The court of appeals reluctantly affirmed, but in a 6-2 decision the Supreme Court reversed. Justice Rehnquist for the majority declared that once a dual system has been dismantled and a neutral pupil assignment plan implemented, subsequent population shifts that produce racial imbalance in the schools are not enough by themselves to warrant additional intervention by the courts; new segregative acts by governmental units are required to reopen the issue.

Two Ohio school cases gave the Court the opportunity to further refine its meaning in this issue area. Remanding a Dayton case for more specific findings of fact, Justice Rehnquist reminded the lower courts that "only if there has been a systemwide impact [of the constitutional violations] may there be a systemwide remedy." (*Dayton Board of Education* v. *Brinkman*, 433 U.S. 406, 1977, at 420). In the second round from Dayton, the majority approved a systemwide remedy based on findings that in 1954 Dayton had operated a dual system and had continued to do so despite an affirmative duty to dismantle that system. Chief Justice Burger, and Justices Stewart, Powell, and Rehnquist dissented. (*Dayton Board of Education* v. *Brinkman*, 443 U.S. 526, 1979) Columbus, Ohio, schools were found deficient for much the same reason—a dual system in 1954, failure to end segregation, and additional acts to perpetuate the dual system. (*Columbus Board of Education* v. *Penick*, 443 U.S. 449, 1979)

President Richard M. Nixon, Address to the Nation on Equal Opportunities and School Busing. March 16, 1972

Good evening:

Tonight I want to talk to you about one of the most difficult issues of our time—the issue of busing.

Across this Nation—in the North, East, West, and South—States, cities, and local school districts have been torn apart in debate over this issue.

My own position is well known. I am opposed to busing for the purpose of achieving racial balance in our schools. I have spoken out against busing scores of times over many years.

And I believe most Americans, white and black, share that view.

But what we need now is not just speaking out against more busing. We need action to stop it. Above all, we need to stop it in the right way— in a way that will provide better education for every child in America in a desegregated school system.

The reason action is so urgent is because of a number of recent decisions of the lower Federal courts. Those courts have gone too far—in some cases beyond the requirements laid down by the Supreme Court—in ordering massive busing to achieve racial balance. The decisions have left in their wake confusion and contradiction in the law; anger, fear, and turmoil in local communities; and, worst of all, agonized concern among hundreds of thousands of parents for the education and the safety of their children who have been forced by court order to be bused miles away from their neighborhood schools.

What is the answer?

There are many who believe that a constitutional amendment is the only way to deal with this problem. The constitutional amendment proposal deserves a thorough consideration by the Congress on its merits. But as an answer to the immediate problem we face of stopping more busing now, the constitutional amendment approach has a fatal flaw: It takes too long.

A constitutional amendment would take between a year and 18 months, at the very least, to become effective. This means that hundreds of thousands of schoolchildren will be ordered by the courts to be bused away from their neighborhood schools in the next school year, with no hope for relief.

What we need is action now—not action 2, 3, or 4 years from now. And there is only one effective way to deal with the problem now. That is for the Congress to act. That is why I am sending a special message to the Congress tomorrow urging immediate consideration and action on two measures.

First, I shall propose legislation that would call an immediate halt to all new busing orders by Federal courts—a moratorium on new busing.

Next, I shall propose a companion measure—the Equal Educational Opportunities Act of 1972.

This act would require that every State or locality grant equal educational opportunity to every person, regardless of race, color, or national origin. For the first time in our history, the cherished American ideal of equality of educational opportunity would be affirmed in the law of the land by the elected representatives of the people in Congress. . . .

What I am proposing is that at the same time we stop more busing, we move forward to guarantee that the children currently attending the poorest schools in our cities and in rural areas be provided with education equal to that of good schools in their communities.

Taken together, the two elements of my proposal—the moratorium on new busing and the Equal Educational Opportunities Act, would focus our efforts where they really belong: on better education for all of our children, rather than on more busing for some of our children.

In addition, I am directing all agencies and departments of the Federal Government at every level to carry out the spirit as well as the letter of the message in all of their actions. I am directing that the Justice Department intervene in selected cases where the lower courts have gone beyond the Supreme Court's requirements in ordering busing.

These are the highlights of the new approach I propose. Let me now go to the heart of the problem that confronts us. I want to tell you why I feel that busing for the purpose of achieving racial balance in our schools is wrong, and why the great majority of Americans are right in wanting to bring it to an end.

The purpose of such busing is to help end segregation. But experience in case after case has shown that busing is a bad means to a good end. The frank recognition of that fact does not reduce our commitment to desegregation; it simply tells us that we have to come up with a better means to that good end.

The great majority of Americans, white and black, feel strongly that the busing of schoolchildren away from their own neighborhoods for the purpose of achieving racial balance is wrong.

But the great majority, black and white, also are determined that the process of desegregation must go forward until the goal of genuinely equal educational opportunity is achieved.

161

The question, then, is "How can we end segregation in a way that does not result in more busing?" The proposals I am sending to the Congress provide an answer to that question. . . .

There are right reasons for opposing busing, and there are wrong reasons—and most people, including large and increasing numbers of blacks, oppose it for reasons that have little or nothing to do with race. It would compound an injustice to persist in massive busing simply because some people oppose it for the wrong reasons. . . .

I submit these proposals to the Congress, and I commend them to all of you listening tonight, mindful of the profound importance and the special complexity of the issues they address. The key is action, and action now. And Congress holds that key. If you agree with the goals I have described tonight—to stop more busing now and provide equality of education for all of our children—I urge you to let your Congressman and Senators know your views so that Congress will act promptly to deal with this problem.

[Public Papers of the Presidents of the United States: Richard M. Nixon, 1972 (Washington: Government Printing Office, 1974), pp. 425-429 passim.]

· · ·

House Bill 13916
92nd Congress, 2nd Session

House Bill 13916, 92nd Congress, 2nd Session was the response by Congress to the president's speech. It was never reported out of the House Judiciary Committee.

· · ·

Be it enacted by the Senate and House of Representatives of the United States of America in Congress assembled, That this Act may be cited as the "Student Transportation Moratorium Act of 1972."

FINDINGS AND PURPOSE

Sec. 2.a. The Congress finds that:

1. For the purpose of desegregation, many local educational agencies have been required to reorganize their school systems, to reassign students, and to engage in the extensive transportation of students.

2. In many cases these reorganizations, with attendant increases in student transportation, have caused substantial hardship to the children thereby affected, have impinged on the educational process in which they are involved, and have required increases in student transportation often in excess of that necessary to accomplish desegregation.

3. There is a need to establish a clear, rational, and uniform standard for determining the extent to which a local educational agency is required to reassign and transport its students in discharging its obligation under the fourteenth amendment to the United States Constitution to desegregate its schools.

4. The Congress is presently considering legislation to establish such a standard and define that obligation.

5. There is a substantial likelihood that, pending enactment of such legislation, many local educational agencies will be required to implement desegregation plans that impose a greater obligation than required by the fourteenth amendment and permitted by such pending legislation and that these plans will require modification in light of the legislation's requirements.

6. Implementation of desegregation plans will in many cases require local educational agencies to expend large amounts of funds for transportation equipment, which may be utilized only temporarily, and for its operation, thus diverting those funds from improvements in educational facilities and instruction which otherwise would be provided.

7. The modification of school schedules and student assignments resulting from implementation of desegregation plans and any subsequent modification in light of the legislation's requirements would place substantial unnecessary administrative burdens on local educational agencies and unduly disrupt the educational process.

b. It is, therefore, the purpose of this Act to impose a moratorium on the implementation of Federal court orders that require local educational agencies to transport students and on the implementation of certain desegregation plans under Title VI of the Civil Rights Act of 1964, in order to provide Congress time to fashion such a standard, and to define such an obligation.

MORATORIUM ON ORDERS AND PLANS

Sec. 3.a. During the period beginning with the day after the date of enactment of this Act and ending with July 1, 1973, or the date of enactment of legislation which the Congress declares to be that contemplated by section 2(a) (4), whichever is earlier, the implementation of any order of a court of the United States entered during such period shall be stayed to the extent it requires, directly or indirectly, a local educational agency—

1. to transport a student who was not being transported by such local educational agency immediately prior to the entry of such order; or
2. to transport a student to or from a school to which or from which such student was not being transported by such local educational agency immediately prior to the entry of such order.

b. During the period described in subsection (a) of this section, a local educational agency shall not be required to implement a desegregation plan submitted to a department or agency of the United States during such period pursuant to title VI of the Civil Rights Act of 1964 to the extent that such plan provides for such local educational agency to carry out any action described in clauses 1 or 2 of subsection (a) of this section.

c. Nothing in this Act shall prohibit an educational agency from proposing, adopting, requiring, or implementing any desegregation plan, otherwise lawful, that exceeds the limitations specified in subsection (a) of this section, nor shall any court of the United States or department or agency of the Federal Government be prohibited from approving implementation of a plan that exceeds the limitations specified in subsection (a) of this section if the plan is voluntarily proposed by the appropriate educational agency.

House Joint Resolution 620
92nd Congress, 2nd Session

House Joint Resolution 620, 92nd Congress, 2nd Session was a proposed constitutional amendment responding to the president's call for action. After hearings were conducted by the House Committee on the Judiciary, the House Rules Committee discharged the Judiciary Committee (took it away from them) but never scheduled the resolution for a floor vote.

No public school student shall, because of his race, creed or color, be assigned to or required to attend a particular school.

Title II - Equal Educational Opportunities and The Transportation of Students

Despite the failure to pass H.B. 13916, Congress did pass the Education Amendments of 1974, Title II of which dealt with busing. [88 Stat. 484, 514-521]

Sec. 201. This title may be cited as the "Equal Educational Opportunities Act of 1974". . . .

Balance Not Required

Sec. 205. The failure of an educational agency to attain a balance, on the basis of race, color, sex, or national origin, of students among its schools shall not constitute a denial of equal educational opportunity, or equal protection of the laws.

Assignment on Neighborhood Basis Not a Denial of Equal Educational Opportunity

Sec. 206. Subject to the other provisions of this part, the assignment by an educational agency of a student to the school nearest his place of residence which provides the appropriate grade level and type of education for such student is not a denial of equal educational opportunity or of equal protection of the laws unless such assignment is for the purpose of segregating students on the basis of race, color, sex, or national origin, or the school to which such student is assigned was located on its site for the purpose of segregating students on such basis. . . .

Effect of Certain Population Changes on Certain Actions

Sec. 208. When a court of competent jurisdiction determines that a school system is desegregated, or that it meets the constitutional requirements, or that it is a unitary system, or that it has no vestiges of a dual system, and thereafter residential shifts in population occur which result in school population changes in any school within such a desegregated school system, such school population changes so occurring shall not, per se, constitute a cause for civil action for a new plan of desegregation or for modification of the court approved plan. . . .

Priority of Remedies

Sec. 214. In formulating a remedy for a denial of equal educational opportunity or a denial of the equal protection of the laws, which may involve directly or indirectly the transportation of students, a court, department, or agency of the United States shall consider and make specific findings on the efficacy in correcting such denial of the following remedies and shall require implementation of the first of the remedies set out below, or of the first combination thereof which would remedy such denial:

(a) assigning students to the schools closest to their places of residence which provide the appropriate grade level and type of education for such students, taking into account school capacities and natural physical barriers;

(b) assigning students to the schools closest to their places of residence which provide the appropriate grade level and type of education for such students, taking into account only school capacities;

(c) permitting students to transfer from a school in which a majority of the students are of their race, color, or national origin to a school in which a minority of the students are of their race, color, or national origin;

(d) the creation or revision of attendance zones or grade structures without requiring transportation beyond that described in section 215;

(e) the construction of new schools or the closing of inferior schools;

(f) the construction or establishment of magnet schools; or

(g) the development and implementation of any other plan which is educationally sound and administratively feasible, subject to the provisions of sections 215 and 216 of this part.

Transportation of Students

Sec. 215. (a) No court, department, or agency of the United States shall, pursuant to section 214, order the implementation of a plan that would require the transportation of any student to a school other than the school closest or next closest to his place of residence which provides the appropriate grade level and type of education for such student.

(b) No court, department, or agency of the United States shall require directly or indirectly the transportation of any student if such transportation poses a risk to the health of such student or constitutes a significant impingement on the educational process with respect to such student.

District Lines

Sec. 216. In the formulation of remedies under section 213 or 214 of this part the lines drawn by a State, subdividing its territory into separate school districts, shall not be ignored or altered except where it is established that the lines were drawn from the purpose, and had the effect, of segregating children among public schools on the basis of race, color, sex, or national origin. . . .

Prohibition Against Assignment or Transportation of Students to Overcome Racial Imbalance

Sec. 251. No provision of this Act shall be construed to require the assignment or transportation of students or teachers in order to overcome racial imbalance. . . .

Additional Priority of Remedies

Sec. 256. Notwithstanding any provision of law, after June 30, 1974 no court of the United States shall order the implementation of any plan to remedy a finding of de jure segregation which involves the transportation of students, unless the court first finds that all alternative remedies are inadequate. . . .

. . .

On March 2, 1982, the struggle with the courts over busing continued as the Senate adopted the Department of Justice Appropriation Authorization Act for fiscal year 1982 (S. 951). It contained the following language on busing.

. . .

Sec. 2. (a) This section may be cited as the "Neighborhood School Act of 1982."

(b) The Congress finds that—

(1) court orders requiring transportation of students to or attendance at public schools other than the one closest to their residences for the purpose of achieving racial balance or racial desegregation have proven to be ineffective remedies to achieve unitary school systems;

(2) such orders frequently result in the exodus from public school systems of children causing even greater racial imbalance and diminished public support for public school systems;

(3) assignment and transportation of students to public schools other than the one closest to their residence is expensive and wasteful of scarce petroleum fuels;

(4) there is an absence of social science evidence to suggest that the costs of school busing outweigh the disruptiveness of busing; and

(5) assignment of students to public schools closest to their residence (neighborhood public schools) is the preferred method of public school attendance.

(c) The Congress is hereby exercising its power under article III, section 1, and under section 5 of the fourteenth amendment.

Limitation of Injunctive Relief

(d) Section 1651 of title 28, United States Code, is amended by adding the following new subsection (c):

"(c)(1) No court of the United States may order or issue any writ directly or indirectly ordering any student to be assigned or to be transported to a public school other than that which is closest to the student's residence unless—

"(i) such assignment of transportation is provided incident to the voluntary attendance of a student at a public school, including a magnet, vocational, technical, or other school or specialized or individualized instruction; or

"(ii) the requirement of such transportation is reasonable.

"(2) The assignment or transportation of students shall not be reasonable if—

"(i) there are reasonable alternatives available which involve less time in travel, distance, danger, or inconveniencing;

"(ii) such assignment or transportation requires a student to cross a school district having the same grade level as that of the student;

"(iii) such transportation plan or order or part thereof is likely to result in a greater degree of racial imbalance in the public school system than was in existence on the date of the order for such assignment or transportation plan or is likely to have a net harmful effect on the quality of education in the public school district;

"(iv) the total actual daily time consumed in travel by schoolbus for any student exceeds 10 miles unless the actual round trip distance traveled by schoolbus is to and from the public school closest to the student's residence with a grade level identical to that of the student"....

(D) No part of any sum authorized to be appropriated by this Act shall be used by the Department of Justice to bring or maintain any sort of action to require directly or indirectly the transportation of any student to a school other than the school which is nearest the student's home, except for a student requiring special education as a result of being mentally or physically handicapped.

.   .   .

On May 7, 1982, the Associated Press reported that the Attorney General had informed the House Judiciary Committee that in his opinion the provisions of this bill limiting the power of the courts to order busing were constitutional. The limitations on the Department of Justice, he said, were constitutional but unwise.

Regents of the University of California v. Bakke

438 U.S. 265, 57 L Ed 2d 750, 98 S Ct. 2733(1978)

Bakke, a white male, had twice been denied admission to the Medical School at the University of California at Davis. Persons with significantly lower quantitative qualifications had been admitted through a special admissions program which reserved 16 places in each class of 100 for disadvantaged members of certain minority races. Bakke asserted the invalidity of this program under a provision of the California Constitution, Title VI of the Civil Rights Act of 1964, and the equal protection clause of the Fourteenth Amendment. He contended that the reservation of the 16 places denied him admission solely because of his race. The California courts declared that the University could not consider race in making admissions

169

decisions, and the California Supreme Court ordered Bakke's admission to the medical school since the state could not demonstrate that he would have been denied admission in the absence of the special admissions program. The U.S. Supreme Court granted certiorari.

. . .

Mr. Justice Powell announced the judgment of the Court.

This case presents a challenge to the special admissions program of the petitioner, the Medical School of the University of California at Davis, which is designed to assure the admission of a specified number of students from certain minority groups. . . .

. . .

For the reasons stated in the following opinion, I believe that so much of the judgment of the California court as holds petitioner's special admissions program unlawful and directs that respondent be admitted to the Medical School must be affirmed. For the reasons expressed in a separate opinion, my Brothers The Chief Justice, Mr. Justice Stewart, Mr. Justice Rehnquist, and Mr. Justice Stevens concur in this judgment.

I also conclude for the reasons stated in the following opinion that the portion of the court's judgement enjoining petitioner from according any consideration to race in its admissions process must be reversed. For reasons expressed in separate opinions, my Brothers Mr. Justice Brennan, Mr. Justice White, Mr. Justice Marshall, and Mr. Justice Blackmun concur in this judgment.

Affirmed in part and reversed in part. . . .

. . .

In this Court the parties neither briefed nor argued the applicability of Title VI of the Civil Rights of 1964. Rather, as had the California court, they focused exclusively upon the validity of the special admissions program under the Equal Protection Clause. Because it was possible, however, that a decision on Title VI might obviate resort to constitutional interpretation, we requested supplementary briefing on the statutory issue. . . .

. . .

The language of § 601, like that of the Equal Protection Clause, is majestic in its sweep:

"No person in the United States shall, on the ground of race, color, or national origin, be excluded from participation in, be denied the benefits of, or be subjected to discrimination under any program or activity receiving Federal financial assistance."

The concept of "discrimination," like the phrase "equal protection of the laws," is susceptible to varying interpretations. . . . We must, therefore, seek whatever aid is available in determining the precise meaning of the statute before us. Examination of the voluminous legislative history of Title VI reveals a congressional intent to halt federal funding of entities that violate a prohibition of racial discrimination similar to that of the Constitution. Although isolated statements of various legislators, taken out of context, can be marshalled in support of the proposition that § 601 enacted a purely colorblind scheme, without regard to the reach of the Equal Protection Clause, these comments must be read against the background of both the problem that Congress was addressing and the broader view of the statute that emerges from a full examination of the legislative debates.

The problem confronting Congress was discrimination against Negro citizens at the hands of recipients of federal moneys. Indeed, the colorblindness pronouncements . . . generally occur in the midst of extended remarks dealing with the evils of segregation in federally funded programs. Over and over again, proponents of the bill detailed the plight of Negroes seeking equal treatment in such programs. There simply was no reason for Congress to consider the validity of hypothetical preferences that might be accorded minority citizens; the legislators were dealing with the real and pressing problem of how to guarantee those citizens equal treatment.

In addressing that problem, supporters of Title VI repeatedly declared that the bill enacted constitutional principles. . . .

. . .

[E]vidence of the incorporation of a constitutional standard into Title VI appears in the repeated refusals of the legislation's supporters precisely to define the term "discrimination." Opponents sharply criticized this failure, but proponents of the bill merely replied that the meaning of

171

"discrimination" would be made clear by reference to the Constitution or other existing law. . . .

. . .

In view of the clear legislative intent, Title VI must be held to proscribe only those racial classifications that would violate the Equal Protection Clause or the Fifth Amendment.

Petitioner does not deny that decisions based on race or ethnic origin by faculties and administrations of state universities are reviewable under the Fourteenth Amendment. For his part, respondent does not argue that all racial or ethnic classifications are per se invalid. The parties do disagree as to the level of judicial scrutiny to be applied to the special admissions program. Petitioner argues that the court below erred in applying strict scrutiny, as this inexact term has been applied in our cases. That level of review, petitioner asserts, should be reserved for classifications that disadvantage "discrete and insular minorities." Respondent, on the other hand, contends that the California court correctly rejected the notion that the degree of judicial scrutiny accorded a particular racial or ethnic classification hinges upon membership in a discrete and insular minority and duly recognized that the "rights established [by the Fourteenth Amendment] are personal rights."

En route to this crucial battle over the scope of judicial review, the parties fight a sharp preliminary action over the proper characterization of the special admissions program. Petitioner prefers to view it as establishing a "goal" of minority representation in the medical school. Respondent, echoing the courts below, labels it a racial quota.

This semantic distinction is beside the point; the special admissions program is undeniably a classification based on race and ethnic background. To the extent that there existed a pool of at least minimally qualified minority applicants to fill the 16 special admissions seats, white applicants could compete only for 84 seats in the entering class, rather than the 100 open to minority applicants. Whether this limitation is described as a quota or a goal, it is a line drawn on the basis of race and ethnic status. . . .

. . .

The guarantee of equal protection cannot mean one thing when applied to one individual and something else when applied to a person of another color. If both are not accorded the same protection, then it is not equal. . . .

. . .

Racial and ethnic distinctions of any sort are inherently suspect and thus call for the most exacting judicial examination. . . .

. . .

Although many of the Framers of the Fourteenth Amendment conceived of its primary function as bridging the vast distance between members of the Negro race and the white "majority," the Amendment itself was framed in universal terms, without reference to color, ethnic origin, or condition of prior servitude. . . .

. . .

Over the past 30 years, this Court has embarked upon the crucial mission of interpreting the Equal Protection Clause with the view of assuring to all persons "the protection of equal laws," in a Nation confronting a legacy of slavery and racial discrimination. Because the landmark decisions in this area arose in response to the continued exclusion of Negroes from the mainstream of American society, they could be characterized as involving discrimination by the "majority" white race against the Negro minority. But they need not be read as depending upon that characterization for their results. It suffices to say that "[o]ver the years, this Court consistently repudiated '[d]istinctions between citizens solely because of their ancestry' as being 'odious to a free people whose institutions are founded upon the doctrine of equality.' "

Petitioner urges us to adopt for the first time a more restrictive view of the Equal Protection Clause and hold that discrimination against members of the white "majority" cannot be suspect if its purpose can be characterized as "benign." The clock of our liberties, however, cannot be turned back to 1868. It is far too late to argue that the guarantee of equal protection to *all* persons permits the recognition of special wards entitled to a degree of protection greater than that accorded others. . . .

. . .

If it is the individual who is entitled to judicial protection against classifications based upon his racial or ethnic background because such

173

distinctions impinge upon personal rights, rather than the individual only because of his membership in a particular group, then constitutional standards may be applied consistently. Political judgments regarding the necessity for the particular classification may be weighed in the constitutional balance, but the standard of justification will remain constant. This is as it should be, since those political judgments are the product of rough compromise struck by contending groups within the democratic process. When they touch upon an individual's race or ethnic background, he is entitled to a judicial determination that the burden he is asked to bear on that basis is precisely tailored to serve a compelling governmental interest. The Constitution guarantees that right to every person regardless of his background.

Petitioner contends that on several occasions this Court has approved preferential classifications without applying the most exacting scrutiny. Most of the cases upon which petitioner relies are drawn from three areas: school desegregation, employment discrimination, and sex discrimination. Each of the cases cited presented a situation materially different from the facts of this case.

The school desegregation cases are inapposite. Each involved remedies for clearly determined constitutional violations. Racial classifications thus were designed as remedies for the vindication of constitutional entitlement. Moreover, the scope of the remedies was not permitted to exceed the extent of the violations. Here, there was no judicial determination of constitutional violation as a predicate for the formulation of a remedial classification.

The employment discrimination cases also do not advance petitioner's cause. . . [W]e approved a retroactive award of seniority to a class of Negro truck drivers who had been the victims of discrimination—not just by society at large, but by the respondent in that case. . . Such preferences also have been upheld where a legislative or administrative body charged with the responsibility made determinations of past discrimination by the industries affected, and fashioned remedies deemed appropriate to rectify the discrimination. . . But we have never approved preferential classifications in the absence of proven constitutional or statutory violations.

Nor is petitioner's view as to the applicable standard supported by the fact that gender-based classifications are not subjected to this level of scrutiny. . . .

·   ·   ·

In this case . . . there has been no determination by the legislature or a responsible administrative agency that the University engaged in a discriminatory practice requiring remedial efforts. Moreover, the operation of petitioner's special admissions program is quite different from the remedial measures approved in those cases. It prefers the designated minority groups at the expense of other individuals who are totally foreclosed from competition for the 16 special admissions seats in every medical school class. Because of that foreclosure, some individuals are excluded from enjoyment of a state-provided benefit—admission to the medical school—they otherwise would receive. When a classification denies an individual opportunities or benefits enjoyed by others solely because of his race or ethnic background, it must be regarded as suspect.

We have held that in "order to justify the use of a suspect classification, a State must show that its purpose or interest is both constitutionally permissible and substantial, and that its use of the classification is 'necessary . . . to the accomplishment' of its purpose or the safeguarding of its interest." The special admissions program purports to serve the purposes of: (i) "reducing the historic deficit of traditionally disfavored minorities in medical schools and the medical profession," (ii) countering the effects of societal discrimination; (iii) increasing the number of physicians who will practice in communities currently underserved; and (iv) obtaining the educational benefits that flow from an ethnically diverse student body. It is necessary to decide which, if any, of these purposes is substantial enough to support the use of a suspect classification.

If petitioner's purpose is to assure within its student body some specified percentage of a particular group merely because of its race or ethnic origin, such a preferential purpose must be rejected not as insubstantial but as facially invalid. Preferring members of any one group for no reason other than race or ethnic origin is discrimination for its own sake. This the Constitution forbids.

The State certainly has a legitimate and substantial interest in ameliorating, or eliminating where feasible, the disabling effects of identified discrimination. . . In the school cases, the States were required by court order to redress the wrongs worked by specific instances of racial discrimination. That goal was far more focused than the remedying of the effects of "societal discrimination," an amorphous concept of injury that may be ageless in its reach into the past.

We have never approved a classification that aids persons perceived as members of relatively victimized groups at the expense of other innocent individuals in the absence of judicial, legislative, or administrative findings of constitutional or statutory violations. After such findings have been made, the governmental interest in preferring members of the injured groups at the expense of others is substantial, since the legal rights of the victims must be vindicated. In such a case, the extent of the injury and the consequent remedy will have been judicially, legislatively, or administratively defined. Also, the remedial action usually remains subject to continuing oversight to assure that it will work the least harm possible to other innocent persons competing for the benefit. Without such findings of constitutional or statutory violations, it cannot be said that the government has any greater interest in helping one individual than in refraining from harming another. Thus, the government has no compelling justification for inflicting such harm. . . .

. . .

Hence, the purpose of helping certain groups whom the faculty of the Davis Medical School perceived as victims of "societal discrimination" does not justify a classification that imposes disadvantages upon persons like respondent, who bear no responsibility for whatever harm the beneficiaries of the special admissions program are thought to have suffered. To hold otherwise would be to convert a remedy heretofore reserved for violations of legal rights into a privilege that all institutions throughout the Nation could grant at their pleasure to whatever groups are perceived as victims of societal discrimination. That is a step we have never approved.

Petitioner identifies, as another purpose of its program, improving the delivery of health care services to communities currently underserved. It may be assumed that in some situations a State's interest in facilitating the health care of its citizens is sufficiently compelling to support the use of a suspect classification. But there is virtually no evidence in the record indicating that petitioner's special admissions program is either needed or geared to promote that goal. . . .

. . .

Petitioner simply has not carried its burden of demonstrating that it must prefer members of particular ethnic groups over all other individuals in order to promote better health care delivery to deprived citizens. Indeed, petitioner has not shown that its preferential classification is likely to have any significant effect on the problem.

The fourth goal asserted by petitioner is the attainment of a diverse student body. This clearly is a constitutionally permissible goal for an institution of higher education. Academic freedom, though not a specifically enumerated constitutional right, long has been viewed as a special concern of the First Amendment. The freedom of a university to make its own judgments as to education includes the selection of its student body. . . .

.   .   .

The atmosphere of "speculation, experiment and creation"—so essential to the quality of higher education—is widely believed to be promoted by a diverse student body. . . .

.   .   .

Thus, in arguing that its universities must be accorded the right to select those students who will contribute the most to the "robust exchange of ideas," petitioner invokes a countervailing constitutional interest, that of the First Amendment. In this light, petitioner must be viewed as seeking to achieve a goal that is of paramount importance in the fulfillment of its mission. . . .

.   .   .

Ethnic diversity, however, is only one element in a range of factors a university properly may consider in attaining the goal of a heterogeneous student body. Although a university must have wide discretion in making the sensitive judgments as to who should be admitted, constitutional limitations protecting individual rights may not be disregarded. Respondent urges—and the courts below have held—that petitioner's dual admissions program is a racial classification that impermissibly infringes his rights under the Fourteenth Amendment. As the interest of diversity is compelling in the context of a university's admissions program, the question remains whether the program's racial classification is necessary to promote this interest.

It may be assumed that the reservation of a special number of seats in each class for individuals from the preferred ethnic groups would contribute to the attainment of considerable ethnic diversity in the student body. But petitioner's argument that this is the only effective means of serving the interest of diversity is seriously flawed. In a most fundamental sense the argument misconceives the nature of the state interest that would justify consideration of race or ethnic background. It is not an interest in simple ethnic diversity, in which a specified percentage of the student body is in effect guaranteed to be members of selected ethnic groups, with the remaining percentage an undifferentiated aggregation of students. The diversity that furthers a compelling state interest encompasses a far broader array of qualifications and characteristics of which racial or ethnic origin is but a single though important element. Petitioner's special admissions program, focused *solely* on ethnic diversity, would hinder rather than further attainment of genuine diversity. . . .

. . .

The experience of other university admissions programs, which take race into account in achieving the educational diversity valued by the First Amendment, demonstrates that the assignment of a fixed number of places to a minority group is not a necessary means toward that end. An illuminating example is found in the Harvard College program. . . .

. . .

In such an admissions program, race or ethnic background may be deemed a "plus" in a particular applicant's file, yet it does not insulate the individual from comparison with all other candidates for the available seats. The file of a particular black applicant may be examined for his potential contribution to diversity without the factor of race being decisive when compared, for example, with that of an applicant identified as an Italian-American if the latter is thought to exhibit qualities more likely to promote beneficial educational pluralism. Such qualities could include exceptional personal talents, unique work or service experience, leadership potential, maturity, demonstrated compassion, a history of overcoming disadvantage, ability to communicate with the poor, or other qualifications deemed important. In short, an admissions program operated in this way is flexible enough to consider all pertinent elements of diversity in light of the particular qualifications of each applicant, and to place them on the same footing for consideration, although not necessarily according them the same weight. Indeed, the weight attributed to a particular quality may vary from year to year depending upon the "mix" both of the student body and the applicants for the incoming class.

This kind of program treats each applicant as an individual in the admissions process. The applicant who loses out on the last available seat to another candidate receiving a "plus" on the basis of ethnic background will not have been foreclosed from all consideration for that seat simply because he was not the right color or had the wrong surname. It would mean only that his combined qualifications, which may have included similar nonobjective factors, did not outweigh those of the other applicant. His qualifications would have been weighed fairly and competitively, and he would have no basis to complain of unequal treatment under the Fourteenth Amendment. . . .

． ． ．

A facial intent to discriminate . . . is evident in petitioner's preference program and not denied in this case. No such facial infirmity exists in an admissions program where race or ethnic background is simply one element—to be weighed fairly against other elements—in the selection process. . . And a Court would not assume that a university, professing to employ a facially nondiscriminatory admissions policy, would operate it as a cover for the functional equivalent of a quota system. In short, good faith would be presumed in the absence of a showing to the contrary in the manner permitted by our cases.

In summary, it is evident that the Davis special admissions program involves the use of an explicit racial classification never before countenanced by this Court. It tells applicants who are not Negro, Asian, or "Chicano" that they are totally excluded from a specific percentage of the seats in an entering class. No matter how strong their qualifications, quantitative and extracurricular, including their own potential for contribution to educational diversity, they are never afforded the chance to compete with applicants from the preferred groups for the special admission seats. At the same time, the preferred applicants have the opportunity to compete for every seat in the class.

The fatal flaw in petitioner's preferential program is its disregard of individual rights as guaranteed by the Fourteenth Amendment. Such rights are not absolute. But when a State's distribution of benefits or imposition of burdens hinges on the color of a person's skin or ancestry, that individual is entitled to a demonstration that the challenged classification is necessary to promote a substantial state interest. Petitioner has failed to carry this burden. For this reason, that portion of the California court's judgment holding petitioner's special admissions program invalid under the Fourteenth Amendment must be affirmed.

In enjoining petitioner from ever considering the race of any applicant, however, the courts below failed to recognize that the State has a substantial interest that legitimately may be served by a properly devised admissions program involving the competitive consideration of race and ethnic origin. For this reason, so much of the California court's judgment as enjoins petitioner from any consideration of the race of any applicant must be reversed.

With respect to respondent's entitlement to an injunction directing his admission to the Medical School, petitioner has conceded that it could not carry its burden of proving that, but for the existence of its unlawful special admissions program, respondent still would not have been admitted. Hence, respondent is entitled to the injunction, and that portion of the judgment must be affirmed.

·　·　·

Opinion of Mr. Justice Brennan, Mr. Justice White, Mr. Justice Marshall, and Mr. Justice Blackmun, concurring in the judgment in part and dissenting.

·　·　·

The difficulty of the issue presented—whether Government may use race-conscious programs to redress the continuing effects of past discrimination—and the mature consideration which each of our Brethren has brought to it have resulted in many opinions, no single one speaking for the Court. But this should not and must not mask the central meaning of today's opinions: Government may take race into account when it acts not to demean or insult any racial group, but to remedy disadvantages cast on minorities by past racial prejudice, at least when appropriate findings have been made by judicial, legislative, or administrative bodies with competence to act in this area. . . .

·　·　·

In our view, Title VI prohibits only those uses of racial criteria that would violate the Fourteenth Amendment if employed by a State or its agencies; it does not bar the preferential treatment of racial minorities as a means of remedying past societal discrimination to the extent that such action is consistent with the Fourteenth Amendment. The legislative history of Title VI, administrative regulations interpreting the statute, subsequent congressional and executive action, and the prior decisions of this Court compel this conclusion. None of these sources lends support to the proposition that Congress intended to bar all race conscious efforts to extend the benefits of federally financed programs to minorities who have been historically excluded from the full benefits of American life. . . .

. . .

Of course it might be argued that the Congress which enacted Title VI understood the Constitution to require strict racial neutrality or color blindness, and then enshrined that concept as a rule of statutory law. Later interpretation and clarification of the Constitution to permit remedial use of race would then not dislodge Title VI's prohibition upon race-conscious action. But there are three compelling reasons to reject such an hypothesis.

First, no decision of this Court has ever adopted the proposition that the Constitution must be colorblind.

Second, even if it could be argued in 1964 that the Constitution might conceivably require color blindness, Congress surely would not have chosen to codify such a view unless the Constitution clearly required it. . . It is inconceivable that Congress intended to encourage voluntary efforts to eliminate the evil of racial discrimination while at the same time forbidding the voluntary use of race-conscious remedies to cure acknowledged or obvious statutory violations. . . Indeed, such an interpretation of Title VI would prevent recipients of federal funds from taking race into account even when necessary to bring their programs into compliance with federal constitutional requirements. This would be a remarkable reading of a statute designed to eliminate constitutional violations, especially in light of judicial decisions holding that under certain circumstances the remedial use of racial criteria is not only permissible but is constitutionally required to eradicate constitutional violations. . . .

. . .

Third, the legislative history shows that Congress specifically eschewed any static definition of discrimination in favor of broad language that could be shaped by experience, administrative necessity, and evolving judicial doctrine. . . .

. . .

[T]here was a strong emphasis throughout Congress' consideration of Title VI on providing the Executive Branch with considerable flexibility in interpreting and applying the prohibition against racial discrimination. Attorney General Robert Kennedy testified that regulations had not been written into the legislation itself because the rules and regulations defining discrimination might differ from one program to another so that the term would assume different meanings in different contexts. . . .

. . .

In sum, Congress' equating of Title VI's prohibition with the commands of the Fifth and Fourteenth Amendments, its refusal precisely to define that racial discrimination which it intended to prohibit, and its expectation that the statute would be administered in a flexible manner, compel the conclusion that Congress intended the meaning of the statute's prohibition to evolve with the interpretation of the commands of the Constitution. Thus any claim that the use of racial criteria is barred by the plain language of the statute must fail in light of the remedial purpose of Title VI and its legislative history. . . .

. . .

We turn, therefore, to our analysis of the Equal Protection Clause of the Fourteenth Amendment.

. . .

[R]acial classifications are not per se invalid under the Fourteenth Amendment. Accordingly, we turn to the problem of articulating what our role should be in reviewing state action that expressly classifies by race.

Respondent argues that racial classifications are always suspect and, consequently, that this Court should weigh the importance of the objectives served by Davis' special admissions program to see if they are compelling. In addition, he asserts that this Court must inquire whether, in its judgment, there are alternatives to racial classifications which would suit Davis' purposes. Petitioner, on the other hand, states that our proper role is simply to accept petitioner's determination that the racial classifications used by its program are reasonably related to what it tells us are its benign purposes. We reject petitioner's view, but, because our prior cases are in many respects inapposite to that before us now, we find it necessary to define with precision the meaning of that inexact term, "strict scrutiny."

Unquestionably we have held that a government practice or statute which restricts "fundamental rights" or which contains "suspect classifications" is to be subjected to "strict scrutiny" and can be justified only if it furthers a compelling government purpose and, even then, only if no less restrictive alternative is available. But no fundamental right is involved here. Nor do whites as a class have any of the "traditional indicia of suspectness: the class is not saddled with such disabilities, or subjected to such a history of purposeful unequal treatment, or relegated to such a position of political powerlessness as to command extraordinary protection from the majoritarian political process."

Moreover, if the University's representations are credited, this is not a case where racial classifications are "irrelevant and therefore prohibited." Nor has anyone suggested that the University's purposes contravene the cardinal principle that racial classifications that stigmatize—because they are drawn on the presumption that one race is inferior to another or because they put the weight of government behind racial hatred and separatism—are invalid without more.

On the other hand, the fact that this case does not fit neatly into our prior analytic framework for race cases does not mean that it should be analyzed by applying the very loose rational-basis standard of review that is the very least that is always applied in equal protection cases. . . Instead, a number of considerations . . . lead us to conclude that racial classifications designed to further remedial purposes " 'must serve important governmental objectives and must be substantially related to achievement of those objectives.' ". . .

. . .

State programs designed ostensibly to ameliorate the effects of past racial discrimination obviously create the . . . hazard of stigma, since they may promote racial separatism and reinforce the views of those who believe that members of racial minorities are inherently incapable of succeeding on their own. . . .

. . .

[R]ace ... is an immutable characteristic which its possessors are powerless to escape or set aside. While a classification is not per se invalid because it divides classes on the basis of an immutable characteristic, it is nevertheless true that such divisions are contrary to our deep belief that "legal burdens should bear some relationship to individual responsibility or wrongdoing," and that advancement sanctioned, sponsored, or approved by the State should ideally be based on individual merit or achievement, or at the least on factors within the control of an individual. . . .

. . .

In sum, because of the significant risk that racial classifications established for ostensibly benign purposes can be misused, causing effects not unlike those created by invidious classifications, it is inappropriate to inquire only whether there is any conceivable basis that might sustain such a classification. Instead, to justify such a classification an important and articulated purpose for its use must be shown. In addition, any statute must be stricken that stigmatizes any group or that singles out those least well represented in the political process to bear the brunt of a benign program. Thus our review under the Fourteenth Amendment should be strict—not " 'strict' in theory and fatal in fact," because it is stigma that causes fatality—but strict and searching nonetheless.

Davis' articulated purpose of remedying the effects of past societal discrimination is, under our cases, sufficiently important to justify the use of race-conscious admissions programs where there is a sound basis for concluding that minority under-representation is substantial and chronic, and that the handicap of past discrimination is impeding access of minorities to the medical school. . . .

. . .

[S]tate educational institutions may constitutionally adopt admissions programs designed to avoid exclusion of historically disadvantaged minorities, even when such programs explicitly take race into account, finds direct support in our cases construing congressional legislation designed to overcome the present effects of past discrimination. Congress can and has outlawed actions which have a disproportionately adverse and unjustified impact upon members of racial minorities and has required or authorized race-conscious action to put individuals disadvantaged by such impact in the position they otherwise might have enjoyed. Such relief does not require as a predicate proof that recipients of preferential advancement have been individually discriminated against; it is enough that each recipient is within a general class of persons likely to have been the victims of discrimination. Nor is it an objection to such relief that preference for minorities will upset the settled expectations of nonminorities. In addition, we have held that Congress, to remove barriers to equal opportunity, can and has required employers to use test criteria that fairly reflect the qualifications of minority applicants vis-a-vis nonminority applicants, even if this means interpreting the qualifications of an applicant in light of his race. . . .

. . .

[T]he requirement of a judicial determination of a constitutional or statutory violation as a predicate for race-conscious remedial actions would be self-defeating. Such a requirement would severely undermine efforts to achieve voluntary compliance with the requirements of law. And, our society and jurisprudence have always stressed the value of voluntary efforts to further the objectives of the law. Judicial intervention is a last resort to achieve cessation of illegal conduct or the remedying of its effects rather than a prerequisite to action. . . .

. . .

Properly construed, therefore, our prior cases unequivocally show that a state government may adopt race-conscious programs if the purpose of such programs is to remove the disparate racial impact its actions might otherwise have and if there is reason to believe that the disparate impact is itself the product of past discrimination, whether its own or that of society at large. There is no question that Davis' program is valid under this test.

Certainly, on the basis of the undisputed factual submissions before this Court, Davis had a sound basis for believing that the problem of underrepresentation of minorities was substantial and chronic and that the problem was attributable to handicaps imposed on minority applicants by past and present racial discrimination. Until at least 1973, the practice of medicine in this country was, in fact, if not in law, largely the prerogative of whites. In 1950, for example, while Negroes comprised 10% of the total population, Negro physicians constituted only 2.2% of the total number of physicians. . . .

. . .

Moreover, Davis had very good reason to believe that the national pattern of underrepresentation of minorities in medicine would be perpetuated if it retained a single admissions standard. . . .

. . .

Davis clearly could conclude that the serious and persistent underrepresentation of minorities in medicine depicted by these statistics is the result of handicaps under which minority applicants labor as a consequence of a background of deliberate, purposeful discrimination against minorities in education and in society generally, as well as in the medical profession. . . .

. . .

Since separation of school children by race "generates a feeling of inferiority as to their status in the community that may affect their hearts and minds in a way unlikely ever to be undone," Brown I, the conclusion is inescapable that applicants to medical school must be few indeed who endured the effects of de jure segregation, the resistance to Brown I, or the equally debilitating pervasive private discrimination fostered by our long history of official discrimination and yet come to the starting line with an education equal to whites. . . .

. . .

The second prong of our test—whether the Davis program stigmatizes any discrete group or individual and whether race is reasonably used in light of the program's objectives—is clearly satisfied by the Davis program.

It is not even claimed that Davis' program in any way operates to stigmatize or single out any discrete and insular, or even any identifiable, nonminority group. Nor will harm comparable to that imposed upon racial minorities by exclusion or separation on grounds of race be the likely result of the program. It does not, for example, establish an exclusive preserve for minority students apart from and exclusive of whites. Rather, its purpose is to overcome the effects of segregation by bringing the races together. True, whites are excluded from participation in the special admissions program, but this fact only operates to reduce the number of whites to be admitted in the regular admissions program in order to permit admission of a reasonable percentage—less than their proportion of the California population—of otherwise underrepresented qualified minority applicants.

Nor was Bakke in any sense stamped as inferior by the Medical School's rejection of him. Indeed, it is conceded by all that he satisfied those criteria regarded by the School as generally relevant to academic performance better than most of the minority members who were admitted. Moreover, there is absolutely no basis for concluding that Bakke's rejection as a result of Davis' use of racial preference will affect him throughout his life in the same way as the segregation of the Negro school children in Brown I would have affected them. Unlike discrimination against racial minorities, the use of racial preferences for remedial purposes does not inflict a pervasive injury upon individual whites in the sense that wherever they go or whatever they do there is a significant likelihood that they will be treated as second-class citizens because of their color. This distinction does not mean that the exclusion of a white resulting from the preferential use of race is not sufficiently serious to require justification; but it does mean that the injury inflicted by such a policy is not distinguishable from disadvantages caused by a wide range of government actions, none of which has ever been thought impermissible for that reason alone. . . .

.　.　.

Nor can the program reasonably be regarded as stigmatizing the program's beneficiaries or their race as inferior. The Davis program does not simply advance less qualified applicants; rather, it compensates applicants, whom it is uncontested are fully qualified to study medicine, for educational disadvantage which it was reasonable to conclude was a product of state-fostered discrimination. Once admitted, these students must satisfy the same degree requirements as regularly admitted students; they are taught by the same faculty in the same classes; and their performance is evaluated by the same standards by which regularly admitted students are judged. Under these circumstances, their performance and degrees must be regarded equally with the regularly admitted students with whom they compete for standing. Since minority graduates cannot justifiably be regarded as less well qualified than nonminority graduates by virtue of the special admissions program, there is no reasonable basis to conclude that minority graduates at schools using such programs would be stigmatized as inferior by the existence of such programs.

We disagree with the lower courts' conclusion that the Davis program's use of race was unreasonable in light of its objectives. First, as petitioner argues, there are no practical means by which it could achieve its ends in the foreseeable future without the use of race-conscious measures. . . .

.   .   .

Second, the Davis admissions program does not simply equate minority status with disadvantage. Rather, Davis considers on an individual basis each applicant's personal history to determine whether he or she has likely been disadvantaged by racial discrimination. The record makes clear that only minority applicants likely to have been isolated from the mainstream of American life are considered in the special program; other minority applicants are eligible only through the regular admissions program. . . .

.   .   .

Finally, Davis' special admissions program cannot be said to violate the Constitution simply because it has set aside a predetermined number of places for qualified minority applicants rather than using minority status as a positive factor to be considered in evaluating the applications of disadvantaged minority applicants. . . There is no sensible, and certainly no constitutional, distinction between, for example, adding a set number of points to the admissions rating of disadvantaged minority applicants as an expression of the preference with the expectation that this will result in the admission of an approximately determined number of qualified minority applicants and setting a fixed number of places for such applicants as was done here. . . .

.   .   .

Separate opinion of Mr. Justice White.

. . .

Mr. Justice Marshall.

I agree with the judgment of the Court only insofar as it permits a university to consider the race of an applicant in making admissions decisions. I do not agree that petitioner's admissions program violates the Constitution. For it must be remembered that, during most of the past 200 years, the Constitution as interpreted by this Court did not prohibit the most ingenious and pervasive forms of discrimination against the Negro. Now, when a State acts to remedy the effects of that legacy of discrimination, I cannot believe that this same Constitution stands as a barrier. . . .

. . .

As has been demonstrated in our joint opinion, this Court's past cases establish the constitutionality of race-conscious remedial measures. Beginning with the school desegregation cases, we recognized that even absent a judicial or legislative finding of constitutional violation, a school board constitutionally could consider the race of students in making school assignment decisions. . . .

. . .

There is thus ample support for the conclusion that a university can employ race-conscious measures to remedy past societal discrimination, without the need for a finding that those benefited were actually victims of that discrimination.

While I applaud the judgment of the Court that a university may consider race in its admissions process, it is more than a little ironic that, after several hundred years of class-based discrimination against Negroes, the Court is unwilling to hold that a class-based remedy for that discrimination is permissible. In declining to so hold, today's judgment ignores the fact that for several hundred years Negroes have been discriminated against, not as individuals, but rather solely because of the color of their skins. It is unnecessary in 20th century America to have individual Negroes demonstrate that they have been victims of racial discrimination; the racism of our society has been so pervasive that none, regardless of wealth or position, has managed to escape its impact. The experience of Negroes in America has been different in kind, not just in degree, from that of other ethnic groups. It is not merely the history of

189

slavery alone but also that a whole people were marked as inferior by the law. And that mark has endured. The dream of America as the great melting pot has not been realized for the Negro; because of his skin color he never even made it into the pot. . . .

. . .

I fear that we have come full circle. After the Civil War our government started several "affirmative action" programs. This Court in the Civil Rights Cases and Plessy v Ferguson destroyed the movement toward complete equality. For almost a century no action was taken, and this nonaction was with the tacit approval of the courts. Then we had Brown v Board of Education and the Civil Rights Acts of Congress, followed by numerous affirmative action programs. *Now,* we have this Court again stepping in, this time to stop affirmative action programs of the type used by the University of California.

. . .

Mr. Justice Blackmun.

. . .

I yield to no one in my earnest hope that the time will come when an "affirmative action" program is unnecessary and is, in truth, only a relic of the past. I would hope that we could reach this stage within a decade at the most. But the story of Brown v Board of Education, decided almost a quarter of a century ago, suggests that that hope is a slim one. At some time, however, beyond any period of what some would claim is only transitional inequality, the United States must and will reach a stage of maturity where action along this line is no longer necessary. Then persons will be regarded as persons, and discrimination of the type we address today will be an ugly feature of history that is instructive but that is behind us. . . .

. . .

It is somewhat ironic to have us so deeply disturbed over a program where race is an element of consciousness, and yet to be aware of the fact, as we are, that institutions of higher learning, albeit more on the undergraduate than the graduate level, have given conceded preferences up to a point to those possessed of athletic skills, to the children of alumni, to the affluent who may bestow their largess on the institutions, and to those having connections with celebrities, the famous, and the powerful.

Programs of admission to institutions of higher learning are basically a responsibility for academicians and for administrators and the specialists they employ. The judiciary, in contrast, is ill-equipped and poorly trained for this. The administration and management of educational institutions are beyond the competence of judges and are within the special competence of educators, provided always that the educators perform within legal and constitutional bounds. For me, therefore, interference by the judiciary must be the rare exception and not the rule. . . .

. . .

I am not convinced, as Mr. Justice Powell seems to be, that the difference between the Davis program and the one employed by Harvard is very profound or constitutionally significant. The line between the two is a thin and indistinct one. In each, subjective application is at work. Because of my conviction that admission programs are primarily for the educators, I am willing to accept the representation that the Harvard program is one where good faith in its administration is practiced as well as professed. I agree that such a program, where race or ethnic background is only one of many factors, is a program better formulated than Davis' two-track system. The cynical, of course, may say that under a program such as Harvard's one may accomplish covertly what Davis concedes it does openly. I need not go that far, for despite its two-track aspect, the Davis program, for me, is within constitutional bounds, though perhaps barely so. . . .

. . .

I suspect that it would be impossible to arrange an affirmative action program in a racially neutral way and have it successful. To ask that this be so is to demand the impossible. In order to get beyond racism, we must first take account of race. There is no other way. And in order to treat some persons equally, we must treat them differently. We cannot—we dare not—let the Equal Protection Clause perpetrate racial supremacy.

So the ultimate question, as it was at the beginning of this litigation, is: Among the qualified, how does one choose? . . .

. . .

Mr. Justice Stevens, with whom The Chief Justice, Mr. Justice Stewart, and Mr. Justice Rehnquist join, concurring in the judgment in part and dissenting in part.

. . .

It is . . . perfectly clear that the question whether race can ever be used as a factor in an admissions decision is not an issue in this case, and that discussion of that issue is inappropriate.

Both petitioner and respondent have asked us to determine the legality of the University's special admissions program by reference to the Constitution. Our settled practice, however, is to avoid the decision of a constitutional issue if a case can be fairly decided on a statutory ground. . . The more important the issue, the more force there is to this doctrine. In this case, we are presented with a constitutional question of undoubted and unusual importance. Since, however, a dispositive statutory claim was raised at the very inception of this case, and squarely decided in the portion of the trial court judgment affirmed by the California Supreme Court, it is our plain duty to confront it. Only if petitioner should prevail on the statutory issue would it be necessary to decide whether the University's admissions program violated the Equal Protection Clause of the Fourteenth Amendment.

Section 601 of the Civil Rights Act of 1964 provides:

"No person in the United States shall, on the ground of race, color, or national origin, be exluded from participation in, be denied the benefits of, or be subjected to discrimination under any program or activity receiving Federal financial assistance."

The University, through its special admissions policy, excluded Bakke from participation in its program of medical education because of his race. The University also acknowledges that it was, and still is, receiving federal financial assistance. The plain language of the statute therefore requires affirmance of the judgment below. A different result cannot be justified unless that language misstates the actual intent of the Congress that enacted the statute or the statute is not enforceable in a private action. Neither conclusion is warranted. . . .

. . .

No doubt, when this legislation was being debated, Congress was not directly concerned with the legality of "reverse discrimination" or "affirmative action" programs. Its attention was focused on the problem at hand, "the glaring ... discrimination against Negroes which exists throughout our Nation," and, with respect to Title VI, the federal funding of segregated facilities. . . .

. . .

Petitioner contends, however, that exclusion of applicants on the basis of race does not violate Title VI if the exclusion carries with it no racial stigma. No such qualification or limitation of § 601's categorical prohibition of "exclusion" is justified by the statute or its history. The language of the entire section is perfectly clear; the words that follow "excluded from" do not modify or qualify the explicit outlawing of any exclusion on the stated grounds. . . .

. . .

[T]he meaning of the Title VI ban on exclusion is crystal clear: Race cannot be the basis of excluding anyone from participation in a federally funded program. . . .

. . .

The University's special admissions program violated Title VI of the Civil Rights Act of 1964 by excluding Bakke from the medical school because of his race. It is therefore our duty to affirm the judgment ordering Bakke admitted to the University.

Accordingly, I concur in the Court's judgment insofar as it affirms the judgment of the Supreme Court of California. To the extent that it purports to do anything else, I respectfully dissent.

. . .

Two other "affirmative action/reverse discrimination" cases deserve comment. The Kaiser Aluminum Co. entered into a contract with the United Steelworkers of America, bargaining agent for Kaiser employees, to eliminate racial imbalances in the almost totally white group of craft employees. Basically, the program committed the company to admitting one black for each white allowed to enter on-the-job training programs. Several white workers were passed over for training in favor of blacks with less seniority with the company. Brian

193

Weber brought suit against both the union and the company alleging that the agreement violated Title VII of the Civil Rights Act that prohibits racial discrimination in admission to on-the-job training programs. The district court and the court of appeals agreed that the Kaiser program violated the provisions of Title VII. The Supreme Court reversed. Emphasizing that the program was temporary, did not require the dismissal of any white workers, and did not totally bar whites from on-the-job training, Justice Brennan for the majority closely examined the legislative history of the act. This led him to the conclusion that Congress did not intend to bar purely voluntary efforts by employers in the private sector to eliminate the effects of past patterns of racial segregation in the work force. Chief Justice Burger and Justice Rehnquist reached a contrary conclusion while Justices Powell and Stevens did not participate in the decision. *United Steelworkers of America* v. *Weber,* 443 U.S. 193 (1979).

Fullilove v. *Klutznick,* 448 U.S. 448 (1980), involved an earmarking of ten percent of Public Works Employment Act funds for procuring services or supplies from minority business enterprises (MBEs). This requirement was accompanied by a legislative finding that minority businesses were traditionally discriminated against in awarding public works contracts and concluding that this ten percent set aside was the only practicable means for correcting the longstanding discrimination. Despite the Fifth Amendment and various statutory challenges, the Court upheld the provision but was unable to agree on a majority opinion. The various opinions concluded that Congress had a compelling interest in ensuring MBE access to public works funds and had chosen the only effective means for reaching that result. Chief Justice Burger, speaking for himself and Justices White and Powell, emphasized the remedial nature of the legislation and applied a standard of "close examination" and "careful judicial examination" to determine whether Congress had gone too far. Justice Powell, writing separately, applied the same "compelling state interest" test that he had used in Bakke. And Justice Marshall, joined by Justices Brennan and Blackmun, rejected (as he had done in Bakke) strict scrutiny as the proper test for legislation providing "benefits to minorities for the purpose of remedying the present effects of post racial discrimination." Justices Stewart, Rehnquist, and Stevens dissented, with the first two insisting on a color-blind award of contracts and the last asserting that Congress had inadequately justified the preference in the Act.

Frontiero v. Richardson

411 U.S. 677, 36 L Ed 2d 583, 93 S Ct 1764 (1973)

Defense Department regulations permit male armed service personnel to receive increased allowances for quarters and medical benefits upon a mere showing that they are married. A service woman may receive these increased allowances only upon showing that her spouse is in fact dependent upon her for more than one-half of his support. Appellant's due process challenge to this distinction was rejected by a three-judge district court and direct appeal was taken.

. . .

Mr. Justice Brennan announced the judgment of the Court and an opinion in which Mr. Justice Douglas, Mr. Justice White, and Mr. Justice Marshall join.

The question before us concerns the right of a female member of the uniformed services to claim her spouse as a "dependent" for the purposes of obtaining increased quarters allowances and medical and dental benefits on an equal footing with male members. Under these statutes, a serviceman may claim his wife as a "dependent" without regard to whether she is in fact dependent upon him for any part of her support. A servicewoman, on the other hand, may not claim her husband as a "dependent" under these programs unless he is in fact dependent upon her for over one-half of his support. Thus, the question for decision is whether this difference in treatment constitutes an unconstitutional discrimination against servicewomen in violation of the Due Process Clause of the Fifth Amendment. . . .

. . .

In an effort to attract career personnel through re-enlistment, Congress established a scheme for the provision of fringe benefits to members of the uniformed services on a competitive basis with business and industry. Thus, a member of the uniformed services with dependents is entitled to an increased "basic allowance for quarters" and a member's dependents are provided comprehensive medical and dental care. . . .

195

.   .   .

Although the legislative history of these statutes sheds virtually no light on the purposes underlying the differential treatment accorded male and female members, a majority of the three-judge District Court surmised that Congress might reasonably have concluded that, since the husband in our society is generally the "breadwinner" in the family—and the wife typically the "dependent" partner—"it would be more economical to require married female members claiming husbands to prove actual dependency than to extend the presumption of dependency to such members." Indeed, given the fact that approximately 99% of all members of the uniformed services are male, the District Court speculated that such differential treatment might conceivably lead to a "considerable saving of administrative expense and manpower."

At the outset, appellants contend that classifications based on sex, like classifications based upon race, alienage, and national origin, are inherently suspect and must therefore be subjected to close judicial scrutiny. We agree. . . .

.   .   .

There can be no doubt that our Nation has had a long and unfortunate history of sex discrimination. Traditionally, such descrimination was rationalized by an attitude of "romantic paternalism" which, in practical effect, put women not on a pedestal, but in a cage. . . .

.   .   .

As a result of notions such as these, our statute books gradually became laden with gross, stereotypical distinctions between the sexes and, indeed, throughout much of the 19th century the position of women in our society was, in many respects, comparable to that of blacks under the pre-Civil War slave codes. Neither slaves nor women could hold office, serve on juries, or bring suit in their own names, and married women traditionally were denied the legal capacity to hold or convey property or to serve as legal guardians of their own children. And although blacks were guaranteed the right to vote in 1870, women were denied even that right—which is itself "preservative of other basic civil and political rights"—until adoption on the Nineteenth Amendment half a century later.

It is true, of course, that the position of women in America has improved markedly in recent decades. Nevertheless, it can hardly be doubted that, in part because of the high visibility of the sex characteristic, women still face pervasive, although at times more subtle, discrimination in our educational institutions, on the job market and, perhaps most conspicuously, in the political arena.

Moreover, since sex, like race and national origin, is an immutable characteristic determined solely by the accident of birth, the imposition of special disabilities upon the members of a particular sex because of their sex would seem to violate "the basic concept of our system that legal burdens should bear some relationship to individual responsibility. . ." And what differentiates sex from such nonsuspect statuses as intelligence or physical disability, and aligns it with the recognized suspect criteria, is that the sex characteristic frequently bears no relation to ability to perform or contribute to society. As a result, statutory distinctions between the sexes often have the effect of invidiously relegating the entire class of females to inferior legal status without regard to the actual capabilities of its individual members. . . .

. . .

With these considerations in mind, we can only conclude that classifications based upon sex, like classifications based upon national origin, are inherently suspect, and must therefore be subjected to strict judicial scrutiny. Applying the analysis mandated by that stricter standard of review, it is clear that the statutory scheme now before us is constitutionally invalid.

The sole basis of the classification established in the challenged statutes is the sex of the individuals involved. . . [A] female member of the uniformed services seeking to obtain housing and medical benefits for her spouse must prove his dependency in fact, whereas no such burden is imposed upon male members. In addition, the statutes operate so as to deny benefits to a female member, such as appellant Sharron Frontiero, who provides less than one-half of her spouse's support, while at the same time granting such benefits to a male member who likewise provides less than one-half of his spouse's support. Thus, to this extent at least, it may fairly be said that these statutes command "disimilar treatment for men and women who are . . . similarly situated."

Moreover, the Government concedes that the differential treatment accorded men and women under these statutes serves no purpose other than mere "administrative convenience.". . .

The Government offers no concrete evidence, however, tending to support its view that such differential treatment in fact saves the Government any money. In order to satisfy the demands of strict judicial scrutiny, the Government must demonstrate, for example, that it is actually cheaper to grant increased benefits with respect to *all* male members, than it is to determine which male members are in fact entitled to such benefits and to grant increased benefits only to those members whose wives actually meet the dependency requirement. Here, however, there is substantial evidence that, if put to the test, many of the wives of male members would fail to qualify for benefits. . . .

· · ·

In any case, our prior decisions make clear that, although efficacious administration of governmental programs is not without some importance, "the Constitution recognizes higher values than speed and efficiency." And when we enter the realm of "strict judicial scrutiny," there can be no doubt that "administrative convenience" is not a shibboleth, the mere recitation of which dictates constitutionality. . . We therefore conclude that, by according differential treatment to male and female members of the uniformed services for the sole purpose of achieving administrative convenience, the challenged statutes violate the Due Process Clause of the Fifth Amendment insofar as they require a female member to prove the dependency of her husband.

Reversed.

· · ·

Mr. Justice Stewart concurs in the judgment.

· · ·

Mr. Justice Rehnquist dissents.

· · ·

Mr. Justice Powell, with whom The Chief Justice and Mr. Justice Blackmun join, concurring in the judgment.

I agree that the challenged statutes constitute an unconstitutional discrimination against service women in violation of the Due Process Clause of the Fifth Amendment, but I cannot join the opinion of Mr. Justice Brennan, which would hold that all classifications based upon sex, "like classifications based upon race, alienage, and national origin," are "inherently suspect and must therefore be subjected to close judicial scrutiny." It is unnecessary for the Court in this case to characterize sex as a suspect classification, with all of the far-reaching implications of such a holding . . . which abundantly supports our decision today, did not add sex to the narrowly limited group of classifications which are inherently suspect. In my view, we can and should decide this case on the authority of Reed and reserve for the future any expansion of its rationale.

. . .

There is another, and I find compelling, reason for deferring a general categorizing of sex classifications as invoking the strictest test of judicial scrutiny. The Equal Rights Amendment, which if adopted will resolve the substance of this precise question, has been approved by the Congress and submitted for ratification by the States. If this Amendment is duly adopted, it will represent the will of the people accomplished in the manner prescribed by the Constitution. By acting prematurely and unnecessarily, as I view it, the Court has assumed a decisional responsibility at the very time when state legislatures, functioning within the traditional democratic process, are debating the proposed Amendment. It seems to me that this reaching out to pre-empt by judicial action a major political decision which is currently in process of resolution does not reflect appropriate respect for duly prescribed legislative processes. . . .

. . .

There are times when this Court, under our system, cannot avoid a constitutional decision on issues which normally should be resolved by the elected representatives of the people. But the democratic institutions are weakened, and confidence in the restraint of the Court is impaired, when we appear unnecessarily to decide sensitive issues of broad social and political importance at the very time they are under consideration within the prescribed constitutional processes.

San Antonio Independent School District v. Rodriguez

411 U.S. 1, 36 L Ed 2d 16, 93 S Ct 1278 (1973)

This "wealth discrimination" case arose out of a challenge to the methods of financing public education used in the state of Texas. Each school district is authorized to impose an ad valorem property tax to raise revenues to supplement state education funds. Significant interdistrict disparities in per pupil expenditures result largely because of differences in the property tax yield. The revenues of two districts in San Antonio illustrate the disparities. The Englewood district is located in the core city, is almost totally without commercial or industrial property, and is largely Mexican-American in population. Property taxes are at the highest rate in the metropolitan area ($1.05 per $100 assessed value) but yielded only $26 per pupil in the 1967-68 school year; state and federal funds raised the per pupil expenditure to $356 in that school year. Alamo Heights, an affluent, residential, Anglo district, raised $333 per pupil by the property tax (with a rate of $0.85 per $100) and with state and federal funds had $594 per pupil to spend in 1967-68. The three-judge district court found an equal protection violation and invalidated the financing scheme because wealth is a suspect classification, education is a fundamental right, and the state failed to show a compelling reason for its system. Direct appeal was taken.

. . .

Mr. Justice Powell delivered the opinion of the Court.

. . .

The first Texas Constitution, promulgated upon Texas' entry into the Union in 1845, provided for the establishment of a system of free schools. Early in its history, Texas adopted a dual approach to the financing of its schools, relying on mutual participation by the local school districts and the State. As early as 1883 the state constitution was amended to provide for the creation of local school districts empowered to levy ad valorem taxes with the consent of local taxpayers for the "erection of school buildings" and for the "further maintenance of public free schools." Such local funds as were raised were supplemented by funds distributed to each district from the State's Permanent and Available School Funds. . . .

. . .

Until recent times Texas was a predominantly rural State and its population and property wealth were spread relatively evenly across the State. Sizable differences in the value of assessable property between local school districts became increasingly evident as the State became more industrialized and as rural-to-urban population shifts became more pronounced. The location of commercial and industrial property began to play a significant role in determining the amount of tax resources available to each school district. These growing disparities in population and taxable property between districts were responsible in part for increasingly notable differences in levels of local expenditure for education. . . .

. . .

Texas virtually concedes that its historically rooted dual system of financing education could not withstand the strict judicial scrutiny that this Court has found appropriate in reviewing legislative judgments that interfere with fundamental constitutional rights or that involve suspect classifications. If, as previous decisions have indicated, strict scrutiny means that the State's system is not entitled to the usual presumption of validity, that the State rather than the complainants must carry a "heavy burden of justification," that the State must demonstrate that its educational system has been structured with "precision" and is "tailored" narrowly to serve legitimate objectives and that it has selected the "least drastic means" for effectuating its objectives, the Texas financing system and its counterpart in virtually every other State will not pass muster. The State candidly admits that "[n]o one familiar with the Texas system would contend that it has yet achieved perfection." Apart from its concession that educational finance in Texas has "defects" and "imperfections," the State defends the system's rationality with vigor and disputes the District Court's finding that it lacks a "reasonable basis."

This, then, establishes the framework for our analysis. We must decide, first, whether the Texas system of financing public education operates to the disadvantage of some suspect class or impinges upon a fundamental right explicitly or implicitly protected by the Constitution, thereby requiring strict judicial scrutiny. If so, the judgment of the District Court should be affirmed. If not, the Texas scheme must still be examined to determine whether it rationally furthers some legitimate, articulated state purpose and therefore does not constitute an invidious discrimination in violation of the Equal Protection Clause of the Fourteenth Amendment. . . .

. . .

The wealth discrimination discovered by the District Court in this case, and by several other courts that have recently struck down school financing laws in other States, is quite unlike any of the forms of wealth discrimination heretofore reviewed by this Court. Rather than focusing on the unique features of the alleged discrimination, the courts in these cases have virtually assumed their findings of a suspect classification through a simplistic process of analysis: since, under the traditional systems of financing public schools, some poorer people receive less expensive educations than other more affluent people, these systems discriminate on the basis of wealth. This approach largely ignores the hard threshold questions, including whether it makes a difference for purposes of consideration under the Constitution that the class of disadvantaged "poor" cannot be identified or defined in customary equal protection terms, and whether the relative—rather than absolute—nature of the asserted deprivation is of significant consequence. Before a State's laws and the justifications for the classifications they create are subjected to strict judicial scrutiny, we think these threshold considerations must be analyzed more closely than they were in the court below. . . .

. . .

The precedents of this Court provide the proper starting point. The individuals or groups of individuals who constituted the class discriminated against in our prior cases shared two distinguishing characteristics: because of their impecunity they were completely unable to pay for some desired benefit, and as a consequence, they sustained an absolute deprivation of a meaningful opportunity to enjoy that benefit. . . .

. . .

Even a cursory examination ... demonstrates that neither of the two distinguishing characteristics of wealth classifications can be found here. First, in support of their charge that the system discriminates against the "poor," appellees have made no effort to demonstrate that it operates to the peculiar disadvantage of any class fairly definable as indigent, or as composed of persons whose incomes are beneath any designated poverty level. Indeed, there is reason to believe that the poorest families are not necessarily clustered in the poorest property districts. . . .

. . .

Second, neither appellees nor the District Court addressed the fact that, unlike each of the foregoing cases, lack of personal resources has not occasioned an absolute deprivation of the desired benefit. The argument here is not that the children in districts having relatively low assessable property values are receiving no public education; rather, it is that they are receiving a poorer quality education than that available to children in districts having more assessable wealth. Apart from the unsettled and disputed question whether the quality of education may be determined by the amount of money expended for it, a sufficient answer to appellees' argument is that at least where wealth is involved the Equal Protection Clause does not require absolute equality or precisely equal advantages. Nor, indeed, in view of the infinite variables affecting the educational process, can any system assure equal quality of education except in the most relative sense. . . .

. . .

However described, it is clear that appellees' suit asks this Court to extend its most exacting scrutiny to review a system that allegedly discriminates against a large, diverse, and amorphous class, unified only by the common factor of residence in districts that happen to have less taxable wealth than other districts. The system of alleged discrimination and the class it defines have none of the traditional indicia of suspectness: the class is not saddled with such disabilities, or subjected to such a history of purposeful unequal treatment, or relegated to such a position of political powerlessness as to command extraordinary protection from the majoritarian political process.

We thus conclude that the Texas system does not operate to the peculiar disadvantage of any suspect class. But in recognition of the fact that this Court has never heretofore held that wealth discrimination alone provides an adequate basis for invoking strict scrutiny, appellees have not relied solely on this contention. They also assert that the State's system impermissibly interferes with the exercise of a "fundamental" right and that accordingly the prior decisions of this Court require the application of the strict standard of judicial review. . . .

. . .

Nothing this Court holds today in any way detracts from our historic dedication to public education. We are in complete agreement with the conclusion of the three-judge panel below that "the grave significance of education both to the individual and to our society" cannot be doubted. But the importance of a service performed by the State does not determine whether it must be regarded as fundamental for purposes of examination under the Equal Protection Clause. . . .

. . .

It is not the province of this Court to create substantive constitutional rights in the name of guaranteeing equal protection of the laws. Thus the key to discovering whether education is "fundamental" is not to be found in comparisons of the relative societal significance of education as opposed to subsistence or housing. Nor is it to be found by weighing whether education is as important as the right to travel. Rather, the answer lies in assessing whether there is a right to education explicitly or implicitly guaranteed by the Constitution. . . .

. . .

Education, of course, is not among the rights afforded explicit protection under our Federal Constitution. Nor do we find any basis for saying it is implicitly so protected. As we have said, the undisputed importance of education will not alone cause this Court to depart from the usual standard for reviewing a State's social and economic legislation. It is appellees' contention, however, that education is distinguishable from other services and benefits provided by the State because it bears a peculiarly close relationship to other rights and liberties accorded protection under the Constitution. Specifically, they insist that education is itself a fundamental personal right because it is essential to the effective exercise of First Amendment freedoms and to intelligent utilization of the right to vote. In asserting a nexus between speech and education, appellees urge that the right to speak is meaningless unless the speaker is capable of articulating his thoughts intelligently and persuasively. The "marketplace of ideas" is an empty forum for those lacking basic communicative tools. Likewise, they argue that the corollary right to receive information becomes little more than a hollow privilege when the recipient has not been taught to read, assimilate, and utilize available knowledge.

A similar line of reasoning is pursued with respect to the right to vote. Exercise of the franchise, it is contended, cannot be divorced from the educational foundation of the voter. The electoral process, if reality is to conform to the democratic ideal, depends on an informed electorate: a voter cannot cast his ballot intelligently unless his reading skills and thought processes have been adequately developed.

We need not dispute any of these propositions. The Court has long afforded zealous protection against unjustifiable governmental interference with the individual's rights to speak and to vote. Yet we have never presumed to possess either the ability or the authority to guarantee to the citizenry the most *effective* speech or the most *informed* electoral choice. That these may be desirable goals of a system of freedom of expression and of a representative form of government is not to be doubted. These are indeed goals to be pursued by a people whose thoughts and beliefs are freed from governmental interference. But they are not values to be implemented by judicial intrusion into otherwise legitimate state activities.

Even if it were conceded that some identifiable quantum of education is a constitutionally protected prerequisite to the meaningful exercise of either right, we have no indication that the present levels of educational expenditure in Texas provide an education that falls short. . . .

. . .

We have carefully considered each of the arguments supportive of the District Court's finding that education is a fundamental right or liberty and have found those arguments unpersuasive. In one further respect we find this a particularly inappropriate case in which to subject state action to strict judicial scrutiny. The present case, in another basic sense, is significantly different from any of the cases in which the Court has applied strict scrutiny to state or federal legislation touching upon constitutionally protected rights. Each of our prior cases involved legislation which "deprived," "infringed," or "interfered" with the free exercise of some such fundamental personal right or liberty. . . .

. . .

Every step leading to the establishment of the system Texas utilizes to-day—including the decisions permitting localities to tax and expend locally, and creating and continuously expanding state aid—was implemented in an effort to *extend* public education and to improve its quality. Of course, every reform that benefits some more than others may be criticized for what it fails to accomplish. But we think it plain that, in substance, the thrust of the Texas system is affirmative and reformatory and, therefore, should be scrutinized under judicial principles sensitive to the nature of the State's efforts and to the rights reserved to the States under the Constitution.

It should be clear, for the reasons stated above and in accord with the prior decisions of this Court, that this is not a case in which the challenged state action must be subjected to the searching judicial scrutiny reserved for laws that create suspect classifications or impinge upon constitutionally protected rights.

We need not rest our decision, however, solely on the inappropriateness of the strict scrutiny test. A century of Supreme Court adjudication under the Equal Protection Clause affirmatively supports the application of the traditional standard of review, which requires only that the State's system be shown to bear some rational relationship to legitimate state purposes. This case represents far more than a challenge to the manner in which Texas provides for the education of its children. We have here nothing less than a direct attack on the way in which Texas has chosen to raise and disburse state and local tax revenues. We are asked to condemn the State's judgment in conferring on political subdivisions the power to tax local property to supply revenues for local interests. In so doing, appellees would have the Court intrude in an area in which it has traditionally deferred to state legislatures. . . .

Thus we stand on familiar ground when we continue to acknowledge that the Justices of this Court lack both the expertise and the familiarity with local problems so necessary to the making of wise decisions with respect to the raising and disposition of public revenues. . . .

. . .

In addition to matters of fiscal policy, this case also involves the most persistent and difficult questions of educational policy, another area in which this Court's lack of specialized knowledge and experience counsels against premature interference with the informed judgments made at the state and local levels. Education, perhaps even more than welfare assistance, presents a myriad of "intractable economic, social and even philosophical problems." The very complexity of the problems of financing and managing a statewide public school system suggest that "there will be more than one constitutionally permissible method of solving them," and that, within the limits of rationality, "the legislature's efforts to tackle the problems" should be entitled to respect. On even the most basic questions in this area the scholars and educational experts are divided. Indeed, one of the hottest sources of controversy concerns the extent to which there is a demonstrable correlation between educational expenditures and the quality of education—an assumed correlation underlying virtually every legal conclusion drawn by the District Court in this case. Related to the questioned relationship between cost and quality is the equally unsettled controversy as to the proper goals of a system of public education. And the question regarding the most effective relationship between state boards of education and local school boards, in terms of their respective responsibilities and degrees of control, is now undergoing searching re-examination. The ultimate wisdom as to these and related problems of education is not likely to be divined for all time even by the scholars who now so earnestly debate the issues. In such circumstances the judiciary is well advised to refrain from imposing on the States inflexible constitutional restraints that could circumscribe or handicap the continued research and experimentation so vital to finding even partial solutions to educational problems and to keeping abreast of ever changing conditions.

It must be remembered also that every claim arising under the Equal Protection Clause has implications for the relationship between national and state power under our federal system. Questions of federalism are always inherent in the process of determining whether a State's laws are to be accorded the traditional presumption of constitutionality, or are to be subjected instead to rigorous judicial scrutiny. While "[t]he maintenance of the principles of federalism is a foremost consideration in interpreting any of the pertinent constitutional provisions under which this Court examines state action," it would be difficult to imagine a case having a greater potential impact on our federal system than the one now before us, in

207

which we are urged to abrogate systems of financing public education presently in existence in virtually every State.

The foregoing considerations buttress our conclusion that Texas' system of public school finance is an inappropriate candidate for strict judicial scrutiny. These same considerations are relevant to the determination whether that system, with its conceded imperfections, nevertheless bears some rational relationship to a legitimate state purpose. . . .

. . .

In its reliance on state as well as local resources, the Texas system is comparable to the systems employed in virtually every other State. The power to tax local property for educational purposes has been recognized in Texas at least since 1883. When the growth of commercial and industrial centers and accompanying shifts in population began to create disparities in local resources, Texas undertook a program calling for a considerable investment of state funds. . . .

. . .

While assuring a basic education for every child in the State, it permits and encourages a large measure of participation in and control of each district's schools at the local level. In an era that has witnessed a consistent trend toward centralization of the functions of government, local sharing of responsibility for public education has survived. . . .

. . .

The persistence of attachment to government at the lowest level where education is concerned reflects the depth of commitment of its supporters. In part, local control means . . . the freedom to devote more money to the education of one's children. Equally important, however, is the opportunity it offers for participation in the decision-making process that determines how those local tax dollars will be spent. Each locality is free to tailor local programs to local needs. Pluralism also affords some opportunity for experimentation, innovation, and a healthy competition for educational excellence. An analogy to the Nation-State relationship in our federal system seems uniquely appropriate. Mr. Justice Brandeis identified as one of the peculiar strengths of our form of government each State's freedom to "serve as a laboratory . . . and try novel social and economic experiments." No area of social concern stands to profit more from a multiplicity of viewpoints and from a diversity of approaches than does public education. . . .

.   .   .

It is also well to remember that even those districts that have reduced ability to make free decisions with respect to how much they spend on education still retain under the present system a large measure of authority as to how available funds will be allocated. They further enjoy the power to make numerous other decisions with respect to the operation of the schools. The people of Texas may be justified in believing that other systems of school finance, which place more of the financial responsibility in the hands of the State, will result in a comparable lessening of desired local autonomy. That is, they may believe that along with increased control of the purse strings at the state level will go increased control over local policies. . . .

.   .   .

In sum, to the extent that the Texas system of school finance results in unequal expenditures between children who happen to reside in different districts, we cannot say that such disparities are the product of a system that is so irrational as to be invidiously discriminatory. Texas has acknowledged its shortcomings and has persistently endeavored—not without some success—to ameliorate the differences in levels of expenditures without sacrificing the benefits of local participation. The Texas plan is not the result of hurried, ill-conceived legislation. It certainly is not the product of purposeful discrimination against any group or class. On the contrary, it is rooted in decades of experience in Texas and elsewhere, and in major part is the product of responsible studies by qualified people. . . The constitutional standard under the Equal Protection Clause is whether the challenged state action rationally furthers a legitimate state purpose or interest. We hold that the Texas plan abundantly satisfies this standard. . . .

.   .   .

[A] cautionary postscript seems appropriate. It cannot be questioned that the constitutional judgment reached by the District Court and approved by our dissenting brothers today would occasion in Texas and elsewhere an unprecedented upheaval in public education. Some commentators have concluded that, whatever the contours of the alternative financing programs that might be devised and approved, the result could not avoid being a beneficial one. But just as there is nothing simple about the constitutional issues involved in these cases, there is nothing simple or certain about predicting the consequences of massive change in the financing and control of public education. Those who have devoted the most thoughtful attention to the practical ramifications of these cases have found no clear or dependable answers and their scholarship reflects no such unqualified confidence in the desirability of completely uprooting the existing system.

The complexity of these problems is demonstrated by the lack of consensus with respect to whether it may be said with any assurance that the poor, the racial minorities, or the children in overburdened core-city school districts would be benefited by abrogation of traditional modes of financing education. Unless there is to be a substantial increase in state expenditures on education across the board—an event the likelihood of which is open to considerable question—these groups stand to realize gains in terms of increased per pupil expenditures only if they reside in districts that presently spend at relatively low levels, i.e., in those districts that would benefit from the redistribution of existing resources. Yet recent studies have indicated that the poorest families are not invariably clustered in the most impecunious school districts. Nor does it now appear that there is any more than a random chance that racial minorities are concentrated in property-poor districts. Additionally, several research projects have concluded that any financing alternative designed to achieve a greater equality of expenditures is likely to lead to higher taxation and lower educational expenditures in the major urban centers, a result that would exacerbate rather than ameliorate existing conditions in those areas.

These practical considerations, of course, play no role in the adjudication of the constitutional issues presented here. But they serve to highlight the wisdom of the traditional limitations on this Court's function. The consideration and initiation of fundamental reforms with respect to state taxation and education are matters reserved for the legislative processes of the various States, and we do no violence to the values of federalism and separation of powers by staying our hand. . . .

.   .   .

Reversed.

. . .

Mr. Justice Stewart, concurring.

The method of financing public schools in Texas, as in almost every other State, has resulted in a system of public education that can fairly be described as chaotic and unjust. It does not follow, however, and I cannot find, that this system violates the Constitution of the United States. I join the opinion and judgment of the Court because I am convinced that any other course would mark an extraordinary departure from principled adjudication under the Equal Protection Clause of the Fourteenth Amendment. . . .

. . .

There is hardly a law on the books that does not affect some people differently than others. But the basic concern of the Equal Protection Clause is with state legislation whose purpose or effect is to create discrete and objectively identifiable classes. And with respect to such legislation, it has long been settled that the Equal Protection Clause is offended only by laws that are invidiously discriminatory—only by classifications that are wholly arbitrary or capricious. . . .

. . .

First, as the Court points out, the Texas system has hardly created the kind of objectively identifiable classes that are cognizable under the Equal Protection Clause. Second, even assuming the existence of such discernible categories, the classifications are in no sense based upon constitutionally "suspect" criteria. Third, the Texas system does not rest "on grounds wholly irrelevant to the achievement of the State's objective." Finally, the Texas system impinges upon no substantive constitutional rights or liberties. . . .

. . .

Mr. Justice Brennan, dissenting.

Although I agree with my Brother White that the Texas statutory scheme is devoid of any rational basis, and for that reason is violative of the Equal Protection Clause, I also record my disagreement with the Court's rather distressing assertion that a right may be deemed "fundamental" for the purposes of equal protection analysis only if it is "explicitly or implicitly guaranteed by the Constitution."

. . .

Mr. Justice White, with whom Mr. Justice Douglas and Mr. Justice Brennan join, dissenting.

. . .

If the State aims at maximizing local initiative and local choice, by permitting school districts to resort to the real property tax if they choose to do so, it utterly fails in achieving its purpose in districts with property tax bases so low that there is little if any opportunity for interested parents, rich or poor, to augment school district revenues. Requiring the State to establish only that unequal treatment is in furtherance of a permissible goal, without also requiring the State to show that the means chosen to effectuate that goal are rationally related to its achievement, makes equal protection analysis no more than an empty gesture. In my view, the parents and children in Edgewood, and in like districts, suffer from an invidious discrimination violative of the Equal Protection Clause. . . .

. . .

[W]e would blink reality to ignore the fact that school districts, and students in the end, are differentially affected by the Texas school financing scheme with respect to their capability to supplement the Minimum Foundation School Program. At the very least, the law discriminates against those children and their parents who live in districts where the per-pupil tax base is sufficiently low to make impossible the provision of comparable school revenues by resort to the real property tax which is the only device the State extends for this purpose.

. . .

Mr. Justice Marshall, with whom Mr. Justice Douglas concurs, dissenting.

. . .

In my judgment, the right of every American to an equal start in life, so far as the provision of a state service as important as education is concerned, is far too vital to permit state discrimination on grounds as tenuous as those presented by this record. Nor can I accept the notion that it is sufficient to remit these appellees to the vagaries of the political process which, contrary to the majority's suggestion, has proven singularly unsuited to the task of providing a remedy for this discrimination. I, for one, am unsatisfied with the hope of an ultimate "political" solution sometime in the indefinite future while, in the meantime, countless children unjustifiably receive inferior educations that "may affect their hearts and minds in a way unlikely ever to be undone." I must therefore respectfully dissent. . . .

. . .

[H]owever praiseworthy Texas' equalizing efforts, the issue in this case is not whether Texas is doing its best to ameliorate the worst features of a discriminatory scheme, but rather whether the scheme itself is in fact unconstitutionally discriminatory in the face of the Fourteenth Amendment's guarantee of equal protection of the laws. When the Texas financing scheme is taken as a whole, I do not think it can be doubted that it produces a discriminatory impact on substantial numbers of the school-age children of the State of Texas.

Funds to support public education in Texas are derived from three sources: local ad valorem property taxes; the Federal Government; and the state government. It is enlightening to consider these in order. . . .

. . .

The significance of the local property tax element of the Texas financing scheme is apparent from the fact that it provides the funds to meet some 40% of the cost of public education for Texas as a whole. Yet the amount of revenue that any particular Texas district can raise is dependent on two factors—its tax rate and its amount of taxable property. . . The necessary effect of the Texas local property tax is, in short, to favor property rich districts and to disfavor property poor ones. . . .

. . .

The Federal Government provides funds sufficient to cover only some 10% of the total cost of public education in Texas. Furthermore, while these federal funds are not distributed in Texas solely on a per pupil basis, appellants do not here contend that they are used in such a way as to ameliorate significantly the widely varying consequences for Texas school districts and school children of the local property tax element of the state financing scheme.

State funds provide the remaining some 50% of the monies spent on public education in Texas. . . .

· · ·

The stated purpose of the Minimum Foundation School Program is to provide certain basic funding for each local Texas school district. At the same time, the Program was apparently intended to improve, to some degree, the financial position of property poor districts relative to property rich districts, since—through the use of the economic index—an effort is made to charge a disproportionate share of the costs of the Program to rich districts. It bears noting, however, that substantial criticism has been leveled at the practical effectiveness of the economic index system of local cost allocation. . . .

· · ·

Moreover, even putting aside these criticisms of the economic index as a device for achieving meaningful district wealth equalization through cost allocation, poor districts still do not necessarily *receive* more state aid than property rich districts. For the standards which currently determine the amount received from the Foundation Program by any particular district favor property rich districts. . . .

· · ·

The appellants do not deny the disparities in educational funding caused by variations in taxable district property wealth. They do contend, however, that whatever the differences in per pupil spending among Texas districts, there are no discriminatory consequences for the children of the disadvantaged districts. They recognize that what is at stake in this case is the quality of the public education provided Texas children in the districts in which they live. But appellants reject the suggestion that the quality of education in any particular district is determined by money—beyond some minimal level of funding which they believe to be assured every Texas district by the Minimum Foundation School Program. In their view, there is simply no denial of equal educational opportunity to any

Texas school children as a result of the widely varying per pupil spending power provided districts under the current financing scheme. . . .

. . .

In my view, though, even an unadorned restatement of this contention is sufficient to reveal its absurdity. Authorities concerned with educational quality no doubt disagree as to the significance of variations in per pupil spending. . . We sit, however, not to resolve disputes over educational theory but to enforce our Constitution. It is an inescapable fact that if one district has more funds available per pupil than another district, the former will have greater choice in educational planning than will the latter. In this regard, I believe the question of discrimination in educational quality must be deemed to be an objective one that looks to what the State provides its children, not to what the children are able to do with what they receive. That a child forced to attend an underfunded school with poorer physical facilities, less experienced teachers, larger classes, and a narrower range of courses than a school with substantially more funds—and thus with greater choice in educational planning—may nevertheless excel is to the credit of the child, not the State. Indeed, who can ever measure for such a child the opportunities lost and the talents wasted for want of a broader, more enriched education? Discrimination in the opportunity to learn that is afforded a child must be our standard. . . .

. . .

At the very least, in view of the substantial inter-district disparities in funding and in resulting educational inputes [sic] shown by appellees to exist under the Texas financing scheme, the burden of proving that these disparities do not in fact affect the quality of children's education must fall upon the appellants. Yet appellants made no effort in the District Court to demonstrate that educational quality is not affected by variations in funding and in resulting inputs. And, in this Court, they have argued no more than that the relationship is ambiguous. This is hardly sufficient to overcome appellees' prima facie showing of state created discrimination between the schoolchildren of Texas with respect to objective educational opportunity. . . .

. . .

Alternatively, the appellants and the majority may believe that the Equal Protection Clause cannot be offended by substantially unequal state treatment of persons who are similarly situated so long as the State provides everyone with some unspecified amount of education which evidently is "enough." The basis for such a novel view is far from clear. It is, of course, true that the Constitution does not require precise equality in the treatment of all persons. . . But this Court has never suggested that because some "adequate" level of benefits is provided to all, discrimination in the provision of services is therefore constitutionally excusable. The Equal Protection Clause is not addressed to the minimal sufficiency but rather to the unjustifiable inequalities of state action. It mandates nothing less than that "all persons similarly circumstanced shall be treated alike.". . .

· · ·

In my view, then, it is inequality—not some notion of gross inadequacy—of educational opportunity that raises a question of denial of equal protection of the laws. I find any other approach to the issue unintelligible and without directing principle. Here appellees have made a substantial showing of wide variations in educational opportunity afforded to the school children of Texas. This discrimination is, in large measure, attributable to significant disparities in the taxable wealth of local Texas school districts. This is a sufficient showing to raise a substantial question of discriminatory state action in violation of the Equal Protection Clause. . . .

· · ·

[H]aving established public education for its citizens, the State, as a direct consequence of the variations in local property wealth endemic to Texas' financing scheme, has provided some Texas school children with substantially less resources for their education than others. Thus, while on its face the Texas scheme may merely discriminate between local districts, the impact of that discrimination falls directly upon the children whose educational opportunity is dependent upon where they happen to live. Consequently, the District Court correctly concluded that the Texas financing scheme discriminates, from a constitutional perspective, between school age children on the basis of the amount of taxable property located within their local districts. . . .

· · ·

I believe it is sufficient that the overarching form of discrimination in this case is between the school children of Texas on the basis of the taxable property wealth of the districts in which they happen to live. To understand both the precise nature of this discrimination and the parameters of the disadvantaged class it is sufficient to consider the constitutional principle which appellees contend is controlling in the context of educational financing. In their complaint appellees asserted that the Constitution does not permit local district wealth to be determinative of educational opportunity. This is simply another way of saying, as the District Court concluded, that consistent with the guarantee of equal protection of the laws, "the quality of public education may not be a function of wealth, other than the wealth of the state as a whole." Under such a principle, the children of a district are excessively advantaged if that district has more taxable property per pupil than the average amount of taxable property per pupil considering the State as a whole. By contrast, the children of a district are disadvantaged if that district has less taxable property per pupil than the state average. The majority attempts to disparage such a definition of the disadvantaged class as the product of an "artificially defined level" of district wealth. But such is clearly not the case, for this is the definition unmistakably dictated by the constitutional principle for which appellees have argued throughout the course of this litigation. And I do not believe that a clearer definition of either the disadvantaged class of Texas school children or the allegedly unconstitutional discrimination suffered by the members of that class under the present Texas financing scheme could be asked for, much less needed. Whether this discrimination, against the school children of property poor districts, inherent in the Texas financing scheme is violative of the Equal Protection Clause is the question to which we must now turn. . . .

. . .

To begin, I must once more voice my disagreement with the Court's rigidified approach to equal protection analysis. The Court apparently seeks to establish today that equal protection cases fall into one of two neat categories which dictate the appropriate standard of review—strict scrutiny or mere rationality. But this Court's decisions in the field of equal protection defy such easy categorization. A principled reading of what this Court has done reveals that it has applied a spectrum of standards in reviewing discrimination allegedly violative of the Equal Protection Clause.

This spectrum clearly comprehends variations in the degree of care with which the Court will scrutinize particular classifications, depending, I believe, on the constitutional and societal importance of the interest adversely affected and the recognized invidiousness of the basis upon which the particular classification is drawn. I find in fact that many of the Court's recent decisions embody the very sort of reasoned approach to equal protection analysis for which I previously argued—that is, an approach in which "concentration [is] placed upon the character of the classification in question, the relative importance to the individuals in the class discriminated against of the governmental benefits they do not receive, and the asserted state interests in support of the classification."

I therefore cannot accept the majority's labored efforts to demonstrate that fundamental interests, which call for strict scrutiny of the challenged classification, encompass only established rights which we are somehow bound to recognize from the text of the Constitution itself. To be sure, some interests which the Court has deemed to be fundamental for purposes of equal protection analysis are themselves constitutionally protected rights... But it will not do to suggest that the "answer" to whether an interest is fundamental for purposes of equal protection analysis is *always* determined by whether that interest "is a right ... explicitly or implicitly guaranteed by the Constitution.". . .

.   .   .

The majority is, of course, correct when it suggests that the process of determining which interests are fundamental is a difficult one. But I do not think the problem is insurmountable. And I certainly do not accept the view that the process need necessarily degenerate into an unprincipled, subjective "picking-and-choosing" between various interests or that it must involve this Court in creating "substantive constitutional rights in the name of guaranteeing equal protection of the laws." Although not all fundamental interests are constitutionally guaranteed, the determination of which interests are fundamental should be firmly rooted in the text of the Constitution. The task in every case should be to determine the extent to which constitutionally guaranteed rights are dependent on interests not mentioned in the Constitution. As the nexus between the specific constitutional guarantee and the nonconstitutional interest draws closer, the nonconstitutional interest becomes more fundamental and the degree of judicial scrutiny applied when the interest is infringed on a discriminatory basis must be adjusted accordingly. . . .

.   .   .

In summary, it seems to me inescapably clear that this Court has consistently adjusted the care with which it will review state discrimination in light of the constitutional significance of the interests affected and the invidiousness of the particular classification. In the context of economic interests, we find that discriminatory state action is almost always sustained for such interests are generally far removed from constitutional guarantees. Moreover, "[t]he extremes to which the Court has gone in dreaming up rational bases for state regulation in that area may in many instances be ascribed to a healthy revulsion from the Court's earlier excesses in using the Constitution to protect interests that have more than enough power to protect themselves in the legislative halls." But the situation differs markedly when discrimination against important individual interests with constitutional implications and against particularly disadvantaged or powerless classes is involved. The majority suggests, however, that a variable standard of review would give this Court the appearance of a "super-legislature." I cannot agree. Such an approach seems to me a part of the guarantee of our Constitution and of the historic experiences with oppression of and discrimination against discrete, powerless minorities which underlie that Document. In truth, the Court itself will be open to the criticism raised by the majority so long as it continues on its present course of effectively selecting in private which cases will be afforded special consideration without acknowledging the true basis of its action. . . Such obfuscated action may be appropriate to a political body such as a legislature, but it is not appropriate to this Court. Open debate of the bases for the Court's action is essential to the rationality and consistency of our decisionmaking process. Only in this way can we avoid the label of legislature and ensure the integrity of the judicial process.

Nevertheless, the majority today attempts to force this case into the same category for purposes of equal protection analysis as decisions involving discrimination affecting commercial interests. By so doing, the majority singles this case out for analytic treatment at odds with what seems to me to be the clear trend of recent decisions in this Court, and thereby ignores the constitutional importance of the interest at stake and the invidiousness of the particular classification, factors that call for far more than the lenient scrutiny of the Texas financing scheme which the majority pursues. Yet if the discrimination inherent in the Texas scheme is scrutinized with the care demanded by the interest and classification present in this case, the unconstitutionality of that scheme is unmistakable. . . .

.   .   .

Education directly affects the ability of a child to exercise his First Amendment interests both as a source and as a receiver of information and ideas, whatever interests he may pursue in life. . . The opportunity for formal education may not necessarily be the essential determinant of an individual's ability to enjoy throughout his life the rights of free speech and association guaranteed to him by the First Amendment. But such an opportunity may enhance the individual's enjoyment of those rights, not only during but also following school attendance. Thus, in the final analysis, "the pivotal position of education to success in American society and its essential role in opening up to the individual the central experiences of our culture lend it an importance that is undeniable.". . .

.   .   .

Education serves the essential function of instilling in our young an understanding of and appreciation for the principles and operation of our governmental processes. Education may instill the interest and provide the tools necessary for political discourse and debate. Indeed, it has frequently been suggested that education is the dominant factor affecting political consciousness and participation. . . But of most immediate and direct concern must be the demonstrated effect of education on the exercise of the franchise by the electorate. The right to vote in federal elections is conferred by Art I, § 2, and the Seventeenth Amendment of the Constitution, and access to the state franchise has been afforded special protection because it is "preservative of other basic civil and political rights." Data from the Presidential Election of 1968 clearly demonstrates a direct relationship between participation in the electoral process and level of educational attainment. . . .

.   .   .

While ultimately disputing little of this, the majority seeks refuge in the fact that the Court has "never presumed to possess either the ability or the authority to guarantee to the citizenry the most *effective* speech or the most *informed* electoral choice." This serves only to blur what is in fact at stake. With due respect, the issue is neither provision of the most *effective* speech nor of the most *informed* vote. Appellees do not now seek the best education Texas might provide. They do seek, however, an end to state discrimination resulting from the unequal distribution of taxable district property wealth that directly impairs the ability of some districts to provide the same educational opportunity that other districts can provide with the same or even substantially less tax effort. The issue is, in other words, one of discrimination that affects the quality of the education which Texas has chosen to provide its children; and, the precise question here is what importance should attach to education for purposes of equal protection analysis of that discrimination... The factors just considered, including the relationship between education and the social and political interests enshrined within the Constitution, compel us to recognize the fundamentality of education and to scrutinize with appropriate care the bases for state discrimination affecting equality of educational opportunity in Texas' school districts—a conclusion which is only strengthened when we consider the character of the classification in this case. . . .

.　　.　　.

[I]t seems to me that discrimination on the basis of group wealth in this case likewise calls for careful judicial scrutiny. First, it must be recognized that while local district wealth may serve other interests, it bears no relationship whatsoever to the interest of Texas school children in the educational opportunity afforded them by the State of Texas. Given the importance of that interest, we must be particularly sensitive to the invidious characteristics of any form of discrimination that is not clearly intended to serve it, as opposed to some other distinct state interest. Discrimination on the basis of group wealth may not, to be sure, reflect the social stigma frequently attached to personal property. Nevertheless, insofar as group wealth discrimination involves wealth over which the disadvantaged individual has no significant control, it represents in fact a more serious basis of discrimination than does personal wealth. For such discrimination is no reflection of the individual's characteristics or his abilities. And thus—particularly in the context of a disadvantaged class composed of children—we have previously treated discrimination on a

221

basis which the individual cannot control as constitutionally disfavored. . . .

      ·   ·   ·

Nor can we ignore the extent to which, in contrast to our prior decisions, the State is responsible for the wealth discrimination in this instance. . . [P]rior cases have dealt with discrimination on the basis of indigency which was attributable to the operation of the private sector. But we have no such simple de facto wealth discrimination here. The means for financing public education in Texas are selected and specified by the State. It is the State that has created local school districts, and tied educational funding to the local property tax and thereby to local district wealth. At the same time, governmentally imposed land use controls have undoubtedly encouraged and rigidified natural trends in the allocation of particular areas for residential or commercial use, and thus determined each district's amount of taxable property wealth. In short, this case, in contrast to the Court's previous wealth discrimination decisions, can only be seen as "unusual in the extent to which governmental action *is* the cause of the wealth classifications."

In the final analysis, then, the invidious characteristics of the group wealth classification present in this case merely serves to emphasize the need for careful judicial scrutiny of the State's justifications for the resulting inter-district discrimination in the educational opportunity afforded to the school children of Texas. . . .

      ·   ·   ·

Whatever the differences, if any, in . . . descriptions of the character of the state interest necessary to sustain such discrimination, basic to each is, I believe, a concern with the legitimacy and the reality of the asserted state interests. Thus, when interests of constitutional importance are at stake, the Court does not stand ready to credit the State's classification with any conceivable legitimate purpose, but demands a clear showing that there are legitimate state interests which the classification was in fact intended to serve. Beyond the question of the adequacy of the state's purpose for the classification, the Court traditionally has become increasingly sensitive to the means by which a State chooses to act as its action affects more directly interests of constitutional significance. Thus, by now, "less restrictive alternatives" analysis is firmly established in equal protection jurisprudence. It seems to me that the range of choice we are willing to accord the State in selecting the means by which it will act and the care with which we scrutinize the effectiveness of the means which the State selects also must reflect the constitutional importance of the interest affected and the invidiousness of the particular classification. Here both the nature of the interest and the classification dictate close judicial scrutiny of the purposes which Texas seeks to serve with its present educational financing scheme and of the means it has selected to serve that purpose.

The only justification offered by appellants to sustain the discrimination in educational opportunity caused by the Texas financing scheme is local educational control. Presented with this justification, the District Court concluded that "[n]ot only are defendants unable to demonstrate compelling state interests for their classification based on wealth, they fail even to establish a reasonable basis for these classifications." I must agree with this conclusion. . . .

*   *   *

In my judgment, any substantial degree of scrutiny of the operation of the Texas financing scheme reveals that the State has selected means wholly inappropriate to secure its purported interest in assuring its school districts local fiscal control. At the same time, appellees have pointed out a variety of alternative financing schemes which may serve the State's purported interest in local control as well, if not better, than the present scheme without the current impairment of the educational opportunity of vast numbers of Texas school children. I see no need, however, to explore the practical or constitutional merits of those suggested alternatives at this time, for whatever their positive or negative features, experience with the present financing scheme impugns any suggestion that it constitutes a serious effort to provide local fiscal control. If, for the sake of local education control, this Court is to sustain interdistrict discrimination in the educational opportunity afforded Texas school children, it should require that the State present something more than the mere sham now before us. . . .

*   *   *

In conclusion it is essential to recognize that an end to the wide variations in taxable district property wealth inherent in the Texas financing scheme would entail none of the untoward consequences suggested by the Court or by the appellants.

County of Washington v. Gunther

452 U.S. 161, 68 L Ed 2d 751, 101 S Ct 2242 (1981)

Four women guards in the Washington County, Oregon, jail brought suit for back pay alleging that they were paid substantially lower wages than their male counterparts because of sex discrimination as proscribed by Title VII of the Civil Rights Act and by the Equal Pay Act. The district court held that the women's jobs were not substantially equal to those of the male guards, that they were not, therefore, entitled to equal pay, and that there was insufficient proof of sex discrimination. The court of appeals reversed and certiorari was granted.

. . .

Justice Brennan delivered the opinion of the Court.

. . .

We emphasize at the outset the narrowness of the question before us in this case. Respondents' claim is not based on the controversial concept of "comparable worth," under which plaintiffs might claim increased compensation on the basis of a comparison of the intrinsic worth or difficulty of their job with that of other jobs in the same organization or community. Rather, respondents seek to prove, by direct evidence, that their wages were depressed because of intentional sex discrimination, consisting of setting the wage scale for female guards, but not for male guards, at a level lower than its own survey of outside markets and the worth of the jobs warranted. . . .

. . .

Title VII makes it an unlawful employment practice for an employer "to discriminate against any individual with respect to his compensation, terms, conditions, or privileges of employment, because of such individual's . . . sex." The Bennett Amendment to Title VII, however, provides:
"It shall not be an unlawful employment practice under this subchapter for any employer to differentiate upon the basis of sex

in determining the amount of the wages or compensation paid or
to be paid to employees of such employer if such differentiation is
authorized by the provisions of [the Equal Pay Act]."
To discover what practices are exempted from Title VII's prohibitions by
the Bennett Amendment, we must turn to ... the Equal Pay Act...

"No employer having employees subject to any provisions of
this section shall discriminate, within any establishment in which
such employees are employed, between employees on the basis of
sex by paying wages to employees in such establishment at a rate
less than the rate at which he pays wages to employees of the
opposite sex in such establishment for equal work on jobs the
performance of which requires equal skill, effort, and responsibility, and which are performed under similar working conditions,
except where such payment is made pursuant to (i) a seniority
system; (ii) a merit system; (iii) a system which measures earnings
by quantity or quality of production; or (iv) a differential based on
any other factor other than sex.". . .

. . .

Petitioner argues that the purpose of the Bennett Amendment was to
restrict Title VII sex-based wage discrimination claims to those that could
also be brought under the Equal Pay Act, and thus that claims not arising
from "equal work" are precluded. Respondents, in contrast, argue that the
Bennett Amendment was designed merely to incorporate the four affirmative defenses of the Equal Pay Act into Title VII for sex-based wage
discrimination claims. Respondents thus contend that claims for sex-based
wage discrimination can be brought under Title VII even though no
member of the opposite sex holds an equal but higher-paying job,
provided that the challenged wage rate is not based on seniority, merit,
quantity or quality of production, or "any other factor other than sex."
The Court of Appeals found respondents' interpretation the "more
persuasive." While recognizing that the language and legislative history of
the provision are not unambiguous, we conclude that the Court of Appeals
was correct. . . .

. . .

The Equal Pay Act is divided into two parts: a definition of the
violation, followed by four affirmative defenses. The first part can hardly
be said to "authorize" anything at all: it is purely prohibitory. The second

part, however, in essence "authorizes" employers to differentiate in pay on the basis of seniority, merit, quantity or quality of production, or any other factor other than sex, even though such differentiation might otherwise violate the Act. . . .

. . .

Petitioner argues that this construction of the Bennett Amendment would render it superfluous. Petitioner claims that the first three affirmative defenses are simply redundant of the provisions elsewhere in § 703(h) of Title VII that already exempt bona fide seniority and merit systems and systems measuring earnings by quantity or quality of production, and that the fourth defense—"any other factor other than sex"—is implicit in Title VII's general prohibition of sex-based discrimination.

We cannot agree. The Bennett Amendment was offered as a "technical amendment" designed to resolve any potential conflicts between Title VII and the Equal Pay Act. Thus, with respect to the first three defenses, the Bennett Amendment has the effect of guaranteeing that courts and administrative agencies adopt a consistent interpretation of like provisions in both statutes. Otherwise, they might develop inconsistent bodies of case law interpreting two sets of nearly identical language.

More importantly, incorporation of the fourth affirmative defense could have significant consequences for Title VII litigation. Title VII's prohibition of discriminatory employment practices was intended to be broadly inclusive, proscribing "not only overt discrimination but also practices that are fair in form, but discriminatory in operation." The structure of Title VII litigation, including presumptions, burdens of proof, and defenses, has been designed to reflect this approach. The fourth affirmative defense of the Equal Pay Act, however, was designed differently, to confine the application of the Act to wage differentials attributable to sex discrimination. Equal Pay Act litigation, therefore, has been structured to permit employers to defend against charges of discrimination where their pay differentials are based on a bona fide use of "other factors other than sex." Under the Equal Pay Act, the courts and administrative agencies are not permitted "to substitute their judgment for the judgment of the employer . . . who [has] established and employed a bona fide job rating system," so long as it does not discriminate on the basis of sex. . . .

226

. . .

We therefore conclude that only differentials attributable to the four affirmative defenses of the Equal Pay Act are "authorized" by that Act within the meaning of § 703(h) of Title VII. . . .

. . .

Our interpretation of the Bennett Amendment draws additional support from the remedial purposes of Title VII and the Equal Pay Act. . . As Congress itself has indicated, a "broad approach" to the definition of equal employment opportunity is essential to overcoming and undoing the effect of discrimination. We must therefore avoid interpretations of Title VII that deprive victims of discrimination of a remedy, without clear congressional mandate.

Under petitioner's reading of the Bennett Amendment, only those sex-based wage discrimination claims that satisfy the "equal work" standard of the Equal Pay Act could be brought under Title VII. In practical terms, this means that a woman who is discriminatorily underpaid could obtain no relief—no matter how egregious the discrimination might be—unless her employer also employed a man in an equal job in the same establishment, at a higher rate of pay. Thus, if an employer hired a woman for a unique position in the company and then admitted that her salary would have been higher had she been male, the woman would be unable to obtain legal redress under petitioner's interpretation. Similarly, if an employer used a transparently sex-biased system for wage determination, women holding jobs not equal to those held by men would be denied the right to prove that the system is a pretext for discrimination. Moreover, to cite an example arising from a recent case, if the employer required its female workers to pay more into its pension program than male workers were required to pay, the only women who could bring a Title VII action under petitioner's interpretation would be those who could establish that a man performed equal work: a female auditor thus might have a cause of action while a female secretary might not. Congress surely did not intend the Bennett Amendment to insulate such blatantly discriminatory practices from judicial redress under Title VII.

Moreover, petitioner's interpretation would have other far-reaching consequences. Since it rests on the proposition that any wage differentials not prohibited by the Equal Pay Act are "authorized" by it, petitioner's interpretation would lead to the conclusion that discriminatory compensation by employers not covered by the Fair Labor Standards Act is "authorized"—since not prohibited—by the Equal Pay Act. Thus it would deny Title VII protection against sex-based wage discrimination by those employers not subject to the Fair Labor Standards Act but covered by Title VII. . . .

. . .

"In forbidding employers to discriminate against individuals because of their sex, Congress intended to strike at the *entire spectrum* of disparate treatment of men and women resulting from sex stereotypes." (Emphasis added.) We must therefore reject petitioner's interpretation of the Bennett Amendment.

Petitioner argues strenuously that the approach of the Court of Appeals places "the pay structure of virtually every employer and the entire economy . . . at risk and subject to scrutiny by the federal courts." It raises the spectre that "Title VII plaintiffs could draw any type of comparison imaginable concerning job duties and pay between any job predominantly performed by women and any job predominantly performed by men." But whatever the merit of petitioner's arguments in other contexts, they are inapplicable here, for claims based on the type of job comparisons petitioner describes are manifestly different from respondents' claim. Respondents contend that the County of Washington evaluated the worth of their jobs; that the county determined that they should be paid approximately 95% as much as the male correctional officers; that it paid them only about 70% as much, while paying the male officers the full evaluated worth of their jobs; and that the failure of the county to pay respondents the full evaluated worth of their jobs can be proven to be attributable to intentional sex discrimination. Thus, respondents' suit does not require a court to make its own subjective assessment of the value of the male and female guard jobs, or to attempt by statistical technique or other method to quantify the effect of sex discrimination on the wage rates. . . .

. . .

The judgment of the Court of Appeals is therefore affirmed.

. . .

Justice Rehnquist, with whom the Chief Justice, Justice Stewart, and Justice Powell join, dissenting.

The Court today holds a plaintiff may state a claim of sex-based wage discrimination under Title VII without even establishing that she has performed "equal or substantially equal work" to that of males as defined in the Equal Pay Act. Because I believe that the legislative history of both the Equal Pay Act and Title VII clearly establish that there can be no Title VII claim of sex-based wage discrimination without proof of "equal work," I dissent. . . .

. . .

Petitioners argue that Congress in adopting the Equal Pay Act of 1963 specifically addressed the problem of sex-based wage discrimination and determined that there should be a remedy for claims of unequal pay for equal work, but not for "comparable" work. Petitioners further observe that nothing in the legislative history of Title VII, enacted just one year later in 1964, reveals an intent to overrule that determination. . . .

. . .

In rejecting that argument, the Court ignores traditional canons of statutory construction and relevant legislative history. Although I had thought it well settled that the legislative history of a statute is a useful guide to the intent of Congress, the Court today claims that the legislative history "has no bearing on the meaning of the Act, does not provide a solution to our present problem," and is simply of "no weight." Instead, the Court rests its decision on its unshakable belief that any other result would be unsound public policy. It insists that there simply *must* be a remedy for wage discrimination *beyond* that provided in the Equal Pay Act. The Court does not explain *why* that must be so, nor does it explain *what* that remedy might be. And, of course, the Court cannot explain why it and not Congress is charged with determining what is and what is not sound public policy. . . .

. . .

It has long been the rule that when a legislature enacts a statute to protect a class of persons, the burden is on the plaintiff to show statutory coverage, not on the defendant to show that there is a "clear congressional mandate" for *excluding* the plaintiff from coverage. Such a departure from traditional rules is particularly unwarranted in this case, where the doctrine of in pari materia suggests that all claims of sex-based wage discrimination are governed by the substantive standards of the previously enacted and more specific legislation, the Equal Pay Act. . . .

. . .

In the end, however, the flaw with today's decision is not so much that it is so narrowly written as to be virtually meaningless, but rather that its legal analysis is wrong. The Court is obviously more interested in the consequences of its decision than in discerning the intention of Congress. In reaching its desired result, the Court conveniently and persistently ignores relevant legislative history and instead relies wholly on what it believes Congress *should* have enacted. . . .

. . .

In adopting the "equal pay for equal work" formula, Congress carefully considered and ultimately rejected the "equal pay for comparable worth" standard advanced by respondents and several amici. As the legislative history of the Equal Pay Act amply demonstrates, Congress realized that the adoption of the comparable worth doctrine would ignore the economic realities of supply and demand and would involve both governmental agencies and courts in the impossible task of ascertaining the worth of comparable work, an area in which they have little expertise. . . .

. . .

The congressional debate on that legislation leaves no doubt that Congress clearly rejected the entire notion of "comparable worth." For example, Representative Goodell, a cosponsor of the Act, stressed the significance of the change from "comparable work" to "equal work."

"I think it is important that we have a clear legislative history at this point. *Last year when the House changed the word 'comparable' to 'equal' the intention was to narrow the whole concept.* We went from 'comparable' to 'equal' meaning that the jobs involved should be virtually identical, that is that they would be very much alike or closely related to each other.

"We do not expect the Labor Department to go into an establishment and attempt to rate jobs that are not equal. We do not want to hear the Department say, 'well, they amount to the same thing,' and evaluate them so that they come up to the same skill or point. We expect this to apply only to jobs that are substantially identical or equal.". . . .

. . .

Thus, the legislative history of the Equal Pay Act clearly reveals that Congress was unwilling to give either the Federal Government or the courts broad authority to determine comparable wage rates. Congress recognized that the adoption of such a theory would ignore economic realities and would result in major restructuring of the American economy. Instead, Congress concluded that governmental intervention to equalize wage differentials was to be undertaken only within one circumstance; when men's and women's jobs were identical or nearly so, hence unarguably of equal worth. . . .

. . .

The question is whether Congress intended to completely turn its back on the "equal work" standard enacted in the Equal Pay Act of 1963 when it adopted Title VII only one year later.

The Court answers that question in the affirmative, concluding that Title VII must be read more broadly than the Equal Pay Act. In so holding, the majority wholly ignores this Court's repeated adherence to the doctrine of in pari materia, namely, that "where there is no clear intention otherwise, a specific statute will not be controlled or nullified by a general one, regardless of the priority of enactment.". . .

. . .

The Equal Pay Act is the more specific piece of legislation, dealing solely with sex-based wage discrimination, and was the product of exhaustive congressional study. Title VII, by contrast, is a general antidiscrimination provision, passed with virtually no consideration of the specific problem of sex-based wage discrimination. . . Most significantly, there is absolutely nothing in the legislative history of Title VII which reveals an intent by Congress to repeal by implication the provisions of the Equal Pay Act. Quite the contrary, what little legislative history there is on the subject . . . indicates that Congress intended to incorporate the substantive standards of the Equal Pay Act into Title VII so that sex-based wage discrimination claims would be governed by equal work standard of the Equal Pay Act and by that standard alone. . . .

. . .

If plaintiffs can proceed under Title VII without showing that they satisfy the "equal work" criterion of the Equal Pay Act, one would expect all plaintiffs to file suit under the "broader" Title VII standard. Such a result would, for all practical purposes, constitute an implied repeal of the equal work standard of the Equal Pay Act and render that Act a nullity. This was precisely the result Congress sought to avert when it adopted the Bennett Amendment, and the result the Court today embraces. . . .

. . .

The Court blithely ignores all of this legislative history and chooses to interpret the Bennett Amendment as incorporating only the Equal Pay Act's four affirmative defenses, and not the equal work requirement. That argument does not survive scrutiny. In the first place, the language of the amendment draws no distinction between the Equal Pay Act's standard for liability—equal pay for equal work—and the Act's defenses. Nor does any Senator or Congressman even come close to suggesting that the Amendment incorporates the Equal Pay Act's affirmative defenses into Title VII, but not the equal work standard itself. Quite the contrary, the concern was that Title VII would render the Equal Pay Act a nullity. It is only too obvious that reading just the four affirmative defenses of the Equal Pay Act into Title VII does not protect the careful draftsmanship of the Equal Pay Act. . . .

. . .

In sum, Title VII and the Equal Pay Act, read together, provide a balanced approach to resolving sex-based wage discrimination claims. Title VII guarantees that qualified female employees will have access to all jobs, and the Equal Pay Act assures that men and women performing the same work will be paid equally. Congress intended to remedy wage discrimination through the Equal Pay Act standards, whether suit is brought under that statute or under Title VII. What emerges is that Title VII would have been construed in pari materia even without the Bennett Amendment, and that the Amendment serves simply to insure that the equal work standard would be the standard by which all wage compensation claims would be judged. . . .

. . .

[T]he Court contends that a separate Title VII remedy is necessary to remedy the situation where an employer admits to a female worker, hired for a unique position, that her compensation would have been higher had she been male. Stated differently, the Court insists that an employer could isolate a predominantly female job category and arbitrarily cut its wages because no men currently perform equal or substantially equal work. But a Title VII remedy is unnecessary in these cases because an Equal Pay Act remedy is available. Under the Equal Pay Act, it is not necessary that every Equal Pay Act violation be established through proof that members of the opposite sex are *currently* performing equal work for greater pay. However unlikely such an admission might be in the bullpen of litigation, an employer's statement that "if my female employees performing a particular job were males, I would pay them more simply because they are males" would be admissible in a suit under the Act. Overt discrimination does not go unremedied by the Equal Pay Act. . . .

. . .

There is of course a situation in which petitioners' position *would* deny women a remedy for claims of sex-based wage discrimination. A remedy would not be available where a lower paying job held primarily by women is "comparable," but not substantially equal to, a higher paying job performed by men. That is, plaintiffs would be foreclosed from showing that they received unequal pay for work of "comparable worth" or that dissimilar jobs are of "equal worth." The short, and best, answer to that contention is that Congress in 1963 explicitly chose not to provide a remedy in such cases. . . .

. . .

Even though today's opinion reaches what I believe to be the wrong result, its narrow holding is perhaps its saving feature. The opinion does not endorse the so-called "comparable worth" theory: though the Court does not indicate how a plaintiff might establish a prima facie case under Title VII, the Court does suggest that allegations of unequal pay for unequal, but comparable, work will not state a claim on which relief may be granted. The Court, for example, repeatedly emphasizes that this is not a case where plaintiffs ask the court to compare the value of dissimilar jobs or to quantify the effect of sex discrimination on wage rates. . . .

. . .

Because there are no logical underpinnings to the Court's opinion, all we may conclude is that even absent a showing of equal work, there is a cause of action under Title VII where there is direct evidence that an employer has *intentionally* depressed a woman's salary because she is a woman. The decision today does not approve a cause of action based on a *comparison* of the wage rates of dissimilar jobs.

For the foregoing reasons, however, I believe that even that narrow holding cannot be supported by the legislative history of the Equal Pay Act and Title VII. This is simply a case where the Court has superimposed upon Title VII a "gloss of its own choosing."

IV

Capital Punishment

Now, therefore, you are hereby ordered, commanded and required to execute the said sentence upon him, . . . upon some day within the week commencing on Monday, the 24th day of June, in the year of our Lord one thousand eight hundred and eighty-nine, and within the walls of Auburn state prison, or within the yard or enclosure adjoining thereto, by then and there causing to pass through the body of him, . . . a current of electricity of sufficient intensity to cause death, and that the application of such current of electricity be continued until he be dead.[1]

This order from a New York court to a prison warden could be duplicated in every legal system; virtually every society has prescribed death as a punishment for one or another class of crimes. The Code of Hammurabi (fl. 1792-1750 B.C.) and the Laws of Alfred (c. 890 A.D.) are in agreement with the twenty-first chapter of Exodus in the Bible: "He that smiteth a man, so that he shall die, shall surely be put to death." Despite the near universality of capital punishment, a policymaker is confronted with a wide range of moral, political, legal, and penological issues when deciding whether or when to use the death penalty. None of these issues have clear answers. Crimes are offenses against society, and society must mete out punishment after it defines those crimes. Some crimes are minor and draw only fines; others are so disruptive of the peace and good order of society that lawmakers seriously consider death as the only appropriate penalty.

In Great Britain, the use of capital punishment expanded regularly between the sixteenth and eighteenth centuries. At the beginning of the sixteenth century, only eight crimes were heinous enough to warrant death: treason, petty treason, murder, larceny, robbery, burglary, rape, and arson. By the beginning of the seventeenth century the number had increased to 50, and by 1800, more than 200 capital offenses had been defined in Great Britain. Beginning in 1800, Parliament slowly reduced the number of capital offenses, and finally abolished the death penalty in 1970.

The American colonies never established as many capital crimes as did the mother country. The earliest known listing of crimes, "The Capital Laws of New-England," published in 1636, shows the theocratic origins of the Massachusetts Bay Colony. It declares death as a penalty for idolatry, witchcraft, blasphemy, murder, assault in anger, sodomy, buggery, adultery, statutory rape, rape, man stealing, perjury in a capital case, and rebellion. By the time of Independence, the average colony had identified 12 capital offenses, and had secularized the listing. Since then, the number of capital crimes has varied from generation to generation and from state to state.

Most American debate on capital punishment has contained four interconnected lines of argument. The first strand is based on a proportionality theme: Which crimes are so offensive to society that death is an appropriate penalty? The second or moral argument stems from the Biblical assertion that "venegeance is mine saith the Lord; I shall repay." This has been secularized by the assertion that no person has the right to take the life of another even when acting as a servant of the state. The third strand questions the effectiveness of the death penalty as a means of detering others from committing the same sort of crime. And finally, the constitutional strand argues whether or not capital punishment is "cruel and unusual" and therefore forbidden by the Eighth Amendment.

The proportionality debate is reflected in various legislative actions that increase or reduce the number and type of offenses subject to the penalty. This lawmaking activity to a real degree reflects societal judgments about the seriousness of a particular crime. Hence, idolatry or blasphemy was a capital crime for the Massachusetts Puritan, but assassination of a president was not included in the federal catalog of capital offenses until after 1963. In *Coker* v. *Georgia* (p. 291), this basic proportionality debate took place within the Court rather than in a legislative chamber.

In addition to changes in the number of capital crimes, legislators have tried to meet the problem of proportionality by basing the degree of the crime on the intent and state of mind of the accused. For example, first degree murder, defined as involving premeditation with a deliberate intent to kill, is usually a capital offense, while lesser degrees involving the spontaneous taking of life are not. Efforts to determine the state of mind of an accused person are fraught with uncertainty, so legislators have developed a second approach to the issue: the jury is supposed to be a reflection of, and spokesman for, society in criminal cases. To avoid the inherent problems in classification, some states have vested the jury with the power to determine not only guilt or innocence, but also the penalty. The hope is that society will speak through the jury and that more severe punishments will be meted out for crimes that society believes are more serious. A practical reason also exists for the adoption of these jury discretion statutes. Juries often avoided the death penalty verdict by refusing to convict or by convicting on a non-capital offense in defiance of the evidence and of the judge's instructions (jury nullification). Leaving the decision and the penalty to the jury avoids this problem. These jury discretion statutes have been upheld by the Supreme Court in a number of instances, most recently in *McGautha* v. *California,* 402 U.S. 183 (1971), which was decided just a year before the Court's decisions calling the whole death penalty into question. However, some of the decisions in this chapter are specifically aimed at limiting the types of discretion a jury may exercise. The cases also show that some justices even seem to doubt if the jury is an appropriate voice of society.

Underlying the proportionality theme is the often unstated motive of revenge or retribution. Society's outrage at some crimes is presumed to be so great that only death will assuage it, but legislators and juries are reluctant to admit these motives. Even so, it seems perfectly consistent with the theory that crimes are committed against society as a whole, to take revenge into account. One Tennessee legislator expressed this idea when he objected to the injection method of execution because it was "too easy."

Opponents of capital punishment who base their argument on moral or ethical reasons begin with the Old Testament and move on in one of two directions. Some argue about the incongruity of the state using a form of punishment that has the same result as the crime for which the person was convicted. That which is a crime when committed by a private person also should be a crime when committed by the state; to hold otherwise is to render the law nothing more than an expression of force rather than of justice. The second approach condemns the use of so final a punishment when the decision to use it is based on human fallibility. In many instances, new evidence proving innocence is unearthed long after conviction; had the death penalty been imposed, correction of the mistake would have been impossible. Interestingly enough, this moral line of argument has not been particularly effective in legislatures when it is used by itself; it usually has been joined with one of the other arguments.

The effectiveness or deterrence issue appears to be the dominant one for the legislative policymakers. Does the existence and use of the death penalty keep others from committing similar crimes? Proponents argue that a criminal will consider the possible consequences of getting caught before committing a crime. Therefore, the existence of the death penalty will induce second thoughts. Opponents counter by noting that many crimes, even capital ones, are committed impulsively. The statistical evidence, much of which is collected in Justice Thurgood Marshall's concurring opinion in *Furman* v. *Georgia* (p. 242), is inconclusive. At most, the data do not show that the presence of the capital sanction deters commission of a crime. However, the converse has not been convincingly proven either. Without indulging in methodological niceties, it is important to observe that holding factors other than the presence or absence of the death penalty constant across several jurisdictions is nearly impossible. It is unlikely that statisticians will be able to establish a legitimate case one way or the other.

A second branch of the deterrence argument holds that the certainty and swiftness of punishment is more of a deterrent than is an extreme penalty. The observed criminal tendency is to assume that it is the other person who will get caught. Also undercutting the determent effects of the death penalty is the belief in acquittal, the pervasive nature of plea bargaining, the delays while appeals are taken, and the substitution by the jury of a lesser penalty. Two experienced judges have viewed differently the effect of frequency and certainty of punishment. According to Justice Byron White: "But common sense and experience tell us that seldom-enforced laws become ineffective measures for controlling human conduct and that the death penalty, unless imposed with sufficient frequency, will make little contribution to deterring those crimes for which it may be exacted." [2] On the other hand, Sir Edward Coke wrote: "And true it is, that we have found by wofull experience, that it is not frequent and often punishment that doth prevent like offenses, for the frequency of the punishment makes it so familiar as it is not feared." [3] In sum, the deterrence argument is inconclusive, and it is persuasive only to the extent that one accepts one or the other set of these mutually exclusive premises.

The constitutional argument, based on the cruel and unusual punishment clause of the Eighth Amendment, is of more recent vintage, as are most of the judicial challenges to the death penalty. Most of these arguments are contained in the decisions excerpted in this chapter, but a few preliminary observations are necessary. No clear catalog exists of the punishments considered cruel and unusual in 1791, although it is generally agreed that the term included punishments like burning at the stake, drawing and quartering, and earcropping of thieves. It also generally is agreed that capital punishment was not considered cruel and unusual punishment in 1791. If it had been, there would have been no references to it in the Fifth Amendment ("No person shall be held to answer for a capital, or otherwise infamous crime...."). There is further agreement that any penalty involves some degree of cruelty.

The Court's first two efforts to define the meaning of this clause as it relates to the death penalty were inconclusive. In both cases there was a challenge to the method of execution, not capital punishment itself, and the Court assumed the validity of the penalty in its analysis. In *Wilkerson* v. *Utah,* 99 U.S. 130 (1879), the justices approved the use of a firing squad in Utah Territory even though the statute was silent on the manner of execution. After examining practices under military law in the United States and other countries, Justice Nathan Clifford concluded that shooting was not an unusual means of inflicting death. Nor was it cruel, according to the Court, because it did not involve torture or "unnecessary cruelty." On the other hand, *Ex parte Kemmler,* 136 U.S. 436 (1890), presented a clearly unusual method of execution—electrocution. New York had just adopted this means of execution, and was the first state to do so. Chief Justice Melville W. Fuller passed rapidly over the "unusual" part of the clause by admitting that electrocution was unusual only because it was new. He asserted that courts must defer to legislative judgment in adapting to technological change unless cruelty also could be shown. Unusual punishments are not forbidden if the legislature has a legitimate motive for adopting them; in this instance, the lawmakers had testimony that the electric chair was more humane than was hanging as a method of execution. Cruelty was not present in this case because "punishments are cruel when they involve torture or a lingering death..." It means "something inhuman and barbarous, something more than the mere extinguishment of life."

After these two decisions, "unusual" came to connote a punishment so different as to be unacceptable to society at large, but a "cruel" punishment remained only hazily defined. Justice Stephen J. Field tried in a later case to define "cruel" when he said that punishments are cruel if "by their excessive length or severity, [they] are greatly disproportioned to the offenses charged." [4] A cruel punishment, then, is one that is more severe than the nature of the crime warrants. Field's suggestion that a requirement of proportionality between crime and punishment be applied was supplemented by an "evolutionary" definition in 1910. Justice Joseph McKenna for the Court observed that "the clause ... may be therefore progressive, and is not fastened to the obsolete, but may acquire meaning as public opinion becomes enlightened by a humane justice." [5] These proportionality and evolutionary definitions of "cruel" have led to the prevailing interpretation of the clause, which gives wide scope to the courts in making policy. According to this interpretation, the clause derives "its meaning from the evolving standards of decency that mark the progress of a maturing society." [6]

The cases in this chapter illuminate some of the problems inherent in standards such as the one just quoted. In *Furman,* the majority found that society had evolved to the point where capital punishment was undesirable either all of the time (Brennan and Marshall) or at least part of the time (Douglas, Stewart, and White). This finding was reached despite the fact that 39 states plus the District of Columbia had the death penalty, that Congress between 1961 and 1970 had added by lopsided votes three capital crimes to the federal criminal code, that public opinion polls showed a slight majority of the public in favor of the death penalty, and that juries had imposed the penalty in these cases. The issue here is not the rightness or wrongness of the majority position but rather how those "evolving standards of decency" are to be determined. It also is significant that in the wake of *Furman,* 35 states reenacted capital punishment statutes in an effort to retain the penalty within the somewhat obscure guidelines established by the Court. In 1976, the Court was confronted with these new statutes in *Gregg* v. *Georgia* (p. 267) and *Woodson* v. *North Carolina* (p. 281). In addition, California voters by referendum effectively overturned a state court decision abolishing the death penalty. These developments have left the Court in a state of disarray on the issue. The multiple opinions in the decisions reprinted in this chapter emphasize the present confusion and uncertainty in this area of the law; Justice White even suggests in *Lockett* v. *Ohio* (p. 300) that the Court has done an "about face" in its decisions since *Furman.*

One last word needs to be added about a facet of the death penalty not discussed in detail by the Court: There is an equal protection problem potentially present in these cases. The contention has been advanced that the poor, the friendless, the powerless, and the minorities have the penalty imposed on them more frequently than do other segments of the population, even for the commission of the same crimes. Some of the opinions in *Furman* hint at this problem in their references to "freakish," "wanton," "capricious," and "arbitrary" imposition of the penalty. The statistics are persuasive but not clear enough to command unqualified assent for this proposition. That may be why the Court chose to explore the capital punishment issue on the grounds of the Eighth Amendment rather than on the Fourteenth. It also may be that new death penalty statutes, such as the one in *Gregg,* provided for automatic state appellate review to ensure consistency to cut off the equal protection claim. However, it should not be assumed that equal protection can now be dismissed from consideration; it could easily be the next point of contention if total abolition on cruel and unusual punishment grounds cannot be accomplished.

These decisions emphasize the variety of means available to the justices when confronted with a swift, contrary response from legislatures. They can, as do Marshall and Brennan, hold the line, insist that they are right, and hope for the best. Or they can, as does the majority after the *Furman* decision, give a little on some parts of the issue *(Gregg)*, hold the line on the core of their position *(Coker, Woodson)*, and retreat behind the protection of procedural requirements *(Lockett)*. In these instances, the partial retreat may be the most successful strategy for the justices to follow. They have managed to void mandatory death penalty statutes and to confine the unfettered discretion of juries, but they may not be able to do more in the face of vigorous legislative opposition. Applying a constitutional standard that, by their own admission, is defined in terms of public attitudes, makes it difficult for the justices to ignore the rapid repassage of capital punishment statutes in so many states. In these decisions, the Justices used the strategy of claiming more than they expected to be able to hold and then retreating to what they wanted in the first place when an attack materialized.

NOTES

1. *Ex parte Kemmler,* 136 U.S. 436 (1890), at 441.
2. Justice Byron White concurring in *Furman* v. *Georgia.*
3. C. D. Bowen, *The Lion and the Throne* (Boston: Little, Brown & Co., 1956), p. 64.
4. *O'Neill* v. *Vermont,* 144 U.S. 323 (1892), dissenting at 340-341.
5. *Weems* v. *United States,* 217 U.S. 349 (1919), at 378.
6. *Trop* v. *Dulles,* 356 U.S. 86 (1958), at 100-101.

SELECTED BIBLIOGRAPHY

Bedau, Hugo A. *The Courts, the Constitution, and Capital Punishment.* Lexington, Mass.: D. C. Heath, 1977.
_____. *The Death Penalty in America.* New York: Doubleday Anchor, 1964, rev. ed., 1967.
_____. and Pierce, C. M., eds., *Capital Punishment in the United States.* New York: AMS Press, 1976.
Black, Charles L. Jr. *Capital Punishment: The Inevitability of Caprice and Mistake.* 2nd ed. New York: Norton, 1981.
Bowers, William J. *Executions in America.* Lexington, Mass.: D. C. Heath, 1974.
Erskine, Hazel. "The Polls: Capital Punishment," 34 *Public Opinion Quarterly* 290 (1970).
Murchison, Kenneth M. "Toward a Perspective on the Death Penalty Cases," 27 *Emory Law Journal* 469 (1978).
Packer, Herbert. "Making the Punishment Fit the Crime," 77 *Harvard Law Review* 1071 (1964).

Prettyman, Barrett Jr. *Death and the Supreme Court*. New York: Harcourt, Brace & World, 1961.

Sarat, Austin and Vidmar, Neil. "Public Opinion, the Death Penalty, and the Eighth Amendment: Testing the Marshall Hypothesis," 1976 *Wisconsin Law Review* 171 (1976).

Sellin, Thorstein. *The Death Penalty*. Philadelphia: American Law Institute, 1959.

Shipley, Maynard. "Does Capital Punishment Prevent Convictions?" 43 *American Law Review* 321 (1909).

Thomas, Charles W. "Eighth Amendment Challenges to the Death Penalty: The Relevance of Informed Public Opinion," 30 *Vanderbilt Law Review* 1005 (1977).

Vidmar, Neil and Ellsworth, Phoebe. "Public Opinion and the Death Penalty," 26 *Stanford Law Review* 1245 (1974).

Yunker, James A. "Is the Death Penalty a Deterrent to Homicide? Some Time-Series Evidence," 5 *Journal of Behavioral Economics* 45 (1976).

Furman v. Georgia

408 U.S. 238, 33 L Ed 2d 346, 92 S Ct 2726 (1972)

Each of the three petitioners was black, was convicted of a capital crime (murder in one instance, rape in the other two) after a trial by jury, and was sentenced to death by those juries which had the discretion to select that or some lesser sentence. State appellate courts upheld the death sentences and the Supreme Court issued a limited grant of certiorari.

·   ·   ·

Per Curiam.

·   ·   ·

Certiorari was granted limited to the following question: "Does the imposition and carrying out of the death penalty in [these cases] constitute cruel and unusual punishment in violation of the Eighth and Fourteenth Amendments? The Court holds that the imposition and carrying out of the death penalty in these cases constitutes cruel and unusual punishment in violation of the Eighth and Fourteenth Amendments. The judgment in each case is therefore reversed insofar as it leaves undisturbed the death sentence imposed, and the cases are remanded for further proceedings.

So ordered.

. . .

Mr. Justice Douglas, Mr. Justice Brennan, Mr. Justice Stewart, Mr. Justice White, and Mr. Justice Marshall have filed separate opinions in support of the judgments. The Chief Justice, Mr. Justice Blackmun, Mr. Justice Powell, and Mr. Justice Rehnquist have filed separate dissenting opinions.

. . .

Mr. Justice Douglas, concurring.

In these three cases the death penalty was imposed, one of them for murder, and two for rape. In each the determination of whether the penalty should be death or a lighter punishment was left by the State to the discretion of the judge or of the jury. In each of the three cases the trial was to a jury. They are here on petitions for certiorari which we granted limited to the question whether the imposition and execution of the death penalty constitutes "cruel and unusual punishments" within the meaning of the Eighth Amendment as applied to the States by the Fourteenth. I vote to vacate each judgment, believing that the exaction of the death penalty does violate the Eighth and Fourteenth Amendments. . . .

. . .

It has been assumed in our decisions that punishment by death is not cruel, unless the manner of execution can be said to be inhuman and barbarous. It is also said in our opinions that the proscription of cruel and unusual punishments "is not fastened to the obsolete but may acquire meaning as public opinion becomes enlightened by a humane justice." . . .

. . .

The generalities of a law inflicting capital punishment is one thing. What may be said of the validity of a law on the books and what may be done with the law in its application do or may lead to quite different conclusions.

It would seem to be incontestable that the death penalty inflicted on one defendant is "unusual" if it discriminates against him by reason of his race, religion, wealth, social position, or class, or if it is imposed under a procedure that gives room for the play of such prejudices. . . .

· · ·

The words "cruel and unusual" certainly include penalties that are barbaric. But the words, at least when read in light of the English proscription against selective and irregular use of penalties, suggest that it is "cruel and unusual" to apply the death penalty—or any other penalty—selectively to minorities whose numbers are few, who are outcasts of society, and who are unpopular, but whom society is willing to see suffer though it would not countenance general application of the same penalty across the boards. . . .

· · ·

There is increasing recognition of the fact that the basic theme of equal protection is implicit in "cruel and unusual" punishments. "A penalty . . . should be considered 'unusually' imposed if it is administered arbitrarily or discriminatorily." The same authors add that "The extreme rarity with which applicable death penalty provisions are put to use raises a strong inference of arbitrariness." The President's Commission on Law Enforcement and Administration of Justice recently concluded:

> "Finally there is evidence that the imposition of the death sentence and the exercise of dispensing power by the courts and the executive follow discriminatory patterns. The death sentence is disproportionately imposed and carried out on the poor, the Negro, and the members of unpopular groups."

· · ·

We cannot say from facts disclosed in these records that these defendants were sentenced to death because they were Black. Yet our task is not restricted to an effort to divine what motives impelled these death penalties. Rather we deal with a system of law and of justice that leaves to the uncontrolled discretion of judges or juries the determination whether defendants committing these crimes should die or be imprisoned. Under these laws no standards govern the selection of the penalty. People live or die, dependent on the whim of one man or of 12. . . .

244

. . .

In a Nation committed to Equal Protection of the laws there is no permissible "caste" aspect of law enforcement. Yet we know that the discretion of judges and juries in imposing the death penalty enables the penalty to be selectively applied, feeding prejudices against the accused if he is poor and despised, poor and lacking political clout, or if he is a member of a suspect or unpopular minority, and saving those who by social position may be in a more protected position. In ancient Hindu law a Brahmin was exempt from capital punishment. And in those days, "Generally, in the law books, punishment increased in severity as social status diminished." We have, I fear, taken in practice the same position, partially as a result of making the death penalty discretionary and partially as a result of the ability of the rich to purchase the services of the most respected and most resourceful legal talent in the Nation.

The high service rendered by the "cruel and unusual" punishment clause of the Eighth Amendment is to require legislatures to write penal laws that are evenhanded, non-selective, and nonarbitrary, and to require judges to see to it that general laws are not applied sparsely, selectively, and spottily to unpopular groups. . . .

. . .

Thus, these discretionary statutes are unconstitutional in their operation. They are pregnant with discrimination and discrimination is an ingredient not compatible with the idea of equal protection of the laws that is implicit in the ban on "cruel and unusual" punishments. . . .

. . .

I concur in the judgments of the Court.

. . .

Mr. Justice Brennan, concurring.

. . .

Ours would indeed be a simple task were we required merely to measure a challenged punishment against those that history has long condemned. That narrow and unwarranted view of the Clause, however, was left behind with the 19th century. Our task today is more complex. We know "that the words of the [Clause] are not precise, and that their

245

scope is not static." We know, therefore, that the Clause "must draw its meaning from the evolving standards of decency that mark the progress of a maturing society." . . .That knowledge, of course, is but the beginning of the inquiry. . . .

.   .   .

At bottom, . . . the Cruel and Unusual Punishments Clause prohibits the infliction of uncivilized and inhuman punishments. The State, even as it punishes, must treat its members with respect for their intrinsic worth as human beings. A punishment is "cruel and unusual," therefore, if it does not comport with human dignity.

This formulation, of course, does not of itself yield principles for assessing the constitutional validity of particular punishments. Nevertheless, even though "[t]his Court has had little occasion to give precise content to the [Clause]," . . . there are principles recognized in our cases and inherent in the Clause sufficient to permit a judicial determination whether a challenged punishment comports with human dignity.

The primary principle is that a punishment must not be so severe as to be degrading to the dignity of human beings. Pain, certainly, may be a factor in the judgment. The infliction of an extremely severe punishment will often entail physical suffering. Yet the Framers also knew "that there could be exercises of cruelty by laws other than those which inflicted bodily pain or mutilation." . . .

.   .   .

In determining whether a punishment comports with human dignity, we are aided also by a second principle inherent in the Clause—that the State must not arbitrarily inflict a severe punishment. This principle derives from the notion that the State does not respect human dignity when, without reason, it inflicts upon some people a severe punishment that it does not inflict upon others. Indeed, the very words "cruel and unusual punishments" imply condemnation of the arbitrary infliction of severe punishments. . . .

.   .   .

A third principle inherent in the Clause is that a severe punishment must not be unacceptable to contemporary society. Rejection by society, of course, is a strong indication that a severe punishment does not comport

246

with human dignity. In applying this principle, however, we must make certain that the judicial determination is as objective as possible... [O]ne factor that may be considered is the existence of the punishment in jurisdictions other than those before the Court. [A]nother factor to be considered is the historic usage of the punishment....

    .   .   .

The question under this principle, then, is whether there are objective indicators from which a court can conclude that contemporary society considers a severe punishment unacceptable. Accordingly, the judicial task is to review the history of a challenged punishment and to examine society's present practices with respect to its use. Legislative authorization, of course, does not establish acceptance. The acceptability of a severe punishment is measured not by its availability, for it might become so offensive to society as never to be inflicted, but by its use.

The final principle inherent in the Clause is that a severe punishment must not be excessive. A punishment is excessive under this principle if it is unnecessary: The infliction of a severe punishment by the State cannot comport with human dignity when it is nothing more than the pointless infliction of suffering. If there is a significantly less severe punishment adequate to achieve the purposes for which the punishment is inflicted, the punishment inflicted is unnecessary and therefore excessive.

    .   .   .

Although the determination that a severe punishment is excessive may be grounded in a judgment that it is disproportionate to the crime, the more significant basis is that the punishment serves no penal purpose more effectively than a less severe punishment....

    .   .   .

There are, then, four principles by which we may determine whether a particular punishment is "cruel and unusual."...

    .   .   .

The test, ... will ordinarily be a cumulative one: If a punishment is unusually severe, if there is a strong probability that it is inflicted arbitrarily, if it is substantially rejected by contemporary society, and if there is no reason to believe that it serves any penal purpose more effectively than some less severe punishment, then the continued infliction of that punishment violates the command of the Clause that the State may not inflict inhuman and uncivilized punishments upon those convicted of crimes. . . .

. . .

The question, then, is whether the deliberate infliction of death is today consistent with the command of the Clause that the State may not inflict punishments that do not comport with human dignity. I will analyze the punishment of death in terms of the principles set out above and the cumulative test to which they lead: It is a denial of human dignity for the State arbitrarily to subject a person to an unusually severe punishment that society has indicated it does not regard as acceptable and that cannot be shown to serve any penal purpose more effectively than a significantly less drastic punishment. Under these principles and this test, death is today a "cruel and unusual" punishment.

Death is a unique punishment in the United States. In a society that so strongly affirms the sanctity of life, not surprisingly the common view is that death is the ultimate sanction. This natural human feeling appears all about us. There has been no national debate about punishment, in general or by imprisonment, comparable to the debate about the punishment of death. No other punishment has been so continuously restricted, nor has any State yet abolished prisons, as some have abolished this punishment. And those States that still inflict death reserve it for the most heinous crimes. Juries, of course, have always treated death cases differently, as have governors exercising their commutation powers. . . [L]egislatures have required particular procedures, such as two-stage trials and automatic appeals, applicable only in death cases. . . This court, too, almost always treats death cases as a class apart. . . .

. . .

Death is truly an awesome punishment. The calculated killing of a human being by the State involves, by its very nature, a denial of the executed person's humanity. The contrast with the plight of a person punished by imprisonment is evident. An individual in prison does not lose "the right to have rights." A prisoner retains, for example, the constitutional rights to the free exercise of religion, to be free of cruel and unusual punishments, and to treatment as a "person" for purposes of due process of law and the equal protection of the laws. A prisoner remains a member of the human family. Moreover, he retains the right of access to the courts. His punishment is not irrevocable. Apart from the common charge, grounded upon the recognition of human fallibility, that the punishment of death must inevitably be inflicted upon innocent men, we know that death has been the lot of men whose convictions were unconstitutionally secured in view of later, retroactively applied, holdings of this Court. The punishment itself may have been unconstitutionally inflicted, yet the finality of death precludes relief. An executed person has indeed "lost the right to have rights." As one 19th century proponent of punishing criminals by death declared, "When a man is hung, there is an end of our relations with him. His execution is a way of saying, 'You are not fit for this world. Take your chance elsewhere.' "

In comparison to all other punishments today, then, the deliberate extinguishment of human life by the State is uniquely degrading to human dignity. I would not hesitate to hold, on that ground alone, that death is today a "cruel and unusual" punishment, were it not that death is a punishment of longstanding usage and acceptance in this country. I therefore turn to the second principle—that the State may not arbitrarily inflict an unusually severe punishment.

The outstanding characteristic of our present practice of punishing criminals by death is the infrequency with which we resort to it. The evidence is conclusive that death is not the ordinary punishment for any crime. . . .

. . .

When a country of over 200 million people inflicts an unusually severe punishment no more than 50 times a year, the inference is strong that the punishment is not being regularly and fairly applied. To dispel it would indeed require a clear showing of nonarbitrary infliction.

Although there are no exact figures available, we know that thousands of murders and rapes are committed annually in States where death is an authorized punishment for those crimes. However the rate of infliction is characterized—as "freakishly" or "spectacularly" rare, or simply as rare—it would take the purest sophistry to deny that death is inflicted in only a minute fraction of these cases. How much rarer, after all, could the infliction of death be?

When the punishment of death is inflicted in a trivial number of the cases in which it is legally available, the conclusion is virtually inescapable that it is being inflicted arbitrarily. Indeed, it smacks of little more than a lottery system. . . .

. . .

When there is a strong probability that an unusually severe and degrading punishment is being inflicted arbitrarily, we may well expect that society will disapprove of its infliction. I turn, therefore, to the third principle. An examination of the history and present operation of the American practice of punishing criminals by death reveals that this punishment has been almost totally rejected by contemporary society. . . .

. . .

The progressive decline in and the current rarity of the infliction of death demonstrate that our society seriously questions the appropriateness of this punishment today. The States point out that many legislatures authorize death as the punishment for certain crimes and that substantial segments of the public, as reflected in opinion polls and referendum votes, continue to support it. Yet the availability of this punishment through statutory authorization, as well as the polls and referenda, which amount simply to approval of that authorization, simply underscores the extent to which our society in fact rejected this punishment. When an unusually severe punishment is authorized for widescale application but not, because of society's refusal, inflicted save in a few instances, the inference is compelling that there is a deep-seated reluctance to inflict it. Indeed, the likelihood is great that the punishment is tolerated only because of its disuse. The objective indicator of society's view of an unusually severe punishment is what society does with it. And today society will inflict death upon only a small sample of the eligible criminals. Rejection could hardly be more complete without becoming absolute. At the very least, I must conclude that contemporary society views this punishment with substantial doubt. . . .

. . .

In sum, the punishment of death is inconsistent with all four principles: Death is an unusually severe and degrading punishment; there is a strong probability that it is inflicted arbitrarily; its rejection by contemporary society is virtually total; and there is no reason to believe that it serves any penal purpose more effectively than the less severe punishment of imprisonment. The function of these principles is to enable a court to determine whether a punishment comports with human dignity. Death, quite simply, does not. . . .

. . .

I concur in the judgments of the Court.

. . .

Mr. Justice Stewart, concurring.

The penalty of death differs from all other forms of criminal punishment, not in degree but in kind. It is unique in its total irrevocability. It is unique in its rejection of rehabilitation of the convict as a basic purpose of criminal justice. And it is unique, finally, in its absolute renunciation of all that is embodied in our concept of humanity.

For these and other reasons, at least two of my Brothers have concluded that the infliction of the death penalty is constitutionally impermissible in all circumstances under the Eighth and Fourteenth Amendments. Their case is a strong one. But I find it unnecessary to reach the ultimate question they would decide. . . .

. . .

[T]he death sentences now before us are the product of a legal system that brings them, I believe, within the very core of the Eighth Amendment's guarantee against cruel and unusual punishments, a guarantee applicable against the States through the Fourteenth Amendment. In the first place, it is clear that these sentences are "cruel" in the sense that they excessively go beyond, not in degree but in kind, the punishments that the state legislatures have determined to be necessary. In the second place, it is equally clear that these sentences are "unusual" in the sense that the penalty of death is infrequently imposed for murder, and that its imposition for rape is extraordinarily rare. But I do not rest my conclusion upon these two propositions alone.

These death sentences are cruel and unusual in the same way that being struck by lightning is cruel and unusual. For, of all the people convicted of rapes and murders in 1967 and 1968, many just as reprehensible as these, the petitioners are among a capriciously selected

251

random handful upon whom the sentence of death has in fact been imposed... I simply conclude that the Eighth and Fourteenth Amendments cannot tolerate the infliction of a sentence of death under legal systems that permit this unique penalty to be so wantonly and so freakishly imposed.

For these reasons I concur in the judgments of the Court.

.   .   .

Mr. Justice White, concurring.

The facial constitutionality of statutes requiring the imposition of the death penalty for first degree murder, for more narrowly defined categories of murder or for rape would present quite different issues under the Eighth Amendment than are posed by the cases before us. In joining the Court's judgment, therefore, I do not at all intimate that the death penalty is unconstitutional per se or that there is no system of capital punishment that would comport with the Eighth Amendment. That question, ably argued by several of my Brethren, is not presented by these cases and need not be decided.

The narrow question to which I address myself concerns the constitutionality of capital punishment statutes under which (1) the legislature authorizes the imposition of the death penalty for murder or rape; (2) the legislature does not itself mandate the penalty in any particular class or kind of case (that is, legislative will is not frustrated if the penalty is never imposed) but delegates to judges or juries the decisions as to those cases, if any, in which the penalty will be utilized; and (3) judges and juries have ordered the death penalty with such infrequency that the odds are now very much against imposition and execution of the penalty with respect to any convicted murderer or rapist. It is in this context that we must consider whether the execution of these petitioners violates the Eighth Amendment....

.   .   .

[I]t is difficult to prove as a general proposition that capital punishment, however administered, more effectively serves the ends of the criminal law than does imprisonment. But however that may be, I cannot avoid the conclusion that as the statutes before us are now administered, the penalty is so infrequently imposed that the threat of execution is too attenuated to be of substantial service to criminal justice....

. . .

The short of it is that the policy of vesting sentencing authority primarily in juries—a decision largely motivated by the desire to mitigate the harshness of the law and to bring community judgment to bear on the sentence as well as guilt or innocence—has so effectively achieved its aims that capital punishment within the confines of the statutes now before us has for all practical purposes run its course. . . .

. . .

I add only that past and present legislative judgment with respect to the death penalty loses much of its force when viewed in light of the recurring practice of delegating sentencing authority to the jury and the fact that a jury, in its own discretion and without violating its trust or any statutory policy, may refuse to impose the death penalty no matter what the circumstances of the crime. Legislative "policy" is thus necessarily defined not by what is legislatively authorized but by what juries and judges do in exercising the discretion so regularly conferred upon them. In my judgment what was done in these cases violated the Eighth Amendment.

I concur in the judgments of the Court.

. . .

Mr. Justice Marshall, concurring.

. . .

The criminal acts with which we are confronted are ugly, vicious, reprehensible acts. Their sheer brutality cannot and should not be minimized. But, we are not called upon to condone the penalized conduct; we are asked only to examine the penalty imposed on each of the petitioners and to determine whether or not it violates the Eighth Amendment. The question then is not whether we condone rape or murder, for surely we do not; it is whether capital punishment is "a punishment no longer consistent with our self-respect" and, therefore, violative of the Eighth Amendment. . . .

. . .

Faced with an open question, we must establish our standards for decision. The decisions . . . imply that a punishment may be deemed cruel and unusual for any one of four distinct reasons.

First, there are certain punishments which inherently involve so much physical pain and suffering that civilized people cannot tolerate them— e.g., use of the rack, the thumbscrew, or other modes of torture. Regardless of public sentiment with respect to imposition of one of these punishments in a particular case or at any one moment in history, the Constitution prohibits it. These are punishments that have been barred since the adoption of the Bill of Rights.

Second, there are punishments which are unusual, signifying that they were previously unknown as penalties for a given offense. . . .

·   ·   ·

Third, a penalty may be cruel and unusual because it is excessive and serves no valid legislative purpose. . . The decisions previously discussed are replete with assertions that one of the primary functions of the cruel and unusual punishments clause is to prevent excessive or unnecessary penalties; these punishments are unconstitutional even though popular sentiment may favor them. . . .

·   ·   ·

Fourth, where a punishment is not excessive and serves a valid legislative purpose, it still may be invalid if popular sentiment abhors it. For example, if the evidence clearly demonstrated that capital punishment served valid legislative purposes, such punishment would, nevertheless, be unconstitutional if citizens found it to be morally unacceptable. A general abhorrence on the part of the public would, in effect, equate a modern punishment with those barred since the adoption of the Eighth Amendment. There are no prior cases in this Court striking down a penalty on this ground, but the very notion of changing values requires that we recognize its existence. . . .

·   ·   ·

In order to assess whether or not death is an excessive or unnecessary penalty, it is necessary to consider the reasons why a legislature might select it as punishment for one or more offenses, and examine whether less severe penalties would satisfy the legitimate legislative wants as well as capital punishment. If they would, then the death penalty is unnecessary cruelty, and, therefore, unconstitutional.

There are six purposes conceivably served by capital punishment: retribution, deterrence, prevention of repetitive criminal acts, encouragement of guilty pleas and confessions, eugenics, and economy....

. . .

[Justice Marshall considers each purpose in detail and concludes that none is sufficient to support the death penalty.]

. . .

In addition, even if capital punishment is not excessive, it nonetheless violates the Eighth Amendment because it is morally unacceptable to the people of the United States at this time in their history.

In judging whether or not a given penalty is morally acceptable, most courts have said that the punishment is valid unless "it shocks the conscience and sense of justice of the people."...

. . .

While a public opinion poll obviously is of some assistance in indicating public acceptance or rejection of a specific penalty, its utility cannot be very great. This is because whether or not a punishment is cruel and unusual depends, not on whether its mere mention "shocks the conscience and sense of justice of the people," but on whether people who were fully informed as to the purposes of the penalty and its liabilities would find the penalty shocking, unjust, and unacceptable....

. . .

Assuming knowledge of all the facts presently available regarding capital punishment, the average citizen would, in my opinion, find it shocking to his conscience and sense of justice. For this reason alone capital punishment cannot stand....

. . .

I concur in the judgments of the Court.

. . .

Mr. Chief Justice Burger, with whom Mr. Justice Blackmun, Mr. Justice Powell, and Mr. Justice Rehnquist join, dissenting.

. . .

If we were possessed of legislative power, I would either join with Mr. Justice Brennan and Mr. Justice Marshall or, at the very least, restrict the use of capital punishment to a small category of the most heinous crimes. Our constitutional inquiry, however, must be divorced from personal feelings as to the morality and efficacy of the death penalty and be confined to the meaning and applicability of the uncertain language of the Eighth Amendment. There is no novelty in being called upon to interpret a constitutional provision that is less than self-defining, but of all our fundamental guarantees, the ban on "cruel and unusual punishments" is one of the most difficult to translate into judicially manageable terms. The widely divergent views of the Amendment expressed in today's opinions reveals the haze that surrounds this constitutional command. Yet it is essential to our role as a court that we not seize upon the enigmatic character of the guarantee as an invitation to enact our personal predilections into law. . . .

. . .

However, the inquiry cannot end here. For reasons unrelated to any change in intrinsic cruelty, the Eighth Amendment prohibition cannot fairly be limited to those punishments thought excessively cruel and barbarous at the time of the adoption of the Eighth Amendment. A punishment is inordinately cruel, in the sense we must deal with it in these cases, chiefly as perceived by the society so characterizing it. The standard of extreme cruelty is not merely descriptive, but necessarily embodies a moral judgment. The standard itself remains the same, but its applicability must change as the basic mores of society change. . . Nevertheless, the Court up to now has never actually held that a punishment has become impermissibly cruel due to a shift in the weight of accepted social values; nor has the Court suggested judicially manageable criteria for measuring such a shift in moral consensus.

The Court's quiescence in this area can be attributed to the fact that in a democratic society legislatures, not courts, are constituted to respond to the will and consequently the moral values of the people. . . Accordingly, punishments such as branding and the cutting off of ears, which were commonplace at the time of the adoption of the Constitution, passed from the penal scene without judicial intervention because they became basically offensive to the people and the legislatures responded to this sentiment. . . .

. . .

The paucity of judicial decisions invalidating legislatively prescribed punishments is powerful evidence that in this country legislatures have in fact been responsive—albeit belatedly at times—to changes in social attitudes and moral values.

I do not suggest that the validity of legislatively authorized punishments presents no justiciable issue under the Eighth Amendment, but rather that the primacy of the legislative role narrowly confines the scope of judicial inquiry. Whether or not provable, and whether or not true at all times, in a democracy the legislative judgment is presumed to embody the basic standards of decency prevailing in the society. This presumption can only be negated by unambiguous and compelling evidence of legislative default.

There are no obvious indications that capital punishment offends the conscience of society to such a degree that our traditional deference to the legislative judgment must be abandoned. It is not a punishment such as burning at the stake that everyone would ineffably find to be repugnant to all civilized standards. Nor is it a punishment so roundly condemned that only a few aberrant legislatures have retained it on the statute books. Capital punishment is authorized by statute in 40 States, the District of Columbia and in the federal courts for the commission of certain crimes. On four occasions in the last 11 years Congress has added to the list of federal crimes punishable by death. In looking for reliable indicia of contemporary attitude, none more trustworthy has been advanced....

. . .

The selectivity of juries in imposing the punishment of death is properly viewed as a refinement on, rather than a repudiation of, the statutory authorization for that penalty. Legislatures prescribe the categories of crimes for which the death penalty should be available, and, acting as "the conscience of the community," juries are entrusted to determine in individual cases that the ultimate punishment is warranted. Juries are undoubtedly influenced in this judgment by myriad factors. The motive or lack of motive of the perpetrator, the degree of injury or suffering of the victim or victims and the degree of brutality in the commission of the crime would seem to be prominent among these factors. Given the general awareness that death is no longer a routine punishment for the crimes for which it is made available, it is hardly surprising that juries have been increasingly meticulous in their imposition of the penalty. But to assume from the mere fact of relative infrequency that only a random assortment of pariahs are sentenced to death, is to cast grave doubt on the basic integrity of our jury system. . . .

.   .   .

Two of the several aims of punishment are generally associated with capital punishment—retribution and deterrence. It is argued that retribution can be discounted because that, after all, is what the Eighth Amendment seeks to eliminate. There is no authority suggesting that the Eighth Amendment was intended to purge the law of its retributive elements, and the Court has consistently assumed that retribution is a legitimate dimension of the punishment of crimes. . . Furthermore, responsible legal thinkers of widely varying persuasions have debated the sociological and philosophical aspects of the retribution question for generations, neither side being able to convince the other. It would be reading a great deal into the Eighth Amendment to hold that the punishments authorized by legislatures cannot constitutionally reflect a retributive purpose.

The less esoteric but no less controversial question is whether the death penalty acts as a superior deterrent. Those favoring abolition find no evidence that it does. Those favoring retention start from the intuitive notion that capital punishment should act as the most effective deterrent and note that there is no convincing evidence that it does not. . . If the States are unable to adduce convincing proof rebutting such assertions, does it then follow that all punishments are suspect of being "cruel and unusual" within the meaning of the Constitution? On the contrary, I submit that the questions raised by the necessity approach are beyond the pale of judicial inquiry under the Eighth Amendment.

Today the Court has not ruled that capital punishment is per se violative of the Eighth Amendment; nor has it ruled that the punishment is barred for any particular class or classes of crimes. The substantially similar concurring opinions of Mr. Justice Stewart and Mr. Justice White, which are necessary to support the judgment setting aside petitioners' sentences, stop short of reaching the ultimate question. The actual scope of the Court's ruling, which I take to be embodied in these concurring opinions, is not entirely clear. This much, however, seems apparent: if the legislatures are to continue to authorize capital punishment for some crimes, juries and judges can no longer be permitted to make the sentencing determination in the same manner they have in the past. . . .

. . .

The critical factor in the concurring opinions of both Mr. Justice Stewart and Mr. Justice White is the infrequency with which the penalty is imposed. This factor is taken not as evidence of society's abhorrence of capital punishment—the inference that petitioners would have the Court draw—but as the earmark of a deteriorated system of sentencing. It is concluded that petitioners' sentences must be set aside, not because the punishment is impermissibly cruel, but because juries and judges have failed to exercise their sentencing discretion in acceptable fashion.

To be sure, there is a recitation cast in Eighth Amendment terms: petitioners' sentences are "cruel" because they exceed that which the legislatures have deemed necessary for all cases; petitioners' sentences are "unusual" because they exceed that which is imposed in most cases. This application of the words of the Eighth Amendment suggests that capital punishment can be made to satisfy Eighth Amendment values if its rate of imposition is somehow multiplied; it seemingly follows that the flexible sentencing system created by the legislatures, and carried out by juries and judges, has yielded more mercy than the Eighth Amendment can stand. The implications of this approach are mildly ironical. . . .

. . .

While I would not undertake to make a definitive statement as to the parameters of the Court's ruling, it is clear that if state legislatures and the Congress wish to maintain the availability of capital punishment, significant statutory changes will have to be made. Since the two pivotal concurring opinions turn on the assumption that the punishment of death is now meted out in a random and unpredictable manner, legislative bodies may seek to bring their laws into compliance with the Court's ruling by providing standards for juries and judges to follow in determining the sentence in capital cases or by more narrowly defining the crimes for which the penalty is to be imposed. If such standards can be devised or the crimes more meticulously defined, the result cannot be detrimental. . . .

. . .

259

Real change could clearly be brought about if legislatures provided mandatory death sentences in such a way as to deny juries the opportunity to bring in a verdict on a lesser charge; under such a system, the death sentence could only be avoided by a verdict of acquittal. If this is the only alternative that the legislatures can safely pursue under today's ruling, I would have preferred that the Court opt for total abolition. . . .

. . .

Since there is no majority of the Court on the ultimate issue presented in these cases, the future of capital punishment in this country has been left in an uncertain limbo. Rather than providing a final and unambiguous answer on the basic constitutional question, the collective impact of the majority's ruling is to demand an undetermined measure of change from the various state legislatures and the Congress. While I cannot endorse the process of decisionmaking that has yielded today's result and the restraints which that result imposes on legislative action, I am not altogether displeased that legislative bodies have been given the opportunity, and indeed unavoidable responsibility, to make a thorough re-evaluation of the entire subject of capital punishment. If today's opinions demonstrate nothing else, they starkly show that this is an area where legislatures can act far more effectively than courts.

The legislatures are free to eliminate capital punishment for specific crimes or to carve-out limited exceptions to a general abolition of the penalty, without adherence to the conceptual strictures of the Eighth Amendment. The legislatures can and should make an assessment of the deterrent influence of capital punishment, both generally and as affecting the commission of specific types of crimes. If legislatures come to doubt the efficacy of capital punishment, they can abolish it, either completely or on a selective basis. If new evidence persuades them that they have acted unwisely, they can reverse their field and reinstate the penalty to the extent it is thought warranted. An Eighth Amendment ruling by judges cannot be made with such flexibility or discriminating precision. . . .

. . .

The highest judicial duty is to recognize the limits on judicial power and to permit the democratic processes to deal with matters falling outside of those limits. The "hydraulic pressures" that Holmes spoke of as being generated by cases of great import have propelled the Court to go beyond the limits of judicial power, while fortunately leaving some room for legislative judgment.

. . .

Mr. Justice Blackmun, dissenting.

. . .

Cases such as these provide for me an excruciating agony of the spirit. I yield to no one in the depth of my distaste, antipathy, and, indeed, abhorrence, for the death penalty, with all its aspects of physical distress and fear and of moral judgment exercised by finite minds. That distaste is buttressed by a belief that capital punishment serves no useful purpose that can be demonstrated. For me, it violates childhood's training and life's experiences, and is not compatible with the philosophical convictions I have been able to develop. It is antagonistic to any sense of "reverence for life." Were I a legislator, I would vote against the death penalty for the policy reasons argued by counsel for the respective petitioners and expressed and adopted in the several opinions filed by the Justices who vote to reverse these convictions. . . .

. . .

To reverse the judgments in these cases is, of course, the easy choice. It is easier to strike the balance in favor of life and against death. It is comforting to relax in the thoughts—perhaps the rationalizations—that this is the compassionate decision for a maturing society; that this is the moral and the "right" thing to do; that thereby we convince ourselves that we are moving down the road toward human decency; that we value life even though that life has taken another or others or has grievously scarred another or others and their families; and that we are less barbaric than we were in 1878 or in 1890 or in 1910 or in 1947 or in 1958 or in 1963 or a year ago in 1971. . . .

. . .

This, for me, is good argument, and it makes some sense. But it is good argument and it makes sense only in a legislative and executive way and not as a judicial expedient. . . .

. . .

I do not sit on these cases, however, as a legislator, responsive, at least in part, to the will of constituents. Our task here, as must so frequently be emphasized and re-emphasized, is to pass upon the constitutionality of legislation that has been enacted and that is challenged. This is the sole task for judges. We should not allow our personal preferences as to the wisdom of legislative and congressional action, or our distaste for such action, to guide our judicial decision in cases such as these. The temptations to cross that policy line are very great. In fact, as today's decision reveals, they are almost irresistible. . . .

· · ·

I trust the Court fully appreciates what it is doing when it decides these cases the way it does today. Not only are the capital punishment laws of 39 States and the District of Columbia stricken down, but also all those provisions of the federal statutory structure that permit the death penalty apparently are voided. No longer is capital punishment possible, I suspect, for, among other crimes, treason; or assassination of the President, the Vice President, or those who stand elected to those positions; or assassination of a Member or member-elect of Congress; or espionage; or rape within the special maritime jurisdiction; or aircraft or motor vehicle destruction where death occurs; or explosives offenses where death results; or train wrecking; or aircraft piracy. . . .

· · ·

Although personally I may rejoice at the Court's result, I find it difficult to accept or to justify as a matter of history, of law, or of constitutional pronouncement. I fear the Court has overstepped. It has sought and has achieved an end.

· · ·

Mr. Justice Powell, with whom The Chief Justice, Mr. Justice Blackmun, and Mr. Justice Rehnquist join, dissenting.

· · ·

It is the judgment of five Justices that the death penalty, as customarily prescribed and implemented in this country today, offends the constitutional prohibition against cruel and unusual punishment. The reasons for that judgment are stated in five separate opinions, expressing as many separate rationales. In my view, none of these opinions provides a constitutionally adequate foundation for the Court's decision. . . .

.   .   .

Whatever uncertainties may hereafter surface, several of the consequences of today's decision are unmistakably clear. The decision is plainly one of the greatest importance. The Court's judgment removes the death sentences previously imposed on some 600 persons awaiting punishment in state and federal prisons throughout the country. At least for the present, it also bars the States and the Federal Government from seeking sentences of death for defendants awaiting trial on charges for which capital punishment was heretofore a potential alternative. The happy event for these countable few constitutes, however, only the most visible consequence of this decision. Less measurable, but certainly of no less significance, is the shattering effect this collection of views has on the root principles of stare decisis, federalism, judicial restraint and—most importantly—separation of powers. . . .

.   .   .

In terms of the constitutional role of this Court, the impact of the majority's ruling is all the greater because the decision encroaches upon an area squarely within the historic prerogative of the legislative branch—both state and federal—to protect the citizenry through the designation of penalties for prohibitable conduct. It is the very sort of judgment that the legislative branch is competent to make and for which the judiciary is ill-equipped. Throughout our history, Justices of this Court have emphasized the gravity of decisions invalidating legislative judgments, admonishing the nine men who sit on this bench of the duty of self-restraint, especially when called upon to apply the expansive due process and cruel and unusual punishment rubrics. I can recall no case in which, in the name of deciding constitutional questions, this Court has subordinated national and local democratic processes to such an extent. . . .

.   .   .

The prior opinions of this Court point with great clarity to reasons why those of us who sit on this Court at a particular time should act with restraint before assuming, contrary to a century of precedent, that we now know the answer for all time to come. First, where as here, the language of the applicable provision provides great leeway and where the underlying social policies are felt to be of vital importance, the temptation to read personal preference into the Constitution is understandably great. It is too easy to propound our subjective standards of wise policy under the rubric of more or less universally held standards of decency.

The second consideration dictating judicial self-restraint arises from a proper recognition of the respective roles of the legislative and judicial branches. The designation of punishments for crimes is a matter peculiarly within the sphere of the state and federal legislative bodies. When asked to encroach on the legislative prerogative we are well counseled to proceed with the utmost reticence. The review of legislative choices, in the performance of our duty to enforce the Constitution, has been characterized most appropriately by Mr. Justice Holmes as "the gravest and most delicate duty that the Court is called on to perform." . . .

How much graver is that duty when we are not asked to pass on the constitutionality of a single penalty under the facts of a single case but instead are urged to overturn the legislative judgments of 40 State legislatures as well as those of Congress. . . .

. . .

[L]egislative judgments as to the efficacy of particular punishments are presumptively rational and may not be struck down under the Eighth Amendment because this Court may think that some alternate sanction would be more appropriate. Even if such judgments were within the judicial prerogative, petitioners have failed to show that there exist no justifications for the legislative enactments challenged in these cases. While the evidence and arguments advanced by petitioners might have proved profoundly persuasive if addressed to a legislative body, they do not approach the showing traditionally required before a court declares that the legislature has acted irrationally. . . .

. . .

I now return to the overriding question in these cases: whether this Court, acting in conformity with the Constitution, can justify its judgment to abolish capital punishment as heretofore known in this country. It is important to keep in focus the enormity of the step undertaken by the Court today. Not only does it invalidate hundreds of state and federal laws, it deprives those jurisdictions of the power to legislate with respect to capital punishment in the future, except in a manner consistent with the cloudily outlined views of those Justices who do not purport to undertake total abolition. Nothing short of an amendment to the United States Constitution can reverse the Court's judgment. Meanwhile, all flexibility is foreclosed. The normal democratic process, as well as the opportunities for the several States to respond to the will of their people expressed through ballot referenda, is now shut off.

The sobering disadvantage of constitutional adjudication of this magnitude is the universality and permanence of the judgment. The enduring merit of legislative action is its responsiveness to the democratic process, and to revision and change: mistaken judgments may be corrected and refinements perfected. . . .

. . .

It seems to me that the sweeping judicial action undertaken today reflects a basic lack of faith and confidence in the democratic process. Many may regret, as I do, the failure of some legislative bodies to address the capital punishment issue with greater frankness or effectiveness. Many might decry their failure either to abolish the penalty entirely or selectively, or to establish standards for its enforcement. But impatience with the slowness, and even the unresponsiveness, of legislatures is no justification for judicial intrusion upon their historic powers. . . .

. . .

Mr. Justice Rehnquist, with whom The Chief Justice, Mr. Justice Blackmun, and Mr. Justice Powell join, dissenting.

. . .

Whatever its precise rationale, today's holding necessarily brings into sharp relief the fundamental question of the role of judicial review in a democratic society. How can government by the elected representatives of the people co-exist with the power of the federal judiciary, whose members are constitutionally insulated from responsiveness to the popular will, to declare invalid laws duly enacted by the popular branches of government? . . .

. . .

The courts in cases properly before them have been entrusted under the Constitution with the last word, short of constitutional amendment, as to whether a law passed by the legislature conforms to the Constitution. . . .

. . .

Rigorous attention to the limits of this Court's authority is likewise enjoined because of the natural desire that beguiles judges along with other human beings into imposing their own views of goodness, truth, and justice upon others. Judges differ only in that they have the power, if not the authority, to enforce their desires. This is doubtless why nearly two centuries of judicial precedent from this Court counsel the sparing use of that power. The most expansive reading of the leading constitutional cases does not remotely suggest that this court has been granted a roving commission, either by the Founding Fathers or by the framers of the Fourteenth Amendment, to strike down laws that are based upon notions of policy or morality suddenly found unacceptable by a majority of the Court. . . .

. . .

A separate reason for deference to the legislative judgment is the consequence of human error on the part of the judiciary with respect to the constitutional issue before it. Human error there is bound to be, judges being men and women, and men and women being what they are. But an error in mistakenly sustaining the constitutionality of a particular enactment, while wrongfully depriving the individual of a right secured to him by the Constitution, nonetheless does so by simply letting stand a duly enacted law of a democratically chosen legislative body. The error resulting from a mistaken upholding of an individual constitutional claim against the validity of a legislative enactment is a good deal more serious. For the result in such a case is not to leave standing a law duly enacted by a representative assembly, but to impose upon the Nation the judicial fiat of a majority of a court of judges whose connection with the popular will is remote at best. . . .

. . .

While overreaching by the Legislative and Executive Branches may result in the sacrifice of individual protections that the Constitution was designed to secure against action of the State, judicial overreaching may result in sacrifice of the equally important right of the people to govern themselves.

Gregg v. Georgia

428 U.S. 153, 49 L Ed 2d 859, 96 S Ct 2909 (1976)

After the decision in *Furman,* Georgia was one of the 35 states that rewrote its capital punishment statutes. The new scheme utilizes a bifurcated trial in which the jury first determines guilt or innocence. In a second, separate hearing the same jury, if a guilty verdict has been reached, hears argument and additional evidence (if any) of mitigating or aggravating circumstances. The death penalty may not be imposed as a result of this second hearing unless the jury declares in writing that it finds at least one of ten aggravating circumstances specified by statute to be present. The jury may ignore the presence of aggravating circumstances and recommend a sentence less than death. A death sentence is automatically reviewed by the Georgia Supreme Court which must determine that the sentence is not arbitrary, capricious, or the result of passion or prejudice, that the evidence supports the findings of the aggravating circumstance, and that in similar cases decided by the court the same result had been reached.

Gregg was convicted on two counts of murder and two counts of armed robbery. In the second stage of the bifurcated trial, the jury imposed the death penalty and specified the armed robbery of the victims before their murder as an aggravating circumstance. The Georgia Supreme Court affirmed on automatic appeal and the U.S. Supreme Court granted certiorari.

. . .

Mr. Justice Stewart, Mr. Justice Powell, and Mr. Justice Stevens announced the judgment of the Court and filed an opinion delivered by Mr. Justice Stewart.

The issue in this case is whether the imposition of the sentence of death for the crime of murder under the law of Georgia violates the Eighth and Fourteenth Amendments.

The petitioner, Troy Gregg, was charged with committing armed robbery and murder. In accordance with Georgia procedure in capital cases, the trial was in two stages, a guilt stage and a sentencing stage.

At the penalty stage, which took place before the same jury, neither the prosecutor nor the petitioner's lawyer offered any additional evidence. Both counsel, however, made lengthy arguments dealing generally with the propriety of capital punishment under the circumstances and with the weight of the evidence of guilt. The trial judge instructed the jury that it could recommend either a death sentence or a life prison sentence on each count. The judge further charged the jury that in determining what sentence was appropriate the jury was free to consider the facts and circumstances presented by the parties, if any, in mitigation or aggravation.

Finally, the judge instructed the jury that it "would not be authorized to consider [imposing] the sentence of death" unless it first found beyond a reasonable doubt one of these aggravating circumstances:

"One—That the offense of murder was committed while the offender was engaged in the commission of two other capital felonies, to-wit the armed robbery of [Simmons and Moore].

"Two—That the offender committed the offense of murder for the purpose of receiving money and the automobile described in the indictment.

"Three—The offense of murder was outrageously and wantonly vile, horrible and inhuman, in that th [sic] involved the depravity of [the] mind of the defendant."

Finding the first and second of these circumstances, the jury returned verdicts of death on each count.

The Supreme Court of Georgia affirmed the convictions and the imposition of the death sentences for murder. . . .

.   .   .

We granted the petitioner's application for a writ of certiorari challenging the imposition of the death sentences in this case as "cruel and unusual" punishment in violation of the Eighth and the Fourteenth Amendments.

Before considering the issues presented it is necessary to understand the Georgia statutory scheme for the imposition of the death penalty. The Georgia statute, as amended after our decision in Furman v Georgia . . . retains the death penalty for six categories of crime: murder, kidnapping for ransom or where the victim is harmed, armed robbery, rape, treason, and aircraft hijacking. The capital defendant's guilt or innocence is determined in the traditional manner, either by a trial judge or a jury, in the first stage of a bifurcated trial....

. . .

After a verdict, finding, or plea of guilty to a capital crime, a presentence hearing is conducted before whomever made the determination of guilt. The sentencing procedures are essentially the same in both bench and jury trials. At the hearing,

"the judge [or jury] shall hear additional evidence in extenuation, mitigation, and aggravation of punishment, including the record of any prior criminal convictions and pleas of guilty or pleas of nolo contendere of the defendant, or the absence of any prior conviction and pleas: Provided, however, that only such evidence in aggravation as the State has made known to the defendant prior to his trial shall be admissible. The judge [or jury] shall also hear argument by defendant or his counsel and the prosecuting attorney ... regarding the punishment to be imposed."

The defendant is accorded substantial latitude as to the types of evidence that he may introduce....

. . .

In the assessment of the appropriate sentence to be imposed the judge is also required to consider or to include in his instructions to the jury "any mitigating circumstances or aggravating circumstances otherwise authorized by law and any of [10] statutory aggravating circumstances which may be supported by the evidence." The scope of the nonstatutory aggravating or mitigating circumstances is not delineated in the statute. Before a convicted defendant may be sentenced to death, however, except in cases of treason or aircraft hijacking, the jury, or the trial judge in cases tried without a jury, must find beyond a reasonable doubt one of the 10 aggravating circumstances specified in the statute. The sentence of death may be imposed only if the jury (or judge) finds one of the statutory aggravating circumstances and then elects to impose that sentence. If the verdict is death the jury or judge must specify the aggravating circumstance(s) found. In jury cases, the trial judge is bound by the jury's recommended sentence.

In addition to the conventional appellate process available in all criminal cases, provision is made for special expedited direct review by the Supreme Court of Georgia of the appropriateness of imposing the sentence of death in the particular case. The court is directed to consider "the punishment as well as any errors enumerated by way of appeal," and to determine:

> "(1) Whether the sentence of death was imposed under the influence of passion, prejudice, or any other arbitrary factor, and
> "(2) Whether, in cases other than treason or aircraft hijacking, the evidence supports the jury's or judge's finding of a statutory aggravating circumstance . . .
> "(3) Whether the sentence of death is excessive or disproportionate to the penalty imposed in similar cases, considering both the crime and the defendant."

If the court affirms a death sentence, it is required to include in its decision reference to similar cases that it has taken into consideration. . . .

. . .

The Court on a number of occasions has both assumed and asserted the constitutionality of capital punishment. In several cases that assumption provided a necessary foundation for the decision, as the Court was asked to decide whether a particular method of carrying out a capital sentence would be allowed to stand under the Eighth Amendment. But until Furman v Georgia, the Court never confronted squarely the fundamental claim that the punishment of death always, regardless of the enormity of the offense or the procedure followed in imposing the sentence, is cruel and unusual punishment in violation of the Constitution. Although this issue was presented and addressed in Furman, it was not resolved by the Court. Four Justices would have held that capital punishment is not unconstitutional per se; two Justices would have reached the opposite conclusion; and three Justices, while agreeing that the statutes then before the Court were invalid as applied, left open the question whether such punishment may ever be imposed. We now hold that the punishment of death does not invariably violate the Constitution. . . .

. . .

[I]n assessing a punishment selected by a democratically elected legislature against the constitutional measure, we presume its validity. We may not require the legislature to select the least severe penalty possible so long as the penalty selected is not cruelly inhumane or disproportionate to the crime involved. And a heavy burden rests on those who would attack the judgment of the representatives of the people.

This is true in part because the constitutional test is intertwined with an assessment of contemporary standards and the legislative judgment weighs heavily in ascertaining such standards... The deference we owe to the decisions of the state legislatures under our federal system is enhanced where the specification of punishments is concerned, for "these are peculiarly questions of legislative policy.".... A decision that a given punishment is impermissible under the Eighth Amendment cannot be reversed short of a constitutional amendment. The ability of the people to express their preference through the normal democratic processes, as well as through ballot referenda, is shut off. Revisions cannot be made in the light of further experience....

.   .   .

We now consider specifically whether the sentence of death for the crime of murder is a per se violation of the Eighth and Fourteenth Amendments to the Constitution. We note first that history and precedent strongly support a negative answer to this question.

The imposition of the death penalty for the crime of murder has a long history of acceptance both in the United States and in England. The common-law rule imposed a mandatory death sentence on all convicted murderers. And the penalty continued to be used into the 20th century by most American States, although the breadth of the common-law rule was diminished, initially by narrowing the class of murders to be punished by death and subsequently by widespread adoption of laws expressly granting juries the discretion to recommend mercy.

It is apparent from the text of the Constitution itself that the existence of capital punishment was accepted by the Framers. At the time the Eighth Amendment was ratified, capital punishment was a common sanction in every State. Indeed, the First Congress of the United States enacted legislation providing death as the penalty for specified crimes. The Fifth Amendment, adopted at the same time as the Eighth, contemplated the continued existence of the capital sanction by imposing certain limits on the prosecution of capital cases... And the Fourteenth Amendment, adopted over three-quarters of a century later, similarly contemplates the existence of the capital sanction in providing that no

State shall deprive any person of "life, liberty, or property" without due process of law. . . .

. . .

The petitioners in the capital cases before the Court today renew the "standards of decency" argument, but developments during the four years since Furman have undercut substantially the assumptions upon which their argument rested. Despite the continuing debate, dating back to the 19th century, over the morality and utility of capital punishment, it is now evident that a large proportion of American society continues to regard it as an appropriate and necessary criminal sanction.

The most marked indication of society's endorsement of the death penalty for murder is the legislative response to Furman. The legislatures of at least 35 States have enacted new statutes that provide for the death penalty for at least some crimes that result in the death of another person. And the Congress of the United States, in 1974, enacted a statute providing the death penalty for aircraft piracy that results in death. These recently adopted statutes have attempted to address the concerns expressed by the Court in Furman primarily (i) by specifying the factors to be weighed and the procedures to be followed in deciding when to impose a capital sentence, or (ii) by making the death penalty mandatory for specified crimes. But all of the post-Furman statutes make clear that capital punishment itself has not been rejected by the elected representatives of the people.

In the only statewide referendum occurring since Furman and brought to our attention, the people of California adopted a constitutional amendment that authorized capital punishment, in effect negating a prior ruling by the Supreme Court of California that the death penalty violated the California Constitution.

. . .

It may be true that evolving standards have influenced juries in recent decades to be more discriminating in imposing the sentence of death. But the relative infrequency of jury verdicts imposing the death sentence does not indicate rejection of capital punishment per se. Rather, the reluctance of juries in many cases to impose the sentence may well reflect the humane feeling that this most irrevocable of sanctions should be reserved for a small number of extreme cases. Indeed, the actions of juries in many

States since Furman is fully compatible with the legislative judgments, reflected in the new statutes, as to the continued utility and necessity of capital punishment in appropriate cases. At the close of 1974 at least 254 persons had been sentenced to death since Furman, and by the end of March 1976, more than 460 persons were subject to death sentences.

As we have seen, however, the Eighth Amendment demands more than that a challenged punishment be acceptable to contemporary society. The Court also must ask whether it comports with the basic concept of human dignity at the core of the Amendment. . . .

.　　.　　.

The death penalty is said to serve two principal social purposes: retribution and deterrence of capital crimes by prospective offenders.

In part, capital punishment is an expression of society's moral outrage at particularly offensive conduct. This function may be unappealing to many, but it is essential in an ordered society that asks its citizens to rely on legal processes rather than self-help to vindicate their wrongs. . . .

.　　.　　.

Indeed, the decision that capital punishment may be the appropriate sanction in extreme cases is an expression of the community's belief that certain crimes are themselves so grievous an affront to humanity that the only adequate response may be the penalty of death.

Statistical attempts to evaluate the worth of the death penalty as a deterrent to crimes by potential offenders have occasioned a great deal of debate. The results simply have been inconclusive. . . .

.　　.　　.

Although some of the studies suggest that the death penalty may not function as a significantly greater deterrent than lesser penalties, there is no convincing empirical evidence either supporting or refuting this view. . . .

.　　.　　.

In sum, we cannot say that the judgment of the Georgia legislature that capital punishment may be necessary in some cases is clearly wrong. Considerations of federalism, as well as respect for the ability of a legislature to evaluate, in terms of its particular state the moral consensus concerning the death penalty and its social utility as a sanction, require us to conclude, in the absence of more convincing evidence, that the infliction of death as a punishment for murder is not without justification and thus is not unconstitutionally severe. . . .

. . .

We hold that the death penalty is not a form of punishment that may never be imposed, regardless of the circumstances of the offense, regardless of the character of the offender, and regardless of the procedure followed in reaching the decision to impose it.

We now consider whether Georgia may impose the death penalty on the petitioner in this case.

While Furman did not hold that the infliction of the death penalty per se violates the Constitution's ban on cruel and unusual punishments, it did recognize that the penalty of death is different in kind from any other punishment imposed under our system of criminal justice. Because of the uniqueness of the death penalty, Furman held that it could not be imposed under sentencing procedures that created a substantial risk that it would be inflicted in an arbitrary and capricious manner. . . .

. . .

Furman mandates that where discretion is afforded a sentencing body on a matter so grave as the determination of whether a human life should be taken or spared, that discretion must be suitably directed and limited so as to minimize the risk of wholly arbitrary and capricious action.

It is certainly not a novel proposition that discretion in the area of sentencing be exercised in an informed manner. We have long recognized that "[f]or the determination of sentences, justice generally requires . . . that there be taken into account the circumstances of the offense together with the character and propensities of the offender." . . .

. . .

But the provision of relevant information under fair procedural rules is not alone sufficient to guarantee that the information will be properly used in the imposition of punishment, especially if sentencing is performed by a jury. Since the members of a jury will have had little, if any, previous experience in sentencing, they are unlikely to be skilled in dealing with the information they are given. . . To the extent that this problem is inherent in jury sentencing, it may not be totally correctible. It seems clear, however, that the problem will be alleviated if the jury is given guidance regarding the factors about the crime and the defendant that the State, representing organized society, deems particularly relevant to the sentencing decision.

The idea that a jury should be given guidance in its decisionmaking is also hardly a novel proposition. Juries are invariably given careful instructions on the law and how to apply it before they are authorized to decide the merits of a lawsuit. It would be virtually unthinkable to follow any other course in a legal system that has traditionally operated by following prior precedents and fixed rules of law. . . .

. . .

While such standards are by necessity somewhat general, they do provide guidance to the sentencing authority and thereby reduce the likelihood that it will impose a sentence that fairly can be called capricious or arbitrary. Where the sentencing authority is required to specify the factors it relied upon in reaching its decision, the further safeguard of meaningful appellate review is available to ensure that death sentences are not imposed capriciously or in a freakish manner.

In summary, the concerns expressed in Furman that the penalty of death not be imposed in an arbitrary or capricious manner can be met by a carefully drafted statute that ensures that the sentencing authority is given adequate information and guidance. As a general proposition these concerns are best met by a system that provides for a bifurcated proceeding at which the sentencing authority is apprised of the information relevant to the imposition of sentence and provided with standards to guide its use of the information.

We do not intend to suggest that only the above-described procedures would be permissible under Furman or that any sentencing system constructed along these general lines would inevitably satisfy the concerns of Furman, for each distinct system must be examined on an individual basis. Rather, we have embarked upon this general exposition to make clear that it is possible to construct capital-sentencing systems capable of meeting Furman's constitutional concerns. . . .

. . .

275

Georgia did act [after Furman] to narrow the class of murderers subject to capital punishment by specifying 10 statutory aggravating circumstances, one of which must be found by the jury to exist beyond a reasonable doubt before a death sentence can ever be imposed. In addition, the jury is authorized to consider any other appropriate aggravating or mitigating circumstances. The jury is not required to find any mitigating circumstance in order to make a recommendation of mercy that is binding on the trial court, but it must find a *statutory* aggravating circumstance before recommending a sentence of death.

These procedures require the jury to consider the circumstances of the crime and the criminal before it recommends sentence. No longer can a Georgia jury do as Furman's jury did: reach a finding of the defendant's guilt and then, without guidance or direction, decide whether he should live or die. Instead, the jury's attention is directed to the specific circumstances of the crime: Was it committed in the course of another capital felony? Was it committed for money? Was it committed upon a peace officer or judicial officer? Was it committed in a particularly heinous way or in a manner that endangered the lives of many persons? In addition, the jury's attention is focused on the characteristics of the person who committed the crime: Does he have a record of prior convictions for capital offenses? Are there any special facts about this defendant that mitigate against imposing capital punishment (e.g., his youth, the extent of his cooperation with the police, his emotional state at the time of the crime). As a result, while some jury discretion still exists, "the discretion to be exercised is controlled by clear and objective standards so as to produce nondiscriminatory application."

As an important additional safeguard against arbitrariness and caprice, the Georgia statutory scheme provides for automatic appeal of all death sentences to the State's supreme court. That court is required by statute to review each sentence of death and determine whether it was imposed under the influence of passion or prejudice, whether the evidence supports the jury's finding of a statutory aggravating circumstance, and whether the sentence is disproportionate compared to those sentences imposed in similar cases. . . .

·   ·   ·

Finally, the Georgia statute has an additional provision designed to assure that the death penalty will not be imposed on a capriciously selected group of convicted defendants. The new sentencing procedures require that the state supreme court review every death sentence to determine whether it was imposed under the influence of passion, prejudice, or any other arbitrary factor, whether the evidence supports the findings of a statutory aggravating circumstance, and "[w]hether the sentence of death is excessive or disproportionate to the penalty imposed in similar cases, considering both the crime and the defendant." ... In performing its sentence-review function, the Georgia court has held that "if the death penalty is only rarely imposed for an act or it is substantially out of line with sentences imposed for other acts it will be set aside as excessive." ... The court on another occasion stated that "we view it to be our duty under the similarity standard to assure that no death sentence is affirmed unless in similar cases throughout the state the death penalty has been imposed generally" ....

It is apparent that the Supreme Court of Georgia has taken its review responsibilities seriously. In Coley, it held that "[t]he prior cases indicate that the past practice among juries faced with similar factual situations and like aggravating circumstances has been to impose only the sentence of life imprisonment for the offense of rape, rather than death." ... It thereupon reduced Coley's sentence from death to life imprisonment. Similarly, although armed robbery is a capital offense under Georgia law, ... the Georgia court concluded that the death sentences imposed in this case for that crime were "unusual in that they are rarely imposed for [armed robbery]. Thus, under the test provided by statute, ... they must be considered to be excessive or disproportionate to the penalties imposed in similar cases." ... The court therefore vacated Gregg's death sentences for armed robbery and has followed a similar course in every other armed robbery death penalty case to come before it.

The provision for appellate review in the Georgia capital-sentencing system serves as a check against the random or arbitrary imposition of the death penalty. In particular, the proportionality review substantially eliminates the possibility that a person will be sentenced to die by the action of an aberrant jury. If a time comes when juries generally do not impose the death sentence in a certain kind of murder case, the appellate review procedures assures that no defendant convicted under such circumstances will suffer a sentence of death....

•   •   •

For the reasons expressed in this opinion, we hold that the statutory system under which Gregg was sentenced to death does not violate the Constitution. Accordingly, the judgment of the Georgia Supreme Court is affirmed.

· · ·

Mr. Justice White, with whom The Chief Justice and Mr. Justice Rehnquist join, concurring in the judgment.

· · ·

The Georgia Legislature has made an effort to identify those aggravating factors which it considers necessary and relevant to the question whether a defendant convicted of capital murder should be sentenced to death. The jury which imposes sentence is instructed on all statutory aggravating factors which are supported by the evidence, and is told that it may not impose the death penalty unless it unanimously finds at least one of those factors to have been established beyond a reasonable doubt. The Georgia Legislature has plainly made an effort to guide the jury in the exercise of its discretion, while at the same time permitting the jury to dispense mercy on the basis of factors too intangible to write into a statute and I cannot accept the naked assertion that the effort is bound to fail. As the types of murders for which the death penalty may be imposed become more narrowly defined and are limited to those which are particularly serious or for which the death penalty is peculiarly appropriate as they are in Georgia by reason of the aggravating circumstance requirement, it becomes reasonable to expect that juries—even given discretion *not* to impose the death penalty—will impose the death penalty in a substantial portion of the cases so defined. If they do, it can no longer be said that the penalty is being imposed wantonly and freakishly or so infrequently that it loses its usefulness as a sentencing device. There is, therefore, reason to expect that Georgia's current system would escape the infirmities which invalidated its previous system under Furman. However, the Georgia Legislature was not satisfied with a system which might but might not turn out in practice to result in death sentences being imposed with reasonable consistency for certain serious murders. Instead, it gave the Georgia Supreme Court the power and the obligation to perform precisely the task which three Justices of this Court, whose opinions were necessary to the result, performed in Furman: namely the task of deciding whether *in fact* the death penalty was being administered for any given class of crime in a discriminatory, standardless, or rare fashion. . . .

. . .

Statement of The Chief Justice and Mr. Justice Rehnquist.

. . .

Mr. Justice Blackmun, concurring in the judgment.

. . .

Mr. Justice Brennan, dissenting.

. . .

This Court inescapably has the duty, as the ultimate arbiter of the meaning of our Constitution, to say whether, when individuals condemned to death stand before our Bar, "moral concepts" require us to hold that the law has progressed to the point where we should declare that the punishment of death, like punishments on the rack, the screw and the wheel, is no longer morally tolerable in our civilized society. My opinion in Furman v Georgia concluded that our civilization and the law had progressed to this point and that therefore the punishment of death, for whatever crime and under all circumstances, is "cruel and unusual" in violation of the Eighth and Fourteenth Amendments of the Constitution. I shall not again canvass the reasons that led to that conclusion. I emphasize only that foremost among the "moral concepts" recognized in our cases and inherent in the Clause is the primary moral principle that the State, even as it punishes, must treat its citizens in a manner consistent with their intrinsic worth as human beings—a punishment must not be so severe as to be degrading to human dignity. A judicial determination whether the punishment of death comports with human dignity is therefore not only permitted but compelled by the Clause. . . .

. . .

Mr. Justice Marshall, dissenting.

. . .

Since the decision in Furman, the legislatures of 35 States have enacted new statutes authorizing the imposition of the death sentence for certain crimes, and Congress has enacted a law providing the death penalty for air piracy resulting in death. I would be less than candid if I did not acknowledge that these developments have a significant bearing on a realistic assessment of the moral acceptability of the death penalty to the American people. But if the constitutionality of the death penalty turns, as I have urged, on the opinion of an *informed* citizenry, then even the enactment of new death statutes cannot be viewed as conclusive. In Furman, I observed that the American people are largely unaware of the information critical to a judgment on the morality of the death penalty, and concluded that if they were better informed they would consider it shocking, unjust, and unacceptable. A recent study, conducted after the enactment of the post-Furman statutes, has confirmed that the American people know little about the death penalty, and that the opinions of an informed public would differ significantly from those of a public unaware of the consequences and effects of the death penalty.[1]

Even assuming, however, that the post-Furman enactment of statutes authorizing the death penalty renders the prediction of the views of an informed citizenry an uncertain basis for a constitutional decision, the enactment of those statutes has no bearing whatsoever on the conclusion that the death penalty is unconstitutional because it is excessive. An excessive penalty is invalid under the Cruel and Unusual Punishments Clause "even though popular sentiment may favor" it. . . .

· · ·

The death penalty, unnecessary to promote the goal of deterrence or to further any legitimate notion of retribution, is an excessive penalty forbidden by the Eighth and Fourteenth Amendments. I respectfully dissent from the Court's judgment upholding the sentences of death imposed upon the petitioners in these cases.

· · ·

Like Georgia, Florida and Texas had adopted new death penalty statutes in the wake of Furman. These new statutes were similar to the Georgia one in that they provided for bifurcated proceedings and attempted to spell out aggravating and mitigating circumstances for the jurors and trial judges. On the same day as Gregg but in separate

---

1. Sarat and Vidmar, Public Opinion, The Death Penalty, and the Eighth Amendment: Testing the Marshall Hypothesis, 1976 Wisc L Rev 171.

opinions the Court upheld these two statutes with the same division of opinion as in Gregg. (*Proffitt* v. *Florida,* 428 U.S. 242, 1976; *Jurek* v. *Texas,* 428 U.S. 262, 1976.)

Woodson v. North Carolina

428 U.S. 280, 49 L Ed 2d 944, 96 S Ct 2978 (1976)

After the decision in *Furman v. Georgia,* the North Carolina Supreme Court held invalid that part of its state's statute that gave juries unbridled discretion to impose or withhold the death penalty in first-degree murder cases; the rest of the statute remained as a mandatory death sentence law. Subsequently, the legislature rewrote the law prescribing a mandatory death penalty upon a finding of guilt in first-degree murder cases. Woodson and a co-defendant were convicted of murder occurring during an armed robbery and were sentenced to death. The North Carolina Supreme Court affirmed.

. . .

Mr. Justice Stewart, Mr. Justice Powell, and Mr. Justice Stevens announced the judgment of the Court and filed an opinion delivered by Mr. Justice Stewart.

. . .

At the time of this Court's decision in Furman v Georgia, North Carolina law provided that in cases of first-degree murder, the jury in its unbridled discretion could choose whether the convicted defendant should be sentenced to death or to life imprisonment. After the Furman decision the Supreme Court of North Carolina held unconstitutional the provision of the death penalty statute that gave the jury the option of returning a verdict of guilty without capital punishment, but held further that this provision was severable so that the statute survived as a mandatory death penalty law.

The North Carolina General Assembly in 1974 followed the court's lead and enacted a new statute that was essentially unchanged from the old one except that it made the death penalty mandatory. . . .

. . .

North Carolina, unlike Florida, Georgia, and Texas, has thus responded to the Furman decision by making death the mandatory sentence for all persons convicted of first-degree murder. In ruling on the constitutionality of the sentences imposed on the petitioners under this North Carolina statute, the Court now addresses for the first time the question whether a death sentence returned pursuant to a law imposing a mandatory death penalty for a broad category of homicidal offenses constitutes cruel and unusual punishment within the meaning of the Eighth and Fourteenth Amendments. The issue, like that explored in Furman, involves the procedure employed by the State to select persons for the unique and irreversible penalty of death. . . .

. . .

[W]e begin by sketching the history of mandatory death penalty statutes in the United States. At the time the Eighth Amendment was adopted in 1791, the States uniformly followed the common-law practice of making death the exclusive and mandatory sentence for certain specified offenses. Although the range of capital offenses in the American colonies was quite limited in comparison to the more than 200 offenses then punishable by death in England, the colonies at the time of the Revolution imposed death sentences on all persons convicted of any of a considerable number of crimes. . . Almost from the outset jurors reacted unfavorably to the harshness of mandatory death sentences. The States initially responded to this expression of public dissatisfaction with mandatory statutes by limiting the classes of capital offenses.

This reform, however, left unresolved the problem posed by the not infrequent refusal of juries to convict murderers rather than subject them to automatic death sentences. . . .

. . .

Despite the broad acceptance of the division of murder into degrees, the reform proved to be an unsatisfactory means of identifying persons appropriately punishable by death. . . Juries continued to find the death penalty inappropriate in a significant number of first-degree murder cases and refused to return guilty verdicts for that crime.

The inadequacy of distinguishing between murderers solely on the basis of legislative criteria narrowing the definition of the capital offense led the States to grant juries sentencing discretion in capital cases. Tennessee in 1838, followed by Alabama in 1841, and Louisiana in 1846, were the first States to abandon mandatory death sentences in favor of discretionary death penalty statutes. This flexibility remedied the harshness of mandatory statutes by permitting the jury to respond to mitigating factors by withholding the death penalty. By the turn of the century, 23 States and the Federal Government had made death sentences discretionary for first-degree murder and other capital offenses. During the next two decades 14 additional States replaced their mandatory death penalty statutes. Thus, by the end of World War I, all but eight States, Hawaii, and the District of Columbia either had adopted discretionary death penalty schemes or abolished the death penalty altogether. By 1963, all of these remaining jurisdictions had replaced their automatic death penalty statutes with discretionary jury sentencing. . . .

. . .

The history of mandatory death penalty statutes in the United States thus reveals that the practice of sentencing to death all persons convicted of a particular offense has been rejected as unduly harsh and unworkably rigid. . . .

. . .

As we have noted today in Gregg v Georgia, legislative measures adopted by the people's chosen representatives weigh heavily in ascertaining contemporary standards of decency. The consistent course charted by the state legislatures and by Congress since the middle of the past century demonstrates that the aversion of jurors to mandatory death penalty statutes is shared by society at large.

Still further evidence of the incompatibility of mandatory death penalties with contemporary values is provided by the results of jury sentencing under discretionary statutes. . . Various studies indicate that even in first-degree murder cases juries with sentencing discretion do not impose the death penalty "with any great frequency." The actions of sentencing juries suggest that under contemporary standards of decency death is viewed as an inappropriate punishment for a substantial portion of convicted first-degree murderers. . . .

. . .

Although it seems beyond dispute that, at the time of the Furman decision in 1972, mandatory death penalty statutes had been renounced by American juries and legislatures, there remains the question whether the mandatory statutes adopted by North Carolina and a number of other States following Furman evince a sudden reversal of societal values regarding the imposition of capital punishment. In view of the persistent and unswerving legislative rejection of mandatory death penalty statutes beginning in 1838 and continuing for more than 130 years until Furman, it seems evident that the post-Furman enactments reflect attempts by the States to retain the death penalty in a form consistent with the Constitution, rather than a renewed societal acceptance of mandatory death sentencing. The fact that some States have adopted mandatory measures following Furman while others have legislated standards to guide jury discretion appears attributable to diverse readings of this Court's multi-opinioned decision in that case. . . .

. . .

As the above discussion makes clear, one of the most significant developments in our society's treatment of capital punishment has been the rejection of the common-law practice of inexorably imposing a death sentence upon every person convicted of a specified offense. North Carolina's mandatory death penalty statute for first-degree murder departs markedly from contemporary standards respecting the imposition of the punishment of death and thus cannot be applied consistently with the Eighth and Fourteenth Amendments' requirement that the State's power to punish "be exercised within the limits of civilized standards."

A separate deficiency of North Carolina's mandatory death sentence statute is its failure to provide a constitutionally tolerable response to Furman's rejection of unbridled jury discretion in the imposition of capital sentences. Central to the limited holding in Furman was the conviction that the vesting of standardless sentencing power in the jury violated the Eighth and Fourteenth Amendments. It is argued that North Carolina has remedied the inadequacies of the death penalty statutes held unconstitutional in Furman by withdrawing all sentencing discretion from juries in capital cases. But when one considers the long and consistent American experience with the death penalty in first-degree murder cases, it becomes evident that mandatory statutes enacted in response to Furman have simply papered over the problem of unguided and unchecked jury discretion. . . .

. . .

[T]here is general agreement that American juries have persistently refused to convict a significant portion of persons charged with first-degree murder of that offense under mandatory death penalty statutes. . . In view of the historic record, it is only reasonable to assume that many juries under mandatory statutes will continue to consider the grave consequences of a conviction in reaching a verdict. North Carolina's mandatory death penalty statute provides no standards to guide the jury in its inevitable exercise of the power to determine which first-degree murderers shall live and which shall die. And there is no way under the North Carolina law for the judiciary to check arbitrary and capricious exercise of that power through a review of death sentences. Instead of rationalizing the sentencing process, a mandatory scheme may well exacerbate the problem identified in Furman by resting the penalty determination on the particular jury's willingness to act lawlessly. While a mandatory death penalty statute may reasonably be expected to increase the number of persons sentenced to death, it does not fulfill Furman's basic requirement by replacing arbitrary and wanton jury discretion with objective standards to guide, regularize, and make rationally reviewable the process for imposing a sentence of death.

A third constitutional shortcoming of the North Carolina statute is its failure to allow the particularized consideration of relevant aspects of the character and record of each convicted defendant before the imposition upon him of a sentence of death. . . A process that accords no significance to relevant facets of the character and record of the individual offender or the circumstances of the particular offense excludes from consideration in fixing the ultimate punishment of death the possibility of compassionate or mitigating factors stemming from the diverse frailties of humankind. It treats all persons convicted of a designated offense not as uniquely individual human beings, but as members of a faceless, undifferentiated mass to be subjected to the blind infliction of the penalty of death. . . .

. . .

While the prevailing practice of individualizing sentencing determinations generally reflects simply enlightened policy rather than a constitutional imperative, we believe that in capital cases the fundamental respect for humanity underlying the Eighth Amendment requires consideration of the character and record of the individual offender and the circumstances of the particular offense as a constitutionally indispensable part of the process of inflicting the penalty of death.

This conclusion rests squarely on the predicate that the penalty of death is qualitatively different from a sentence of imprisonment, however long. Death, in its finality, differs more from life imprisonment than a 100-year prison term differs from one of only a year or two. Because of that qualitative difference, there is a corresponding difference in the need for reliability in the determination that death is the appropriate punishment in a specific case. . . .

. . .

The judgment of the Supreme Court of North Carolina is reversed insofar as it upheld the death sentences imposed upon the petitioners, and the case is remanded for further proceedings not inconsistent with this opinion.

. . .

Mr. Justice Brennan, concurring in the judgment.

For the reasons stated in my dissenting opinion in Gregg v Georgia, I concur in the judgment that sets aside the death sentences imposed under the North Carolina death sentence statute as violative of the Eighth and Fourteenth Amendments.

. . .

Mr. Justice Marshall, concurring in the judgment.

For the reasons stated in my dissenting opinion in Gregg v Georgia, I am of the view that the death penalty is a cruel and unusual punishment forbidden by the Eighth and Fourteenth Amendments. I therefore concur in the Court's judgment.

Mr. Justice White, with whom The Chief Justice and Mr. Justice Rehnquist join, dissenting.

. . .

Mr. Justice Blackmun, dissenting.

. . .

Mr. Justice Rehnquist, dissenting.

The difficulties which attend the plurality's explanation for the result it reaches tend at first to obscure difficulties at least as significant which inhere in the unarticulated premises which necessarily underlie that explanation. . . .

. . .

The plurality relies first upon its conclusion that society has turned away from the mandatory imposition of death sentences, and second upon its conclusion that the North Carolina system has "simply papered over" the problem of unbridled jury discretion. . . The third "constitutional shortcoming" of the North Carolina statute is said to be "its failure to allow the particularized consideration of relevant aspects of the character and record of each convicted defendant before the imposition upon him of a sentence of death."

I do not believe that any one of these reasons singly, nor all of them together, can withstand careful analysis. Contrary to the plurality's assertions, they would import into the Cruel and Unusual Punishment Clause procedural requirements which find no support in our cases. Their application will result in the invalidation of a death sentence imposed upon a defendant convicted of first-degree murder under the North Carolina system, and the upholding of the same sentence imposed on an identical defendant convicted on identical evidence of first-degree murder under the Florida, Georgia, or Texas systems—a result surely as "freakish" as that condemned in the separate opinions in Furman.

The plurality is simply mistaken in its assertion that "[t]he history of mandatory death penalty statutes in the United States thus reveals that the practice of sentencing to death all persons convicted of a particular offense have been rejected as unduly harsh and unworkably rigid.". . .

. . .

The legislative narrowing of the spectrum of capital crimes, therefore, while very arguably representing a general societal judgment since the trend was so widespread, simply never reached far enough to exclude the sort of aggravated homicide of which petitioners stand convicted.

The second string to the plurality's analytical bow is that legislative change from mandatory to discretionary imposition of the death sentence likewise evidences societal rejection of mandatory death penalties. The plurality simply does not make out this part of its case, however, in large part because it treats as being of equal dignity with legislative judgments the judgments of particular juries and of individual jurors.

There was undoubted dissatisfaction, from more than one sector of 19th century society, with the operation of mandatory death sentences. One segment of that society was totally opposed to capital punishment, and was apparently willing to accept the substitution of discretionary imposition of that penalty for its mandatory imposition as a halfway house on the road to total abolition. Another segment was equally unhappy with the operation of the mandatory system, but for an entirely different reason. As the plurality recognizes, this second segment of society was unhappy with the operation of the mandatory system, not because of the death sentences imposed under it, but because people obviously guilty of criminal offenses were not being convicted under it. Change to a discretionary system was accepted by these persons not because they thought mandatory imposition of the death penalty was cruel and unusual, but because they thought that if jurors were permitted to return a sentence other than death upon the conviction of a capital crime, fewer guilty defendants would be acquitted.

So far as the action of juries is concerned, the fact that in some cases juries operating under the mandatory system refused to convict obviously guilty defendants does not reflect any "turning away" from the death penalty, or the mandatory death penalty, supporting the proposition that it is "cruel and unusual." Given the requirement of unanimity with respect to jury verdicts in capital cases, ... it is apparent that a single juror could prevent a jury from returning a verdict of conviction. Occasional refusals to convict, therefore, may just as easily have represented the intransigence of only a small minority of 12 jurors as well as the unanimous judgment of all 12. The fact that the presence of such jurors could prevent conviction in a given case, even though the majority of society, speaking through legislatures, had decreed that it should be imposed, certainly does not indicate that society as a whole rejected mandatory punishment for such offenders; it does not even indicate that those few members of society who serve on juries, as a whole, had done so.

The introduction of discretionary sentencing likewise creates no inference that contemporary society had rejected the mandatory system as unduly severe. Legislatures enacting discretionary sentencing statutes had no reason to think that there would not be roughly the same number of capital convictions under the new system as under the old. The same subjective juror responses which resulted in juror nullification under the old system were legitimized, but in the absence of those subjective responses to a particular set of facts, a capital sentence could as likely be anticipated under the discretionary system as under the mandatory. And at least some of those who would have been acquitted under the mandatory system would be subjected to at least some punishment under the discretionary system, rather than escaping altogether a penalty for the crime of which they were guilty. That society was unwilling to accept the paradox presented to it by the actions of some maverick juries or jurors—the acquittal of palpably guilty defendants—hardly reflects the sort of an "evolving standard of decency" to which the plurality professes obeisance. . . .

. . .

The plurality concedes, as they must, that following Furman 10 States enacted laws providing for mandatory capital punishment. . . These enactments the plurality seeks to explain as due to a wrong-headed reading of the holding in Furman. But this explanation simply does not wash. While those States may be presumed to have preferred their prior systems reposing sentencing discretion in juries or judges, they indisputably preferred mandatory capital punishment to no capital punishment at all. Their willingness to enact statutes providing that penalty is utterly inconsistent with the notion that they regarded mandatory capital sentencing as beyond "evolving standards of decency." The plurality's glib rejection of these legislative decisions as having little weight on the scale which it finds in the Eighth Amendment seems to me more an instance of their desire to save the people from themselves than a conscientious effort to ascertain the content of any "evolving standard of decency."

The second constitutional flaw which the plurality finds in North Carolina's mandatory system is that it has simply "papered over" the problem of unchecked jury discretion. . . .

. . .

In North Carolina jurors unwilling to impose the death penalty may simply hang a jury or they may so assert themselves that a verdict of not guilty is brought in; in Louisiana they will have a similar effect in causing some juries to bring in a verdict of guilty of a lesser included offense even though all the jurors are satisfied that the elements of the greater offense are made out. Such jurors, of course, are violating their oath, but such violation is not only consistent with the majority's hypothesis; the majority's hypothesis is bottomed on its occurrence.

For purposes of argument, I accept the plurality's hypothesis: but it seems to me impossible to conclude from it that a mandatory death sentence statute such as North Carolina enacted is any less sound constitutionally than are the systems enacted by Georgia, Florida, and Texas which the Court upholds.

In Georgia juries are entitled to return a sentence of life, rather than death, for no reason whatever, simply based upon their own subjective notions of what is right and what is wrong. In Florida the judge and jury are required to weigh legislatively enacted aggravating factors against legislatively enacted mitigating factors, and then base their choice between life or death on an estimate of the result of that weighing. Substantial discretion exists here, too, though it is somewhat more canalized than it is in Georgia. Why these types of discretion are regarded by the plurality as constitutionally permissible, while that which may occur in the North Carolina system is not, is not readily apparent... To conclude that the North Carolina system is bad because juror nullification may permit jury discretion while concluding that the Georgia and Florida systems are sound because they *require* this same discretion, is, as the plurality opinion demonstrates, inexplicable....

· · ·

The plurality's insistence on individualized consideration of the sentencing ... depends not upon any traditional application of the prohibition against cruel and unusual punishment contained in the Eighth Amendment. The punishment here is concededly not cruel and unusual, and that determination has traditionally ended judicial inquiry in our cases construing the Cruel and Unusual Punishment Clause. What the plurality opinion has actually done is to import into the Due Process Clause of the Fourteenth Amendment what it conceives to be desirable procedural guarantees where the punishment of death, concededly not cruel and unusual for the crime of which the defendant was convicted, is to be imposed....

· · ·

[T]he judgments of conviction should be affirmed.

. . .

Louisiana had also adopted a mandatory death sentence statute following the decision in *Furman* and in *Roberts* v. *Louisiana,* 428 U.S. 325 (1976), it suffered the same fate as the North Carolina statute. July 2, 1976, was a busy day for death penalty decisions. Three states had statutes enacted in response to Furman upheld, and two other states had their new efforts invalidated. It also was clear that the justices were uncertain just where they were going in this group of decisions; three was the largest number who could agree on an opinion.

Coker v. Georgia

433 U.S. 584, 53 L Ed 2d 982, 97 S Ct 2861 (1977)

Petitioner escaped from a Georgia correctional institution where he was serving sentences (including consecutive life sentences) for murder, rape, kidnapping, and aggravated assault. While free, he raped a woman during an armed robbery. He was sentenced to death by a jury that found as aggravating circumstances that he was a person previously convicted of a capital felony and that he had committed this felony (the rape) during the commission of still another capital felony (the armed robbery). The Georgia Supreme Court affirmed.

. . .

Mr. Justice White announced the judgment of the Court and filed an opinion in which Mr. Justice Stewart, Mr. Justice Blackmun, and Mr. Justice Stevens, joined.

Georgia Code Ann § 26-2001 (1972) provides that "[a] person convicted of rape shall be punished by death or by imprisonment for life, or by imprisonment for not less than 20 years." Punishment is determined by a jury in a separate sentencing proceeding in which at least one of the statutory aggravating circumstances must be found before the death penalty may be imposed. Petitioner Coker was convicted of rape and sentenced to death. Both conviction and sentence were affirmed by the Georgia Supreme Court. Coker was granted a writ of certiorari, limited to the single claim, rejected by the Georgia court, that the punishment of death for rape violates the Eighth Amendment, which proscribes "cruel and unusual punishments" and which must be observed by the States as well as the Federal Government. . . .

. . .

It is now settled that the death penalty is not invariably cruel and unusual punishment within the meaning of the Eighth Amendment; it is not inherently barbaric or an unacceptable mode of punishment for crime; neither is it always disproportionate to the crime for which it is imposed. It is also established that imposing capital punishment, at least for murder, in accordance with the procedures provided under the Georgia statutes saves the sentence from the infirmities which led the Court to invalidate the prior Georgia capital punishment statute in Furman v Georgia. [See Gregg v. Georgia] . . . .

. . .

Under Gregg, a punishment is "excessive" and unconstitutional if it (1) makes no measurable contribution to acceptable goals of punishment and hence is nothing more than the purposeless and needless imposition of pain and suffering; or (2) is grossly out of proportion to the severity of the crime. A punishment might fail the test on either ground. Furthermore, these Eighth Amendment judgments should not be, or appear to be, merely the subjective views of individual Justices; judgment should be informed by objective factors to the maximum possible extent. To this end, attention must be given to the public attitudes concerning a particular sentence—history and precedent, legislative attitudes, and the response of juries reflected in their sentencing decisions are to be consulted. In Gregg, after giving due regard to such sources, the Court's judgment was that the death penalty for deliberate murder was neither the purposeless imposition of severe punishment nor a punishment grossly disproportionate to the crime. But the Court reserved the question of the constitutionality of the death penalty when imposed for other crimes.

That question, with respect to rape of an adult woman, is now before us. We have concluded that a sentence of death is grossly disproportionate and excessive punishment for the crime of rape and is therefore forbidden by the Eighth Amendment as cruel and unusual punishment.

As advised by recent cases, we seek guidance in history and from the objective evidence of the country's present judgment concerning the acceptability of death as a penalty for rape of an adult woman. At no time in the last 50 years has a majority of the States authorized death as a punishment for rape. In 1925, 18 States, the District of Columbia, and the Federal Government authorized capital punishment for the rape of an adult female. By 1971 just prior to the decision in Furman v Georgia, that number had declined, but not substantially, to 16 States plus the Federal Government. Furman then invalidated most of the capital punishment statutes in this country. . . .

. . .

Thirty-five States immediately reinstituted the death penalty for at least limited kinds of crime. . . .

. . .

In reviving death penalty laws to satisfy Furman's mandate, none of the States that had not previously authorized death for rape chose to include rape among capital felonies. Of the 16 States in which rape had been a capital offense, only three provided the death penalty for rape of an adult woman in their revised statutes—Georgia, North Carolina, and Louisiana. In the latter two States, the death penalty was mandatory for those found guilty, and those laws were invalidated by Woodson and Roberts. When Louisiana and North Carolina, responding to those decisions, again revised their capital punishment laws, they reenacted the death penalty for murder but not for rape; none of the seven other legislatures that to our knowledge have amended or replaced their death penalty statutes since July 2, 1976, including four States (in addition to Louisiana and North Carolina) that had authorized the death sentence for rape prior to 1972 and had reacted to Furman with mandatory statutes, included rape among the crimes for which death was an authorized punishment. . . .

. . .

The upshot is that Georgia is the sole jurisdiction in the United States at the present time that authorizes a sentence of death when the rape victim is an adult woman, and only two other jurisdictions provide capital punishment when the victim is a child.

The current judgment with respect to the death penalty for rape is not wholly unanimous among state legislatures, but it obviously weighs very heavily on the side of rejecting capital punishment as a suitable penalty for raping an adult woman. . . .

.   .   .

According to the factual submissions in this Court, out of all rape convictions in Georgia since 1973—and that total number has not been tendered—63 cases had been reviewed by the Georgia Supreme Court as of the time of oral argument; and of these, six involved a death sentence, one of which was set aside, leaving five convicted rapists now under sentence of death in the State of Georgia. Georgia juries have thus sentenced rapists to death six times since 1973. This obviously is not a negligible number; and the State argues that as a practical matter juries simply reserve the extreme sanction for extreme cases of rape and that recent experience surely does not prove that jurors consider the death penalty to be a disproportionate punishment for every conceivable instance of rape, no matter how aggravated. Nevertheless, it is true that in the vast majority of cases, at least nine out of 10, juries have not imposed the death sentence. . . .

.   .   .

[T]he legislative rejection of capital punishment for rape strongly confirms our own judgment, which is that death is indeed a disproportionate penalty for the crime of raping an adult woman.

We do not discount the seriousness of rape as a crime. It is highly reprehensible, both in a moral sense and in its almost total contempt for the personal integrity and autonomy of the female victim and for the latter's privilege of choosing those with whom intimate relationships are to be established. Short of homicide, it is the "ultimate violation of self." It is also a violent crime because it normally involves force, or the threat of force or intimidation, to overcome the will and the capacity of the victim to resist. Rape is very often accompanied by physical injury to the female and can also inflict mental and psychological damage. Because it undermines the community's sense of security, there is public injury as well.

Rape is without doubt deserving of serious punishment; but in terms of moral depravity and of the injury to the person and to the public, it does not compare with murder, which does involve the unjustified taking of human life. Although it may be accompanied by another crime, rape by definition does not include the death or even the serious injury to another person. The murderer kills; the rapist, if no more than that, does not. Life is over for the victim of the murderers; for the rape victim, life may not be nearly so happy as it was, but it is not over and normally is not beyond repair. We have the abiding conviction that the death penalty, which "is unique in its severity and revocability," is an excessive penalty for the rapist who, as such, does not take human life. . . .

. . .

The judgment of the Georgia Supreme Court upholding the death sentence is reversed and the case is remanded to that court for further proceedings not inconsistent with this opinion.

. . .

Mr. Justice Brennan, concurring in the judgment.

. . .

Mr. Justice Marshall, concurring in the judgment of the Court.

. . .

Mr. Justice Powell, concurring in part and dissenting in part.

I concur in the judgment of the Court on the facts of this case, and also in its reasoning supporting the view that ordinarily death is disproportionate punishment for the crime of raping an adult woman. Although rape invariably is a reprehensible crime, there is no indication that petitioner's offense was committed with excessive brutality or that the victim sustained serious or lasting injury. The plurality, however, does not limit its holding to the case before us or to similar cases. Rather, in an opinion that ranges well beyond what is necessary, it holds that capital punishment *always*—regardless of the circumstances—is a disproportionate penalty for the crime of rape. . . .

. . .

It is . . . quite unnecessary for the plurality to write in terms so sweeping as to foreclose each of the 50 state legislatures from creating a narrowly defined substantive crime of aggravated rape punishable by death. . . .

. . .

Mr. Chief Justice Burger, with whom Mr. Justice Rehnquist joins, dissenting.

In a case such as this, confusion often arises as to the Court's proper role in reaching a decision. Our task is not to give effect to our individual views on capital punishment; rather, we must determine what the Constitution permits a State to do under its reserved powers. In striking down the death penalty imposed upon the petitioner in this case, the Court has overstepped the bounds of proper constitutional adjudication by substituting its policy judgment for that of the state legislature. I accept that the Eighth Amendment's concept of disproportionality bars the death penalty for minor crimes. But rape is not a minor crime; hence the Cruel and Unusual Punishment Clause does not give the Members of this Court license to engraft their conceptions of proper public policy onto the considered legislative judgments of the States. Since I cannot agree that Georgia lacked the constitutional power to impose the penalty of death for rape, I dissent from the Court's judgment.

. . .

My first disagreement with the Court's holding is its unnecessary breadth. . . .

. . .

Unlike the Court, I would narrow the inquiry in this case to the question actually presented: Does the Eight Amendment's ban against cruel and unusual punishment prohibit the State of Georgia from executing a person who has, within the space of three years, raped three separate women, killing one and attempting to kill another, who is serving prison terms exceeding his probable lifetime and who has not hesitated to escape confinement at the first available opportunity? Whatever one's view may be as to the State's constitutional power to impose the death penalty upon a rapist who stands before a court convicted for the first time, this case reveals a chronic rapist whose continuing danger to the community is abundantly clear. . . .

. . .

[O]nce the Court has held that "the punishment of death does not invariably violate the Constitution," Gregg v Georgia, it seriously impinges upon the State's legislative judgment to hold that it may not impose such sentence upon an individual who has shown total and repeated disregard for the welfare, safety, personal integrity and human worth of others, and who seemingly cannot be deterred from continuing such conduct. I therefore would hold that the death sentence here imposed is within the power reserved to the State and leave for another day the question of whether such sanction would be proper under other circumstances. The dangers which inhere whenever the Court casts its constitutional decisions in terms sweeping beyond the facts of the case presented, are magnified in the context of the Eighth Amendment... Since the Court now invalidates the death penalty as a sanction for all rapes of adults at all times under all circumstances, I reluctantly turn to what I see as the broader issues raised by this holding....

.   .   .

Despite its strong condemnation of rape, the Court reaches the inexplicable conclusion that "the death penalty ... is an excessive penalty" for the perpetrator of this heinous offense. This, the Court holds, is true even though in Georgia the death penalty may be imposed only where the rape is coupled with one or more aggravating circumstances. The process by which this conclusion is reached is as startling as it is disquieting. It represents a clear departure from precedent by making this Court "under the aegis of the Cruel and Unusual Punishment Clause, the ultimate arbiter of the standards of criminal responsibility in diverse areas of the criminal law, throughout the country." This seriously strains and distorts our federal system, removing much of the flexibility from which it has drawn strength for two centuries....

.   .   .

The plurality opinion bases its analysis, in part, on the fact that "Georgia is the sole jurisdiction in the United States at the present time that authorizes the sentence of death when the rape victim is an adult woman." Surely, however, this statistic cannot be deemed determinative, or even particularly relevant....

.   .   .

[I]t is myopic to base sweeping constitutional principles upon the narrow experience of the past five years. Considerable uncertainty was introduced into this area of the law by this Court's Furman decision. A large number of States found their death penalty statutes invalidated; legislatures were left in serious doubt by the expressions vacillating between discretionary and mandatory death penalties, as to whether this Court would sustain *any* statute imposing death as a criminal sanction. Failure of more States to enact statutes imposing death for rape of an adult woman may thus reflect hasty legislative compromise occasioned by time pressures following Furman, a desire to wait on the experience of those States which did enact such statutes, or simply an accurate forecast of today's holding.

In any case, when considered in light of the experience since the turn of this century, where more than one-third of American jurisdictions have consistently provided the death penalty for rape, the plurality's focus on the experience of the immediate past must be viewed as truly disingenuous. Having in mind the swift changes in positions of some Members of this Court in the short span of five years, can it rationally be considered a relevant indicator of what our society deems "cruel and unusual" to look solely to what legislatures have *refrained* from doing under conditions of great uncertainty arising from our less than lucid holdings on the Eighth Amendment? Far more representative of societal mores of the 20th Century is the accepted practice in a substantial number of jurisdictions preceding the Furman decision. . . .

. . .

The Court has repeatedly pointed to the reserve strength of our federal system which allows state legislatures, within broad limits, to experiment with laws, both criminal and civil, in the effort to achieve socially desirable results. . . .

. . .

Statutory provisions in criminal justice applied in one part of the country can be carefully watched by other state legislatures, so that the experience of one State becomes available to all. Although human lives are in the balance, it must be remembered that failure to allow flexibility may also jeopardize human lives—those of the victims of undeterred criminal conduct. Our concern for the accused ought not foreclose legislative judgments showing a modicum of consideration for the potential victims. . . .

.   .   .

The question of whether the death penalty is an appropriate punishment for rape is surely an open one. It is arguable that many prospective rapists would be deterred by the possibility that they could suffer death for their offense; it is also arguable that the death penalty would have only minimal deterrent effect. It may well be that rape victims would become more willing to report the crime and aid in the apprehension of the criminals if they knew that community disapproval of rapists was sufficiently strong to inflict the extreme penalty; or perhaps they would be reluctant to cooperate in the prosecution of rapists if they knew that a conviction might result in the imposition of the death penalty. Quite possibly, the occasional, well-publicized execution of egregious rapists may cause citizens to feel greater security in their daily lives, or, on the contrary, it may be that members of a civilized community will suffer the pangs of a heavy conscience because such punishment will be perceived as excessive. We cannot know which among this range of possibilities is correct, but today's holding forecloses the very exploration we have said federalism was intended to foster. It is difficult to believe that Georgia would long remain alone in punishing rape by death if the next decade demonstrated a drastic reduction in its incidence of rape, an increased cooperation by rape victims in the apprehension and prosecution of rapists, and a greater confidence in the rule of law on the part of the populace. . . .

.   .   .

The subjective judgment that the death penalty is simply disproportionate for the crime of rape is even more disturbing than the "objective" analysis discussed supra. The plurality's conclusion on this point is based upon the bare fact that murder necessarily results in the physical death of the victim, while rape does not. However, no Member of the Court explains why this distinction has relevance, much less constitutional significance. It is, after all, not irrational—nor constitutionally impermissible—for a legislature to make the penalty more severe than the criminal act it punishes in the hope it would deter wrongdoing: . . .

.   .   .

Until now, the issue under the Eighth Amendment has not been the state of any particular victim after the crime, but rather whether the punishment imposed is grossly disproportionate to the evil committed by the perpetrator. As a matter of constitutional principle, that test cannot have the primitive simplicity of "life for life, eye for eye, tooth for tooth." Rather States must be permitted to engage in a more sophisticated weighing of values in dealing with criminal activity which consistently poses serious danger of death or grave bodily harm. If innocent life and limb is to be preserved I see no constitutional barrier in punishing by death all who engage in such activity, regardless of whether the risk comes to fruition in any particular instance.

Lockett v. Ohio

438 U.S. 586, 57 L Ed 2d 973, 98 S Ct 2954 (1978)

The Ohio statute requires imposition of the death penalty in an aggravated murder case unless it is shown that 1) the victim induced or aided in the offense, 2) the offender was under duress or coercion, or 3) the offender was psychotic but not legally insane. Lockett was convicted of aggravated murder growing out of an armed robbery which she helped to plan and during which she was in the escape car. Another defendant fired the actual shot that produced the death. The trial judge found that none of the three mitigating factors was present and imposed the death penalty expressing some distaste for the task as he performed it. The Ohio Supreme Court affirmed.

. . .

Mr. Chief Justice Burger delivered the opinion of the Court with respect to the constitutionality of the petitioner's conviction (Parts I and II), together with an opinion (Part III), in which Mr. Justice Stewart, Mr. Justice Powell, and Mr. Justice Stevens, joined, on the constitutionality of the statute under which petitioner was sentenced to death and announced the judgment of the Court.

We granted certiorari in this case to consider, among other questions, whether Ohio violated the Eighth and Fourteenth Amendments by sentencing Sandra Lockett to death pursuant to a statute that narrowly limits the sentencer's discretion to consider the circumstances of the crime and the record and character of the offender as mitigating factors.

I

Lockett was charged with aggravated murder with the aggravating specifications (1) that the murder was "committed for the purpose of escaping detection, apprehension, trial, or punishment" for aggravated robbery, and (2) that the murder was "committed . . . while committing, attempting to commit, or fleeing immediately after committing or attempting to commit aggravated robbery." That offense was punishable by death in Ohio. . . .

. . .

The Court instructed the jury that, before it could find Lockett guilty, it had to find that she purposely had killed the pawnbroker while committing or attempting to commit aggravated robbery. The jury was further charged that one who

"purposely aids, helps, associates himself or herself with another for the purpose of committing a crime is regarded as if he or she were the principal offender and is just as guilty as if the person performed every act constituting the offense. . . ."

Regarding the intent requirement, the court instructed:

"[A] person engaged in a common design with others to rob by force and violence an individual or individuals of their property is presumed to acquiesce in whatever may reasonably be necessary to accomplish the object of their enterprise. . . .

"If the conspired robbery and the manner of its accomplishment would be reasonably likely to produce death, each plotter is equally guilty with the principal offender as an aider and abettor in the homicide. . . An intent to kill by an aider and abettor may be found to exist beyond a reasonable doubt under such circumstances."

The jury found Lockett guilty as charged. . . .

II

[In this section The Chief Justice disposes of three procedural objections to the conduct of the trial.]

III

Lockett challenges the constitutionality of Ohio's death penalty statute on a number of grounds. We find it necessary to consider only her contention that her death sentence is invalid because the statute under which it was imposed did not permit the sentencing judge to consider, as mitigating factors, her character, prior record, age, lack of specific intent to cause death, and her relatively minor part in the crime. . . .

. . .

In the last decade many of the States have been obliged to revise their death penalty statutes in response to the various opinions supporting the judgments in Furman, supra, and Gregg, supra, and its companion cases. The signals from this Court have not, however, always been easy to decipher. The States now deserve the clearest guidance that the Court can provide; we have an obligation to reconcile previously differing views in order to provide that guidance. . . .

. . .

We begin by recognizing that the concept of individualized sentencing in criminal cases generally, although not constitutionally required, has long been accepted in this country. Consistent with that concept, sentencing judges traditionally have taken a wide range of factors into account. That States have authority to make aiders and abettors equally responsible, as a matter of law, with principals, or to enact felony murder statutes is beyond constitutional challenge. But the definition of crimes generally has not been thought automatically to dictate what should be the proper penalty. And where sentencing discretion is granted, it generally has been agreed that the sentencing judge's "possession of the fullest information possible concerning the defendant's life and characteristics" is "[h]ighly relevant—*if not essential*—[to the] selection of an appropriate sentence. . . ."

. . .

We are satisfied that this qualitative difference between death and other penalties calls for a great degree of reliability when the death sentence is imposed. The mandatory death penalty statute in Woodson was held invalid because it permitted *no* consideration of "relevant facets of the character and record of the individual offender or the circumstances of the particular offense." The plurality did not attempt to indicate, however, which facets of an offender or his offense it deemed "relevant" in capital sentencing or what degree of consideration of "relevant facets" it would require.

We are now faced with those questions and we conclude that the Eighth and Fourteenth Amendments require that the sentencer, in all but the rarest kind of capital case, not be precluded from considering *as a mitigating factor,* any aspect of a defendant's character or record and any of the circumstances of the offense that the defendant proffers as a basis for a sentence less than death. We recognize that, in noncapital cases, the established practice of individualized sentences rests not on constitutional commands but public policy enacted into statutes. The considerations that account for the wide acceptance of individualization of sentences in noncapital cases surely cannot be thought less important in capital cases. Given that the imposition of death by public authority is so profoundly different from all other penalties, we cannot avoid the conclusion that an individualized decision is essential in capital cases. The need for treating each defendant in a capital case with that degree of respect due the uniqueness of the individual is far more important than in noncapital cases. A variety of flexible techniques—probation, parole, work furloughs, to name a few—and various post conviction remedies, may be available to modify an initial sentence of confinement in noncapital cases. The nonavailability of corrective or modifying mechanisms with respect to an executed capital sentence underscores the need for individualized consideration as a constitutional requirement in imposing the death sentence.

There is no perfect procedure for deciding in which cases governmental authority should be used to impose death. But a statute that prevents the sentencer in all capital cases from giving independent mitigating weight to aspects of the defendant's character and record and to circumstances of the offense proffered in mitigation creates the risk that the death penalty will be imposed in spite of factors which may call for a less severe penalty. When the choice is between life and death, that risk is

303

unacceptable and incompatible with the commands of the Eighth and Fourteenth Amendments.

The Ohio death penalty statute does not permit the type of individualized consideration of mitigating factors we now hold to be required by the Eighth and Fourteenth Amendments in capital cases....

. . .

None of the statutes we sustained in Gregg and the companion cases clearly operated at that time to prevent the sentencer from considering any aspect of the defendant's character and record or any circumstances of his offense as an independently mitigating factor.

In this regard the statute now before us is significantly different. Once a defendant is found guilty of aggravated murder with at least one of seven specified aggravating circumstances, the death penalty must be imposed unless, considering "the nature and circumstances of the offense and the history, character, and conditions of the offender," the sentencing judge determines that at least one of the following mitigating circumstances is established by a preponderance of the evidence:

"(1) The victim of the offense induced or facilitated it.

"(2) It is unlikely that the offense would have been committed but for the fact that the offender was under duress, coercion, or strong provocation.

"(3) The offense was primarily the product of the offender's psychosis or mental deficiency, though such condition is insufficient to establish the defense of insanity."

. . .

The limited range of mitigating circumstances which may be considered by the sentencer under the Ohio statute is incompatible with the Eighth and Fourteenth Amendments. To meet constitutional requirements, a death penalty statute must not preclude consideration of relevant mitigating factors.

Accordingly, the judgment under review is reversed to the extent that it sustains the imposition of the death penalty; the case is remanded for further proceedings.

. . .

Mr. Justice Brennan took no part in the consideration or decision of this case.

. . .

Mr. Justice Blackmun, concurring in part and concurring in the judgment.

I join the Court's judgment, but only Parts I and II of its opinion. I, too, would reverse the judgment of the Supreme Court of Ohio insofar as it upheld the imposition of the death penalty on petitioner Sandra Lockett, but I would do so for a reason more limited than that which the plurality espouses, . . .

. . .

[I]n my view, the Ohio judgment in this case improperly provided the death sentence for a defendant who only aided and abetted a murder, without permitting any consideration by the sentencing authority of the extent of her involvement, or the degree of her mens rea, in the commission of the homicide. The Ohio capital statute, together with that State's aiding and abetting statute, and its statutory definition of "purposefulness" as including reckless endangerment, allow for a particularly harsh application of the death penalty to any defendant who has aided or abetted the commission of an armed robbery in the course of which a person is killed, even though accidentally. . . .

. . .

The more manageable alternative, in my view, is to follow a proceduralist tack, and require, as Ohio does not, in the case of a nontriggerman such as Lockett, that the sentencing authority have discretion to consider the degree of the defendant's participation in the acts leading to the homicide and the character of the defendant's mens rea. That approach does not interfere with the States' individual statutory categories for assessing legal guilt, but merely requires that the sentencing authority be permitted to weigh any available evidence, adduced at trial or at the sentencing hearing, concerning the defendant's degree of participation in the homicide and the nature of his mens rea in regard to the commission of the homicidal act. A defendant would be permitted to adduce evidence, if any be available, that he had little or no reason to anticipate that a gun would be fired, or that he played only a minor part in the course of events leading to the use of fatal force. Though heretofore I have been unwilling to interfere with the legislative judgment of the States in regard to capital-sentencing procedures, this Court's judgment as to

305

disproportionality in Coker, in which I joined, and the unusual degree to which Ohio requires capital punishment of a mere aider and abettor in an armed felony resulting in a fatality even where *no* participant specifically intended the fatal use of a weapon, provides a significant occasion for setting some limit to the method by which the States assess punishment for actions less immediately connected to the deliberate taking of human life.

· · ·

Mr. Justice Marshall, concurring in the judgment.

I continue to adhere to my view that the death penalty is, under all circumstances, a cruel and unusual punishment prohibited by the Eighth Amendment. . . .

· · ·

When a death sentence is imposed under the circumstances presented here, I fail to understand how any of my Brethren—even those who believe that the death penalty is not wholly inconsistent with the Constitution—can disagree that it must be vacated. Under the Ohio death penalty statute, this 21-year-old Negro woman was sentenced to death for a killing that she did not actually commit or intend to commit. She was convicted under a theory of vicarious liability. The imposition of the death penalty for this crime totally violates the principle of proportionality embodied in the Eighth Amendment's prohibition; it makes no distinction between a willful and malicious murderer and an accomplice to an armed robbery in which a killing unintentionally occurs. . . .

· · ·

Where life itself is what hangs in the balance, a fine precision in the process must be insisted upon. The Ohio statute, with its blunderbuss, virtually mandatory approach to imposition of the death penalty for certain crimes, wholly fails to recognize the unique individuality of every criminal defendant who comes before its courts.

· · ·

Mr. Justice White, dissenting in part and concurring in the judgments of the Court.

· · ·

The Court has now completed its about-face since Furman v Georgia, ... Furman held that as a result of permitting the sentencer to exercise unfettered discretion to impose or not to impose the death penalty for murder, the penalty was then being imposed discriminatorily, wantonly and freakishly, and so infrequently that any given death sentence was cruel and unusual. The Court began its retreat in Woodson v North Carolina, where a plurality held that statutes which imposed mandatory death sentences even for first-degree murders were constitutionally invalid because the Eighth Amendment required that consideration be given by the sentencer to aspects of character of the individual offender and the circumstances of the particular offense in deciding whether to impose the punishment of death. Today the Court holds, again through a plurality, that the sentencer may constitutionally impose the death penalty only as an exercise of his unguided discretion after being presented with all circumstances which the defendant might believe to be conceivably relevant to the appropriateness of the penalty for the individual offender. . . .

. . .

I greatly fear that the effect of the Court's decision today will be to constitutionally compel a restoration of the state of affairs at the time Furman was decided, where the death penalty is imposed so erratically and the threat of execution is so attenuated for even the most atrocious murders that "its imposition would then be the pointless and needless extinction of life with only marginal contributions to any discernible social or public purposes." By requiring as a matter of constitutional law that sentencing authorities must be permitted to consider and in their discretion to act upon any and all mitigating circumstances, the Court permits them to refuse to impose the death penalty no matter what the circumstances of the crime. This invites a return to the pre-Furman days when the death penalty was generally reserved for those very few for whom society has least consideration. . . .

. . .

I nevertheless concur in the judgment of the Court reversing the imposition of the death sentences because I agree with the contention of the petitioners, ignored by the plurality, that it violates the Eighth

Amendment to impose the penalty of death without a finding that the defendant possessed a purpose to cause the death of the victim.

It is now established that a penalty constitutes cruel and unusual punishment if it is excessive in relation to the crime for which it is imposed. A punishment is disproportionate "if it (1) makes no measurable contribution to acceptable goals of punishment and hence is nothing more than the purposeless and needless imposition of pain and suffering; or (2) is grossly out of proportion to the severity of the crime. A punishment might fail the test on either ground." Because it has been extremely rare that the death penalty has been imposed upon those who were not found to have intended the death of the victim, the punishment of death violates both tests under the circumstances present here. . . .

*   *   *

Mr. Justice Rehnquist, concurring in part and dissenting.

*   *   *

[A]s I believe both the opinion of The Chief Justice and the opinion of my Brother White seem to concede, the Court has gone from pillar to post, with the result that the sort of reasonable predictability upon which legislatures, trial courts, and appellate courts must of necessity rely has been all but completely sacrificed.

The Chief Justice states, "We do not write on a 'clean slate,' " [b]ut it can scarcely be maintained that today's decision is the logical application of a coherent doctrine first espoused by the opinions leading to the Court's judgment in Furman, and later elaborated in the Woodson series of cases decided two Terms ago. Indeed, it cannot even be responsibly maintained that it is a principled application of the plurality opinions in the Woodson series of cases, without regard to Furman. The opinion strives manfully to appear as a logical exegesis of those plurality opinions, but I believe that it fails in the effort. We are now told, in effect, that in order to impose a death sentence the judge or jury must receive in evidence whatever the defense attorney wishes them to hear. I do not think The Chief Justice's effort to trace this quite novel constitutional principle back to the plurality opinions in the Woodson cases succeeds. . . .

*   *   *

It seems to me indisputably clear from today's opinion that, while we may not be writing on a clean slate, the Court is scarcely faithful to what has been written before. Rather, it makes a third distinct effort to address the same question, an effort which derives little support from any of the various opinions in Furman or from the prevailing opinions in the Woodson cases. As a practical matter, I doubt that today's opinion will make a great deal of difference in the manner in which trials in capital cases are conducted, since I would suspect that it has been the practice of most trial judges to permit a defendant to offer virtually any sort of evidence in his own defense as he wished. But as my Brother White points out in his dissent, the theme of today's opinion, far from supporting those views expressed in Furman which did appear to be carried over to the Woodson cases, tends to undercut those views. If a defendant as a matter of constitutional law is to be permitted to offer as evidence in the sentencing hearing any fact, however bizarre, which he wishes, even though the most sympathetically disposed trial judge could conceive of no basis upon which the jury might take it into account in imposing a sentence, the new constitutional doctrine will not eliminate arbitrariness or freakishness in the imposition of sentences, but will codify and institutionalize it. By encouraging defendants in capital cases, and presumably sentencing judges and juries, to take into consideration anything under the sun as a "mitigating circumstance," it will not guide sentencing discretion but will totally unleash it. It thus appears that the evil described by the Woodson plurality—that mandatory capital sentencing "papered over the problem of unguided and unchecked jury discretion," was in truth not the unchecked discretion, but a system which "papered over" its exercise rather than spreading it on the record. . . .

. . .

I am frank to say that I am uncertain whether today's opinion represents the seminal case in the exposition by this Court of the Eighth and Fourteenth Amendments as they apply to capital punishment, or whether instead it represents the third false start in this direction within the past six years. . . .

. . .

Sandra Lockett was fairly tried, and was found guilty of aggravated murder. I do not think Ohio was required to receive any sort of mitigating evidence which an accused or his lawyer wishes to offer, and therefore I disagree with Part III of the Court's opinion. . . .

. . .

Since all of petitioner's claims appear to me to be without merit, I would affirm the judgment of the Supreme Court of Ohio.

. . .

On July 2, 1982, the Court held invalid a Florida felony murder aiding and abetting statute similar to the one at issue in Lockett. Justice White, joined by Justices Brennan, Marshall, Blackmun, and Stevens, held that abettors and aiders lack the requisite intent for imposition of the death penalty on some theory of vicarious liability. Justice O'Connor, joined by Chief Justice Burger and Justices Powell and Rehnquist, dissented. *Enmund* v. *Florida,* 73 L Ed 2d 1140 (1982).

Godfrey v. Georgia

446 U.S. 420, 64 L Ed 2d 398, 100 S Ct 1759 (1980)

Petitioner's wife had left him to file suit for divorce and was living with her mother. Godfrey killed his wife by firing a shotgun through a window, killing her instantly. He reloaded the gun, entered the house trailer, and shot and killed his mother-in-law. He then called the sheriff, admitted the acts, and asked to be arrested. He told a police officer, "I've done a hideous crime—but I have been thinking about it for eight years—I'd do it again."

The jury found petitioner guilty and in the sentencing hearing determined on death as the proper penalty. As required by the Georgia capital punishment statute, the jury found that an aggravating circumstance was present; viz., that the offense "was outrageously or wantonly vile, horrible or inhuman in that it involved torture, depravity of mind, or an aggravated battery to the victim." The Georgia Supreme Court upheld the conviction despite contentions by petitioner that this section of the statute was impermissibly vague and provided inadequate guidance for the jury. The Supreme Court granted certiorari.

. . .

Mr. Justice Stewart announced the judgment of the Court and delivered an opinion in which Mr. Justice Blackmun, Mr. Justice Powell, and Mr. Justice Stevens join.

. . .

In Furman v Georgia, the Court held that the penalty of death may not be imposed under sentencing procedures that create a substantial risk that the punishment will be inflicted in an arbitrary and capricious manner. Gregg v Georgia, supra, reaffirmed this holding: . . A capital sentencing scheme must, in short, provide a "meaningful basis for distinguishing the few cases in which [the penalty] is imposed from the many cases in which it is not."

This means that if a State wishes to authorize capital punishment it has a constitutional responsibility to tailor and apply its law in a manner that avoids the arbitrary and capricious infliction of the death penalty. Part of a State's responsibility in this regard is to define the crimes for which death may be the sentence in a way that obviates "standardless [sentencing] discretion. . ."

It must channel the sentencer's discretion by "clear and objective standards" that provide "specific and detailed guidance," and that "make rationally reviewable the process for imposing a sentence of death." As was made clear in Gregg, a death penalty "system could have standards so vague that they would fail adequately to channel the sentencing decision patterns of juries with the result that a pattern of arbitrary and capricious sentencing like that found unconstitutional in Furman could occur."

In the case before us, the Georgia Supreme Court has affirmed a sentence of death based upon no more than a finding that the offense was "outrageously or wantonly vile, horrible and inhuman." There is nothing in these few words, standing alone, that implies any inherent restraint on the arbitrary and capricious infliction of the death sentence. A person of ordinary sensibility could fairly characterize almost every murder as "outrageously or wantonly vile, horrible and inhuman." Such a view may, in fact, have been one to which the members of the jury in this case subscribed. If so, their preconceptions were not dispelled by the trial judge's sentencing instructions. . . .

. . .

No claim was made, and nothing in the record before us suggests, that the petitioner committed an aggravated battery upon his wife or mother-in-law or, in fact, caused either of them to suffer any physical injury preceding their deaths. Moreover, in the trial court, the prosecutor repeatedly told the jury—and the trial judge wrote in his sentencing report—that the murders did not involve "torture." Nothing said on appeal by the Georgia Supreme Court indicates that it took a different view of the evidence. . . .

· · ·

Thus, the validity of the petitioner's death sentences turns on whether, in light of the facts and circumstances of the murders that Godfrey was convicted of committing, the Georgia Supreme Court can be said to have applied a constitutional construction of the phrase "outrageously or wantonly vile, horrible or inhuman in that [they] involved . . . depravity of mind. . ." We conclude that the answer must be no. The petitioner's crimes cannot be said to have reflected a consciousness materially more "depraved" than that of any person guilty of murder. His victims were killed instantaneously. They were members of his family who were causing him extreme emotional trauma. Shortly after the killings, he acknowledged his responsibility and the heinous nature of his crimes. These factors certainly did not remove the criminality from the petitioner's acts. But, it "is of vital importance to the defendant and to the community that any decision to impose the death sentence be, and appear to be, based on reason rather than caprice or emotion."

That cannot be said here. There is no principled way to distinguish this case, in which the death penalty was imposed, from the many cases in which it was not. Accordingly, the judgment of the Georgia Supreme Court insofar as it leaves standing the petitioner's death sentences is reversed, and the case is remanded to that court for further proceedings.

· · ·

Mr. Justice Marshall, with whom Mr. Justice Brennan joins, concurring in the judgment.

· · ·

The Georgia court's inability to administer its capital punishment statute in an even-handed fashion is not necessarily attributable to any bad faith on its part; it is, I believe, symptomatic of a deeper problem that is proving to be genuinely intractable. Just five years before Gregg, Mr.

Justice Harlan stated for the Court that the task of identifying "before the fact those characteristics of criminal homicides and their perpetrators which call for the death penalty, and [of] express[ing] these characteristics in language which can be fairly understood and applied by the sentencing authority, appear to be . . . beyond present human ability." . . .

. . .

I believe that the Court . . . was substantially correct in concluding that the task of selecting in some objective way those persons who should be condemned to die is one that remains beyond the capacities of the criminal justice system. For this reason, I remain hopeful that even if the Court is unwilling to accept the view that the death penalty is so barbaric that it is in all circumstances cruel and unusual punishment forbidden by the Eighth and Fourteenth Amendments, it may eventually conclude that the effort to eliminate arbitrariness in the infliction of that ultimate sanction is so plainly doomed to failure that it—and the death penalty—must be abandoned altogether.

. . .

Mr. Justice White, with whom Mr. Justice Rehnquist joins, dissenting.

. . .

Our role is to correct genuine errors of constitutional significance resulting from the application of Georgia's capital sentencing procedures; our role is not to peer majestically over the lower court's shoulder so that we might second-guess its interpretation of facts that quite reasonably—perhaps even quite plainly—fit within the statutory language. . . .

. . .

The point is not that, in my view, petitioner's crimes were definitively vile, horrible, or inhuman, or that, as I assay the evidence, they beyond any doubt involved torture, depravity of mind, or an aggravated battery to the victims. Rather, the lesson is a much more elementary one, an instruction that, I should have thought, this Court would have taken to heart long ago. Our mandate does not extend to interfering with factfinders in state criminal proceedings or with state courts that are responsibly and consistently interpreting state law, unless that interference

313

is predicated on a violation of the Constitution. No convincing showing of such a violation is made here. . . Faithful adherence to this standard of reviewing compels our affirmance of the judgment below.

. . .

Mr. Chief Justice Burger, dissenting.

. . .

I am convinced that the course the plurality embarks on today is sadly mistaken—indeed confused. It is this Court's function to insure that the rights of a defendant are scrupulously respected; and in capital cases we must see to it that the jury has rendered its decision with meticulous care. But it is emphatically not our province to second guess the jury's judgment or to tell the States which of their "hideous," intentional murderers may be given the ultimate penalty. Because the plurality does both, I dissent.

V

Free Press and Fair Trial

Americans have always prided themselves on the freedom of their press although, lamentably, it has been less than free at times. The first major attempt to protect this right occurred in 1735. That year, an American jury refused to convict John Peter Zenger of seditious libel, a convenient common law doctrine that enabled the Crown to stifle criticism at will. This protection expressed the American belief that a free and responsible press lies at the foundation of free government. As Thomas Jefferson wrote in 1816: "When the press is free, and every man able to read, all is safe." [1] Jefferson phrased his opinion even more sharply in 1787, the same year the Constitution was written: "The basis of our government being the opinion of the people, the first object shall be to keep that right; and were it left for me to decide whether we should have a government without newspapers, or newspapers without government, I should not hesitate a moment to choose the latter." [2]

The Supreme Court in the twentieth century has vigorously embraced these Jeffersonian concepts and has applied them in a variety of ways to protect the press from governmental interference. *Near* v. *Minnesota*, 283 U.S. 697 (1931), in which Chief Justice Charles Evans Hughes established two major principles, is the first landmark decision. First, Hughes made it clear that the First Amendment protection—which obviously limits national power—also limits state power through the Fourteenth Amendment. Second, Hughes stated that neither national nor state government ordinarily may prohibit publication of anything by the press; after-the-fact sanctions against wrongdoing by the press are available and usually are sufficient. The majority asserted that "it is the chief purpose of the guaranty to prevent previous restraints upon publication." [3] The presumption that prepublication control of the press is constitutionally infirm arises in *Nebraska Press Association* v. *Stuart* (p. 328) and was the hinge on which the Pentagon

Papers decision turned (*New York Times* v. *United States*, 403 U.S. 713, 1971). In the latter case, the Court held that the government could not suppress publication of documents stolen from the Pentagon and relating to the Vietnam War. The potential threat to national security interests was not clear enough to justify the attempt at prior restraint. The generalization drawn from the cases is that any efforts to prevent publication by the press are likely to fail; the compelling state interest required for the government to censor the press has not yet been found by the justices, although it might be given the proper set of circumstances.

Not only can the press publish without censorship, it also is immune to several postpublication sanctions including the law of libel, at least when the subject of the publication is a public official or a public figure. Even for the publication of falsehoods, such a person may not collect damages in a defamation suit against the press unless it can be shown that "the statement was made with actual malice—that is, with the knowledge that it was false or with reckless disregard of whether it was false or not." [4] In a later decision, the Court suggested what was meant by "reckless disregard." Justice John Marshall Harlan said that damages could be recovered by a public figure only if there were a "showing of highly unreasonable conduct constituting an extreme departure from the standards of investigation and reporting ordinarily adhered to by responsible publishers." [5] Although the justices have had difficulty defining who might be a "public figure" (*Time, Inc.* v. *Hill*, 385 U.S. 374, 1967; *Gertz* v. *Robert Welch, Inc.*, 418 U.S. 323, 1974; *Time Inc.* v. *Firestone*, 424 U.S. 448, 1976), the overall effect of the *Sullivan* rule was to hold the press relatively free from harassment from libel suits brought by the subjects of its stories.

Judges are, of course, public figures and thus would have considerable difficulty recovering damages from comments made about them in the press. In three earlier decisions, the Court severely curtailed another weapon used by judges against the press—the contempt power. In *Bridges* v. *California*, 314 U.S. 252 (1941); *Pennekamp* v. *Florida*, 328 U.S. 331 (1946); and *Craig* v. *Harney*, 331 U.S. 367 (1947), the Court reversed contempt convictions brought on by critical out-of-court press comments about the manner in which the judge was handling a pending case. Not only did the Court find a lack of clear and present danger to the administration of justice in these cases, but Justice Stanley Reed also noted in one case that for the offensive editorials to affect the judge's performance of his duties, he would have to have been "of less than ordinary fortitude." [6]

Although press comment on a judge's motives or actions is immunized from both libel and contempt proceedings, some press activities threaten the fair and orderly administration of justice. Press comment on the investigation of a criminal offense may so "poison the well" that the accused cannot receive a fair trial. This is especially true when the trial is held before a jury influenced by what has been said in the press.

In the criminal courts, two fundamental rights—fair trial and free press—may seriously conflict. Fortunately, the Court has agreed that, by definition, trials dominated by mob pressure and the threat of violence cannot be fair trials. It began its consideration of the clash between fair trial and free press with this facet of the problem. [7] A short step from that conclusion is that in some instances pretrial publicity could have the same effect as mob domination of the proceedings. As might be expected, the Court's concern with "trial by newspaper" was focused on the effect of publicity on a jury or on potential jurors rather than on the judge. The jury makes its decision on the basis of evidence produced in court, not on speculation and innuendo published in the press before the jurors are even selected. One way to ensure that the jury is unaffected by pretrial publicity is to adopt the British practice of banning publication of anything about a pending criminal case except that which is brought out in open court; the First Amendment prevented the justices from adopting this extreme solution. Therefore, the Court, in early cases, assumed that the press must be left alone and contented itself with prescribing ways of mitigating the effect of extensive pretrial publicity. The Court's methods included: continuance, change of venue, careful conduct of the examination of potential jurors, and control of disruptive behavior by reporters in the courtroom. [8] Some members of the Court were not satisfied by the application of these partial solutions to the problem. Justice Felix Frankfurter summed up his own conclusions:

> Not a term passes without this Court being importuned to review convictions . . . in which substantial claims are made that a jury trial has been distorted because of inflammatory newspaper accounts. . . . The Court has not yet decided that the fair administration of criminal justice must be subordinated to another safeguard of our constitutional system—freedom of the press properly conceived. The Court has not yet decided that, while convictions must be reversed and miscarriage of justice result because the minds of jurors or potential jurors were poisoned, the poisoner is constitutionally protected in plying his trade. [9]

The decisions excerpted in this chapter show that the Court has not yet accepted Frankfurter's invitation to make an unequivocal choice.

The press and bar associations have reacted to these decisions more than have the legislative and executive branches of state and national governments. The other branches of government have long since tacitly or explicitly delegated to the courts the authority to make rules for the conduct of their own business, and these decisions place special obligations on trial court judges, prosecutors, and defense counsel. No sense of shared policymaking responsibility exists, so the press and bar must deal directly with the courts rather than with a combination of courts and legislators.

The most notable and useful reactions to these decisions came in the wake of *Sheppard* v. *Maxwell* (p. 321). The American Bar Association's Advisory Committee on Fair Trial and a Free Press, chaired by Justice Paul Reardon of the Supreme Judicial Court of Massachusetts, produced an elaborate set of recommendations in three general categories: 1) rules governing the conduct of attorneys and public officials to be enforced by courts and bar associations, 2) improvement in jury selection and protection procedures, and 3) adoption of a limited contempt of power to punish intentional press interference with an ongoing trial.

More specifically, the committee proposed in the first group of recommendations that police, prosecutors, and defense counsel be limited in their comments to the press to a description of the nature of the offense charged, the identity of the accused, and the circumstances of the arrest. Defense counsel also could announce that the defendant denied the charges. In many ways these guidelines duplicate the British rules, except that they apply to the other participants in the process rather than to the press. It was proposed that these rules be enforced first by local bar associations and later by the contempt power. They were immediately challenged as being unduly secretive and as giving the police and prosecutors too great an opportunity to abuse the criminal justice process. The limited contempt power was not widely adopted in large part because the Court believed that the press would not and, indeed, could not, disrupt an ongoing trial unless the presiding judge had completely lost control of the proceedings. The suggested rules on jury selection were mostly those suggested in *Sheppard,* and they have been adopted in virtually all courts. The other major changes proposed by the American Bar Association's advisory committee have not been followed in most jurisdictions because of the storm of criticism leveled at them.

Two other committees were active in 1967 and 1968. One, chaired by Judge Harold Medina, was appointed by the Association of the Bar of the City of New York; the other was created by the Judicial Conference of the United States under the leadership of Judge Irving R. Kaufman. Neither of these committees went as far as the American Bar Association's committee, although both endorsed some degree of control over what police and lawyers could tell the press. Neither suggested any direct control over the activities of the media. Finally, a report by the Special Committee on Free Press and Fair Trial of the American Newspaper Publishers Association, chaired by D. Tennant Bryan, publisher of the *Richmond Times-Dispatch and News Leader,* took the predictable position of opposing any restriction on what might be published. It went on to oppose any limitation on access to information by the press. This last issue is pointedly presented in *Gannett* v. *de Pasquale* (p. 340) and *Richmond Newspapers* v. *Virginia* (p. 362).

The net effect of this reaction to the *Sheppard* decision has been the thorough canvassing of the free press and fair trial issue by several groups, the adoption of rules on jury selection and protection by some courts, and the adoption of ethical standards by some bar associations or joint bar-press committees. The important fact emerging from these studies is that the groups realized they must concentrate their efforts on devising a system that protects a defendant's right to a fair trial and at the same time prohibits any substantial restrictions on what the media may publish. Even so, the issue is not resolved. In May 1982 the Court denied certiorari in two cases that tested the limits of the *Gannett* and *Richmond Newspapers* decisions. More probing of those limits can be expected.

The last decision in this chapter represents a variation of the free press and fair trial dilemma. The Court had found in *Estes* v. *Texas,* 381 U.S. 532 (1965), that the presence of television cameras in the courtroom and the confusion attendant upon their use was so disruptive as to make a fair trial improbable if not impossible. In this decision, the plurality followed Canon 35 of the American Bar Association's Canons of Professional Ethics, adopted in 1937 and later amended to include television within its scope:

> The taking of photographs in the courtroom during sessions of the court or recesses between sessions, and the broadcasting or televising of court proceedings are calculated to detract from the essential dignity of the proceedings, distract the witness in giving his testimony, degrade the court, and create misconceptions with respect thereto in the mind of the public and should not be permitted.

Despite this admonition that does not have the force of law, Justice Harlan in his decision to reverse the conviction in *Estes,* indicated that he was not prepared to issue a blanket prohibition on the use of television cameras in the courtroom. Encouraged by Harlan's position and by technological changes that have produced smaller, less obtrusive cameras, several states have experimented with television coverage of court sessions. A challenge to Florida's ambitious and carefully monitored experiment with television coverage produced *Chandler* v. *Florida* (p. 371).

The Court's pattern in making rules for the conduct of judicial business has been fairly clear and consistent. The press can be kept uninformed of what is happening only under unusual circumstances and under almost no circumstances can it be forbidden to publish what it learns about a trial. *Chandler* even suggests a judicial tendency to maximize the press's access to the judicial process. At the same time, the Court has insisted on maintaining the criminal trial's purity by developing prophylactic procedures such as those suggested in *Sheppard* and *Nebraska Press.* The Court performs an interesting balancing act to protect these two potentially conflicting constitutional rights.

The decisions in this chapter illustrate the Court in its strongest role as an independent policymaker. On this issue, the Court applies and interprets two unusually clear constitutional commands expressing deeply engrained American values. It does so in an area, the administration of justice, in which the judges are presumed to have special knowledge and expertise. It expresses its policy conclusions in clear and unambiguous terms and operates in an arena from which competing policymakers have voluntarily withdrawn. The courts have a virtual monopoly on making rules governing the conduct of their own proceedings, and the resolution of the conflict has been accomplished, for the most part, by controlling that part of the process that is most directly under the control of the courts. At the same time, the courts leave the other participants free in hopes that their power will breed responsibility. The directing of press demands for policy change to the Court alone and the justices' undertaking in public speeches to explain the precise holding in *Gannett* have shown a recognition that the press, the bar, and the judges are the only important actors in this particular area of conflict. The strong reaction by the press to *Gannett,* however, demonstrates that the Court is not immune from criticism, even in this policy area.

NOTES

1. Thomas Jefferson to Colonel Yancey, January 6, 1816.
2. Thomas Jefferson to Colonel Edward Carrington, January 16, 1787.
3. *Near* v. *Minnesota,* 283 U.S. 697 (1931), at 713.
4. *New York Times* v. *Sullivan,* 376 U.S. 254 (1964), at 279-280.
5. *Curtis Publishing Co.* v. *Butts,* 388 U.S. 130 (1967), at 155.
6. *Pennekamp* v. *Florida,* 328 U.S. 331 (1946), at 349.
7. *Frank* v. *Mangrum,* 237 U.S. 309 (1915); *Moore* v. *Dempsey,* 261 U.S. 86 (1923); *Sheppard* v. *Florida,* 341 U.S. 50 (1951).
8. See e.g. *Stroble* v. *California,* 343 U.S. 181 (1952); *Irwin* v. *Dowd,* 336 U.S. 717 (1961); *Rideau* v. *Louisiana,* 373 U.S. 723 (1963); *Estes* v. *Texas,* 381 U.S. 532 (1965).
9. Justice Felix Frankfurter concurring in *Irwin* v. *Dowd,* 336 U.S. 717 (1961), at 730.

SELECTED BIBLIOGRAPHY

American Bar Association Advisory Committee on Fair Trial and Free Press. "Standards Relating to Fair Trial and Free Press," 54 *American Bar Association Journal* 347 (1968). (Reardon Report)

American Newspaper Publishers Association. *Free Press and Fair Trial.* New York: American Newspaper Publishers Association, 1967.

Association of the Bar of the City of New York. *Freedom of the Press and Fair Trial: Final Report with Recommendations.* New York: Association of the Bar of the City of New York, 1967. (Medina Report)

Drechsel, Robert E. *Newsmaking in the Trial Courts.* New York: Longmans, 1982.

Felsher, Howard and Rosen, Michael. *Justice, U.S.A.?* New York: Collier, 1967.

Friendly, Alfred and Goldfard, Ronald L. *Crime and Publicity.* New York: Twentieth Century Fund, 1967.

"The Impartial Jury—Twentieth Century Dilemma: Some Solutions to the Conflict Between Free Press and Fair Trial." 51 *Cornell Law Quarterly* 306 (1966).

"Report of the Committee on the Operation of the Jury System to the Judicial Conference of the United States." 45 *F.R.D.* 91 (1968). (Kaufman Report)

Stranga, John E., Jr. "Judicial Protection of the Criminal Defendant Against Adverse Press Coverage," 13 *William and Mary Law Review* 1 (1971).

Twentieth Century Fund. *Rights in Conflict.* New York: McGraw-Hill, 1976.

Sheppard v. Maxwell

384 U.S. 333, 16 L ed 2d 600, 86 S Ct 1507 (1966)

Petitioner was convicted of murdering his wife. Both before and during the trial, media coverage was extensive, generally unfavorable to the defendant, and included much information never used in court as evidence. The trial judge denied requests for continuances or a change of venue. During the trial, reporters interviewed prospective witnesses, eavesdropped on efforts of petitioner and his counsel to confer, openly handled trial exhibits, and generally made so much noise that the trial judge, witnesses, counsel, and the jury often had great difficulty hearing what was being said. The trial judge made no effort to control the activities of the newspersons nor did he attempt

321

to control the release of information to the press by the defense, prosecution, police, and witnesses.

Petitioner's conviction was affirmed by the court of appeals for Cuyahoga County and the Ohio Supreme Court. The U.S. Supreme Court denied certiorari. A number of years later, petitioner filed this habeas corpus action in United States District Court which granted the writ. The court of appeals for the Sixth Circuit reversed and this time the Supreme Court granted certiorari.

. . .

Mr. Justice Clark delivered the opinion of the Court.

This federal habeas corpus application involves the question whether Sheppard was deprived of a fair trial in his state conviction for the second-degree murder of his wife because of the trial judge's failure to protect Sheppard sufficiently from the massive, pervasive and prejudicial publicity that attended his prosecution. . . .

. . .

A responsible press has always been regarded as the handmaiden of effective judicial administration, especially in the criminal field. Its function in this regard is documented by an impressive record of service over several centuries. The press does not simply publish information about trials but guards against the miscarriage of justice by subjecting the police, prosecutors, and judicial processes to extensive public scrutiny and criticism. This Court has, therefore, been unwilling to place any direct limitations on the freedom traditionally exercised by the news media for "[w]hat transpires in the court room is public property.". . .

. . .

But the Court has also pointed out that "[l]egal trials are not like elections, to be won through the use of the meeting-hall, the radio, and the newspaper." And the Court has insisted that no one be punished for a crime without "a charge fairly made and fairly tried in a public tribunal free of prejudice, passion, excitement, and tyranical power." "Freedom of discussion should be given the widest range compatible with the essential requirement of the fair and orderly administration of justice." But it must not be allowed to divert the trial from the "very purpose of a court system . . . to adjudicate controversies, both criminal and civil, in the calmness and solemnity of the courtroom according to legal procedures." Among these "legal procedures" is the requirement that the jury's verdict be based on evidence received in open court, not from outside sources. Thus, we set aside a federal conviction where the jurors were exposed "through news accounts" to information that was not admitted at trial. We held that the prejudice from such material "may indeed be greater" than when it is part of the prosecution's evidence "for it is then not tempered by protective procedures.". . .

. . .

The undeviating rule of this Court was expressed by Mr. Justice Holmes over half a century ago in Patterson v Colorado:

"The theory of our system is that the conclusions to be reached in a case will be induced only by evidence and argument in open court, and not by any outside influence, whether of private talk or public print.". . .

. . .

Sheppard was not granted a change of venue to a locale away from where the publicity originated; nor was his jury sequestered. . . The Sheppard jurors were subjected to newspaper, radio and television coverage of the trial while not taking part in the proceedings. They were allowed to go their separate ways outside of the courtroom, without adequate directions not to read or listen to anything concerning the case. The judge's "admonitions" at the beginning of the trial are representative:

"I would suggest to you and caution you that you do not read any newspapers during the progress of this trial, that you do not listen to radio comments nor watch or listen to television comments, insofar as this case is concerned. You will feel very much better as the trial proceeds. . . I am sure that we shall all feel very much better if we do not indulge in any newspaper reading or listening to any comments whatever about the matter while the case is in progress. After it is all over, you can read it all to your heart's content. . ."

At intervals during the trial, the judge simply repeated his "suggestions" and "requests" that the jury not expose themselves to comment upon the case. Moreover, the jurors were thrust into the role of celebrities by the judge's failure to insulate them from reporters and photographers. The numerous pictures of the jurors, with their addresses, which appeared in the newspapers before and during the trial itself exposed them to expressions of opinion from both cranks and friends. The fact that anonymous letters had been received by prospective jurors should have made the judge aware that this publicity seriously threatened the jurors' privacy....

.   .   .

For months the virulent publicity about Sheppard and the murder had made the case notorious. Charges and countercharges were aired in the news media besides those for which Sheppard was called to trial. In addition, only three months before trial, Sheppard was examined for more than five hours without counsel during a three-day inquest which ended in a public brawl. The inquest was televised live from a high school gymnasium seating hundreds of people. Furthermore, the trial began two weeks before a hotly contested election at which both Chief Prosecutor Mahon and Judge Blythin were candidates for judgeships.

While we cannot say that Sheppard was denied due process by the judge's refusal to take precautions against the influence of pretrial publicity alone, the court's later rulings must be considered against the setting in which the trial was held. In light of this background, we believe that the arrangements made by the judge with the news media caused Sheppard to be deprived of that "judicial serenity and calm to which [he] was entitled." The fact is that bedlam reigned at the courthouse during the trial and newsmen took over practically the entire courtroom, hounding most of the participants in the trial, especially Sheppard. At a temporary table within a few feet of the jury box and counsel table sat some 20 reporters staring at Sheppard and taking notes. The erection of a press table for reporters inside the bar is unprecedented. The bar of the court is reserved for counsel, providing them a safe place in which to keep papers and exhibits, and to confer privately with client and co-counsel. It is designed to protect the witness and the jury from any distractions, intrusions or influences, and to permit bench discussions of the judge's rulings away from the hearing of the public and the jury. Having assigned almost all of the available seats in the courtroom to the news media the judge lost his ability to supervise that environment. The movement of the reporters in and out of the courtroom caused frequent confusion and disruption of the trial. And the record reveals constant commotion within the bar. Moreover, the judge gave the throng of newsmen gathered in the corridors of the courthouse absolute free rein. Participants in the trial, including the jury, were forced to run a gantlet of reporters and photographers each time they entered or left the courtroom. The total lack of consideration for the privacy of the jury was demonstrated by the assignment to a broadcasting station of space next to the jury room on the floor above the courtroom, as well as the fact that jurors were allowed to make telephone calls during their five-day deliberation. . . .

. . .

Nor is there doubt that this deluge of publicity reached at least some of the jury. On the only occasion that the jury was queried, two jurors admitted in open court to hearing the highly inflammatory charge that a prison inmate claimed Sheppard as the father of her illegitimate child. Despite the extent and nature of the publicity to which the jury was exposed during trial, the judge refused defense counsel's other requests that the jury be asked whether they had read or heard specific prejudicial comment about the case, . . .

. . .

The court's fundamental error is compounded by the holding that it lacked power to control the publicity about the trial. From the very inception of the proceedings the judge announced that neither he nor anyone else could restrict prejudicial news accounts. And he reiterated this view on numerous occasions. Since he viewed the news media as his target, the judge never considered other means that are often utilized to reduce the appearance of prejudicial material and to protect the jury from outside influence. We conclude that these procedures would have been sufficient to guarantee Sheppard a fair trial and so do not consider what sanctions might be available against a recalcitrant press nor the charges of bias now made against the state trial judge.

The carnival atmosphere at trial could easily have been avoided since the courtroom and courthouse premises are subject to the control of the court. . . . Bearing in mind the massive pretrial publicity, the judge should have adopted stricter rules governing the use of the courtroom by newsmen, as Sheppard's counsel requested. The number of reporters in the courtroom itself could have been limited at the first sign that their presence would disrupt the trial. They certainly should not have been placed inside the bar. Furthermore, the judge should have more closely regulated the conduct of newsmen in the courtroom. . . .

.   .   .

Secondly, the court should have insulated the witnesses. All of the newspapers and radio stations apparently interviewed prospective witnesses at will, and in many instances disclosed their testimony. . . .

.   .   .

Thirdly, the court should have made some effort to control the release of leads, information, and gossip to the press by police officers, witnesses, and the counsel for both sides. Much of the information thus disclosed was inaccurate, leading to groundless rumors and confusion. . . .

.   .   .

Defense counsel immediately brought to the court's attention the tremendous amount of publicity in the Cleveland press that "misrepresented entirely the testimony" in the case. Under such circumstances, the judge should have at least warned the newspapers to check the accuracy of their accounts. And it is obvious that the judge should have further sought to alleviate this problem by imposing control over the statements made to the news media by counsel, witnesses, and especially the Coroner and police officers. The prosecution repeatedly made evidence available to the news media which was never offered in the trial. Much of the "evidence" disseminated in this fashion was clearly inadmissible. The exclusion of such evidence in court is rendered meaningless when news media makes it available to the public. . . .

.   .   .

More specifically, the trial court might well have proscribed extrajudicial statements by any lawyer, party, witness, or court official which divulged prejudicial matters, such as the refusal of Sheppard to submit to interrogation or take any lie detector tests; any statement made by Sheppard to officials; the identity of prospective witnesses or their probable testimony; any belief in guilt or innocence; or like statements concerning the merits of the case. . . Being advised of the great public interest in the case, the mass coverage of the press, and the potential prejudicial impact of publicity, the court could also have requested the appropriate city and county officials to promulgate a regulation with respect to dissemination of information about the case by their employees. In addition, reporters who wrote or broadcasted prejudicial stories, could have been warned as to the impropriety of publishing material not introduced in the proceedings... In this manner, Sheppard's right to a trial free from outside interference would have been given added protection without corresponding curtailment of the news media. Had the judge, the other officers of the court, and the police placed the interest of justice first, the news media would have soon learned to be content with the task of reporting the case as it unfolded in the courtroom—not pieced together from extra-judicial statements.

From the cases coming here we note that unfair and prejudicial news comment on pending trials has become increasingly prevalent. Due process requires that the accused receive a trial by an impartial jury free from outside influences. Given the pervasiveness of modern communications and the difficulty of effacing prejudicial publicity from the minds of the jurors, the trial courts must take strong measures to ensure that the balance is never weighed against the accused. And appellate tribunals have the duty to make an independent evaluation of the circumstances. Of course, there is nothing that proscribes the press from reporting events that transpire in the courtroom. But where there is a reasonable likelihood that prejudicial news prior to trial will prevent a fair trial, the judge should continue the case until the threat abates, or transfer it to another county not so permeated with publicity. In addition, sequestration of the jury was something the judge should have raised sua sponte with counsel. If publicity during the proceedings threatens the fairness of the trial, a new trial should be ordered. But we must remember that reversals are but palliatives; the cure lies in those remedial measures that will prevent the prejudice at its inception. The courts must take such steps by rule and regulation that will protect their processes from prejudicial outside interferences. Neither prosecutors, counsel for defense, the accused, witnesses, court staff nor enforcement officers coming under the jurisdiction of the court should be permitted to frustrate its function. Collaboration between counsel and the press as to information affecting the fairness of a criminal trial is not only subject to regulation, but is highly censurable and worthy of disciplinary measures.

Since the state trial judge did not fulfill his duty to protect Sheppard from the inherently prejudicial publicity which saturated the community and to control disruptive influences in the courtroom, we must reverse the denial of the habeas petition. The case is remanded to the District Court with instructions to issue the writ and order that Sheppard be released from custody unless the State puts him to its charges again within a reasonable time.

It is so ordered.

· · ·

Mr. Justice Black dissents.

[After the remand Sheppard was retried with less publicity and was acquitted.]

Nebraska Press Association v. Stuart

427 U.S. 539, 49 L Ed 2d 683, 96 S Ct 2791 (1976)

The facts are contained in the opinion of the Court.

· · ·

Mr. Chief Justice Burger delivered the opinion of the Court.

The respondent State District Judge entered an order restraining the petitioners from publishing or broadcasting accounts of confessions or admissions made by the accused or facts "strongly implicative" of the accused in a widely reported murder of six persons. We granted certiorari to decide whether the entry of such an order on the showing made before the state court violated the constitutional guarantee of freedom of the press. . . .

· · ·

The order applied only until the jury was impaneled, and specifically prohibited petitioners from reporting five subjects: (1) the existence or contents of a confession Simants had made to law enforcement officers, which had been introduced in open court at arraignment; (2) the fact or nature of statements Simants had made to other persons; (3) the contents of a note he had written the night of the crime; (4) certain aspects of the medical testimony at the preliminary hearing; (5) the identity of the victims of the alleged sexual assault and the nature of the assault. It also prohibited reporting the exact nature of the restrictive order itself. . . .

. . .

The Nebraska Supreme Court . . . modified the District Court's order to accommodate the defendant's right to a fair trial and the petitioners' interest in reporting pretrial events. The order as modified prohibited reporting of only three matters: (a) the existence and nature of any confessions or admissions made by the defendant to law enforcement officers, (b) any confessions or admissions made to any third parties, except members of the press, and (c) other facts "strongly implicative" of the accused. . . .

. . .

The problems presented by this case are almost as old as the Republic. Neither in the Constitution nor in contemporaneous writings do we find that the conflict between these two important rights was anticipated, yet it is inconceivable that the authors of the Constitution were unaware of the potential conflicts between the right to an unbiased jury and the guarantee of freedom of the press. . . [T]hey were intimately familiar with the clash of the adversary system and the part that passions of the populace sometimes play in influencing potential jurors. They did not address themselves directly to the situation presented by this case; their chief concern was the need for freedom of expression in the political arena and the dialogue in ideas. But they recognized that there were risks to private rights from an unfettered press. . . .

. . .

The speed of communication and the pervasiveness of the modern news media have exacerbated these problems, however, as numerous appeals demonstrate. . . .

. . .

The excesses of press and radio and lack of responsibility of those in authority . . . led to efforts to develop voluntary guidelines for courts, lawyers, press and broadcasters. . . In the wake of these efforts, the cooperation between bar associations and members of the press led to the adoption of the voluntary guidelines. . . .

. . .

In practice, of course, even the most ideal guidelines are subjected to powerful strains when a case such as Simants' arises, with reporters from many parts of the country on the scene. Reporters from distant places are unlikely to consider themselves bound by local standards. They report to editors outside the area covered by the guidelines, and their editors are likely to be guided only by their own standards. To contemplate how a state court can control acts of a newspaper or broadcaster outside its jurisdiction, even though the newspapers and broadcasts reach the very community from which jurors are to be selected, suggests something of the practical difficulties of managing such guidelines.

The problems presented in this case have a substantial history outside the reported decisions of courts, in the efforts of many responsible people to accommodate the competing interests. We cannot resolve all of them, for it is not the function of this Court to write a code. We look instead to this particular case and the legal context in which it arises. . . .

. . .

In the overwhelming majority of criminal trials, pretrial publicity presents few unmanageable threats to this important right. But when the case is a "sensational" one tensions develop between the right of the accused to trial by an impartial jury and the rights guaranteed others by the First Amendment. . . .

. . .

[The opinion then surveys several prior decisions of the Court.]

. . .

Taken together, these cases demonstrate that pretrial publicity—even pervasive, adverse publicity—does not inevitably lead to an unfair trial. The capacity of the jury eventually impaneled to decide the case fairly is influenced by the tone and extent of the publicity, which is in part, and often in large part, shaped by what attorneys, police, and other officials do to precipitate news coverage. The trial judge has a major responsibility. What the judge says about a case, in or out of the courtroom, is likely to appear in newspapers and broadcasts. More important, the measures a judge takes or fails to take to mitigate the effects of pretrial publicity—the measures described in Sheppard—may well determine whether the defendant receives a trial consistent with the requirements of due process. That this responsibility has not always been properly discharged is apparent from the decisions just reviewed. . . .

.   .   .

The state trial judge in the case before us acted responsibly, out of a legitimate concern, in an effort to protect the defendant's right to a fair trial. What we must decide is not simply whether the Nebraska courts erred in seeing the possibility of real danger to the defendant's rights, but whether in the circumstances of this case the means employed were foreclosed by another provision of the Constitution. . . .

.   .   .

The thread running through all these cases is that prior restraints on speech and publication are the most serious and the least tolerable infringement on First Amendment rights. A criminal penalty or a judgment in a defamation case is subject to the whole panoply of protections afforded by deferring the impact of the judgment until all avenues of appellate review have been exhausted. Only after judgment has become final, correct or otherwise, does the law's sanction become fully operative.

A prior restraint, by contrast and by definition, has an immediate and irreversible sanction. If it can be said that a threat of criminal or civil sanctions after publication "chills" speech, prior restraint "freezes" it at least for the time.

The damage can be particularly great when the prior restraint falls upon the communication of news and commentary on current events. Truthful reports of public judicial proceedings have been afforded special protection against subsequent punishment. . . For the same reasons the protection against prior restraint should have particular force as applied to reporting of criminal proceedings, whether the crime in question is a single isolated act or a pattern of criminal conduct. . . .

.   .   .

The extraordinary protections afforded by the First Amendment carry with them something in the nature of a fiduciary duty to exercise the protected rights responsibly—a duty widely acknowledged but not always observed by editors and publishers. It is not asking too much to suggest that those who exercise First Amendment rights in newspapers or broadcasting enterprises direct some effort to protect the rights of an accused to a fair trial by unbiased jurors.

Of course, the order at issue . . . does not prohibit but only postpones publication. Some news can be delayed and most commentary can even more readily be delayed without serious injury, and there often is a self-imposed delay when responsible editors call for verification of information. But such delays are normally slight and they are self-imposed. Delays imposed by governmental authority are a different matter. . . .

. . .

The authors of the Bill of Rights did not undertake to assign priorities as between First Amendment and Sixth Amendment rights, ranking one as superior to the other. In this case, the petitioners would have us declare the right of an accused subordinate to their right to publish in all circumstances. But if the authors of these guarantees, fully aware of the potential conflicts between them, were unwilling or unable to resolve the issue by assigning to one priority over the other, it is not for us to rewrite the Constitution by undertaking what they declined. It is unnecessary, after nearly two centuries, to establish a priority applicable in all circumstances. Yet it is nonetheless clear that the barriers to prior restraint remain high unless we are to abandon what the Court has said for nearly a quarter of our national existence and implied throughout all of it. . . .

. . .

In assessing the probable extent of publicity, the trial judge had before him newspapers demonstrating that the crime had already drawn intensive news coverage, and the testimony of the County Judge, who had entered the initial restraining order based on the local and national attention the case had attracted. The District Judge was required to assess the probable publicity that would be given these shocking crimes prior to the time a jury was selected and sequestered. He then had to examine the probable nature of the publicity and determine how it would affect prospective jurors.

Our review of the pretrial record persuades us that the trial judge was justified in concluding that there would be intense and pervasive pretrial publicity concerning this case. He could also reasonably conclude, based on common human experience, that publicity might impair the defendant's right to a fair trial. He did not purport to say more, for he found only "a clear and present danger that pretrial publicity *could* impinge upon the defendant's right to a fair trial." (Emphasis added.) His conclusion as to the impact of such publicity on prospective jurors was of necessity speculative, dealing as he was with factors unknown and unknowable. . . .

. . .

Most of the alternatives to prior restraint of publication in these circumstances were discussed with obvious approval in Sheppard v Maxwell, (a) change of trial venue to a place less exposed to the intense publicity that seemed imminent in Lincoln County; (b) postponement of the trial to allow public attention to subside; (c) use of searching questioning of prospective jurors, (d) the use of emphatic and clear instructions on the sworn duty of each juror to decide the issues only on evidence presented in open court. Sequestration of jurors is, of course, always available. Although that measure insulates jurors only after they are sworn, it also enhances the likelihood of dissipating the impact of pretrial publicity and emphasizes the elements of the jurors' oaths.

This Court has outlined other measures short of prior restraints on publication tending to blunt the impact of pretrial publicity. See Sheppard v Maxwell. . . Professional studies have filled out these suggestions, recommending that trial courts in appropriate cases limit what the contending lawyers, the police and witnesses may say to anyone. . . .

. . .

[W]e note that the events disclosed by the record took place in a community of 850 people. It is reasonable to assume that, without any news accounts being printed or broadcast, rumors would travel swiftly by word of mouth. One can only speculate on the accuracy of such reports, given the generative propensities of rumors; they could well be more damaging than reasonably accurate news accounts. But plainly a whole community cannot be restrained from discussing a subject intimately affecting life within it.

Given these practical problems, it is far from clear that prior restraint on publication would have protected Simants' rights. . . .

. . .

The record demonstrates, as the Nebraska courts held, that there was indeed a risk that pretrial news accounts, true or false, would have some adverse impact on the attitudes of those who might be called as jurors. But on the record now before us it is not clear that further publicity, unchecked, would so distort the views of potential jurors that 12 could not be found who would, under proper instructions, fulfill their sworn duty to render a just verdict exclusively on the evidence presented in open court. We cannot say on this record that alternatives to a prior restraint on petitioners would not have sufficiently mitigated the adverse effects of pretrial publicity so as to make prior restraint unnecessary. Nor can we conclude that the restraining order actually entered would serve its intended purpose. Reasonable minds can have few doubts about the gravity of the evil pretrial publicity can work, but the probability that it would do so here was not demonstrated with the degree of certainty our cases on prior restraint require. . . .

．　．　．

Our analysis ends as it began, with a confrontation between prior restraint imposed to protect one vital constitutional guarantee and the explicit command of another that the freedom to speak and publish shall not be abridged. We reaffirm that the guarantees of freedom of expression are not an absolute prohibition under all circumstances, but the barriers to prior restraint remain high and the presumption against its use continues intact. We hold that, with respect to the order entered in this case prohibiting reporting or commentary on judicial proceedings held in public, the barriers have not been overcome; to the extent that this order restrained publication of such material, it is clearly invalid. To the extent that it prohibited publication based on information gained from other sources, we conclude that the heavy burden imposed as a condition to securing a prior restraint was not met and the judgment of the Nebraska Supreme Court is therefore reversed.

．　．　．

Mr. Justice White, concurring.

Technically there is no need to go farther than the Court does to dispose of this case, and I join the Court's opinion. I should add, however, that for the reasons which the Court itself canvasses there is grave doubt in my mind whether orders with respect to the press such as were entered in this case would ever be justifiable. . . .

．　．　．

Mr. Justice Powell, concurring.

. . .

Mr. Justice Brennan, with whom Mr. Justice Stewart and Mr. Justice Marshall concur, concurring in the judgment.

. . .

I would hold ... that resort to prior restraints on the freedom of the press is a constitutionally impermissible method for enforcing that right; judges have at their disposal a broad spectrum of devices for ensuring that fundamental fairness is accorded the accused without necessitating so drastic an incursion on the equally fundamental and salutary constitutional mandate that discussion of public affairs in a free society cannot depend on the preliminary grace of judicial censors. ...

. . .

Commentary and reporting on the criminal justice system is at the core of First Amendment values, for the operation and integrity of that system is of crucial import to citizens concerned with the administration of Government. Secrecy of judicial action can only breed ignorance and distrust of courts and suspicion concerning the competence and impartiality of judges; free and robust reporting, criticism, and debate can contribute to public understanding of the rule of law and comprehension of the functioning of the entire criminal justice system, as well as improve the quality of that system by subjecting it to the cleansing effects of exposure and public accountability.

No one can seriously doubt, however, that unmediated prejudicial pretrial publicity may destroy the fairness of a criminal trial and the past decade has witnessed substantial debate, colloquially known as the Free Press/Fair Trial controversy, concerning this interface of First and Sixth Amendment rights. In effect, we are now told by respondents that the two rights can no longer coexist when the press possesses and seeks to publish "confessions and admissions against interest" and other information "strongly implicative" of a criminal defendant as the perpetrator of a crime, and that one or the other right must therefore be subordinated. I disagree. Settled case law concerning the impropriety and constitutional invalidity of prior restraints on the press compels the conclusion that there can be no prohibition on the publication by the press of any information

335

pertaining to pending judicial proceedings or the operation of the criminal justice system, no matter how shabby the means by which the information is obtained. This does not imply, however, any subordination of Sixth Amendment rights, for an accused's right to a fair trial may be adequately assured through methods that do not infringe First Amendment values. . . .

.   .   .

A judge importuned to issue a prior restraint in the pretrial context will be unable to predict the manner in which the potentially prejudicial information would be published, the frequency with which it would be repeated or the emphasis it would be given, the context in which or purpose for which it would be reported, the scope of the audience that would be exposed to the information, or the impact, evaluated in terms of current standards for assessing juror impartiality, the information would have on that audience. These considerations would render speculative the prospective impact on a fair trial of reporting even an alleged confession or other information "strongly implicative" of the accused. Moreover, we can take judicial notice of the fact that given the prevalence of plea bargaining, few criminal cases proceed to trial, and the judge would thus have to predict what the likelihood was that a jury would even have to be impaneled. Indeed, even in cases that do proceed to trial, the material sought to be suppressed before trial will often be admissible and may be admitted in any event. And, more basically, there are adequate devices for screening from jury duty those individuals who have in fact been exposed to prejudicial pretrial publicity.

Initially, it is important to note that once the jury is impaneled, the techniques of sequestration of jurors and control over the courtroom and conduct of trial should prevent prejudicial publicity from infecting the fairness of judicial proceedings. Similarly, judges may stem much of the flow of prejudicial publicity at its source, before it is obtained by representatives of the press. But even if the press nevertheless obtains potentially prejudicial information and decides to publish that information, the Sixth Amendment rights of the accused may still be adequately protected. In particular, the trial judge should employ the voir dire to probe fully into the effect of publicity. The judge should broadly explore such matters as the extent to which prospective jurors had read particular news accounts or whether they had heard about incriminating data such as an alleged confession or statements by purportedly reliable sources concerning the defendant's guilt. Particularly in cases of extensive publicity, defense counsel should be accorded more latitude in personally asking or tendering searching questions that might root out indications of bias, both to facilitate intelligent exercise of peremptory challenges and to help uncover factors that would dictate disqualification for cause. Indeed, it may sometimes be necessary to voir dire prospective jurors individually or in small groups, both to maximize the likelihood that members of the venire will respond honestly to questions concerning bias, and to avoid contaminating unbiased members of the venire when other members disclose prior knowledge of prejudicial information. Moreover, voir dire may indicate the need to grant a brief continuance or to grant a change of venue, techniques that can effectively mitigate any publicity at a particular time or in a particular locale. Finally, if the trial court fails or refuses to utilize these devices effectively, there are the "palliatives" of reversals on appeal and directions for a new trial. . . .

·   ·   ·

Recognition of any judicial authority to impose prior restraints on the basis of harm to the Sixth Amendment rights of particular defendants, especially since that harm must remain speculative, will thus inevitably interject judges at all levels into censorship roles that are simply inappropriate and impermissible under the First Amendment. Indeed, the potential for arbitrary and excessive judicial utilization of any such power would be exacerbated by the fact that judges and committing magistrates might in some cases be determining the propriety of publishing information that reflects on their competence, integrity or general performance on the bench. . . .

·   ·   ·

To hold that courts cannot impose any prior restraints on the reporting of or commentary upon information revealed in open court proceedings, disclosed in public documents, or divulged by other sources with respect to the criminal justice system is not, I must emphasize, to countenance the sacrifice of precious Sixth Amendment rights on the altar of the First Amendment. For although there may in some instances be tension between uninhibited and robust reporting by the press and fair trials for criminal defendants, judges possess adequate tools short of injunctions

337

against reporting for relieving that tension. To be sure, these alternatives may require greater sensitivity and effort on the part of judges conducting criminal trials than would the stifling of publicity through the simple expedient of issuing a restrictive order on the press; but that sensitivity and effort is required in order to ensure the full enjoyment and proper accommodation of both First and Sixth Amendment rights. . . .

.   .   .

[T]he press may be arrogant, tyrannical, abusive, and sensationalist, just as it may be incisive, probing, and informative. But at least in the context of prior restraints on publication, the decision of what, when, and how to publish is for editors, not judges. . . .

.   .   .

Mr. Justice Stevens, concurring in the judgment.

Oklahoma Publishing Co. v. District Court

430 U.S. 308, 51 L Ed 2d 355, 97 S Ct 1045 (1977)

The facts are contained in the opinion of the Court.

.   .   .

Per Curiam.

A pretrial order entered by the District Court of Oklahoma County enjoined members of the news media from "publishing, broadcasting, or disseminating, in any manner, the name or picture of [a] minor child" in connection with a juvenile proceeding involving that child then pending in that court. . . .

.   .   .

Reporters, including one from petitioner's newspapers, were present in the courtroom during the hearing and learned the juvenile's name. As the boy was escorted from the courthouse to a vehicle, one of petitioner's photographers took his picture. Thereafter, a number of stories using the boy's name and photograph were printed in newspapers within the county, including petitioner's three newspapers in Oklahoma City; radio stations broadcast his name and television stations showed film footage of him and identified him by name. . . .

.   .   .

Petitioner asks us only to hold that the First and Fourteenth Amendments will not permit a state court to prohibit the publication of widely disseminated information obtained at court proceedings which were in fact open to the public. We think this result is compelled by our recent decisions in Nebraska Press Assn. v Stuart and Cox Broadcasting Corp. v Cohn.

In Cox Broadcasting the Court held that a State could not impose sanctions on the accurate publication of the name of a rape victim "which was publicly revealed in connection with the prosecution of the crime." There, a reporter learned the identity of the victim from an examination of indictments made available by a clerk for his inspection in the courtroom during a recess of court proceedings against the alleged rapists. The Court expressly refrained from intimating a view on any constitutional questions arising from a state policy of denying the public or the press access to official records of juvenile proceedings but made clear that the press may not be prohibited from "truthfully publishing information released to the public in official court records.". . .

.   .   .

This principle was reaffirmed last Term in Nebraska Press v Stuart. . . The Court noted that under state law the trial court was permitted in certain circumstances to close pretrial proceedings to the public, but indicated that such an option did not allow the trial judge to suppress publication of information from the hearing if the public was allowed to attend: "[O]nce a public hearing had been held, what transpired there could not be subject to prior restraint.". . .

.   .   .

The court below found the rationale of these decisions to be inapplicable here because a state statute provided for closed juvenile hearings unless specifically opened to the public by court order and because "there is no indication that the judge distinctly and expressly ordered the hearing to be public." Whether or not the trial judge expressly made such an order, members of the press were in fact present at the hearing with the full knowledge of the presiding judge, the prosecutor, and the defense counsel. No objection was made to the presence of the press in the courtroom or to the photographing of the juvenile as he left the courthouse. There is no evidence that petitioner acquired the information unlawfully or even without the State's implicit approval. The name and picture of the juvenile here were "publicly revealed in connection with the prosecution of the crime". . . Under these circumstances, the District Court's order abridges the freedom of the press in violation of the First and Fourteenth Amendments.

The petition for certiorari is granted and the judgment is reversed.

Gannett Co. v. DePasquale

443 U.S. 368, 61 L Ed 2d 608, 99 S Ct 2898 (1979)

The respondent trial judge granted an unopposed defense motion to exclude the public and the press from a pretrial hearing on a challenge to the admissibility of evidence in a murder case. Defense counsel cited continuous adverse publicity which threatened the fair trial rights of the accused. A reporter for the two newspapers published by petitioner in Rochester, New York was present in the courtroom at the time and did not protest the granting of the motion. The following day the reporter did object to the exclusion order and requested access to the transcript of the closed hearing. When this request was denied, the publisher filed a motion to set aside the exclusion order. This motion was denied by the trial judge on the ground that the interests of the press and the public in this pretrial hearing were outweighed by the defendants' right to a fair trial. The New York Supreme Court vacated the exclusionary order but the state court of appeals upheld its validity. Certiorari was granted.

. . .

Mr. Justice Stewart delivered the opinion of the Court.

The question presented in this case is whether members of the public have an independent constitutional right to insist upon access to a pretrial judicial proceeding, even though the accused, the prosecutor and the trial judge all have agreed to the closure of that proceeding in order to assure a fair trial. . . .

. . .

Greathouse and Jones [the defendants] moved to suppress statements made to the police. The ground they asserted was that those statements had been given involuntarily. They also sought to suppress physical evidence seized as fruits of the allegedly involuntary confessions; the primary physical evidence they sought to suppress was the gun to which, as petitioner's newspaper had reported, Greathouse had led the Michigan police.

The motions to suppress came on before Judge DePasquale on November 4. At this hearing, defense attorneys argued that the unabated buildup of adverse publicity had jeopardized the ability of the defendants to receive a fair trial. They thus requested that the public and the press be excluded from the hearing. The District Attorney did not oppose the motion. Although Carol Ritter, a reporter employed by the petitioner, was present in the courtroom, no objection was made at the time of the closure motion. The trial judge granted the motion.

The next day, however, Ritter wrote a letter to the trial judge asserting a "right to cover this hearing," and requesting that "we . . . be given access to the transcript." The judge responded later the same day. He stated that the suppression hearing had concluded and that any decision on immediate release of the transcript had been reserved. The petitioner then moved the court to set aside its exclusionary order.

The trial judge scheduled a hearing on this motion for November 16 after allowing the parties to file briefs. At this proceeding, the trial judge stated that, in his view, the press had a constitutional right of access although he deemed it "unfortunate" that no representative of the petitioner had objected at the time of the closure motion. Despite his acceptance of the existence of this right, however, the judge emphasized that it had to be balanced against the constitutional right of the defendants to a fair trial. After finding on the record that an open suppression hearing would pose a "reasonable probability of prejudice to these defendants," the judge ruled that the interest of the press and the public was outweighed in this case by the defendants' right to a fair trial. The judge thus refused to vacate his exclusion order or grant the petitioner immediate access to a transcript of the pretrial hearing. . . .

. . .

This Court has long recognized that adverse publicity can endanger the ability of a defendant to receive a fair trial. To safeguard the due process rights of the accused, a trial judge has an affirmative constitutional duty to minimize the effects of prejudicial pretrial publicity. And because of the Constitution's pervasive concern for these due process rights, a trial judge may surely take protective measures even when they are not strictly and inescapably necessary.

Publicity concerning pretrial suppression hearings such as the one involved in the present case poses special risks of unfairness. The whole purpose of such hearings is to screen out unreliable or illegally obtained evidence and insure that this evidence does not become known to the jury. Publicity concerning the proceedings at a pretrial hearing, however, could influence public opinion against a defendant and inform potential jurors of inculpatory information wholly inadmissible at the actual trial.

The danger of publicity concerning pretrial suppression hearings is particularly acute, because it may be difficult to measure with any degree of certainty the effects of such publicity on the fairness of the trial. After the commencement of the trial itself, inadmissible prejudicial information about a defendant can be kept from a jury by a variety of means. When such information is publicized during a pretrial proceeding, however, it may never be altogether kept from potential jurors. Closure of pretrial proceedings is often one of the most effective methods that a trial judge can employ to attempt to insure that the fairness of a trial will not be jeopardized by the dissemination of such information throughout the community before the trial itself has even begun. . . .

. . .

Among the guarantees that the [Sixth] Amendment provides to a person charged with the commission of a criminal offense, and to him alone, is the "right to a speedy and public trial, by an impartial jury." The Constitution nowhere mentions any right of access to a criminal trial on the part of the public; its guarantee, like the others enumerated, is personal to the accused.

Our cases have uniformly recognized the public trial guarantee as one created for the benefit of the defendant. . . .

.   .   .

[I]n Estes v Texas, the Court held that a defendant was deprived of his right to due process of law under the Fourteenth Amendment by the televising and broadcasting of his trial. In rejecting the claim that the media representatives had a constitutional right to televise the trial, the Court stated that "[t]he purpose of the requirement of a public trial was to guarantee that the accused would be fairly dealt with and not unjustly condemned." "Thus the right of 'public trial' is not one belonging to the public, but one belonging to the accused, and inhering in the institutional process by which justice is administered" (Harlan, J., concurring); "[T]he public trial provision of the Sixth Amendment is a 'guarantee to an accused' . . . [and] a necessary component of an accused's right to a fair trial . . ." (Warren, C. J., concurring).

Thus, both the Oliver and Estes cases recognized that the constitutional guarantee of a public trial is for the benefit of the defendant. There is not the slightest suggestion in either case that there is any correlative right in members of the public to insist upon a public trial.

While the Sixth Amendment guarantees to a defendant in a criminal case the right to a public trial, it does not guarantee the right to compel a private trial. "The ability to waive a constitutional right does not ordinarily carry with it the right to insist upon the opposite of that right." But the issue here is not whether the defendant can compel a private trial. Rather, the issue is whether members of the public have an enforceable right to a public trial that can be asserted independently of the parties in the litigation.

There can be no blinking the fact that there is a strong societal interest in public trials. Openness in court proceedings may improve the quality of testimony, induce unknown witnesses to come forward with relevant testimony, cause all trial participants to perform their duties more conscientiously, and generally give the public an opportunity to observe the judicial system. . . .

.   .   .

Recognition of an independent public interest in the enforcement of Sixth Amendment guarantees is a far cry, however, from the creation of a constitutional right on the part of the public. In an adversary system of criminal justice, the public interest in the administration of justice is protected by the participants in the litigation. Thus, because of the great public interest in jury trials as the preferred mode of fact-finding in criminal cases, a defendant cannot waive a jury trial without the consent of the prosecutor and judge. But if the defendant waives his right to a jury trial, and the prosecutor and the judge consent, it could hardly be seriously argued that a member of the public could demand a jury trial because of the societal interest in that mode of factfinding... Similarly, while a defendant cannot convert his right to a speedy trial into a right to compel an indefinite postponement, a member of the general public surely has no right to prevent a continuance in order to vindicate the public interest in the efficient administration of justice. In short, our adversary system of criminal justice is premised upon the proposition that the public interest is fully protected by the participants in the litigation....

. . .

Our judicial duty in this case is to determine whether the common-law rule of open proceedings was incorporated, rejected, or left undisturbed by the Sixth Amendment. In pursuing this inquiry, it is important to distinguish between what the Constitution permits and what it requires. It has never been suggested that by phrasing the public-trial guarantee as a right of the accused, the Framers intended to reject the common-law rule of open proceedings. There is no question that the Sixth Amendment permits and even presumes open trials as a norm. But the issue here is whether the Constitution *requires* that a pretrial proceeding such as this one be opened to the public, even though the participants in the litigation agree that it should be closed to protect the defendants' right to a fair trial. The history upon which the petitioner and amici rely totally fails to demonstrate that the Framers of the Sixth Amendment intended to create a constitutional right in strangers to attend a pretrial proceeding, when all that they actually did was to confer upon the accused an explicit right to demand a public trial. In conspicuous contrast with some of the early state constitutions that provided for a public right to open civil and criminal trials, the Sixth Amendment confers the right to a public trial only upon a defendant and only in a criminal case.

But even if the Sixth and Fourteenth Amendments could properly be viewed as embodying the common-law right of the public to attend criminal trials, it would not necessarily follow that the petitioner would have a right of access under the circumstances of this case. For there exists no persuasive evidence that at common law members of the public had any right to attend pretrial proceedings; indeed, there is substantial evidence to the contrary. By the time of the adoption of the Constitution, public trials were clearly associated with the protection of the defendant. And pretrial proceedings, precisely because of the same concern for a fair trial, were never characterized by the same degree of openness as were actual trials. . . .

.   .   .

For these reasons, we hold that members of the public have no constitutional right under the Sixth and Fourteenth Amendments to attend criminal trials. . . .

.   .   .

The petitioner in this case urges us to recogniz[e] a First and Fourteenth Amendment right to attend criminal trials. We need not decide in the abstract, however, whether there is any such constitutional right. For even assuming, arguendo, that the First and Fourteenth Amendments may guarantee such access in some situations, a question we do not decide, this putative right was given all appropriate deference by the state nisi prius court in the present case.

Several factors lead to the conclusion that the actions of the trial judge here were consistent with any right of access the petitioner may have had under the First and Fourteenth Amendments. First, none of the spectators present in the courtroom, including the reporter employed by the petitioner, objected when the defendants made the closure motion. Despite this failure to make a contemporaneous objection, counsel for the petitioner was given an opportunity to be heard at a proceeding where he was allowed to voice the petitioner's objections to closure of the pretrial hearing. At this proceeding, which took place after the filing of briefs, the trial court balanced the "constitutional rights of the press and the public" against the "defendants' right to a fair trial." The trial judge concluded after making this appraisal that the press and the public could be excluded from the suppression hearing and could be denied immediate access to a transcript, because an open proceeding would pose a "reasonable probability of prejudice to these defendants." Thus, the trial court found that

345

the representatives of the press did have a right of access of constitutional dimension, but held, under the circumstances of this case, that this right was outweighed by the defendants' right to a fair trial. In short, the closure decision was based "on an assessment of the competing societal interests involved ... rather than on any determination that First Amendment freedoms were not implicated."

Furthermore, any denial of access in this case was not absolute but only temporary. Once the danger of prejudice had dissipated, a transcript of the suppression hearing was made available. The press and the public then had a full opportunity to scrutinize the suppression hearing. Unlike the case of an absolute ban on access, therefore, the press here had the opportunity to inform the public of the details of the pretrial hearing accurately and completely. Under these circumstances, any First and Fourteenth Amendment right of the petitioner to attend a criminal trial was not violated.

We certainly do not disparage the general desirability of open judicial proceedings. But we are not asked here to declare whether open proceedings represent beneficial social policy, or whether there would be a constitutional barrier to a state law that imposed a stricter standard of closure than the one here employed by the New York courts. Rather, we are asked to hold that the Constitution itself gave the petitioner an affirmative right of access to this pretrial proceeding, even though all the participants in the litigation agreed that it should be closed to protect the fair-trial rights of the defendants.

For all of the reasons discussed in this opinion, we hold that the Constitution provides no such right. Accordingly, the judgment of the New York Court of Appeals is affirmed.

.   .   .   .

Mr. Chief Justice Burger, concurring.

I join the opinion of the Court, but I write separately to emphasize my view of the nature of the proceeding involved in today's decision. By definition, a hearing on a motion before trial to suppress evidence is not a trial; it is a pretrial hearing. . . .

.   .   .

When the Sixth Amendment was written, and for more than a century after that, no one could have conceived that the exclusionary rule and pretrial motions to suppress evidence would be part of our criminal jurisprudence. The authors of the Constitution, imaginative, farsighted, and perceptive as they were, could not conceivably have anticipated the paradox inherent in a judge-made rule of evidence that excludes undoubted truth from the truthfinding processes of the adversary system. Nevertheless, as of now, we are confronted not with a legal theory but with the reality of the unique strictures of the exclusionary rule, and they must be taken into account in this setting. To make public the evidence developed in a motion to suppress evidence ... would, so long as the exclusionary rule is not modified, introduce a new dimension to the problem of conducting fair trials.

Even though the draftsmen of the Constitution could not anticipate the 20th-century pretrial proceedings to suppress evidence, pretrial proceedings were not wholly unknown in that day... Thus, it is safe to assume that those lawyers who drafted the Sixth Amendment were not unaware that some testimony was likely to be recorded before trials took place. Yet, no one ever suggested that there was any "right" of the public to be present at such pretrial proceedings as were available in that time; until the trial it could not be known whether and to what extent the pretrial evidence would be offered or received.

Similarly, during the last 40 years in which the pretrial processes have been enormously expanded, it has never occurred to anyone, so far as I am aware, that a pretrial deposition or pretrial interrogatories were other than wholly private to the litigants. A pretrial deposition does not become part of a "trial" until and unless the contents of the deposition are offered in evidence. Pretrial depositions are not uncommon to take the testimony of a witness, either for the defense or for the prosecution. In the entire pretrial period, there is no certainty that a trial will take place. Something in the neighborhood of 85 percent of all criminal charges are resolved by guilty pleas, frequently after pretrial depositions have been taken or motions to suppress evidence have been ruled upon.

For me, the essence of all of this is that by definition "pretrial proceedings" are exactly that.

.   .   .

Mr. Justice Powell, concurring.

Although I join the opinion of the Court, I would address the question that it reserves. Because of the importance of the public's having accurate information concerning the operation of its criminal justice system, I would hold explicitly that petitioner's reporter had an interest protected by the First and Fourteenth Amendments in being present at the pretrial suppression hearing. [T]his constitutional protection derives, not from any special status of members of the press as such, but rather because "[i]n seeking out the news the press . . . acts as an agent of the public at large," each individual member of which cannot obtain for himself "the information needed for the intelligent discharge of his political responsibilities.". . .

. . .

In cases such as this, where competing constitutional rights must be weighed in the context of a criminal trial, the often difficult question is whether unrestrained exercise of First Amendment rights poses a serious danger to the fairness of a defendant's trial. "As we stressed in Estes, the presence of the press at judicial proceedings must be limited when it is apparent that the accused might otherwise be prejudiced or disadvantaged." In striking this balance there are a number of considerations to be weighed. In Nebraska Press Assn. v Stuart, we concluded that there is a strong presumption against prohibiting members of the press from publishing information already in their possession concerning courtroom proceedings. Excluding all members of the press from the courtroom, however, differs substantially from the "gag order" at issue in Nebraska Press, as the latter involved a classic prior restraint, "one of the most extraordinary remedies known to our jurisprudence," and applied to information irrespective of its source. In the present case, on the other hand, we are confronted with a trial court's order that in effect denies access only to one, albeit important, source. It does not in any way tell the press what it may and may not publish. . . .

. . .

The question for the trial court, therefore, in considering a motion to close a pretrial suppression hearing is whether a fair trial for the defendant is likely to be jeopardized by publicity, if members of the press and public are present and free to report prejudicial evidence that will not be presented to the jury. . . .

. . .

[W]here a defendant requests the trial court to exclude the public, it should consider whether there are alternative means reasonably available by which the fairness of the trial might be preserved without interfering substantially with the public's interest in prompt access to information concerning the administration of justice. Similarly, because exclusion is justified only as a protection of the defendant's right to a fair trial and the State's interest in confidentiality, members of the press and public objecting to the exclusion have the right to demand that it extend no farther than is likely to achieve these goals. Thus, for example, the trial court should not withhold the transcript of closed courtroom proceedings past the time when no prejudice is likely to result to the defendant or the State from its release.

It is not enough, however, that trial courts apply a certain standard to requests for closure. If the constitutional right of the press and public to access is to have substance, representatives of these groups must be given an opportunity to be heard on the question of their exclusion. But this opportunity extends no farther than the persons actually present at the time the motion for closure is made, for the alternative would require substantial delays in trial and pretrial proceedings while notice was given to the public. Upon timely objection to the granting of the motion, it is incumbent upon the trial court to afford those present a reasonable opportunity to be heard on the question whether the defendant is likely to be deprived of a fair trial if the press and public are permitted to remain in attendance. At this hearing, it is the defendant's responsibility as the moving party to make some showing that the fairness of his trial likely will be prejudiced by public access to the proceedings. Similarly, if the State joins in the closure request, it should be given the opportunity to show that public access would interfere with its interests in fair proceedings or preserving the confidentiality of sensitive information. On the other hand, members of the press and public who object to closure have the responsibility of showing to the court's satisfaction that alternative procedures are available that would eliminate the dangers shown by the defendant and the State. . . .

.   .   .

In my view, the procedure followed by the trial court fully comported with that required by the Constitution. Moreover, the substantive standard applied was essentially correct, and, giving due deference to the proximity of the trial judge to the surrounding circumstances, I cannot conclude that it was error in this case to exclude petitioner's reporter. . . .

. . .

Mr. Justice Rehnquist, concurring.

In this case, the trial judge closed the suppression hearing because he concluded that an open hearing might have posed a danger to the defendants' ability to receive a fair trial. But the Court's recitation of this fact and its discussion of the need to preserve the defendant's right to a fair trial should not be interpreted to mean that under the Sixth Amendment a trial court can close a pretrial hearing or trial only when there is a danger that prejudicial publicity will harm the defendant. To the contrary, since the Court holds that the public does not have any Sixth Amendment right of access to such proceedings, it necessarily follows that if the parties agree on a closed proceeding, the trial court is not required by the Sixth Amendment to advance any reason whatsoever for declining to open a pretrial hearing or trial to the public. . . .

. . .

Despite the Court's seeming reservation of the question whether the First Amendment guarantees the public a right of access to pretrial proceedings, it is clear that this Court repeatedly has held that there is no First Amendment right of access in the public or the press to judicial or other governmental proceedings. . . "The First and Fourteenth Amendments do not guarantee the public a right of access to information generated or controlled by government, nor do they guarantee the press any basic right of access superior to that of the public generally. The Constitution does no more than assure the public and the press equal access once government has opened its doors." Thus, this Court emphatically has rejected the proposition advanced in Mr. Justice Powell's concurring opinion that the First Amendment is some sort of constitutional "sunshine law" that requires notice, an opportunity to be heard, and substantial reasons before a governmental proceeding may be closed to the public and press. Because this Court has refused to find a First Amendment right of access in the past, lower courts should not assume that after today's decision they must adhere to the procedures employed by the trial court in this case or to those advanced by Mr. Justice Powell in his separate opinion in order to avoid running afoul of the First Amendment. To the contrary, in my view and, I think, in the view of a majority of this Court, the lower courts are under no constitutional constraint either to accept or reject those procedures. They remain, in the best tradition of our federal system, free to determine for themselves the question whether to open or close the proceeding. Hopefully, they will decide the question by accommodating competing interests in a judicious manner. But so far as the Constitution is concerned, the question is for them, not us, to resolve.

.   .   .

Mr. Justice Blackmun, with whom Mr. Justice Brennan, Mr. Justice White, and Mr. Justice Marshall join, concurring in part and dissenting in part.

.   .   .

Today's decision, as I view it, is an unfortunate one. I fear that the Court surrenders to the temptation to overstate and overcolor the actual nature of the pre-August 7, 1976, publicity; that it reaches for a strict and flat result; and that in the process it ignores the important antecedents and significant developmental features of the Sixth Amendment. The result is an inflexible per se rule, as Mr. Justice Rehnquist so appropriately observes in his separate concurrence. . . That rule is to the effect that if the defense and the prosecution merely agree to have the public excluded from a suppression hearing, and the trial judge does not resist—as trial judges may be prone not to do, since nonresistance is easier than resistance—closure shall take place, and there is nothing in the Sixth Amendment that prevents that happily agreed upon event. The result is that the important interests of the public and the press (as a part of that public) in open judicial proceedings are rejected and cast aside as of little value or significance.

Because I think this easy but wooden approach is without support either in legal history or in the intendment of the Sixth Amendment, I dissent. . . .

.   .   .

This Court confronts in this case another aspect of the recurring conflict that arises whenever a defendant in a criminal case asserts that his right to a fair trial clashes with the right of the public in general, and of the press in particular, to an open proceeding. It has considered other aspects of the problem in deciding whether publicity was sufficiently prejudicial to have deprived the defendant of a fair trial. . . And recently it examined the extent to which the First and Fourteenth Amendments protect news organizations' rights to publish, free from prior restraint, information learned in open court during a pretrial suppression hearing. . . . But the Court has not yet addressed the precise issue raised by this case: whether and to what extent the Constitution prohibits the States from excluding, at the request of a defendant, members of the public from such a hearing. . . .

. . .

The issue here, then, is not one of prior restraint on the press but is, rather, one of *access* to a judicial proceeding. . . .

. . .

This Nation's accepted practice of providing open trials in both federal and state courts "has always been recognized as a safeguard against any attempt to employ our courts as instruments of persecution. The knowledge that every criminal trial is subject to contemporaneous review in the forum of public opinion is an effective restraint on possible abuse of judicial power.". . .

. . .

The public-trial guarantee, moreover, ensures that not only judges but all participants in the criminal justice system are subjected to public scrutiny as they conduct the public's business of prosecuting crime. This publicity "guards against the miscarriage of justice by subjecting the police, prosecutors, and judicial processes to extensive public scrutiny and criticism." Publicity "serves to guarantee the fairness of trials and to bring to bear the beneficial effects of public scrutiny upon the administration of justice." "The commission of crime, prosecutions resulting from it, and judicial proceedings arising from the prosecutions . . . are without question events of legitimate concern to the public." Indeed, such information is "of critical importance to our type of government in which the citizenry is the final judge of the proper conduct of public business.". . .

. . .

By its literal terms, the Sixth Amendment secures the right to a public trial only to "the accused." And in this case, the accused were the ones who sought to waive that right, and to have the public removed from the pretrial hearing in order to guard against publicity that possibly would be prejudicial to them. The Court is urged, accordingly, to hold that the decision of respondents Greathouse and Jones to submit to a private hearing is controlling.

The Court, however, previously has recognized that the Sixth Amendment may implicate interests beyond those of the accused. . . .

.　.　.

It is . . . clear . . . that the fact the Sixth Amendment casts the right to a public trial in terms of the right of the accused is not sufficient to permit the inference that the accused may compel a private proceeding simply by waiving that right. Any such right to compel a private proceeding must have some independent basis in the Sixth Amendment. In order to determine whether an independent basis exists, we should examine . . . the common-law and colonial antecedents of the public-trial provision as well as the original understanding of the Sixth Amendment. If no such basis is found, we should then turn to the function of the public trial in our system so that we may decide under what circumstances, if any, a trial court may give effect to a defendant's attempt to waive his right. . . .

.　.　.

Study of [the common-law] heritage reveals that the tradition of conducting the proceedings in public came about as an inescapable concomitant of trial by jury, quite unrelated to the rights of the accused, and that the practice at common law was to conduct all criminal proceedings in public. . . .

.　.　.

[T]he unbroken tradition of the English common law was that criminal trials were conducted "openlie in the presence of the Judges, the Justices, the enquest, the prisoner, and so manie as will or can come so neare as to heare it, and all depositions and witnesses given aloude, that all men may heare from the mouth of the depositors and witnesses what is saide.". . .

.　.　.

It is not surprising, therefore, that both Hale and Blackstone, in identifying the function of publicity at common law, discussed the open-trial requirement not in terms of individual liberties but in terms of the effectiveness of the trial process. Each recognized publicity as an essential of trial at common law. And each emphasized that the requirement that evidence be given in open court deterred perjury, since "a witness may frequently depose that in private, which he will be ashamed to testify in a public and solemn tribunal.". . .

Similarly, both recognized that publicity was an effective check on judicial abuse, since publicity made it certain that "if the judge be PARTIAL, his partiality and injustice will be evident to all bystanders.". . .

. . .

There is no evidence that criminal trials of any sort ever were conducted in private at common law, whether at the request of the defendant or over his objection. And there is strong evidence that the public trial, which developed before other procedural rights now routinely afforded the accused, widely was perceived as serving important social interests, relating to the integrity of the trial process, that exist apart from, and conceivably in opposition to, the interests of the individual defendant. Accordingly, I find no support in the common-law antecedents of the Sixth Amendment public-trial provision for the view that the guarantee of a public trial carries with it a correlative right to compel a private proceeding. . . .

. . .

This practice of conducting judicial proceedings in criminal cases in public took firm hold in all the American Colonies. There is no evidence that any colonial court conducted criminal trials behind closed doors or that any recognized the right of an accused to compel a private trial. . . .

. . .

I consequently find no evidence in the development of the public-trial concept in the American Colonies and in the adoption of the Sixth Amendment to indicate that there was any recognition in this country, any more than in England, of a right to a private proceeding or a power to compel a private trial arising out of the ability to waive the grant of a public one. I shall not indulge in a mere mechanical inference that, by phrasing the public trial as one belonging to the accused, the Framers of the Amendment must have meant the accused to have the power to dispense with publicity.

354

I thus conclude that there is no basis in the Sixth Amendment for the suggested inference. I also find that, because there is a societal interest in the public trial that exists separately from, and at times in opposition to, the interests of the accused, a court may give effect to an accused's attempt to waive his public-trial right only in certain circumstances.

The courts and the scholars of the common law perceived the public-trial tradition as one serving to protect the integrity of the trial and to guard against partiality on the part of the court. The same concerns are generally served by the public trial today. The protection against perjury which publicity provides, and the opportunity publicity offers to unknown witnesses to make themselves known, do not necessarily serve the defendant. The public has an interest in having criminal prosecutions decided on truthful and complete records, and this interest, too, does not necessarily coincide with that of the accused.

Nor does the protection against judicial partiality serve only the defendant. It is true that the public-trial provision serves to protect every accused from the abuses to which secret tribunals would be prone. But the defendant himself may benefit from the partiality of a corrupt, biased, or incompetent judge, "for a secret trial can result in favor to as well as unjust prosecution of a defendant."

Open trials also enable the public to scrutinize the performance of police and prosecutors in the conduct of public judicial business. Trials and particularly suppression hearings typically involve questions concerning the propriety of police and government conduct that took place hidden from the public view. Any interest on the part of the prosecution in hiding police or prosecutorial misconduct or ineptitude may coincide with the defendant's desire to keep the proceedings private, with the result that the public interest is sacrificed from both sides.

Public judicial proceedings have an important educative role as well. The victim of the crime, the family of the victim, others who have suffered similarly, or others accused of like crimes, have an interest in observing the course of a prosecution. Beyond this, however, is the interest of the general public in observing the operation of the criminal justice system. Judges, prosecutors, and police officials often are elected or are subject to some control by elected officials, and a main source of information about how these officials perform is the open trial. And the manner in which criminal justice is administered in this country is in and of itself of interest to all citizens. . . .

.   .   .

The ability of the courts to administer the criminal laws depends in no small part on the confidence of the public in judicial remedies, and on respect for and acquaintance with the processes and deliberations of those courts. Anything that impairs the open nature of judicial proceedings threatens to undermine this confidence and to impede the ability of the courts to function. . . .

.   .   .

I therefore conclude that the Due Process Clause of the Fourteenth Amendment, insofar as it incorporates the public-trial provision of the Sixth Amendment, prohibits the States from excluding the public from a proceeding within the ambit of the Sixth Amendment's guarantee without affording full and fair consideration to the public's interests in maintaining an open proceeding. And I believe that the Sixth and Fourteenth Amendments require this conclusion notwithstanding the fact it is the accused who seeks to close the trial.

Before considering whether and under what circumstances a court may conduct a criminal proceeding in private, one must first decide whether the Sixth Amendment, as applied through the Fourteenth, encompasses the type of pretrial hearing at issue in this case. . . .

.   .   .

I find good reason to hold that even if a State, as it may, chooses to hold a suppression hearing separate from and prior to the full trial, the Sixth Amendment's public-trial provision applies to that hearing. First, the suppression hearing resembles and relates to the full trial in almost every particular. Evidence is presented by means of live testimony, witnesses are sworn, and those witnesses are subject to cross-examination. Determination of the ultimate issue depends in most cases upon the trier of fact's evaluation of the evidence, and credibility is often crucial. Each side has incentive to prevail, with the result that the role of publicity as a testimonial safeguard, as a mechanism to encourage the parties, the witnesses, and the court to a strict conscientiousness in the performance of their duties, and in providing a means whereby unknown witnesses may become known, are just as important for the suppression hearing as they are for the full trial.

Moreover, the pretrial suppression hearing often is critical, and it may be decisive, in the prosecution of a criminal case. If the defendant prevails, he will have dealt the prosecution's case a serious, perhaps fatal, blow; the proceeding often then will be dismissed or negotiated on terms favorable to the defense. If the prosecution successfully resists the motion to suppress, the defendant may have little hope of success at trial (especially where a confession is in issue), with the result that the likelihood of a guilty plea is substantially increased.

The suppression hearing often is the only judicial proceeding of substantial importance that takes place during a criminal prosecution. In this very case, the hearing from which the public was excluded was the only one in which the important factual and legal issues in the prosecution of respondents Greathouse and Jones were considered. It was the only proceeding at which the conduct of the police, prosecution, and the court iself was exposed to scrutiny. Indeed, in 1976, when this case was processed, every felony prosecution in Seneca County—and I say this without criticism—was terminated without a trial on the merits. This statistic is characteristic of our state and federal criminal justice systems as a whole, and it underscores the importance of the suppression hearing in the functioning of those systems.

Further, the issues considered at such hearings are of great moment beyond their importance to the outcome of a particular prosecution. A motion to suppress typically involves, as in this case, allegations of misconduct by police and prosecution that raise constitutional issues. Allegations of this kind, although they may prove to be unfounded, are of importance to the public as well as to the defendant. The searches and interrogations that such hearings evaluate do not take place in public. The hearing therefore usually presents the only opportunity the public has to learn about police and prosecutorial conduct, and about allegations that those responsible to the public for the enforcement of laws themselves are breaking it.

A decision to suppress often involves the exclusion of highly relevant evidence. Because this is so, the decision may generate controversy. It is important that any such decision be made on the basis of evidence and argument offered in open court, so that all who care to see or read about the case may evaluate for themselves the propriety of the exclusion.

These factors lead me to conclude that a pretrial suppression hearing is the close equivalent of the trial on the merits for purposes of applying

357

the public-trial provision of the Sixth Amendment. Unlike almost any other proceeding apart from the trial itself, the suppression hearing implicates all the policies that require that the trial be public. For this reason, I would be loath to hold that a State could conduct a pretrial hearing in private over the *objection* of the defendant. And for this same reason, the public's interest in the openness of judicial proceedings is implicated fully when it is the accused who seeks to exclude the public from such a hearing. Accordingly, I conclude that the Sixth and Fourteenth Amendments prohibit a state from conducting a pretrial suppression hearing in private, even at the request of the accused, unless full and fair consideration is first given to the public's interest, protected by the Amendments, in open trials. . . .

· · ·

I, for one, am unwilling to allow trials and suppression hearings to be closed with no way to ensure that the public interest is protected. Unlike the other provisions of the Sixth Amendment, the public-trial interest cannot adequately be protected by the prosecutor and judge in conjunction, or connivance, with the defendant. The specter of a trial or suppression hearing where a defendant of the same political party as the prosecutor and the judge—both of whom are elected officials perhaps beholden to the very defendant they are to try—obtains closure of the proceeding without any consideration for the substantial public interest at stake is sufficiently real to cause me to reject the Court's suggestion that the parties be given complete discretion to dispose of the public's interest as they see fit. The decision of the parties to close a proceeding in such a circumstance, followed by suppression of vital evidence or acquittal by the bench, destroys the appearance of justice and undermines confidence in the judicial system in a way no subsequent provision of transcript might remedy. But even where no connivance occurs, prosecutors and judges may have their own reasons for preferring a closed proceeding. And a prosecutor, who seeks to obtain a conviction free from error, and a judge who seeks the same while protecting the defendant's rights, may lack incentive to assert some notion of the public interest in the face of a motion by a criminal defendant to close a trial. . . .

· · ·

Although the Sixth Amendment's public-trial provision establishes a strong presumption in favor of open proceedings, it does not require that all proceedings be held in open court when to do so would deprive a defendant of a fair trial.

No court has held that the Sixth Amendment imposes an absolute requirement that courts be open at all times. On the contrary, courts on both the state and federal levels have recognized exceptions to the public-trial requirement even when it is the accused who objects to the exclusion of the public or a portion thereof....

.   .   .

Because of the importance we attach to a fair trial, it is clear that whatever restrictions on access the Sixth Amendment may prohibit in another context, it does not prevent a trial court from restricting access to a pretrial suppression hearing where such restriction is necessary in order to ensure that a defendant not be denied a fair trial as a result of prejudicial publicity flowing from that hearing....

.   .   .

At the same time, however, the public's interest in maintaining open courts requires that any exception to the rule be narrowly drawn. It comports with the Sixth Amendment to require an accused who seeks closure to establish that it is strictly and inescapably necessary in order to protect the fair-trial guarantee. That finding must be made in the first instance, of course, by the trial court. I cannot detail here all the factors to be taken into account in evaluating the defendant's closure request, nor can I predict how the balance should be struck in every hypothetical case. The accused who seeks closure should establish, however, at a minimum the following:

First, he should provide an adequate basis to support a finding that there is a substantial probability that irreparable damage to his fair-trial right will result from conducting the proceeding in public. This showing will depend on the facts. But I think it requires evidence of the nature and extent of the publicity prior to the motion to close in order to establish a basis for the trial court to conclude that further coverage will result in the harm sought to be prevented. In most cases, this will involve a showing of the impact on the jury pool. This seldom can be measured with exactness, but information relating to the size of the pool, the extent of media coverage in the pertinent locality, and the ease with which change of venire can be accomplished or searching voir dire instituted to protect against prejudice, would be relevant. The court also should consider the extent to which the information sought to be suppressed is already known to the public, and the extent to which publication of such information, if unknown, would have an impact in the context of the publicity that has preceded the motion to close.

Second, the accused should show a substantial probability that alternatives to closure will not protect adequately his right to a fair trial. One may suggest numerous alternatives, but I think the following should be considered: continuance, severance, change of venue, change of venire, voir dire, peremptory challenges, sequestration, and admonition of the jury. One or more of these alternatives may adequately protect the accused's interests and relieve the court of any need to close the proceeding in advance. . . .

. . .

Third, the accused should demonstrate that there is a substantial probability that closure will be effective in protecting against the perceived harm. Where significantly prejudicial information already has been made public, there might well be little justification for closing a pretrial hearing in order to prevent only the disclosure of details. . . .

. . .

If, after considering the essential factors, the trial court determines that the accused has carried his burden of establishing that closure is necessary, the Sixth Amendment is no barrier to reasonable restrictions on public access designed to meet that need. Any restrictions imposed, however, should extend no further than the circumstances reasonably require. Thus, it might well be possible to exclude the public from only those portions of the proceeding at which the prejudicial information would be disclosed, while admitting to other portions where the information the accused seeks to suppress would not be revealed. Further, closure should be temporary in that the court should ensure that an accurate record is made of those proceedings held in camera and that the public is permitted proper access to the record as soon as the threat to the defendant's fair-trial right has passed. . . .

. . .

The Sixth Amendment, in establishing the public's right of access to a criminal trial and a pretrial proceeding, also fixes the rights of the press in this regard. Petitioner, as a newspaper publisher, enjoys the same right of access to the . . . hearing at issue in this case as does the general public. And what petitioner sees and hears in the courtroom it may, like any other citizen, publish or report consistent with the First Amendment. . . .

.   .   .

Petitioner acknowledges that it seeks no greater rights than those due the general public. But it argues that, the Sixth Amendment aside, the First Amendment protects the free flow of information about judicial proceedings, and that this flow may not be cut off without meeting the standards required to justify the imposition of a prior restraint under the First Amendment. Specifically, petitioner argues that the First Amendment prohibits closure of a pretrial proceeding except in accord with the standards established in Nebraska Press and only after notice and hearing and a stay pending appeal.

I do not agree. As I have noted, this case involves no restraint upon publication or upon comment about information already in the possession of the public or the press. It involves an issue of access to a judicial proceeding. To the extent the Constitution protects a right of public access to the proceeding, the standards enunciated under the Sixth Amendment suffice to protect that right. I therefore need not reach the issue of First Amendment access.

.   .   .

A short time after this litigation, the Gannett Publishing Co. issued reporters on the staff of its newspapers a wallet-size card with the following statement to be read any time a judge appeared likely to close a judicial proceeding to the public.

"Your honor, I am _____, a reporter for _____, and I would like to object on behalf of my employer and the public to this proposed closing. Our attorney is prepared to make a number of arguments against closings such as this one, and we respectfully ask the Court for a hearing on those issues. I believe our attorney can be here relatively quickly for the Court's convenience and he will be able to demonstrate that closure in this case will violate the First Amendment, and possibly state statutory and constitutional provisions as well. I cannot make the arguments myself, but our attorney can point out several issues for your consideration. If it pleases the Court, we request the opportunity to be heard through counsel."

Richmond Newspapers Inc. v. Virginia

448 U.S. 555, 65 L Ed 2d 973, 100 S Ct 2814 (1973)

After one reversal and two mistrials, a defendant was about to be tried for the fourth time on murder charges. Defense counsel moved that the trial be closed, the prosecutor stated that he had no objection, and the judge ordered that the courtroom be cleared of all persons except the witnesses when they testified. A Virginia statute provided that in criminal cases "the court may, in its discretion, exclude from the trial any persons whose presence would impair the conduct of a fair trial, provided that the right of the accused to a public trial shall not be violated." Petitioner sought a hearing on a motion to vacate the closure order. The motion to vacate was denied in a closed hearing and the trial proceeded with the press and public excluded. Subsequently, the trial judge found the defendant not guilty. The Virginia Supreme Court denied petitions for writs of mandamus and prohibition and upheld the closure order. The U.S. Supreme Court granted certiorari.

. . .

Mr. Chief Justice Burger announced the judgment of the Court and delivered an opinion in which Mr. Justice White and Mr. Justice Stevens joined.

The narrow question presented in this case is whether the right of the public and press to attend criminal trials is guaranteed under the United States Constitution. . . .

. . .

We begin consideration of this case by noting that the precise issue presented here has not previously been before this Court for decision. In Gannett Co., Inc. v DePasquale, the Court was not required to decide whether a right of access to *trials,* as distinguished from hearings on *pre*trial motions, was constitutionally guaranteed. . . .

. . .

But here for the first time the Court is asked to decide whether a criminal trial itself may be closed to the public upon the unopposed request of a defendant, without any demonstration that closure is required to protect the defendant's superior right to a fair trial, or that some other overriding consideration requires closure.

The origins of the proceeding which has become the modern criminal trial in Anglo-American justice can be traced back beyond reliable historical records. We need not here review all details of its development, but a summary of that history is instructive. What is significant for present purposes is that throughout its evolution, the trial has been open to all who cared to observe. . . .

. . .

The early history of open trials in part reflects the widespread acknowledgement, long before there were behavioral scientists, that public trials had significant community therapeutic value. Even without such experts to frame the concept in words, people sensed from experience and observation that, especially in the administration of criminal justice, the means used to achieve justice must have the support derived from public acceptance of both the process and its results.

When a shocking crime occurs, a community reaction of outrage and public protest often follows. Thereafter the open processes of justice serve an important prophylactic purpose, providing an outlet for community concern, hostility, and emotion. Without an awareness that society's responses to criminal conduct are underway, natural human reactions of outrage and protest are frustrated and may manifest themselves in some form of vengeful "self-help," as indeed they did regularly in the activities of vigilante "committees" on our frontiers. . . .

. . .

Civilized societies withdraw both from the victim and the vigilante the enforcement of criminal laws, but they cannot erase from people's consciousness the fundamental, natural yearning to see justice done—or even the urge for retribution. The crucial prophylactic aspects of the administration of justice cannot function in the dark; no community catharsis can occur if justice is "done in a corner [or] in any covert manner." It is not enough to say that results alone will satiate the natural community desire for "satisfaction." A result considered untoward may

363

undermine public confidence, and where the trial has been concealed from public view an unexpected outcome can cause a reaction that the system at best has failed and at worst has been corrupted. To work effectively, it is important that society's criminal process "satisfy the appearance of justice," and the appearance of justice can best be provided by allowing people to observe it.

Looking back, we see that when the ancient "town meeting" form of trial became too cumbersome, twelve members of the community were delegated to act as its surrogates, but the community did not surrender its right to observe the conduct of trials. The people retained a "right of visitation" which enabled them to satisfy themselves that justice was in fact being done.

People in an open society do not demand infallibility from their institutions, but it is difficult for them to accept what they are prohibited from observing. When a criminal trial is conducted in the open, there is at least an opportunity both for understanding the system in general and its workings in a particular case. . . .

·   ·   ·

Instead of acquiring information about trials by firsthand observation or by word of mouth from those who attended, people now acquire it chiefly through the print and electronic media. In a sense, this validates the media claim of functioning as surrogates for the public. While media representatives enjoy the same right of access as the public, they often are provided special seating and priority of entry so that they may report what people in attendance have seen and heard. This "contribute[s] to public understanding of the rule of law and to comprehension of the functioning of the entire criminal justice system. . . ."

·   ·   ·

From this unbroken, uncontradicted history, supported by reasons as valid today as in centuries past, we are bound to conclude that a presumption of openness inheres in the very nature of a criminal trial under our system of justice. This conclusion is hardly novel; without a direct holding on the issue, the Court has voiced its recognition of it in a variety of contexts over the years. . . .

·   ·   ·

Despite the history of criminal trials being presumptively open since long before the Constitution, the State presses its contention that neither the Constitution nor the Bill of Rights contains any provision which by its terms guarantees to the public the right to attend criminal trials. Standing alone, this is correct, but there remains the question whether, absent an explicit provision, the Constitution affords protection against exclusion of the public from criminal trials. . . .

.　.　.

It is not crucial whether we describe this right to attend criminal trials to hear, see, and communicate observations concerning them as a "right of access," or a "right to gather information," for we have recognized that "without some protection for seeking out the news, freedom of the press could be eviscerated." The explicit, guaranteed rights to speak and to publish concerning what takes place at a trial would lose much meaning if access to observe the trial could, as it was here, be foreclosed arbitrarily. . . .

.　.　.

The State argues that the Constitution nowhere spells out a guarantee for the right of the public to attend trials, and that accordingly no such right is protected. The possibility that such a contention could be made did not escape the notice of the Constitution's draftsmen; they were concerned that some important rights might be thought disparaged because not specifically guaranteed. It was even argued that because of this danger no Bill of Rights should be adopted. . . .

.　.　.

But arguments such as the State makes have not precluded recognition of important rights not enumerated. Notwithstanding the appropriate caution against reading into the Constitution rights not explicitly defined, the Court has acknowledged that certain unarticulated rights are implicit in enumerated guarantees. For example, the rights of association and of privacy, the right to be presumed innocent and the right to be judged by a standard of proof beyond a reasonable doubt in a criminal trial, as well as the right to travel, appear nowhere in the Constitution or Bill of Rights. Yet these important but unarticulated rights have nonetheless been found to share constitutional protection in common with explicit guarantees.

[F]undamental rights, even though not expressly guaranteed, have been recognized by the Court as indispensable to the enjoyment of rights explicitly defined.

We hold that the right to attend criminal trials is implicit in the guarantees of the First Amendment; without the freedom to attend such trials, which people have exercised for centuries, important aspects of freedom of speech and "of the press could be eviscerated.". . .

. . .

Absent an overriding interest articulated in findings, the trial of a criminal case must be open to the public. Accordingly, the judgment under review is reversed. . . .

. . .

Mr. Justice Powell took no part in the consideration or decision of this case.

. . .

Mr. Justice White, concurring.

This case would have been unnecessary had Gannett Co. v DePasquale construed the Sixth Amendment to forbid excluding the public from criminal proceedings except in narrowly defined circumstances. But the Court there rejected the submission of four of us to this effect, thus requiring that the First Amendment issue involved here be addressed. On this issue, I concur in the opinion of The Chief Justice.

. . .

Mr. Justice Stevens, concurring.

This is a watershed case. Until today the court has accorded virtually absolute protection to the dissemination of information or ideas, but never before has it squarely held that the acquisition of newsworthy matter is entitled to any constitutional protection whatsoever. . . .

. . .

Mr. Justice Brennan, with whom Mr. Justice Marshall joins, concurring in the judgment.

Gannett Co. v DePasquale . . . held that the Sixth Amendment right to a public trial was personal to the accused, conferring no right of access to pretrial proceedings that is separately enforceable by the public or the press. The instant case raises the question whether the First Amendment, of its own force and as applied to the States through the Fourteenth Amendment, secures the public an independent right of access to trial proceedings. Because I believe that the First Amendment—of itself and as applied to the States through the Fourteenth Amendment—secures such a public right of access, I agree with those of my Brethren who hold that, without more, agreement of the trial judge and the parties cannot constitutionally close a trial to the public. . . .

. . .

The Court's approach in right of access cases simply reflects the special nature of a claim of First Amendment right to gather information. Customarily, First Amendment guarantees are interposed to protect communication between speaker and listener. When so employed against prior restraints, free speech protections are almost insurmountable. But the First Amendment embodies more than a commitment to free expression and communicative interchange for their own sakes; it has a *structural* role to play in securing and fostering our republican system of self-government. Implicit in this structural role is not only "the principle that debate on public issues should be uninhibited, robust, and wide-open," but the antecedent assumption that valuable public debate—as well as other civic behavior—must be informed. The structural model links the First Amendment to that process of communication necessary for a democracy to survive, and thus entails solicitude not only for communication itself, but for the indispensable conditions of meaningful communication.

. . .

An assertion of the prerogative to gather information must accordingly be assayed by considering the information sought and the opposing interests invaded.

This judicial task is as much a matter of sensitivity to practical necessities as it is of abstract reasoning. But at least two helpful principles may be sketched. First, the case for a right of access has special force when drawn from an enduring and vital tradition of public entree to particular proceedings or information. Such a tradition commands respect in part because the Constitution carries the gloss of history. More importantly, a tradition of accessibility implies the favorable judgment of experience. Second, the value of access must be measured in specifics. Analysis is not advanced by rhetorical statements that all information bears upon public issues; what is crucial in individual cases is whether access to a particular government process is important in terms of that very process. . . .

· · ·

[A] special solicitude for the public character of judicial proceedings is evident in the Court's rulings upholding the right to report about the administration of justice. While these decisions are impelled by the classic protections afforded by the First Amendment to pure communication, they are also bottomed upon a keen appreciation of the structural interest served in opening the judicial system to public inspection. . . .

· · ·

Open trials assure the public that procedural rights are respected, and that justice is afforded equally. Closed trials breed suspicion of prejudice and arbitrariness, which in turn spawns disrespect for law. Public access is essential, therefore, if trial adjudication is to achieve the objective of maintaining public confidence in the administration of justice. . . .

· · ·

But the trial is more than a demonstrably just method of adjudicating disputes and protecting rights. It plays a pivotal role in the entire judicial process, and, by extension, in our form of government. Under our system, judges are not mere umpires, but, in their own sphere, lawmakers—a coordinate branch of *government*. While individual cases turn upon the controversies between parties, or involve particular prosecutions, court rulings impose official and practical consequences upon members of society at large. Moreover, judges bear responsibility for the vitally important task of construing and securing constitutional rights. Thus, so far as the trial is the mechanism for judicial factfinding, as well as the initial forum for legal decisionmaking, it is a genuine governmental proceeding.

It follows that the conduct of the trial is preeminently a matter of public interest. . . .

· · ·

Popular attendance at trials, in sum, substantially furthers the particular public purposes of that critical judicial proceeding. In that sense, public access is an indispensable element of the trial process itself. Trial access, therefore, assumes structural importance in our "government of laws,". . .

. . .

Mr. Justice Stewart, concurring in the judgment.

. . .

Mr. Justice Blackmun, concurring in the judgment.

. . .

The decision in this case is gratifying for me for two reasons:

It is gratifying, first, to see the Court now looking to and relying upon legal history in determining the fundamental public character of the criminal trial. . . .

. . .

It is gratifying, second, to see the Court wash away at least some of the graffiti that marred the prevailing opinions in Gannett. No fewer than 12 times in the primary opinion in that case, the Court (albeit in what seems now to have become clear dicta) observed that its Sixth Amendment closure ruling applied to the *trial* itself. The author of the first concurring opinion was fully aware of this and would have restricted the Court's observations and ruling to the suppression hearing. . . Nonetheless, he *joined* the Court's opinion . . . with its multiple references to the trial itself; the opinion was not a mere concurrence in the Court's judgment. And Mr. Justice Rehnquist, in his separate concurring opinion, quite understandably observed, as a consequence, that the Court was holding "without qualification," that " 'members of the public have no constitutional right under the Sixth and Fourteenth Amendments to attend criminal trials,' " quoting from the primary opinion. . . The resulting confusion among commentators and journalists was not surprising. . . .

. . .

I, of course, continue to believe that Gannett was in error, both in its interpretation of the Sixth Amendment generally, and in its application to the suppression hearing, for I remain convinced that the right to a public trial is to be found where the Constitution explicitly placed it—in the Sixth Amendment.

The Court, however, has eschewed the Sixth Amendment route. The plurality turns to other possible constitutional sources and invokes a veritable potpourri of them—the speech clause of the First Amendment, the press clause, the assembly clause, the Ninth Amendment, and a cluster of penumbral guarantees recognized in past decisions. This course is troublesome, but it is the route that has been selected and, at least for now, we must live with it. No purpose would be served by my spelling out at length here the reasons for my saying that the course is troublesome. I need do no more than observe that uncertainty marks the nature—and strictness—of the standard of closure the Court adopts. . . .

•   •   •

Having said all this, and with the Sixth Amendment set to one side in this case, I am driven to conclude, as a secondary position, that the First Amendment must provide some measure of protection for public access to the trial. . . .

•   •   •

Mr. Justice Rehnquist, dissenting.

In the Gilbert & Sullivan operetta Iolanthe, the Lord Chancellor recites:
"The Law is the true embodiment
of everything that's excellent,
It has no kind of fault or flaw,
And I, my lords, embody the law."
It is difficult not to derive more than a little of this flavor from the various opinions supporting the judgment in this case. . . .

•   •   •

For the reasons stated in my separate concurrence in Gannett Co., Inc. v DePasquale, I do not believe that either the First or Sixth Amendments, as made applicable to the States by the Fourteenth, require that a State's reasons for denying public access to a trial, where both the prosecuting attorney and the defendant have consented to an order of closure approved by the judge, are subject to any additional constitutional review at our hands. And I most certainly do not believe that the Ninth Amendment confers upon us any such power to review orders of state trial judges closing trials in such situations.

We have at present 50 state judicial systems and one federal judicial system in the United States, and our authority to reverse a decision by the highest court of the State is limited to only those occasions when the state decision violates some provision of the United States Constitution. And that authority should be exercised with a full sense that the judges whose decisions we review are making the same effort as we to uphold the Constitution. As said by Mr. Justice Jackson, "we are not final because we are infallible, but we are infallible only because we are final."

The proper administration of justice in any nation is bound to be a matter of the highest concern to all thinking citizens. But to gradually rein in, as this Court has done over the past generation, all of the ultimate decisionmaking power over how justice shall be administered, not merely in the federal system but in each of the 50 States, is a task that no Court consisting of nine persons, however gifted, is equal to. Nor is it desirable that such authority be exercised by such a tiny numerical fragment of the 220 million people who compose the population of this country.

Chandler v. Florida

449 U.S. 560, 66 L Ed 2d 740, 101 S Ct 802 (1981)

Defendants in a criminal case that attracted considerable attention attempted to get the trial judge to close their trial to coverage by television. The motion was denied and defendants were convicted. In a motion for a new trial defendants alleged the television coverage denied them a fair trial but they did not point to specific prejudicial acts. The district court of appeals affirmed and the Florida Supreme Court denied review.

· · ·

Chief Justice Burger delivered the opinion of the Court.

371

The question presented on this appeal is whether, consistent with constitutional guarantees, a state may provide for radio, television, and still photographic coverage of a criminal trial for public broadcast, notwithstanding the objection of the accused.

Background. Over the past 50 years, some criminal cases characterized as "sensational" have been subjected to extensive coverage by news media, sometimes seriously interfering with the conduct of the proceedings and creating a setting wholly inappropriate for the administration of justice. Judges, lawyers, and others soon became concerned, and in 1937, after study, the American Bar Association House of Delegates adopted Judicial Canon 35, declaring that all photographic and broadcast coverage of courtroom proceedings should be prohibited. In 1952, the House of Delegates amended Canon 35 to proscribe television coverage as well. The Canon's proscription was reaffirmed in 1972 when the Code of Judicial Conduct replaced the Canons of Judicial Ethics and Canon 3A(7) superseded Canon 35. A majority of the states, including Florida, adopted the substance of the ABA provision and its amendments. In Florida, the rule was embodied in Canon 3A(7) of the Florida Code of Judicial Conduct.

In February 1978, the American Bar Association Committee on Fair Trial-Free Press proposed revised standards. These included a provision permitting courtroom coverage by the electronic media under conditions to be established by local rule and under the control of the trial judge, but only if such coverage was carried out unobtrusively and without affecting the conduct of the trial. The revision was endorsed by the ABA's Standing Committee on Standards for Criminal Justice and by its Committee on Criminal Justice and the Media, but it was rejected by the House of Delegates on February 12, 1979.

In 1978, based upon its own study of the matter, the Conference of State Chief Justices, by a vote of 44 to 1, approved a resolution to allow the highest court of each state to promulgate standards and guidelines regulating radio, television, and other photographic coverage of court proceedings.

The Florida Program. In January 1975, while these developments were unfolding, the Post-Newsweek Stations of Florida petitioned the Supreme Court of Florida urging a change in Florida's Canon 3A(7). In April 1975, the court invited presentations in the nature of a rulemaking proceeding... The Florida Supreme Court ... established a new one-year pilot program during which the electronic media were permitted to cover all judicial proceedings in Florida without reference to the consent of participants, subject to detailed standards with respect to technology and the conduct of operators. . . .

When the pilot program ended, the Florida Supreme Court received and reviewed briefs, reports, letters of comment, and studies. It conducted its own survey of attorneys, witnesses, jurors, and court personnel through the Office of the State Court Coordinator. A separate survey was taken of judges by the Florida Conference of Circuit Judges. The court also studied the experience of six states that had, by 1979, adopted rules relating to electronic coverage of trials, as well as that of the 10 other states that, like Florida, were experimenting with such coverage.

Following its review of this material, the Florida Supreme Court concluded "that on balance there [was] more to be gained than lost by permitting electronic media coverage of judicial proceedings subject to standards for such coverage." The Florida court was of the view that because of the significant effect of the courts on the day-to-day lives of the citizenry, it was essential that the people have confidence in the process. It felt that broadcast coverage of trials would contribute to wider public acceptance and understanding of decisions. Consequently, after revising the 1977 guidelines to reflect its evaluation of the pilot program, the Florida Supreme Court promulgated a revised Canon 3A(7). . . The canon provides:

"Subject at all times to the authority of the presiding judge to (i) control the conduct of proceedings before the court, (ii) ensure decorum and prevent distractions, and (iii) ensure fair administration of justice in the pending cause, electronic media and still photography coverage of public judicial proceedings in the appellate and trial courts of this state shall be allowed in accordance with standards of conduct and technology promulgated by the Supreme Court of Florida."

The implementing guidelines specify in detail the kind of electronic equipment to be used and the manner of its use. For example, no more than one television camera and only one camera technician are allowed. Existing recording systems used by court reporters are used by broadcasters for audio pickup. Where more than one broadcast news organization seeks to cover a trial, the media must pool coverage. No artificial lighting is allowed. The equipment is positioned in a fixed location, and it may not be moved during trial. Videotaping equipment must be remote from the courtroom. Film, videotape, and lenses may not be changed while the court is in session. No audio recording of conferences between lawyers, between parties and counsel, or at the bench is permitted. The judge has sole and plenary discretion to exclude coverage of certain witnesses, and the jury may not be filmed. The judge has discretionary power to forbid coverage whenever satisfied that coverage may have a deleterious effect on the paramount right of the defendant to a fair trial. The Florida Supreme Court has the right to revise these rules as experience dictates, or indeed to bar all broadcast coverage of photography in courtrooms.

In July 1977, appellants were charged with conspiracy to commit burglary, grand larceny, and possession of burglary tools. . . .

.   .   .

The details of the alleged criminal conduct are not relevant to the issue before us, . . .

.   .   .

By pretrial motion, counsel for the appellants sought to have Experimental Canon 3A(7) declared unconstitutional on its face and as applied. The trial court denied relief but certified the issue to the Florida Supreme Court. However, the Supreme Court declined to rule on the question, on the ground that it was not directly relevant to the criminal charges against the appellants.

After several additional fruitless attempts by the appellants to prevent electronic coverage of the trial, the jury was selected. At voir dire, the appellants' counsel asked each prospective juror whether he or she would be able to be "fair and impartial" despite the presence of a television camera during some, or all, of the trial. Each juror selected responded that such coverage would not affect his or her consideration in any way. A television camera recorded the voir dire. . . .

.   .   .

A television camera was in place for one entire afternoon, during which the state presented the testimony of Sion, its chief witness. No camera was present for the presentation of any part of the case for the defense. The camera returned to cover closing arguments. Only two minutes and fifty-five seconds of the trial below were broadcast—and those depicted only the prosecution's side of the case.

The jury returned a guilty verdict on all counts. Appellants moved for a new trial, claiming that because of the television coverage, they had been denied a fair and impartial trial. No evidence of specific prejudice was tendered. . . .

. . .

The Florida Supreme Court predicated the revised Canon 3A(7) upon its supervisory authority over the Florida courts, and not upon any constitutional imperative. Hence, we have before us only the limited question of the Florida Supreme Court's authority to promulgate the canon for the trial of cases in Florida courts.

This Court has no supervisory jurisdiction over state courts, and, in reviewing a state court judgment, we are confined to evaluating it in relation to the Federal Constitution.

Appellants rely chiefly on Estes v Texas. They argue that the televising of criminal trials is inherently a denial of due process, and they read Estes as announcing a per se constitutional rule to that effect. . . .

. . .

The six separate opinions in Estes must be examined carefully to evaluate the claim that it represents a per se constitutional rule forbidding all electronic coverage. Chief Justice Warren and Justices Douglas and Goldberg joined Justice Clark's opinion announcing the judgment, thereby creating only a plurality. Justice Harlan provided the fifth vote necessary in support of the judgment. . . A careful analysis of Justice Harlan's opinion is therefore fundamental to an understanding of the ultimate holding of Estes. . . .

. . .

Parsing the six opinions in Estes, one is left with a sense of doubt as to precisely how much of Justice Clark's opinion was joined in, and supported by, Justice Harlan. In an area charged with constitutional nuances, perhaps more should not be expected. Nonetheless, it is fair to say that Justice Harlan viewed the holding as limited to the proposition that *"what was done in this case* infringed the fundamental right to a fair trial assured by the Due Process Clause of the Fourteenth Amendment," he went on:

"At the present juncture, I can only conclude that televised trials, *at least in cases like this one,* possess such capabilities for interfering with the

375

even course of the judicial process that they are constitutionally banned.". . .

. . .

[W]e conclude that Estes is not to be read as announcing a constitutional rule barring still photographic, radio and television coverage in all cases and under all circumstances. It does not stand as an absolute ban on state experimentation with an evolving technology, which, in terms of modes of mass communication, was in its relative infancy in 1964, and is, even now, in a state of continuing change. . . .

. . .

Any criminal case that generates a great deal of publicity presents some risks that the publicity may compromise the right of the defendant to a fair trial. Trial courts must be especially vigilant to guard against any impairment of the defendant's right to a verdict based solely upon the evidence and the relevant law. Over the years, courts have developed a range of curative devices to prevent publicity about a trial from infecting jury deliberations.

An absolute constitutional ban on broadcast coverage of trials cannot be justified simply because there is a danger that, in some cases, prejudicial broadcast accounts of pretrial and trial events may impair the ability of jurors to decide the issue of guilt or innocence uninfluenced by extraneous matter. The risk of juror prejudice in some cases does not justify an absolute ban on news coverage of trials by the printed media; so also the risk of such prejudice does not warrant an absolute constitutional ban on all broadcast coverage. A case attracts a high level of public attention because of its intrinsic interest to the public and the manner of reporting the event. The risk of juror prejudice is present in any publication of a trial, but the appropriate safeguard against such prejudice is the defendant's right to demonstrate that the media's coverage of his case—be it printed or broadcast—compromised the ability of the particular jury that heard the case to adjudicate fairly. . . .

. . .

In confronting the difficult and sensitive question of the potential psychological prejudice associated with broadcast coverage of trials, we have been aided by amicus briefs submitted by various state officers involved in law enforcement, the Conference of Chief Justices, and the Attorneys General of 17 states in support of continuing experimentation such as that embarked upon by Florida, and by the American Bar Association, the American College of Trial Lawyers, and various members of the defense bar. . . .

.　.　.

Not unimportant to the position asserted by Florida and other states is the change in television technology since 1962, when Estes was tried. It is urged, and some empirical data are presented, that many of the negative factors found in Estes—cumbersome equipment, cables, distracting lighting, numerous camera technicians—are less substantial factors today than they were at that time.

It is also significant that safeguards have been built into the experimental programs in state courts, and into the Florida program, to avoid some of the most egregious problems envisioned by the six opinions in the Estes case. Florida admonishes its courts to take special pains to protect certain witnesses—for example, children, victims of sex crimes, some informants, and even the very timid witness or party—from the glare of publicity and the tensions of being "on camera.". . .

.　.　.

Inherent in electronic coverage of a trial is the risk that the very awareness by the accused of the coverage and the contemplated broadcast may adversely affect the conduct of the participants and the fairness of the trial, yet leave no evidence of how the conduct or the trial's fairness was affected. . . .

.　.　.

[I]t is clear that the general issue of the psychological impact of broadcast coverage upon the participants in a trial, and particularly upon the defendant, is still a subject of sharp debate. . . Comprehensive empirical data is still not available—at least on some aspects of the problem. . . .

.　.　.

Whatever may be the "mischievous potentialities [of broadcast coverage] for intruding upon the detached atmosphere which should always surround the judicial process," Estes v Texas, at present no one has been able to present empirical data sufficient to establish that the mere presence of the broadcast media inherently has an adverse effect on that process. The appellants have offered nothing to demonstrate that their trial was subtly tainted by broadcast coverage—let alone that all broadcast trials would be so tainted. . . .

. . .

It is not necessary either to ignore or to discount the potential danger to the fairness of a trial in a particular case in order to conclude that Florida may permit the electronic media to cover trials in its state courts. Dangers lurk in this, as in most, experiments, but unless we were to conclude that television coverage under all conditions is prohibited by the Constitution, the states must be free to experiment. We are not empowered by the Constitution to oversee or harness state procedural experimentation; only when the state action infringes fundamental guarantees are we authorized to intervene. We must assume state courts will be alert to any factors that impair the fundamental rights of the accused.

The Florida program is inherently evolutional in nature; the initial project has provided guidance for the new canons which can be changed at will, and application of which is subject to control by the trial judge. The risk of prejudice to particular defendants is ever present and must be examined carefully as cases arise. Nothing of the "Roman circus" or "Yankee Stadium" atmosphere, as in Estes, prevailed here, however, nor have appellants attempted to show that the unsequestered jury was exposed to "sensational" coverage, in the sense of Estes or of Sheppard v. Maxwell. Absent a showing of prejudice of constitutional dimensions to these defendants, there is no reason for this Court either to endorse or to invalidate Florida's experiment.

In this setting, because this Court has no supervisory authority over state courts, our review is confined to whether there is a constitutional violation. We hold that the Constitution does not prohibit a state from experimenting with the program authorized by revised Canon 3A(7).

Affirmed.

. . .

Justice Stevens took no part in the decision of this case.

. . .

Justice Stewart, concurring in the result.

Although concurring in the judgment, I cannot join the opinion of the Court because I do not think the convictions in this case can be affirmed without overruling Estes v Texas. . . .

. . .

The Court in Estes found the admittedly unobtrusive presence of television cameras in a criminal trial to be inherently prejudicial, and thus violative of Due Process of Law. Today the Court reaches precisely the opposite conclusion. I have no great trouble in agreeing with the Court today, but I would acknowledge our square departure from precedent.

. . .

Justice White, concurring in the judgment.

. . .

Whether the decision in Estes is read broadly or narrowly, I agree with Justice Stewart that it should be overruled. I was in dissent in that case, and I remain unwilling to assume or conclude without more proof than has been marshalled to date that televising criminal trials is inherently prejudicial even when carried out under properly controlled conditions. . . . But absent some showing of prejudice to the defense, I remain convinced that a conviction obtained in a state court should not be overturned simply because a trial judge refused to exclude television cameras and all or part of the trial was televised to the public. The experience of those States which have, since Estes, permitted televised trials supports this position, and I believe that the accumulated experience of those States has further undermined the assumptions on which the majority rested its judgment in Estes. . . .

. . .

By reducing Estes to an admonition to proceed with some caution, the majority does not underestimate or minimize the risks of televising criminal trials over a defendant's objections. I agree that those risks are real and should not be permitted to develop into the reality of an unfair trial. Nor does the decision today, as I understand it, suggest that any state is any less free than it was to avoid this hazard by not permitting a trial to be televised over the objection of the defendant or by forbidding cameras in its court rooms in any criminal case.

Accordingly, I concur in the judgment.

VI

Abortion

Abortion has evoked more emotional reaction in recent years than any other policy issue dealt with by the courts because "every argument starts from and returns to an ethical or religious assumption." [1] One side of the argument holds that life exists from the moment of conception and that abortion, therefore, is murder. The opposing view is based on the premise that the fetus is not a person—in fact, is not even alive—until fairly late in the pregnancy, and that the mother has a morally unassailable right to control the use of her body. Debaters on the subject usually talk past one another and never come to grips with the public policy issues involved. One basic issue is the extent to which the state should be allowed to control the mother's decision whether or not to terminate a pregnancy.

History does not provide ready-made answers to problems of public policy, but it provides a context within which to place the debate. "The Glory that was Greece and the Grandeur that was Rome" included voluntary abortions, infanticide, and homosexuality as means of curbing unwanted population growth. Plato wrote approvingly of abortion as a means of correcting unplanned results of relations between members of his Guardian class, and Aristotle advanced it as a means of population control. Ancient religion did not ban abortion either in theory or in practice. Abortion simply was not a moral issue to most Greeks and Romans and therefore was not an issue that called for intervention by the state.

The Hippocratic oath is one indication of a contrary attitude in the ancient world. The oath, among other things, requires the physician to swear that he "will not give to a woman an abortive remedy." Today, the oath represents the high point of medical ethics, but it was not generally accepted in its own time. It was *a* point of view, not *the* point of view in the ancient world; Christians found the oath more useful as a guide to ethical behavior than did Hippocrates' contemporaries in 400 B.C.

The English common law declared early and clearly that at some point between conception and birth a process called "quickening" occurred. At this point, a recognizable movement of the fetus within the womb took place. An abortion before that time—usually defined as the sixteenth to eighteenth week of pregnancy—was not an indictable offense because the fetus was defined as part of the mother and no "person" was killed. The common law attitude toward an abortion after quickening was not as clear, but at most it was a misdemeanor rather than a felony. It might not have been a crime at all. The common law was accepted by the American colonies when they were settled, and it remained the law in both Britain and America until the beginning of the nineteenth century. The early statutes (1803 in England and 1821 in America) preserved the before and after quickening distinction, making abortion a misdemeanor in the first instance and a felony in the second.

American legislatures acted only sporadically on this issue until after the Civil War when statutes began to replace the common law. Despite early attempts to preserve the quickening distinction, it had disappeared by the late nineteenth century and the penalties for the crime, now almost uniformly classified as a felony, became more severe. Various explanations have been offered for this change. Some legislators apparently were concerned about the rights of the fetus, although that concern was not necessarily reflected in other areas of the law. Other legislators feared that conventional morality would be subverted if abortions were freely available. In their view, promiscuity would result if the consequences were minimized or if procreation ceased to be the sole reason for sexual activity. Finally, a third group of lawmakers viewed with justifiable alarm the fact that more medical hazards were involved in abortions than in live births; the American Medical Association in 1859 forcefully called this fact to the attention of legislators. Those supporting anti-abortion legislation claimed that this was the primary reason for the change in the law. Whatever the reason, the century between 1850 and 1950 saw practically every American and European jurisdiction ban abortions unless necessary to save the life of the mother.

Having arrived at this position, American attitudes in the late 1960s and early 1970s began to move in a more permissive direction. After calling abortion an "unwarrantable destruction of the human life" in 1859, the American Medical Association in 1970 merely said that "abortion, like any other medical procedure, should not be performed when contrary to the best interests of the patient." The American Public Health Association, also in 1970, declared that "rapid and simple abortion referral must be readily available." By 1972, 14 states had adopted some form of the American Law Institute's proposed Model Penal Code provision liberalizing abortion

statutes. As the Supreme Court prepared to decide *Roe* v. *Wade* (p. 397),
society had entered a period in which "old certainties" were "dissolving"
with new ones yet "unformed." [2]

The degree to which these certainties were dissolving is demonstrated
by comparing two actual and two proposed abortion statutes.

Texas Penal Code. Adopted in 1857 and at issue in *Roe* v. *Wade:*
"Nothing in this chapter [making abortion a crime] applies to an abortion
procured or attempted by medical advice for the purpose of saving the life
of the mother."

Georgia Criminal Code. Adopted in 1968 and at issue in *Doe* v. *Bolton:*
Excepts from criminal penalty "an abortion performed by a physician . . .
based on his best clinical judgment that an abortion is necessary because:
(1) A continuation of the pregnancy would endanger the life of the
pregnant woman or would seriously and permanently injure her
health; or
(2) The fetus would very likely be born with a grave, permanent, and
irremedial physical defect; or
(3) The pregnancy resulted from forcible or statutory rape.

American Law Institute, Model Penal Code (1970):
"A licensed physician is justified in terminating a pregnancy if he believes
there is a substantial risk that a continuance of the pregnancy would
gravely impair the physical or mental health of the mother or that the
child would be born with a grave physical or mental defect, or that the
pregnancy resulted from rape, incest, or other felonious intercourse."

American Bar Association, Proposed Uniform Abortion Act (1972):
"An abortion may be performed . . . by a physician . . . only if the
physician has reasonable cause to believe (i) there is a substantial risk that
continuance of the pregnancy would endanger the life of the mother or
would gravely impair the physical or mental health of the mother, (ii) that
the child would be born with grave physical or mental defect, or (iii) that
the pregnancy resulted from rape or incest, or illicit intercourse with a girl
under the age of 16. . . ."

Notice the shift in these statutes from saving the life of the mother, to
preventing injury to her physical health, to avoiding damage to physical or
mental health. Note also that the Texas statute is unconcerned about the
health of the fetus and that one of the other three has a different view of the
fetal conditions that might justify abortion.

The opinions in *Roe* reflect not only the change in attitudes contained in
these statutes and the highly charged nature of the issue, but also the lack

of precedent to serve as a beginning point for the Court's analysis. Lower federal and state courts had divided almost evenly on earlier challenges to laws banning nontherapeutic abortions. These cases had been brought on such a variety of grounds that the precedents could not be pulled together to mark out a body of developing—even if divided—opinion. It is hard to synthesize a definitive rule from a set of cases attacking statutes on grounds as diverse as being vague in their definitions, overly broad, constituting an excessive use of the police power, failing to protect a compelling state interest, interfering with the right to privacy, interfering with the physician's right to practice medicine, interfering with the doctor-patient relationship, denying equal protection, reversing the traditional presumption of innocence, applying cruel and unusual punishment, and interfering with the right to travel. The judiciary's failure to explore a number of lines of argument emphasizes the Court's difficulty in deciding the issue. The fact that *Roe* required one majority opinion, three concurrences, and two dissents emphasizes this point. It is small wonder that Justice Harry Blackmun begins the majority opinion by citing the attitudinal changes in society as affected by these state statutes.

The basic majority opinion rests upon a right not mentioned in the Constitution. The *Roe* majority asserts that a pregnant woman has, at least in the first trimester, a right to privacy that protects her decision about the future of that pregnancy. The source of this right to privacy—Justice Louis Brandeis called it "the most comprehensive of rights and the right most valued by civilized men"—is not entirely clear. Justice Wililam O. Douglas had found it in the "penumbras"* of several of the provisions of the Bill of Rights; in fact, he combined the First, Third, Fourth, Fifth, and Ninth Amendments to support an argument that such a right exists and was intended to exist. [3]

Others have found this right of privacy in the general provisions of the Fourteenth Amendment. Regardless of its origin, Justice Blackmun asserted that the right "is broad enough to encompass a woman's decision whether or not to terminate her pregnancy." The most troublesome feature of the right to privacy is that the Court has consistently held that it may be invaded, provided that a compelling or substantial state interest can be shown. So here, as in the equal protection cases, the justices must weigh competing interests on scales impossible to calibrate.

The reaction to the Court's decision in *Roe* was as sharp and strong as any in this century. Groups immediately organized under the banner of

---

*A shadowy area around explicit rights that contains other rights inferentially derived from the enumerated right.

"Right to Life" to lobby in any available forum for the reversal of the decision while "Pro-Choice" groups emerged as defenders of the Court's decisions. Religious groups and those advocating family planning became active.

Several approaches were devised by the opponents of *Roe*. One early step in Congress was a drive for a constitutional amendment. Initially, the most popular form of amendment was a "states' rights" one that would have simply returned the decisionmaking authority to the 50 states. The second proposal focused on "human life" and granted full "personhood" to the fetus from "the moment of fertilization." The states' rights proposals have steadily lost support in Congress as their proponents have realized that they would not solve the problem but merely transfer it back to the local jurisdictions. Many states already had been set on a liberalizing course before *Roe*. Therefore, some members of Congress have been placed in an awkward position. On the one hand they want to restrict the use and availability of abortions; on the other hand, they are committed to getting the national government "off the backs of the people." A states' rights amendment could lead to frustration of the first objective while a human life amendment runs counter to reducing the scope of national regulatory activity. For some members of Congress, inactivity is the usual solution to such cross-pressured situations. The human life proposals have gained support in terms of the number of cosponsors the proposals have in each house of Congress (nine senators and 28 representatives in the 93rd Congress, 17 senators and 50 representatives in the 96th). Even so, the suggested amendments, with one exception, have moved no further than committee hearings; the one exception was tabled by the Senate in 1976 on a vote of 47 to 40. The Right to Life groups also have tried, as have the opponents of reapportionment, to use the convention method of amending the Constitution. Despite questions about the mechanics of setting this process in motion, 19 states have adopted resolutions calling for such a convention; in some instances, the resolution passed unanimously while voters, brought to legislatures in church buses, watched from packed galleries.

In the absence of further success on the amendment front, attention has shifted to the possibility of adopting a simple statute to accomplish the same end. S.B. 158 (p. 453) was pending in the Senate as of December 1982. By declaring that life begins at conception, the bill's supporters hope that the due process protections granted to the mother will be attached to the fetus as well.

As early as 1977, Congress discovered an easier way to deal with part of the problem. Prior to that time, the national government had reimbursed states for all abortions of indigents eligible for the Medicaid Program. In the fiscal year 1977 budget, Congress restricted the use of federal funds to abortions necessary to preserve the mother's life (the Hyde Amendment, p. 436). In subsequent years this limitation was broadened to include abortions when the pregnancy was caused by rape or incest (if that had been promptly reported) or when two physicians certified that severe and long-term harm to the mother would result. In *Harris* v. *McRae* (p. 437), the Court accepted these restrictions.

State legislators also have been active in this area since the decision in *Roe*. Forty-one abortion statutes, most of them intended to confine or circumvent *Roe*, were adopted in 1979 alone as contrasted with 15 new statutes in 1975 and 23 in 1976. Much of this legislation has been devoted to denying public funding for voluntary abortions; by mid-1980, only nine states and the District of Columbia were authorizing the use of public funds to pay for abortions other than those necessary to save the life of the mother. *Beal* v. *Doe* and *Maher* v. *Roe* (p. 427) are the Court's responses to these limitations.

In its 1982 term, the Court will review some additional results of this state activity. On the docket are statutes and ordinances requiring the performance of second and third trimester abortions in hospitals, a 24-hour waiting period between the decision and the operation, parental or court approval of a minor's abortion, and a full and complete description of pregnancy, abortion, and fetal development when a woman requests an abortion. *Planned Parenthood of Missouri* v. *Danforth* (p. 412) gives some hints of the Court's views on these issues.

These decisions are the archetype of marginal incursion by the Court into major policymaking. The justices assaulted a traditional set of moral values—sanctity of life and the preservation of the family—in the name of a constitutional guarantee that cannot be found in the document except by inference. The values the Court was promoting—privacy, equal access to medical benefits, consideration of costs and benefits of welfare program alternatives—are issues believed by many to fall under legislative rather than judicial jurisdiction. The subject was on the legislative agenda in New York, Colorado, and the District of Columbia, three jurisdictions where legalization statutes were adopted. Several other states liberalized but did not totally discard rules immediately prior to *Roe*.

It hardly is surprising that a firestorm of criticism arose when *Roe* was decided and that efforts to change it have persisted. A question of timing may have exacerbated the situation. The Warren Court had just spent a decade telling the states how to run their criminal justice systems; now the Burger Court was invading still another area the states had thought was theirs alone.

NOTES

1. *Gleitman* v. *Cosgrove,* 49 N.J. 22, 227 A. 2d 689 (1967), at 709.
2. *Scott* v. *Macy,* 402 F. 3d 644, (D.C. Cir.) (1968), at 649.
3. *Griswold* v. *Connecticut,* 381 U.S. 479 (1965). Justice Arthur Goldberg in concurrence relied solely on the Ninth Amendment.

SELECTED BIBLIOGRAPHY

Callahan, Daniel. *Abortion: Law, Choice, and Morality.* New York: Macmillan, 1969.

Davie, Walhert and Butler, J.D. *Abortion, Society, and the Law.* Cleveland: Case-Western Reserve Press, 1973.

DeCrow, Karen. *Sexist Justice.* New York: Vintage, 1975.

Ely, John Hart. "The Wages of Crying Wolf: A Comment on *Roe* v. *Wade,*" 82 *Yale Law Journal* 920 (1973).

Hansen, Susan B. "State Implementation of Supreme Court Decisions: Abortion Rates Since *Roe* v. *Wade,*" 42 *Journal of Politics* 372 (1980).

Kemmers, Donald V. "Abortion and the Constitution: United States and West Germany," 25 *American Journal of Comparative Law* 257 (1977).

Lader, Lawrence. *Abortion.* Boston: Beacon Press, 1967.

Lister, Charles. "The Right to Control the Use of One's Body." In *The Rights of Americans,* edited by Norman Dorsen. New York: Pantheon Books, 1971.

Mohr, James C. *Abortion in America.* New York: Oxford University Press, 1972.

Noonan, John T. Jr., ed. *The Morality of Abortion: Legal and Historical Perspective.* Cambridge: Harvard University Press, 1970.

Rubin, Eva R. *Abortion, Politics, and the Courts.* Westport, Conn.: Greenwood Press, 1982.

Vietch, Edward and Trace, R. R. S. "Abortion in the Common Law World," 22 *American Journal of Comparative Law* 653 (1974).

Griswold v. Connecticut

381 U.S. 479, 14 L ed 2d 510, 85 S Ct 1678 (1965)

Though it does not involve the abortion issue, this decision sets the stage for those cases by attempting to define a right of privacy. Appellants advised married couples on the use of various contraceptive devices and materials even though state law forbade such activity. The state courts upheld the statute despite claims that it was invalid under the provisions of the Fourteenth Amendment. The Supreme Court accepted the case on appeal.

.   .   .

Mr. Justice Douglas delivered the opinion of the Court.

.   .   .

We do not sit as a super-legislature to determine the wisdom, need, and propriety of laws that touch economic problems, business affairs, or social conditions. This law, however, operates directly on an intimate relation of husband and wife and their physician's role in one aspect of that relation.

The association of people is not mentioned in the Constitution nor in the Bill of Rights. The right to educate a child in a school of the parents' choice—whether public or private or parochial—is also not mentioned. Nor is the right to study any particular subject or any foreign language. Yet the First Amendment has been construed to include certain of those rights. . . .

.   .   .

In NAACP v. Alabama we protected the "freedom to associate and privacy in one's associations," noting that freedom of association was a peripheral First Amendment right. . . In other words, the First Amendment has a penumbra where privacy is protected from governmental intrusion. In like context, we have protected forms of "association" that are not political in the customary sense but pertain to the social, legal, and economic benefit of the members. . . .

.   .   .

The right of "association," like the right of belief is more than the right to attend a meeting; it includes the right to express one's attitudes or philosophies by membership in a group or by affiliation with it or by other lawful means. Association in that context is a form of expression of opinion; and while it is not expressly included in the First Amendment its existence is necessary in making the express guarantees fully meaningful.

The foregoing cases suggest that specific guarantees in the Bill of Rights have penumbras, formed by emanations from those guarantees that help give them life and substance. Various guarantees create zones of privacy. The right of association contained in the penumbra of the First Amendment is one, as we have seen. The Third Amendment in its prohibition against the quartering of soldiers "in any house" in time of peace without the consent of the owner is another facet of that privacy. The Fourth Amendment explicitly affirms the "right of the people to be secure in their persons, houses, papers, and effects, against unreasonable searches and seizures." The Fifth Amendment in its Self-Incrimination Clause enables the citizen to create a zone of privacy which government may not force him to surrender to his detriment. The Ninth Amendment provides: "The enumeration in the Constitution, of certain rights, shall not be construed to deny or disparage others retained by the people.". . .

. . .

The present case, then, concerns a relationship lying within the zone of privacy created by several fundamental constitutional guarantees. And it concerns a law which, in forbidding the *use* of contraceptives rather than regulating their manufacture or sale, seeks to achieve its goals by means having a maximum destructive impact upon that relationship. Such a law cannot stand in light of the familiar principle, so often applied by this Court, that a "governmental purpose to control or prevent activities constitutionally subject to state regulation may not be achieved by means which sweep unnecessarily broadly and thereby invade the area of protected freedoms." Would we allow the police to search the sacred precincts of marital bedrooms for telltale signs of the use of contraceptives? The very idea is repulsive to the notions of privacy surrounding the marriage relationship.

We deal with the right of privacy older than the Bill of Rights—older than our political parties, older than our school system. Marriage is a coming together for better or for worse, hopefully enduring, and intimate to the degree of being sacred. It is an association that promotes a way of life, not causes; a harmony in living, not political faiths; a bilateral loyalty, not commercial or social projects. Yet it is an association for as noble a purpose as any involved in our prior decisions.

Reversed.

. . .

Mr. Justice Goldberg, whom the Chief Justice and Mr. Justice Brennan join, concurring.

I agree with the Court that Connecticut's birth-control law unconstitutionally intrudes upon the right of marital privacy, and I join in its opinion and judgment. Although I have not accepted the view that "due process" as used in the Fourteenth Amendment incorporates all of the first eight Amendments . . . I do agree that the concept of liberty protects those personal rights that are fundamental, and is not confined to the specific terms of the Bill of Rights. My conclusion that the concept of liberty is not so restricted and that it embraces the right of marital privacy though that right is not mentioned explicitly in the Constitution is supported both by numerous decisions of this Court, referred to in the Court's opinion, and by the language and history of the Ninth Amendment. In reaching the conclusion that the right of marital privacy is protected, as being within the protected penumbra of specific guarantees of the Bill of [R]ights, the Court refers to the Ninth Amendment. . . . I add these words to emphasize the relevance of that Amendment to the Court's holding.

·   ·   ·

The Ninth Amendment reads, "The enumeration in the Constitution, of certain rights, shall not be construed to deny or disparage others retained by the people." The Amendment is almost entirely the work of James Madison. It was introduced in Congress by him and passed the House and Senate with little or no debate and virtually no change in language. It was proffered to quiet expressed fears that a bill of specifically enumerated rights could not be sufficiently broad to cover all essential rights and that the specific mention of certain rights would be interpreted as a denial that others were protected. . . .

·   ·   ·

The Ninth Amendment to the Constitution may be regarded by some as a recent discovery and may be forgotten by others, but since 1791 it has been a basic part of the Constitution which we are sworn to uphold. To hold that a right so basic and fundamental and so deep-rooted in our society as the right of privacy in marriage may be infringed because that right is not guaranteed in so many words by the first eight amendments to the Constitution is to ignore the Ninth Amendment and to give it no effect whatsoever. Moreover, a judicial construction that this fundamental right is not protected by the Constitution because it is not mentioned in explicit terms by one of the first eight amendments or elsewhere in the Constitution would violate the Ninth Amendment, which specifically states that "[t]he enumeration in the Constitution, of certain rights, shall not be *construed* to deny or disparage others retained by the people." (Emphasis added.)

A dissenting opinion suggests that my interpretation of the Ninth Amendment somehow "broaden[s] the powers of this Court." With all due respect, I believe that it misses the import of what I am saying. . . I do not mean to imply that the Ninth Amendment is applied against the States by the Fourteenth. Nor do I mean to state that the Ninth Amendment constitutes an independent source of rights protected from infringement by either the States or the Federal Government. Rather, the Ninth Amendment shows a belief of the Constitution's authors that fundamental rights exist that are not expressly enumerated in the first eight amendments and an intent that the list of rights included there not be deemed exhaustive. As any student of this Court's opinions knows, this Court has held, often unanimously, that the Fifth and Fourteenth Amendments protect certain fundamental personal liberties from abridgment by the Federal Government or the States. . . The Ninth Amendment simply shows the intent of the Constitution's authors that other fundamental personal rights should not be denied such protection or disparaged in any other way simply because they are not specifically listed in the first eight constitutional amendments. I do not see how this broadens the authority of the Court; rather it serves to support what this Court has been doing in protecting fundamental rights.

Nor am I turning somersaults with history in arguing that the Ninth Amendment is relevant in a case dealing with a *State's* infringement of a fundamental right. While the Ninth Amendment—and indeed the entire Bill of Rights—originally concerned restrictions upon *federal* power, the subsequently enacted Fourteenth Amendment prohibits the States as well from abridging fundamental personal liberties. And, the Ninth Amendment, in indicating that not all such liberties are specifically mentioned in the first eight amendments, is surely relevant in showing the existence of other fundamental personal rights, now protected from state, as well as federal, infringement. In sum, the Ninth Amendment simply lends strong support to the view that the "liberty" protected by the Fifth and Fourteenth Amendments from infringement by the Federal Government or the States is not restricted to rights specifically mentioned in the first eight amendments. . . .

. . .

The Connecticut statutes here involved deal with a particularly important and sensitive area of privacy—that of the marital relation and the marital home. This Court recognized in Meyer v. Nebraska . . . that the right "to marry, establish a home and bring up children" was an essential part of the liberty guaranteed by the Fourteenth Amendment. . . .

. . .

Although the Constitution does not speak in so many words of the right of privacy in marriage, I cannot believe that it offers these fundamental rights no protection. The fact that no particular provision of the Constitution explicitly forbids the State from disrupting the traditional relation of the family—a relation as old and as fundamental as our entire civilization—surely does not show that the Government was meant to have the power to do so. Rather, as the Ninth Amendment expressly recognizes, there are fundamental personal rights such as this one, which are protected from abridgment by the Government though not specifically mentioned in the Constitution.

. . .

Mr. Justice Harlan, concurring in the judgment.

. . .

I fully agree with the judgment of reversal, but find myself unable to join the Court's opinion. The reason is that it seems to me to evince an approach to this case very much like that taken by my Brothers Black and Stewart in dissent, namely: the Due Process Clause of the Fourteenth Amendment does not touch this Connecticut statute unless the enactment is found to violate some right assured by the letter or penumbra of the Bill of Rights. . . .

. . .

In my view, the proper constitutional inquiry in this case is whether this Connecticut statute infringes the Due Process Clause of the Fourteenth Amendment because the enactment violates basic values "implicit in the concept of ordered liberty,"... While the relevant inquiry may be aided by resort to one or more of the provisions of the Bill of Rights, it is not dependent on them or any of their radiations. The Due Process Clause of the Fourteenth Amendment stands, in my opinion, on its own bottom....

.   .   .

Mr. Justice White, concurring in the judgment.

.   .   .

Mr. Justice Black, with whom Mr. Justice Stewart joins, dissenting.

I agree with my Brother Stewart's dissenting opinion. And like him I do not to any extent whatever base my view that this Connecticut law is constitutional on a belief that the law is wise or that its policy is a good one. In order that there may be no room at all to doubt why I vote as I do, I feel constrained to add that the law is every bit as offensive to me as it is to my Brethren of the majority and my Brothers Harlan, White and Goldberg who, reciting reasons why it is offensive to them, hold it unconstitutional. There is no single one of the graphic and eloquent strictures and criticisms fired at the policy of this Connecticut law either by the Court's opinion or by those of my concurring Brethren to which I cannot subscribe—except their conclusion that the evil qualities they see in the law make it unconstitutional....

.   .   .

The Court talks about a constitutional "right of privacy" as though there is some constitutional provision or provisions forbidding any law ever to be passed which might abridge the "privacy" of individuals. But there is not. There are, of course, guarantees in certain specific constitutional provisions which are designed in part to protect privacy at certain times and places with respect to certain activities. Such, for example, is the Fourth Amendment's guarantee against "unreasonable searches and seizures." But I think it belittles that Amendment to talk about it as though it protects nothing but "privacy."...

.   .   .

One of the most effective ways of diluting or expanding a constitution-ally guaranteed right is to substitute for the crucial word or words of a constitutional guarantee another word or words more or less flexible and more or less restricted in meaning. This fact is well illustrated by the use of the term "right of privacy" as a comprehensive substitute for the Fourth Amendment's guarantee against "unreasonable searches and seizures." "Privacy" is a broad, abstract and ambiguous concept which can easily be shrunken in meaning but which can also, on the other hand, easily be interpreted as a constitutional ban against many things other than searches and seizures. I have expressed the view many times that First Amendment freedoms, for example, have suffered from a failure of the courts to stick to the simple language of the First Amendment in construing it, instead of invoking multitudes of words substituted for those the Framers used. For these reasons I get nowhere in this case by talk about a constitutional "right of privacy" as an emanation from one or more constitutional provisions. I like my privacy as well as the next one, but I am nevertheless compelled to admit that government has a right to invade it unless prohibited by some specific constitutional provision. For these reasons I cannot agree with the Court's judgment and the reasons it gives for holding this Connecticut law unconstitutional.

This brings me to the arguments made by my Brothers Harlan, White and Goldberg for invalidating the Connecticut law. Brothers Harlan and White would invalidate it by reliance on the Due Process Clause of the Fourteenth Amendment, but Brother Goldberg, while agreeing with Brother Harlan, relies also on the Ninth Amendment. I have no doubt that the Connecticut law could be applied in such a way as to abridge freedom of speech and press and therefore violate the First and Fourteenth Amendments. My disagreement with the Court's opinion holding that there is such a violation here is a narrow one, relating to the application of the First Amendment to the facts and circumstances of this particular case. But my disagreement with Brothers Harlan, White and Goldberg is more basic. I think that if properly construed neither the Due Process Clause nor the Ninth Amendment, nor both together, could under any circumstances be a proper basis for invalidating the Connecticut law. I discuss the due process and Ninth Amendment arguments together because on analysis they turn out to be the same thing—merely using different words to claim for this Court and the federal judiciary power to invalidate any legislative act which the judges find irrational, unreasonable or offensive.

The due process argument which my Brothers Harlan and White adopt here is based, as their opinions indicate, on the premise that this

Court is vested with power to invalidate all state laws that it considers to be arbitrary, capricious, unreasonable, or oppressive, or this Court's belief that a particular state law under scrutiny has no "rational or justifying" purpose, or is offensive to a "sense of fairness and justice." If these formulas based on "natural justice," or others which mean the same thing, are to prevail, they require judges to determine what is or is not constitutional on the basis of their own appraisal of what laws are unwise or unnecessary. The power to make such decisions is of course that of a legislative body. Surely it has to be admitted that no provision of the Constitution specifically gives such blanket power to courts to exercise such a supervisory veto over the wisdom and value of legislative policies and to hold unconstitutional those laws which they believe unwise or dangerous. I readily admit that no legislative body, state or national, should pass laws that can justly be given any of the invidious labels invoked as constitutional excuses to strike down state laws. But perhaps it is not too much to say that no legislative body ever does pass laws without believing that they will accomplish a sane, rational, wise and justifiable purpose. . . . I do not believe that we are granted power by the Due Process Clause or any other constitutional provision or provisions to measure constitutionality by our belief that legislation is arbitrary, capricious or unreasonable, or accomplishes no justifiable purpose, or is offensive to our own notions of "civilized standards of conduct." Such an appraisal of the wisdom of legislation is an attribute of the power to make laws, not of the power to interpret them. The use by federal courts of such a formula or doctrine or whatnot to veto federal or state laws simply takes away from Congress and States the power to make laws based on their own judgment of fairness and wisdom and transfers that power to this Court for ultimate determination—a power which was specifically denied to federal courts by the convention that framed the Constitution. . . .

.   .   .

My Brother Goldberg has adopted the recent discovery that the Ninth Amendment as well as the Due Process Clause can be used by this Court as authority to strike down all state legislation which this Court thinks violates "fundamental principles of liberty and justice," or is contrary to the "traditions and [collective] conscience of our people." He also states, without proof satisfactory to me, that in making decisions on this basis judges will not consider "their personal and private notions." One may ask how they can avoid considering them. Our Court certainly has no machinery with which to take a Gallup Poll. And the scientific miracles of this age have not yet produced a gadget which the Court can use to determine what traditions are rooted in the "[collective] conscience of our people." Moreover, one would certainly have to look far beyond the language of the Ninth Amendment to find that the Framers vested in this Court any such awesome veto powers over lawmaking, either by the States or by the Congress. Nor does anything in the history of the Amendment offer any support for such a shocking doctrine... If any broad, unlimited power to hold laws unconstitutional because they offend what this Court conceives to be the "[collective] conscience of our people" is vested in this Court by the Ninth Amendment, the Fourteenth Amendment, or any other provision of the Constitution, it was not given by the Framers, but rather has been bestowed on the Court by the Court. This fact is perhaps responsible for the peculiar phenomenon that for a period of a century and a half no serious suggestion was ever made that the Ninth Amendment, enacted to protect state powers against federal invasion, could be used as a weapon of federal power to prevent state legislatures from passing laws they consider appropriate to govern local affairs. Use of any such broad, unbounded judicial authority would make of this Court's members a day-to-day constitutional convention.

I repeat so as not to be misunderstood that this Court does have power, which it should exercise, to hold laws unconstitutional where they are forbidden by the Federal Constitution. My point is that there is no provision of the Constitution which either expressly or impliedly vests power in this Court to sit as a supervisory agency over acts of duly constituted legislative bodies and set aside their laws because of the Court's belief that the legislative policies adopted are unreasonable, unwise, arbitrary, capricious or irrational. The adoption of such a loose, flexible, uncontrolled standard for holding laws unconstitutional, if ever it is finally achieved, will amount to a great unconstitutional shift of power to the courts which I believe and am constrained to say will be bad for the courts and worse for the country. Subjecting federal and state laws to such an unrestrained and unrestrainable judiciary control as to the wisdom of legislative enactments would, I fear, jeopardize the separation of governmental powers that the Framers set up and at the same time threaten to take away much of the power of States to govern themselves which the Constitution plainly intended them to have.

I realize that many good and able men have eloquently spoken and written, sometimes in rhapsodical strains, about the duty of this Court to keep the Constitution in tune with the times. The idea is that the Constitution must be changed from time to time and that this Court is charged with a duty to make those changes. For myself, I must with all deference reject that philosophy. The Constitution makers knew the need for change and provided for it. Amendments suggested by the people's elected representatives can be submitted to the people or their selected agents for ratification. That method of change was good for our Fathers, and being somewhat old-fashioned I must add it is good enough for me. And so, I cannot rely on the Due Process Clause or the Ninth Amendment or any mysterious and uncertain natural law concept as a reason for striking down this state law. . . .

.   .   .

The late Judge Learned Hand, after emphasizing his view that judges should not use the due process formula suggested in the concurring opinions today or any other formula like it to invalidate legislation offensive to their "personal preferences," made the statement, with which I fully agree, that:

"For myself it would be most irksome to be ruled by a bevy of Platonic Guardians, even if I knew how to choose them, which I assuredly do not."

So far as I am concerned, Connecticut's law as applied here is not forbidden by any provision of the Federal Constitution as that Constitution was written, and I would therefore affirm.

.   .   .

Mr. Justice Stewart, whom Mr. Justice Black joins, dissenting.

Roe v. Wade

410 U.S. 113, 35 L Ed 2d 147, 93 S Ct 705 (1973)

Jane Roe, an unmarried pregnant woman, brought suit against the District Attorney of Dallas County, Texas, seeking a declaratory judgment that the Texas abortion statute was unconstitutional. The statute (adopted in 1857) made it a criminal act to procure or perform an abortion unless "for the purpose of saving the life of the mother." A three-judge district court held that the right to choose whether to have children was protected by the Ninth Amendment and voided the Texas statute as impermissibly broad and vague. The Supreme Court received the case on appeal.

. . .

Mr. Justice Blackmun delivered the opinion of the Court.

This Texas federal appeal and its Georgia companion, Doe v. Bolton present constitutional challenges to state criminal abortion legislation. The Texas statutes under attack here are typical of those that have been in effect in many States for approximately a century. The Georgia statutes, in contrast, have a modern cast and are a legislative product that, to an extent at least, obviously reflects the influences of recent attitudinal change, of advancing medical knowledge and techniques, and of new thinking about an old issue.

We forthwith acknowledge our awareness of the sensitive and emotional nature of the abortion controversy, of the vigorous opposing views, even among physicians, and of the deep and seemingly absolute convictions that the subject inspires. One's philosophy, one's experiences, one's exposure to the raw edges of human existence, one's religious training, one's attitudes toward life and family and their values, and the moral standards one establishes and seeks to observe, are all likely to influence and to color one's thinking and conclusions about abortion.

In addition, population growth, pollution, poverty, and racial overtones tend to complicate and not to simplify the problem.

Our task, of course, is to resolve the issue by constitutional measurement free of emotion and of predilection. We seek earnestly to do this, and, because we do, we have inquired into, and in this opinion place some emphasis upon, medical and medical-legal history and what that history reveals about man's attitudes toward the abortive procedure over the centuries. We bear in mind, too, Mr. Justice Holmes' admonition in his now vindicated dissent in Lochner v New York:

"It [the Constitution] is made for people of fundamentally differing views, and the accident of our finding certain opinions natural and familiar or novel and even shocking ought not to conclude our judgment upon the question whether statutes embodying them conflict with the Constitution of the United States. . . ."

. . .

The principal thrust of appellant's attack on the Texas statutes is that they improperly invade a right, said to be possessed by the pregnant woman, to choose to terminate her pregnancy. Appellant would discover this right in the concept of personal "liberty" embodied in the Fourteenth Amendment's Due Process Clause; or in personal, marital, familial, and sexual privacy said to be protected by the Bill of Rights or its penumbras, [see *Griswold* v. *Connecticut*] or among those rights reserved to the people by the Ninth Amendment. Before addressing this claim, we feel it desirable briefly to survey, in several aspects, the history of abortion, for such insight as that history may afford us, and then to examine the state purposes and interests behind the criminal abortion laws. . . .

. . .

[After an extensive survey of the history of abortion laws, Justice Blackmun moves on to the interests involved.]

. . .

Three reasons have been advanced to explain historically the enactment of criminal abortion laws in the 19th century and to justify their continued existence.

It has been argued occasionally that these laws were the product of a Victorian social concern to discourage illicit sexual conduct. Texas, however, does not advance this justification in the present case, and it appears that no court or commentator has taken the argument seriously. The appellants and amici contend, moreover, that this is not a proper state purpose at all and suggest that, if it were, the Texas statutes are overbroad in protecting it since the law fails to distinguish between married and unwed mothers.

A second reason is concerned with abortion as a medical procedure. When most criminal abortion laws were first enacted, the procedure was a hazardous one for the woman. This was particularly true prior to the development of antisepsis. . . Abortion mortality was high. Even after 1900, and perhaps until as late as the development of antibiotics in the 1940's, standard modern techniques such as dilation and curettage were not nearly so safe as they are today. Thus it has been argued that a State's real concern in enacting a criminal abortion law was to protect the pregnant woman, that is, to restrain her from submitting to a procedure that placed her life in serious jeopardy.

Modern medical techniques have altered this situation. Appellants and various amici refer to medical data indicating that abortion in early pregnancy, that is, prior to the end of first trimester, although not without its risk, is now relatively safe. Mortality rates for women undergoing early abortions, where the procedure is legal, appear to be as low as or lower than the rates for normal childbirth. Consequently, any interest of the State in protecting the woman from an inherently hazardous procedure, except when it would be equally dangerous for her to forgo it, has largely disappeared... The State has a legitimate interest in seeing to it that abortion, like any other medical procedure, is performed under circumstances that insure maximum safety for the patient. This interest obviously extends at least to the performing physician and his staff, to the facilities involved, to the availability of aftercare, and to adequate provision for any complication or emergency that might arise. The prevalence of high mortality rates at illegal "abortion mills" strengthens, rather than weakens, the State's interest in regulating the conditions under which abortions are performed. Moreover, the risk to the woman increases as her pregnancy continues. Thus the State retains a definite interest in protecting the woman's own health and safety when an abortion is proposed at a late stage of pregnancy.

The third reason is the State's interest—some phrase it in terms of duty—in protecting prenatal life. Some of the argument for this justification rests on the theory that a new human life is present from the moment of conception. The State's interest and general obligation to protect life then extends, it is argued, to prenatal life. Only when the life of the pregnant mother herself is at stake, balanced against the life she carries within her, should the interest of the embryo or fetus not prevail. Logically, of course, a legitimate state interest in this area need not stand or fall on acceptance of the belief that life begins at conception or at some other point prior to live birth. In assessing the State's interest, recognition may be given to the less rigid claim that as long as at least *potential* life is involved, the State may assert interests beyond the protection of the pregnant woman alone....

.   .   .

It is with these interests, and the weight to be attached to them, that this case is concerned.

The Constitution does not explicitly mention any right of privacy. In a line of decisions the Court has recognized that a right of personal privacy, or a guarantee of certain areas or zones of privacy, does exist under the Constitution. In varying contexts the Court or individual Justices have indeed found at least the roots of that right in the First Amendment, in the Fourth and Fifth Amendments, in the penumbras of the Bill of Rights, in the Ninth Amendment, or in the concept of liberty guaranteed by the first section of the Fourteenth Amendment. These decisions make it clear that only personal rights that can be deemed "fundamental" or "implicit in the concept of ordered liberty," are included in this guarantee of personal privacy. They also make it clear that the right has some extension to activities relating to marriage, procreation, contraception, family relationships, and child rearing and education.

This right of privacy, whether it be founded in the Fourteenth Amendment's concept of personal liberty and restrictions upon state action, as we feel it is, or, as the District Court determined, in the Ninth Amendment's reservation of rights to the people, is broad enough to encompass a woman's decision whether or not to terminate her pregnancy... Specific and direct harm medically diagnosable even in early pregnancy may be involved. Maternity, or additional offspring, may force upon the woman a distressful life and future. Psychological harm may be imminent. Mental and physical health may be taxed by child care. There is also the distress, for all concerned, associated with the unwanted child, and there is the problem of bringing a child into a family already unable, psychologically and otherwise, to care for it. In other cases, as in this one, the additional difficulties and continuing stigma of unwed motherhood may be involved. All these are factors the woman and her responsible physician necessarily will consider in consultation.

On the basis of elements such as these, appellants and some amici argue that the woman's right is absolute and that she is entitled to terminate her pregnancy at whatever time, in whatever way, and for whatever reason she alone chooses. With this we do not agree... The Court's decisions recognizing a right of privacy also acknowledge that some state regulation in areas protected by that right is appropriate... At some point in pregnancy, these respective interests become sufficiently compelling to sustain regulation of the factors that govern the abortion

401

decision. The privacy right involved, therefore, cannot be said to be absolute. In fact, it is not clear to us that the claim asserted by some amici that one has an unlimited right to do with one's body as one pleases bears a close relationship to the right of privacy previously articulated in the Court's decisions. The Court has refused to recognize an unlimited right of this kind in the past.

We therefore conclude that the right of personal privacy includes the abortion decision, but that t   right is not unqualified and must be considered against important state interests in regulation. . . .

.   .   .

The appellee and certain amici argue that the fetus is a "person" within the language and meaning of the Fourteenth Amendment. In support of this they outline at length and in detail the well-known facts of fetal development. If this suggestion of personhood is established, the appellant's case, of course, collapses, for the fetus' right to life is then guaranteed specifically by the Amendment. The appellant conceded as much on reargument. On the other hand, the appellee conceded on reargument that no case could be cited that holds that a fetus is a person within the meaning of the Fourteenth Amendment.

The Constitution does not define "person" in so many words. Section 1 of the Fourteenth Amendment contains three references to "person.". . The word also appears both in the Due Process Clause and in the Equal Protection Clause. "Person" is used in other places in the Constitution: . . . But in nearly all these instances, the use of the word is such that it has application only postnatally. None indicates, with any assurance, that it has any possible prenatal application.

All this, together with our observation . . . that throughout the major portion of the 19th century prevailing legal abortion practices were far freer than they are today, persuades us that the word "person," as used in the Fourteenth Amendment, does not include the unborn. . . .

.   .   .

The pregnant woman cannot be isolated in her privacy. She carries an embryo and, later, a fetus, if one accepts the medical definitions of the developing young in the human uterus. . . As we have intimated above, it is reasonable and appropriate for a State to decide that at some point in time another interest, that of health of the mother or that of potential human life, becomes significantly involved. The woman's privacy is no longer sole and any right of privacy she possesses must be measured accordingly.

Texas urges that, apart from the Fourteenth Amendment, life begins at conception and is present throughout pregnancy, and that, therefore, the State has a compelling interest in protecting that life from and after conception. We need not resolve the difficult question of when life begins. When those trained in the respective disciplines of medicine, philosophy, and theology are unable to arrive at any consensus, the judiciary, at this point in the development of man's knowledge, is not in a position to speculate as to the answer. . . .

.   .   .

In areas other than criminal abortion the law has been reluctant to endorse any theory that life, as we recognize it, begins before live birth or to accord legal rights to the unborn except in narrowly defined situations and except when the rights are contingent upon live birth. . . [T]he unborn have never been recognized in the law as persons in the whole sense.

In view of all this, we do not agree that, by adopting one theory of life, Texas may override the rights of the pregnant woman that are at stake. We repeat, however, that the State does have an important and legitimate interest in preserving and protecting the health of the pregnant woman, whether she be a resident of the State or a nonresident who seeks medical consultation and treatment there, and that it has still *another* important and legitimate interest in protecting the potentiality of human life. These interests are separate and distinct. Each grows in substantiality as the woman approaches term and, at a point during pregnancy, each becomes "compelling."

With respect to the State's important and legitimate interest in the health of the mother, the "compelling" point, in the light of present medical knowledge, is at approximately the end of the first trimester. This is so because of the now established medical fact . . . that until the end of the first trimester mortality in abortion is less than mortality in normal childbirth. It follows that, from and after this point, a State may regulate the abortion procedure to the extent that the regulation reasonably relates to the preservation and protection of maternal health. Examples of permissible state regulation in this area are requirements as to the qualifications of the person who is to perform the abortion; as to the licensure of that person; as to the facility in which the procedure is to be performed, that is, whether it must be a hospital or may be a clinic or some other place of less-than-hospital status; as to the licensing of the facility; and the like.

This means, on the other hand, that, for the period of pregnancy prior to this "compelling" point, the attending physician, in consultation with his patient, is free to determine, without regulation by the State, that in his medical judgment the patient's pregnancy should be terminated. If that decision is reached, the judgment may be effectuated by an abortion free of interference by the State.

With respect to the State's important and legitimate interest in potential life, the "compelling" point is at viability. This is so because the fetus then presumably has the capability of meaningful life outside the mother's womb. State regulation protective of fetal life after viability thus has both logical and biological justifications. If the State is interested in protecting fetal life after viability, it may go so far as to proscribe abortion during that period except when it is necessary to preserve the life or health of the mother.

Measured against these standards, Art 1196 of the Texas Penal Code, in restricting legal abortions to those "procured or attempted by medical advice for the purpose of saving the life of the mother," sweeps too broadly. The statute makes no distinction between abortions performed early in pregnancy and those performed later, and it limits to a single reason, "saving" the mother's life, the legal justification for the procedure. The statute, therefore, cannot survive the constitutional attack made upon it here. . . .

. . .

To summarize and to repeat:

1. A state criminal abortion statute of the current Texas type, that excepts from criminality only a life saving procedure on behalf of the mother, without regard to pregnancy stage and without recognition of the other interests involved, is violative of the Due Process Clause of the Fourteenth Amendment.

(a) For the stage prior to approximately the end of the first trimester, the abortion decision and its effectuation must be left to the medical judgment of the pregnant woman's attending physician.

(b) For the stage subsequent to approximately the end of the first trimester, the State, in promoting its interest in the health of the mother, may, if it chooses, regulate the abortion procedure in ways that are reasonably related to maternal health.

(c) For the stage subsequent to viability the State, in promoting its interest in the potentiality of human life, may, if it chooses, regulate, and even proscribe, abortion except where it is necessary, in appropriate medical judgment, for the preservation of the life or health of the mother.

. . .

This holding, we feel, is consistent with the relative weights of the respective interests involved, with the lessons and example of medical and legal history, with the lenity of the common law, and with the demands of the profound problems of the present day. The decision leaves the State free to place increasing restrictions on abortion as the period of pregnancy lengthens, so long as those restrictions are tailored to the recognized state interests. The decision vindicates the right of the physician to administer medical treatment according to his professional judgment up to the points where important state interests provide compelling justifications for intervention. Up to those points the abortion decision in all its aspects is inherently, and primarily, a medical decision, and basic responsibility for it must rest with the physician. If an individual practitioner abuses the privilege of exercising proper medical judgment, the usual remedies, judicial and intra-professional, are available. . . .

. . .

[T]he judgment of the District Court is affirmed.

. . .

Mr. Chief Justice Burger, concurring.

I agree that, under the Fourteenth Amendment to the Constitution, the abortion statutes of Georgia and Texas impermissibly limit the performance of abortions necessary to protect the health of pregnant women, using the term health in its broadest medical context. I am somewhat troubled that the Court has taken notice of various scientific and medical data in reaching its conclusion; however, I do not believe that the Court has exceeded the scope of judicial notice accepted in other contexts.

. . .

In oral argument, counsel for the State of Texas informed the Court that early abortive procedures were routinely permitted in certain exceptional cases, such as nonconsensual pregnancies resulting from rape and incest. In the face of a rigid and narrow statute, such as that of Texas, no one in these circumstances should be placed in a posture of dependence on a prosecutorial policy or prosecutorial discretion. Of course, States must have broad power, within the limits indicated in the opinions, to regulate the subject of abortions, but where the consequences of state intervention are so severe, uncertainty must be avoided as much as possible. For my part, I would be inclined to allow a State to require the certification of two physicians to support an abortion, but the Court holds otherwise. . . .

. . .

I do not read the Court's holding today as having the sweeping consequences attributed to it by the dissenting Justices; the dissenting views discount the reality that the vast majority of physicians observe the standards of their profession, and act only on the basis of carefully deliberated medical judgments relating to life and health. Plainly, the Court today rejects any claim that the Constitution requires abortion on demand.

. . .

Mr. Justice Douglas, concurring.

. . .

The Ninth Amendment obviously does not create federally enforceable rights. It merely says, "The enumeration in the Constitution of certain rights shall not be construed to deny or disparage others retained by the people." But a catalogue of these rights includes customary, traditional, and time-honored rights, amenities, privileges, and immunities that come within the sweep of "the Blessings of Liberty" mentioned in the preamble to the Constitution. Many of them in my view come within the meaning of the term "liberty" as used in the Fourteenth Amendment.

First is the autonomous control over the development and expression of one's intellect, interests, tastes, and personality.

These are rights protected by the First Amendment and in my view they are absolute, permitting of no exceptions. . . .

. . .

Second is freedom of choice in the basic decisions of one's life respecting marriage, divorce, procreation, contraception, and the education and upbringing of children.

These rights, unlike those protected by the First Amendment, are subject to some control by the police power. . . .

. . .

Third is the freedom to care for one's health and person, freedom from bodily restraint or compulsion, freedom to walk, stroll, or loaf.

These rights, though fundamental, are likewise subject to regulation on a showing of "compelling state interest.". . .

. . .

Elaborate argument is hardly necessary to demonstrate that childbirth may deprive a woman of her preferred life style and force upon her a radically different and undesired future. . . .

. . .

Such a holding is, however, only the beginning of the problem. . . While childbirth endangers the lives of some women, voluntary abortion at any time and place regardless of medical standards would impinge on a rightful concern of society. The woman's health is part of that concern; as is the life of the fetus after quickening. These concerns justify the State in treating the procedure as a medical one. . . .

. . .

The vicissitudes of life produce pregnancies which may be unwanted, or which may impair "health" in the broad . . . sense of the term, or which may imperil the life of the mother, or which in the full setting of the case may create such suffering, dislocations, misery, or tragedy as to make an early abortion the only civilized step to take. These hardships may be properly embraced in the "health" factor of the mother as appraised by a person of insight. Or they may be part of a broader medical judgment based on what is "appropriate" in a given case, though perhaps not "necessary" in a strict sense.

The "liberty" of the mother, though rooted as it is in the Constitution, may be qualified by the State for the reasons we have stated. But where

407

fundamental personal rights and liberties are involved, the corrective legislation must be "narrowly drawn to prevent the supposed evil." Unless regulatory measures are so confined and are addressed to the specific areas of compelling legislative concern, the police power would become the great leveller of constitutional rights and liberties.

There is no doubt that the State may require abortions to be performed by qualified medical personnel. The legitimate objective of preserving the mother's health clearly supports such laws. . . .

. . .

The present statute has struck the balance between the woman and the State's interests wholly in favor of the latter. I am not prepared to hold that a State may equate all phases of maturation preceding birth. . . .

. . .

The right to seek advice on one's health and the right to place his reliance on the physician of his choice are basic to Fourteenth Amendment values. We deal with fundamental rights and liberties, which, as already noted, can be contained or controlled only by discretely drawn legislation that preserves the "liberty" and regulates only those phases of the problem of compelling legislative concern. The imposition by the State of group controls over the physician-patient relation is not made on any medical procedure apart from abortion, no matter how dangerous the medical step may be. The oversight imposed on the physician and patient in abortion cases denies them their "liberty," viz., their right of privacy, without any compelling, discernible state interest. . . .

. . .

Mr. Justice Stewart, concurring.

. . .

Several decisions of this Court make clear that freedom of personal choice in matters of marriage and family life is one of the liberties protected by the Due Process Clause of the Fourteenth Amendment. As recently as last Term, we recognized "the right of the *individual*, married or single, to be free from unwarranted governmental intrusion into matters so fundamentally affecting a person as the decision whether to bear or beget a child." That right necessarily includes the right of a woman to decide whether or not to terminate her pregnancy. "Certainly the interests of a woman in giving of her physical and emotional self during pregnancy and the interests that will be affected throughout her life by the birth and raising of a child are of a far greater degree of significance and personal intimacy than the right to send a child to private school or the right to teach a foreign language. . . .

Clearly, therefore, the Court today is correct in holding that the right asserted by Jane Roe is embraced within the personal liberty protected by the Due Process Clause of the Fourteenth Amendment.

It is evident that the Texas abortion statute infringes that right directly. Indeed, it is difficult to imagine a more complete abridgment of a constitutional freedom than that worked by the inflexible criminal statute now in force in Texas. The question then becomes whether the state interests advanced to justify this abridgment can survive the "particularly careful scrutiny" that the Fourteenth Amendment here requires.

The asserted state interests are protection of the health and safety of the pregnant woman, and protection of the potential future human life within her. These are legitimate objectives, amply sufficient to permit a State to regulate abortions as it does other surgical procedures, and perhaps sufficient to permit a State to regulate abortions more stringently or even to prohibit them in the late stages of pregnancy. But such legislation is not before us, and I think the Court today has thoroughly demonstrated that these state interests cannot constitutionally support the broad abridgment of personal liberty worked by the existing Texas law. . . .

. . .

Mr. Justice White, with whom Mr. Justice Rehnquist joins, dissenting.

At the heart of the controversy in these cases are those recurring pregnancies that pose no danger whatsoever to the life or health of the mother but are nevertheless unwanted for any one or more of a variety of reasons—convenience, family planning, economics, dislike of children, the embarrassment of illegitimacy, etc. The common claim before us is that for any one of such reasons, or for no reason at all, and without asserting or claiming any threat to life or health, any woman is entitled to an abortion at her request if she is able to find a medical advisor willing to undertake the procedure. . . .

. . .

With all due respect, I dissent. I find nothing in the language or history of the Constitution to support the Court's judgment. The Court simply fashions and announces a new constitutional right for pregnant mothers and, with scarcely any reason or authority for its action, invests that right with sufficient substance to override most existing state abortion statutes. The upshot is that the people and the legislatures of the 50 States are constitutionally disentitled to weigh the relative importance of the continued existence and development of the fetus on the one hand against a spectrum of possible impacts on the mother on the other hand. As an exercise of raw judicial power, the Court perhaps has authority to do what it does today; but in my view its judgment is an improvident and extravagant exercise of the power of judicial review which the Constitution extends to this Court.

The Court apparently values the convenience of the pregnant mother more than the continued existence and development of the life or potential life which she carries. Whether or not I might agree with that marshalling of values, I can in no event join the Court's judgment because I find no constitutional warrant for imposing such an order of priorities on the people and legislatures of the States. In a sensitive area such as this, involving as it does issues over which reasonable men may easily and heatedly differ, I cannot accept the Court's exercise of its clear power of choice by interposing a constitutional barrier to state efforts to protect human life and by investing mothers and doctors with the constitutionally protected right to exterminate it. This issue, for the most part, should be left with the people and to the political processes the people have devised to govern their affairs. . . .

. . .

Mr. Justice Rehnquist, dissenting.

. . .

I have difficulty in concluding, as the Court does, that the right of "privacy" is involved in this case. Texas by the statute here challenged bars the performance of a medical abortion by a licensed physician on a plaintiff such as Roe. A transaction resulting in an operation such as this is not "private" in the ordinary usage of that word. Nor is the "privacy" which the Court finds here even a distant relative of the freedom from searches and seizures protected by the Fourth Amendment to the Constitution which the Court has referred to as embodying a right to privacy.

If the Court means by the term "privacy" no more than that the claim of a person to be free from unwanted state regulation of consensual transactions may be a form of "liberty" protected by the Fourteenth Amendment, there is no doubt that similar claims have been upheld in our earlier decisions on the basis of that liberty... But that liberty is not guaranteed absolutely against deprivation, but only against deprivation without due process of law. The test traditionally applied in the area of social and economic legislation is whether or not a law such as that challenged has a rational relation to a valid state objective... The Due Process Clause of the Fourteenth Amendment undoubtedly does place a limit on legislative power to enact laws such as this, albeit a broad one... But the Court's sweeping invalidation of any restrictions on abortion during the first trimester is impossible to justify under that standard, and the conscious weighing of competing factors which the Court's opinion apparently substitutes for the established test is far more appropriate to a legislative judgment than to a judicial one....

. . .

[T]he adoption of the compelling state interest standard will inevitably require this Court to examine the legislative policies and pass on the wisdom of these policies in the very process of deciding whether a particular state interest put forward may or may not be "compelling." The decision here to break the term of pregnancy into three distinct terms and to outline the permissible restrictions the State may impose in each one, for example, partakes more of judicial legislation than it does of a determination of the intent of the drafters of the Fourteenth Amendment.

The fact that a majority of the States, reflecting after all the majority sentiment in those States, have had restrictions on abortions for at least a century seems to me as strong an indication there is that the asserted right to an abortion is not "so rooted in the traditions and conscience of our people as to be ranked as fundamental, ..." Even today, when society's views on abortion are changing, the very existence of the debate is evidence that the "right" to an abortion is not so universally accepted as the appellants would have us believe....

. . .

Doe v. *Bolton,* decided with Roe, involved a Georgia statute of more recent adoption. It permitted an abortion when a physician determined that 1) a continuation of the pregnancy would imperil the life of the mother or seriously and permanently injure her health, or 2) the fetus was seriously and permanently physically or mentally defective, or 3) the pregnancy resulted from forcible or statutory rape. Several other statutory provisions were noted by the majority as reinforcing the decision to invalidate the statute: the woman had to be a resident of the State of Georgia, two other physicians had to agree with the woman's physician's decision, a hospital abortion committee had to concur, and the facility in which the abortion was to be performed had to be licensed by the state and accredited by the Joint Commission on Accreditation of Hospitals. The district court had invalidated that part of the statute limiting the reasons for an abortion, and the Supreme Court struck down the two-doctor consultation, the abortion committee, the JCAH accreditation, and the residency requirements as unduly limiting the woman's "right to receive medical care in accordance with her licensed physician's best judgment."

Planned Parenthood of Missouri v. Danforth

428 U.S. 52, 49 L Ed 2d 788, 96 S. Ct 2831 (1976)

The facts are contained in the opinion of the Court.

. . .

Mr. Justice Blackmun delivered the opinion of the Court.

This case is a logical and anticipated corollary to Roe v Wade, for it raises issues secondary to those that were then before the Court. . . .

. . .

In June 1974, somewhat more than a year after Roe and Doe had been decided, Missouri's 77th General Assembly, in its Second Regular Session, enacted House Committee Substitute for House Bill No. 1211 (hereinafter referred to as the "Act"). The legislation was approved by the

Governor on June 14, 1974, . . . It imposes a structure for the control and regulation of abortions in Missouri during all stages of pregnancy. . . .

. . .

Our primary task, then, is to consider each of the challenged provisions of the new Missouri abortion statute in the particular light of the opinions and decisions in Roe and in Doe. To this we now turn, with the assistance of helpful briefs from both sides and from some of the amici.

A

The definition of viability. Section 2(2) of the Act defines "viability" as "that stage of fetal development when the life of the unborn child may be continued indefinitely outside the womb by natural or artificial life-supportive systems.". . .

. . .

In Roe, we used the term "viable," properly we thought, to signify the point at which the fetus is "potentially able to live outside the mother's womb, albeit with artificial aid," and presumably capable of "meaningful life outside the mother's womb." We noted that this point "is usually placed" at about seven months or 28 weeks, but may occur earlier.

We agree with the District Court and conclude that the definition of viability in the Act does not conflict with what was said and held in Roe. In fact, we believe that § 2(c), even when read in conjunction with § 5 (proscribing an abortion "not necessary to preserve the life or health of the mother . . . unless the attending physician first certifies with reasonable medical certainty that the fetus is not viable"), the constitutionality of which is not explicitly challenged here, reflects an attempt on the part of the Missouri General Assembly to comply with our observations and discussion in Roe relating to viability. . . [W]e recognized in Roe that viability was a matter of medical judgment, skill, and technical ability, and we preserved the flexibility of the term. Section 2(2) does the same. Indeed, one might argue, as the appellees do, that the presence of the statute's words "continued indefinitely" favor, rather than disfavor, the appellants, for, arguably, the point when life can be "continued indefinitely outside the womb" may well occur later in pregnancy than the point where the fetus is "potentially able to live outside the mother's womb."

In any event, we agree with the District Court that it is not the proper function of the legislature or the courts to place viability, which essentially is a medical concept, at a specific point in the gestation period. The time

413

when viability is achieved may vary with each pregnancy, and the determination of whether a particular fetus is viable is, and must be, a matter for the judgment of the responsible attending physician. The definition of viability in § 2(2) merely reflects this fact. . . .

. . .

We thus do not accept appellants' contention that a specified number of weeks in pregnancy must be fixed by statute as the point of viability.

. . .

B

The woman's consent. Under § 3(2) of the Act, a woman, prior to submitting to an abortion during the first 12 weeks of pregnancy, must certify in writing her consent to the procedure and "that her consent is informed and freely given and is not the result of coercion.". . .

. . .

[T]he District Court's majority relied on the propositions that the decision to terminate a pregnancy, of course, "is often a stressful one," and that the consent requirement of § 3(2) "insures that the pregnant woman retains control over the discretions of her consulting physician." The majority also felt that the consent requirement "does not single out the abortion procedure, but merely includes it within the category of medical operations for which consent is required." The third judge joined the majority in upholding § 3(2), but added that the written consent requirement was "not burdensome or chilling" and manifested "a legitimate interest of the state that this important decision has in fact been made by the person constitutionally empowered to do so.". . .

. . .

We do not disagree with the result reached by the District Court as to § 3(2). It is true that Doe and Roe clearly establish that the State may not restrict the decision of the patient and her physician regarding abortion during the first stage of pregnancy. . . [T]he imposition by § 3(2) of such a requirement for termination of pregnancy even during the first stage, in our view, is not in itself an unconstitutional requirement. The decision to abort, indeed, is an important, and often a stressful one, and it is desirable and imperative that it be made with full knowledge of its nature and consequences. The woman is the one primarily concerned, and her awareness of the decision and its significance may be assured, constitutionally, by the State to the extent of requiring her prior written consent. . . .

. . .

C

The spouse's consent. Section 3(3) requires the prior written consent of the spouse of the woman seeking an abortion during the first 12 weeks of pregnancy, unless "the abortion is certified by a licensed physician to be necessary in order to preserve the life of the mother."

The appellees defend § 3(3) on the ground that it was enacted in the light of the General Assembly's "perception of marriage as an institution," and that any major change in family status is a decision to be made jointly by the marriage partners. . . .

. . .

It is argued that "[r]ecognizing that the consent of both parties is generally necessary . . . to begin a family, the legislature has determined that a change in the family structure set in motion by mutual consent should be terminated only by mutual consent.". . .

. . .

The appellants, on the other hand, contend that § 3(3) obviously is designed to afford the husband the right unilaterally to prevent or veto an abortion, whether or not he is the father of the fetus, and that this not only violates Roe and Doe but is also in conflict with other decided cases. . . .

. . .

In Roe and Doe we specifically reserved decision on the question whether a requirement for consent by the father of the fetus, by the spouse, or by the parents, or a parent, of an unmarried minor, may be constitutionally imposed. . . Clearly, since the State cannot regulate or proscribe abortion during the first stage, when the physician and his patient make that decision, the State cannot delegate authority to any particular person, even the spouse, to prevent abortion during that same period.

We are not unaware of the deep and proper concern and interest that a devoted and protective husband has in his wife's pregnancy and in the growth and development of the fetus she is carrying. Neither has this Court failed to appreciate the importance of the marital relationship in our society. Moreover, we recognize that the decision whether to undergo or to forgo an abortion may have profound effects on the future of any marriage, effects that are both physical and mental, and possibly deleterious. Notwithstanding these factors, we cannot hold that the State has the constitutional authority to give the spouse unilaterally the ability to prohibit the wife from terminating her pregnancy, when the State itself lacks that right. . . .

. . .

It seems manifest that, ideally, the decision to terminate a pregnancy should be one concurred in by both the wife and her husband. No marriage may be viewed as harmonious or successful if the marriage partners are fundamentally divided on so important and vital an issue. But it is difficult to believe that the goal of fostering mutuality and trust in a marriage, and of strengthening the marital relationship and the marriage institution, will be achieved by giving the husband a veto power exercisable for any reason whatsoever or for no reason at all. . . .

. . .

We recognize, of course, that when a woman, with the approval of her physician but without the approval of her husband, decides to terminate her pregnancy, it could be said that she is acting unilaterally. The obvious fact is that when the wife and the husband disagree on this decision, the view of only one of the two marriage partners can prevail. Since it is the woman who physically bears the child and who is the more directly and immediately affected by the pregnancy, as between the two, the balance weighs in her favor. . . .

. . .

D

Parental Consent. Section 3(4) requires, with respect to the first 12 weeks of pregnancy, where the woman is unmarried and under the age of 18 years, the written consent of a parent or person in loco parentis unless, again, "the abortion is certified by a licensed physician as necessary in order to preserve the life of the mother." It is to be observed that only one parent need consent. . . .

416

. . .

Certain decisions are considered by the State to be outside the scope of a minor's ability to act in his own best interest or in the interest of the public, . . . It is pointed out that the record contains testimony to the effect that children of tender years (even ages 10 and 11) have sought abortions. Thus, a State's permitting a child to obtain an abortion without the counsel of an adult "who has responsibility or concern for the child would constitute an irresponsible abdication of the State's duty to protect the welfare of minors.". . .

. . .

We agree with appellants . . . that the State may not impose a blanket provision, such as § 3(4), requiring the consent of a parent or person in loco parentis as a condition for abortion of an unmarried minor during the first 12 weeks of her pregnancy. Just as with the requirement of consent from the spouse, so here, the State does not have the constitutional authority to give a third party an absolute, and possibly arbitrary, veto over the decision of the physician and his patient to terminate the patient's pregnancy, regardless of the reason for withholding the consent.

Constitutional rights do not mature and come into being magically only when one attains the state-defined age of majority. Minors, as well as adults, are protected by the Constitution and possess constitutional rights. . . .

. . .

It is difficult . . . to conclude that providing a parent with absolute power to overrule a determination, made by the physician and his minor patient, to terminate the patient's pregnancy will serve to strengthen the family unit. Neither is it likely that such veto power will enhance parental authority or control where the minor and the nonconsenting parent are so fundamentally in conflict and the very existence of the pregnancy already has fractured the family structure. Any independent interest the parent may have in the termination of the minor daughter's pregnancy is no more weighty than the right of privacy of the competent minor mature enough to have become pregnant. . . .

. . .

E

Saline amniocentesis. Section 9 of the statute prohibits the use of saline amniocentesis, as a method or technique of abortion, after the first 12 weeks of pregnancy. It describes the method as one whereby the amniotic fluid is withdrawn and "a saline or other fluid" is inserted into the amniotic sac. The statute imposes this proscription on the ground that the technique "is deleterious to maternal health," and places it in the form of a legislative finding. Appellants challenge this provision on the ground that it operates to preclude virtually all abortions after the first trimester. This is so, it is claimed, because a substantial percentage, in the neighborhood of 70% according to the testimony, of all abortions performed in the United States after the first trimester are effected through the procedure of saline amniocentesis. . . .

· · ·

We held in Roe that after the first stage, "the state, in promoting its interest in the health of the mother, may, if it chooses, regulate the abortion procedure in ways that are reasonably related to maternal health." The question with respect to § 9 therefore is whether the flat prohibition of saline amniocentesis is a restriction which "reasonably relates to the preservation and protection of maternal health." The appellees urge that what the Missouri General Assembly has done here is consistent with that guideline and is buttressed by substantial supporting medical evidence in the record to which this Court should defer.

The District Court's majority determined, on the basis of the evidence before it, that the maternal mortality rate in childbirth does, indeed, exceed the mortality rate where saline amniocentesis is used. Therefore, the majority acknowledged, § 9 could be upheld only if there were safe alternative methods of inducing abortion after the first 12 weeks. Referring to such methods as hysterotomy, hysterectomy, "mechanical means of inducing abortion," and prostaglandin injection, the majority said that at least the latter two techniques were safer than saline. Consequently, the majority concluded, the restriction in § 9 could be upheld as reasonably related to maternal health.

We feel that the majority, in reaching its conclusion, failed to appreciate and to consider several significant facts. First, it did not recognize the prevalence, as the record conclusively demonstrates, of the use of saline amniocentesis as an accepted medical procedure in this country; the procedure, as noted above, is employed in a substantial majority (the testimony from both sides ranges from 68% to 80%) of all post-first trimester abortions. Second, it failed to recognize that at the time of trial, there were severe limitations on the availability of the prostaglandin technique, which, although promising, was used only on an experimental basis until less than two years before. Third, the statute's reference to the insertion of "a saline or other fluid" appears to include within its proscription the intra-amniotic injection of prostaglandin itself and other methods that may be developed in the future and that may prove highly effective and completely safe. Finally, the majority did not consider the anomaly inherent in § 9 when it proscribes the use of saline but does not prohibit techniques that are many times more likely to result in maternal death.

These unappreciated or overlooked factors place the State's decision to bar use of the saline method in a completely different light. The State, through § 9, would prohibit the use of a method which the record shows is the one most commonly used nationally by physicians after the first trimester and which is safer, with respect to maternal mortality, than even continuation of the pregnancy until normal childbirth. Moreover, as a practical matter, it forces a woman and her physician to terminate her pregnancy by methods more dangerous to her health than the method outlawed.

As so viewed, particularly in the light of the present unavailability—as demonstrated by the record—of the prostaglandin technique, the outright legislative proscription of saline fails as a reasonable regulation for the protection of maternal health. It comes into focus, instead, as an unreasonable or arbitrary regulation designed to inhibit, and having the effect of inhibiting, the vast majority of abortions after the first 12 weeks. As such, it does not withstand constitutional challenge. . . .

. . .

F

Recordkeeping. . . .

. . .

We conclude . . . that the provisions of §§ 10 and 11, while perhaps approaching permissible limits, are not constitutionally offensive in themselves. Recordkeeping of this kind, if not abused or overdone, can be useful to the State's interest in protecting the health of its female citizens, and may be a resource that is relevant to decisions involving medical experience and judgment. The added requirements for confidentiality, with the sole exception for public health officers, and for retention for seven years, a period not unreasonable in length, assist and persuade us in our determination of the constitutional limits. As so regarded, we see no legally significant impact or consequence on the abortion decision or on the physician-patient relationship. We naturally assume, furthermore, that these recordkeeping and record-maintaining provisions will be interpreted and enforced by Missouri's Division of Health in the light of our decision with respect to the Act's other provisions, and that, of course, they will not be utilized in such a way as to accomplish, through the sheer burden of recordkeeping detail, what we have held to be an otherwise unconstitutional restriction....

. . .

G

Standard of care. Appellee Danforth appeals from the unanimous decision of the District Court that § 6(1) of the Act is unconstitutional. That section provides:

"...No person who performs or induces an abortion shall fail to exercise that degree of professional skill, care and diligence to preserve the life and health of the fetus which such person would be required to exercise in order to preserve the life and health of any fetus intended to be born and not aborted. Any physician or person assisting in the abortion who shall fail to take such measures to encourage or to sustain the life of the child, and the death of the child results, shall be deemed guilty of manslaughter.... Further, such physician or other person shall be liable in an action for damages."

The District Court held that the first sentence was unconstitutionally overbroad because it failed to exclude from its reach the stage of pregnancy prior to viability.

The Attorney General argues that the District Court's interpretation is erroneous and unnecessary. He claims that the first sentence of § 6(1) establishes only the general standard of care that applies to the person who performs the abortion, and that the second sentence describes the circumstances when that standard of care applies, namely, when a live child results from the procedure. Thus, the first sentence, it is said, despite its reference to the fetus, has no application until a live birth results.

The appellants, of course, agree with the District Court. They take the position that § 6(1) imposes its standard of care upon the person performing the abortion even though the procedure takes place before viability. They argue that the statute on its face effectively precludes abortion and was meant to do just that. . . .

. . .

As the provision now reads, it impermissibly requires the physician to preserve the life and health of the fetus, whatever the stage of pregnancy. The fact that the second sentence of § 6(1) refers to a criminal penalty where the physician fails "to take such measures to encourage or to sustain the life of the *child*, and the death of the *child* results" (emphasis supplied), simply does not modify the duty imposed by the previous sentence or limit that duty to pregnancies that have reached the stage of viability. . . .

. . .

The judgment of the District Court is affirmed in part and reversed in part and the case is remanded for further proceedings consistent with this opinion.

It is so ordered.

. . .

Mr. Justice Stewart, with whom Mr. Justice Powell joins, concurring.

While joining the Court's opinion, I write separately to indicate my understanding of some of the constitutional issues raised by this case.

With respect to the definition of viability in § 2(2) of the Act, it seems to me that the critical consideration is that the statutory definition has almost no operative significance. The State has merely required physicians performing abortions to *certify* that the fetus to be aborted is not viable. While the physician may be punished for failing to issue a certification, he may not be punished for erroneously concluding that the fetus is not viable. . . .

. . .

As to the provision of the law that requires a husband's consent to an abortion, § 3(3), the primary issue that it raises is whether the State may constitutionally recognize and give effect to a right on his part to participate in the decision to abort a jointly conceived child. This seems to me a rather more difficult problem than the Court acknowledges. Previous decisions have recognized that a man's right to father children and enjoy the association of his offspring is a constitutionally protected freedom. But the Court has recognized as well that the Constitution protects "a *woman's* decision whether or not to terminate her pregnancy." In assessing the constitutional validity of § 3(3) we are called upon to choose between these competing rights. I agree with the Court that since "it is the woman who physically bears the child and who is the more directly and immediately affected by the pregnancy ... the balance weighs in her favor."

With respect to the state law's requirement of parental consent, § 3(4), I think it clear that its primary constitutional deficiency lies in its imposition of an absolute limitation on the minor's right to obtain an abortion. ...

．　．　．

There can be little doubt that the State furthers a constitutionally permissible end by encouraging an unmarried pregnant minor to seek the help and advice of her parents in making the very important decision whether or not to bear a child. That is a grave decision, and a girl of tender years, under emotional stress, may be ill-equipped to make it without mature advice and emotional support. It seems unlikely that she will obtain adequate counsel and support from the attending physician at an abortion clinic, where abortions for pregnant minors frequently take place. ...

．　．　．

Mr. Justice White, with whom The Chief Justice and Mr. Justice Rehnquist join, concurring in part and dissenting in part.

．　．　．

Section 3(3) of the Act provides that a married woman may not obtain an abortion without her husband's consent. The Court strikes down this statute in one sentence. It says that "since the State cannot ... proscribe abortion ... the State cannot delegate authority to any particular person, even the spouse, to prevent abortion. .." But the State is not—under

§ 3(3)—delegating to the husband the power to vindicate the *State's* interest in the future life of the fetus. It is instead recognizing that the husband has an interest of his own in the life of the fetus which should not be extinguished by the unilateral decision of the wife. . . It is truly surprising that the majority finds in the United States Constitution, as it must in order to justify the result it reaches, a rule that the State must assign a greater value to a mother's decision to cut off a potential human life by abortion than to a father's decision to let it mature into a live child. Such a rule cannot be found there, nor can it be found in Roe v. Wade. . . .

. . .

Section 3(4) requires that an unmarried woman under 18 years of age obtain the consent of a parent or a person in loco parentis as a condition to an abortion. Once again the Court strikes the provision down in a sentence. . . The abortion decision is unquestionably important and has irrevocable consequences whichever way it is made. Missouri is entitled to protect the minor unmarried woman from making the decision in a way which is not in her own best interests, and it seeks to achieve this goal by requiring parental consultation and consent. This is the traditional way by which States have sought to protect children from their own immature and improvident decisions; and there is absolutely no reason expressed by the majority why the State may not utilize that method here. . . .

. . .

If section [6(1)] is read in any way other than through a microscope, it is plainly intended to require that, where a "fetus . . . [may have] the capability of meaningful life outside the mother's womb," the abortion be handled in a way which is designed to preserve that life notwithstanding the mother's desire to terminate it. Indeed, even looked at through a microscope the statute seems to go no further. It requires a physician to exercise "*that* degree of professional skill . . . to preserve the fetus," which he would be required to exercise if the mother wanted a live child. Plainly, if the pregnancy is to be terminated at a time when there is no chance of life outside the womb, a physician would not be required to exercise any care or skill to preserve the life of the fetus during abortion no matter what the mother's desires. . . .

. . .

Incredibly, the Court reads the statute instead to require "the physician to preserve the life and health of the fetus, whatever the stage of pregnancy," thereby attributing to the Missouri Legislature the strange intention of passing a statute with absolutely no chance of surviving constitutional challenge under Roe v. Wade, . . .

.   .   .

Mr. Justice Stevens, concurring in part and dissenting in part.

.   .   .

If two abortion procedures had been equally accessible to Missouri women, in my judgment the United States Constitution would not prevent the State legislature from outlawing the one it found to be the less safe even though its conclusion might not reflect a unanimous consensus of informed medical opinion. However, the record indicates that when the Missouri statute was enacted, a prohibition of the saline amniocentesis procedure was almost tantamount to a prohibition of any abortion in the State after the first 12 weeks of pregnancy. Such a prohibition is inconsistent with the essential holding of Roe v Wade and therefore cannot stand.

In my opinion, however, the parental consent requirement is consistent with the holding in Roe. The State's interest in the welfare of its young citizens justifies a variety of protective measures. Because he may not foresee the consequences of his decision, a minor may not make an enforceable bargain. He may not lawfully work or travel where he pleases, or even attend exhibitions of constitutionally protected adult motion pictures. Persons below a certain age may not marry without parental consent. Indeed, such consent is essential even when the young woman is already pregnant. The State's interest in protecting a young person from harm justifies the imposition of restraints on his or her freedom even though comparable restraints on adults would be constitutionally impermissible. Therefore, the holding in Roe v Wade that the abortion decision is entitled to constitutional protection merely emphasizes the importance of the decision; it does not lead to the conclusion that the state legislature has no power to enact legislation for the purpose of protecting a young pregnant woman from the consequences of an incorrect decision. . . .

.   .   .

If there is no parental consent requirement, many minors will submit to the abortion procedure without ever informing their parents. An assumption that the parental reaction will be hostile, disparaging or violent no doubt persuades many children simply to bypass parental counsel which would in fact be loving, supportive and, indeed, for some indispensable. It is unrealistic, in my judgment, to assume that every parent-child relationship is either (a) so perfect that communication and accord will take place routinely or (b) so imperfect that the absence of communication reflects the child's correct prediction that the parent will exercise his or her veto arbitrarily to further a selfish interest rather than the child's interest. A state legislature may conclude that most parents will be primarily interested in the welfare of their children, and further, that the imposition of a parental consent requirement is an appropriate method of giving the parents an opportunity to foster that welfare by helping a pregnant distressed child to make and to implement a correct decision. . . .

·   ·   ·

The Court seems to assume that the capacity to conceive a child and the judgment of the physician are the only constitutionally permissible yardsticks for determining whether a young woman can independently make the abortion decision. I doubt the accuracy of the Court's empirical judgment. Even if it were correct, however, as a matter of constitutional law I think a State has power to conclude otherwise and to select a chronological age as its standard.

In short, the State's interest in the welfare of its young citizens is sufficient, in my judgment, to support the parental consent requirement.

House Joint Resolution 503
(South Dakota)

A typical state call for a constitutional convention is this one from South Dakota, presented to Congress April 4, 1977. [123 *Congressional Record* 10335]

A joint resolution, making application to the Congress of the United States to call a convention for the purpose of proposing a human life amendment to the Constitution of the United States in accordance with article V of said Constitution.

Whereas, millions of abortions have been performed in the United States since the abortion decision of the Supreme Court of January 22, 1973; and

Whereas, the Congress of the United States has not to date proposed, subject to ratification, a human life amendment to the Constitution of the United States; and

Whereas, in the event of such congressional inaction, article V of the Constitution of the United States grants to the states the right to initiate constitutional change by applications from the Legislatures of two-thirds of the several states to the Congress, calling for a constitutional convention; and

Whereas, the Congress of the United States is required by the Constitution to call such a convention upon the receipt of applications from the Legislatures of two-thirds of the several states: be it resolved, by the House of Representatives of the State of South Dakota, the Senate concurring therein:

That the Legislature of the state of South Dakota does hereby make application to the Congress of the United States to call a convention for the sole purpose of proposing an amendment to the Constitution of the United States [which] would protect the life of all human beings, including unborn children; be it further

Resolved, That this application shall constitute a continuing application for such convention pursuant to article V of the Constitution of the United States until the Legislatures of two-thirds of the states shall have made like applications and such convention shall have been called by the Congress of the United States; be it further

Resolved, That certified copies of this resolution be presented to the President of the Senate of the United States, the Speaker of the House of Representatives of the United States, the Clerk of the House of Representatives of the United States, and to each Member of the Congress from this state attesting the adoption of this joint resolution by the Legislature of the state of South Dakota.

·   ·   ·

Maher v. Roe

432 U.S. 464, 53 L Ed 2d 484, 97 S Ct 2376 (1977)

Implementing the Medical Assistance Program (Medicaid) of Title XIX of the Social Security Act, Connecticut refused to fund voluntary abortions. In addition to aiding only medically necessary abortions, the state also required 1) that the physician certify and explain the necessity, 2) that the abortion be performed in an accredited hospital or licensed clinic, 3) that the mother request the abortion in writing, and 4) that prior approval of the Department of Social Services be obtained. Two indigent women desiring nontherapeutic abortions challenged these regulations as denying both equal protection and due process as guaranteed by the Fourteenth Amendment. A three-judge district court granted relief and direct appeal to the Supreme Court followed.

. . .

Mr. Justice Powell delivered the opinion of the Court.

In Beal v Doe, we hold today that Title XIX of the Social Security Act does not require the funding of nontherapeutic abortions as a condition of participation in the joint federal-state medicaid program established by that statute. In this case, as a result of our decision in Beal, we must decide whether the Constitution requires a participating State to pay for nontherapeutic abortions when it pays for childbirth.

A regulation of the Connecticut Welfare Department limits state medicaid benefits for first trimester abortions to those that are "medically necessary," a term defined to include psychiatric necessity. Connecticut enforces this limitation through a system of prior authorization from its Department of Social Services. In order to obtain authorization for a first trimester abortion, the hospital or clinic where the abortion is to be performed must submit, among other things, a certificate from the patient's attending physician stating that the abortion is medically necessary.

This attack on the validity of the Connecticut regulation was brought against Appellant Maher, the Commissioner of Social Services, by

Appellees Doe and Roe, two indigent women who were unable to obtain a physician's certificate of medical necessity. . . .

.   .   .

Although it found no independent constitutional right to a state-financed abortion, the District Court held that the Equal Protection Clause forbids the exclusion of nontherapeutic abortions from a state welfare program that generally subsidizes the medical expenses incident to pregnancy and childbirth. The court found implicit in Roe v Wade, and Doe v Bolton, the view that "abortion and childbirth, when stripped of the sensitive moral arguments surrounding the abortion controversy, are simply two alternative medical methods of dealing with pregnancy. . ." [T]he court held that the Connecticut program "weights the choice of the pregnant mother against choosing to exercise her constitutionally protected right" to a nontherapeutic abortion and "thus infringes upon a fundamental interest." The court found no state interest to justify this infringement. The State's fiscal interest was held to be "wholly chimerical because abortion is the least expensive medical response to a pregnancy." And any moral objection to abortion was deemed constitutionally irrelevant:

> "The state may not justify its refusal to pay for one type of expense arising from pregnancy on the basis that it morally opposes such an expenditure of money. To sanction such a justification would be to permit discrimination against those seeking to exercise a constitutional right on the basis that the state simply does not approve of the exercise of that right."

.   .   .

The Constitution imposes no obligation on the States to pay the pregnancy-related medical expenses of indigent women, or indeed to pay any of the medical expenses of indigents. But when a State decides to alleviate some of the hardships of poverty by providing medical care, the manner in which it dispenses benefits is subject to constitutional limitations. Appellees' claim is that Connecticut must accord equal treatment to both abortion and childbirth, and may not evidence a policy preference by funding only the medical expenses incident to childbirth. This challenge to the classifications established by the Connecticut regulation presents a question arising under the Equal Protection Clause of the Fourteenth Amendment. . . .

. . .

[W]e think the District Court erred in holding that the Connecticut regulation violated the Equal Protection Clause of the Fourteenth Amendment.

This case involves no discrimination against a suspect class. An indigent woman desiring an abortion does not come within the limited category of disadvantaged classes so recognized by our cases. Nor does the fact that the impact of the regulation falls upon those who cannot pay lead to a different conclusion. In a sense, every denial of welfare to an indigent creates a wealth classification as compared to nonindigents who are able to pay for the desired goods or services. But this Court has never held that financial need alone identifies a suspect class for purposes of equal protection analysis. Accordingly, the central question in this case is whether the regulation "impinges upon a fundamental right explicitly or implicitly protected by the Constitution." . . .

. . .

[T]he right in Roe v Wade can be understood only by considering both the woman's interest and the nature of the State's interference with it. Roe did not declare an unqualified "constitutional right to an abortion," as the District Court seemed to think. Rather, the right protects the woman from unduly burdensome interference with her freedom to decide whether to terminate her pregnancy. It implies no limitation on the authority of a State to make a value judgment favoring childbirth over abortion, and to implement that judgment by the allocation of public funds.

The Connecticut regulation before us is different in kind from the laws invalidated in our previous abortion decisions. The Connecticut regulation places no obstacles—absolute or otherwise—in the pregnant woman's path to an abortion. An indigent woman who desires an abortion suffers no disadvantage as a consequence of Connecticut's decision to fund childbirth; she continues as before to be dependent on private sources for the service she desires. The State may have made childbirth a more attractive alternative, thereby influencing the woman's decision, but it has imposed no restriction on access to abortions that was not already there. The indigency that may make it difficult—and in some cases, perhaps, impossible—for some women to have abortions is neither created nor in any way affected by the Connecticut regulation. We conclude that the

Connecticut regulation does not impinge upon the fundamental right recognized in Roe.

Our conclusion signals no retreat from Roe or the cases applying it. There is a basic difference between direct state interference with a protected activity and state encouragement of an alternative activity consonant with legislative policy. Constitutional concerns are greatest when the State attempts to impose its will by force of law; the State's power to encourage actions deemed to be in the public interest is necessarily far broader. . . .

. . .

The question remains whether Connecticut's regulation can be sustained under the less demanding test of rationality that applies in the absence of a suspect classification or the impingement of a fundamental right. This test requires that the distinction drawn between childbirth and nontherapeutic abortion by the regulation be "rationally related" to a "constitutionally permissible" purpose. . . We hold that the Connecticut funding scheme satisfies this standard.

Roe itself explicitly acknowledged the State's strong interest in protecting the potential life of the fetus. That interest exists throughout the pregnancy, "grow[ing] in substantiality as the woman approaches term." Because the pregnant woman carries a potential human being, she "cannot be isolated in her privacy. . . [Her] privacy is no longer sole and any right of privacy she possesses must be measured accordingly." The State unquestionably has a "strong and legitimate interest in encouraging normal childbirth," an interest honored over the centuries.[11] Nor can there be any question that the Connecticut regulation rationally furthers that interest. The medical costs associated with childbirth are substantial, and have increased significantly in recent years. As recognized by the District Court in this case, such costs are significantly greater than those normally associated with elective abortions during the first trimester. The subsidizing of costs incident to childbirth is a rational means of encouraging childbirth.

---

11. In addition to the direct interest in protecting the fetus, a State may have legitimate demographic concerns about its rate of population growth. Such concerns are basic to the future of the State and in some circumstances could constitute a substantial reason for departure from a position of neutrality between abortion and childbirth.

We certainly are not unsympathetic to the plight of an indigent woman who desires an abortion, but "the Constitution does not provide judicial remedies for every social and economic ill..." Our cases uniformly have accorded the States a wider latitude in choosing among competing demands for limited public funds. In Dandridge v Williams, despite recognition that laws and regulations allocating welfare funds involve "the most basic economic needs of impoverished human beings," we held that classifications survive equal protection challenge when a "reasonable basis" for the classification is shown. As the preceding discussion makes clear, the state interest in encouraging normal childbirth exceeds this minimal level.

The decision whether to expend state funds for nontherapeutic abortion is fraught with judgments of policy and value over which opinions are sharply divided. Our conclusion that the Connecticut regulation is constitutional is not based on a weighing of its wisdom or social desirability, for this Court does not strike down state laws "because they may be unwise, improvident, or out of harmony with a particular school of thought." Indeed, when an issue involves policy choices as sensitive as those implicated by public funding of nontherapeutic abortions, the appropriate forum for their resolution in a democracy is the legislature. We should not forget that "legislatures are ultimate guardians of the liberties and welfare of the people in quite as great a degree as the courts."

In conclusion, we emphasize that our decision today does not proscribe government funding of nontherapeutic abortions. It is open to Congress to require provision of medicaid benefits for such abortions as a condition of state participation in the medicaid program. Also, Connecticut is free—through normal democratic processes—to decide that such benefits should be provided. We hold only that the Constitution does not require a judicially imposed resolution of these difficult issues....

• • •

The judgment of the District Court is reversed, and the case is remanded for further proceedings consistent with this opinion.

• • •

Mr. Chief Justice Burger, concurring.

• • •

From time to time, every state legislature determines that, as a matter of sound public policy, the government ought to provide certain health and social services to its citizens. Encouragement of childbirth and child care is not a novel undertaking in this regard. Various governments, both in this country and in others, have made such a determination for centuries. In recent times, they have similarly provided educational services. The decision to provide any one of these services—or not to provide them—is not required by the Federal Constitution. Nor does the providing of a particular service require, as a matter of federal constitutional law, the provision of another....

.   .   .

Mr. Justice Brennan, with whom Mr. Justice Marshall and Mr. Justice Blackmun join, dissenting.

.   .   .

[A] distressing insensitivity to the plight of impoverished pregnant women is inherent in the Court's analysis. The stark reality for too many, not just "some," indigent pregnant women is that indigency makes access to competent licensed physicians not merely "difficult" but "impossible." As a practical matter, many indigent women will feel they have no choice but to carry their pregnancies to term because the State will pay for the associated medical services, even though they would have chosen to have abortions if the State had also provided funds for that procedure, or indeed if the State had provided funds for neither procedure. This disparity in funding by the State clearly operates to coerce indigent pregnant women to bear children they would not otherwise choose to have, and just as clearly, this coercion can only operate upon the poor, who are uniquely the victims of this form of financial pressure. Mr. Justice Frankfurter's words are apt:

> "...To sanction such a ruthless consequence, inevitably resulting from a money hurdle erected by the State, would justify a latter-day Anatole France to add one more item to his ironic comments on the 'majestic equality' of the law. 'The law, in its majestic equality, forbids the rich as well as the poor to sleep under bridges, to beg in the streets, and to steal bread'...."

.   .   .

Roe v Wade and cases following it hold that an area of privacy invulnerable to the State's intrusion surrounds the decision of a pregnant woman whether or not to carry her pregnancy to term. The Connecticut scheme clearly infringes upon that area of privacy by bringing financial pressures on indigent women that force them to bear children they would not otherwise have. That is an obvious impairment of the fundamental right established by Roe. Yet the Court concludes that "the Connecticut regulation does not impinge upon [that] fundamental right." This conclusion is based on a perceived distinction, on the one hand, between the imposition of criminal penalties for the procurement of an abortion present in Roe v Wade and Doe v Bolton and the absolute prohibition present in Planned Parenthood of Missouri v Danforth, and, on the other, the assertedly lesser inhibition imposed by the Connecticut scheme. . . .

.   .   .

Doe v Bolton, the companion to Roe, in addition to striking down the Georgia criminal prohibition against elective abortions, struck down the procedural requirements of certification of hospitals, of approval by a hospital committee, and of concurrence in the abortion decision by two doctors other than the woman's own doctor. None of these requirements operated as an absolute bar to elective abortions in the manner of the criminal prohibitions present in the other aspect of the case or in Roe, but this was not sufficient to save them from unconstitutionality. In Planned Parenthood, supra, we struck down a requirement for spousal consent to an elective abortion which the Court characterizes today simply as an "absolute obstacle" to a woman obtaining an abortion. But the obstacle was "absolute" only in the limited sense that a woman who was unable to persuade her spouse to agree to an elective abortion was prevented from obtaining one. Any woman whose husband agreed, or could be persuaded to agree, was free to obtain an abortion, and the State never imposed directly any prohibition of its own. This requirement was qualitatively different from the criminal statutes that the Court today says are comparable, but we nevertheless found it unconstitutional. . . .

.   .   .

Finally, cases involving other fundamental rights also make clear that the Court's concept of what constitutes an impermissible infringement upon the fundamental right of a pregnant woman to choose to have an abortion makes new law. We have repeatedly found that infringements of fundamental rights are not limited to outright denials of those rights. First Amendment decisions have consistently held in a wide variety of contexts that the compelling state interest test is applicable not only to outright denials but also to restraints that make exercise of those rights more difficult. The compelling state interest test has been applied in voting cases, even where only relatively small infringements upon voting power, such as dilution of voting strength caused by malapportionment, have been involved... And indigents asserting a fundamental right of access to the courts have been excused payment of entry costs without being required first to show that their indigency was an absolute bar to access....

. . .

Until today, I had not thought the nature of the fundamental right established in Roe was open to question, let alone susceptible to the interpretation advanced by the Court. The fact that the Connecticut scheme may not operate as an absolute bar preventing all indigent women from having abortions is not critical. What is critical is that the State has inhibited their fundamental right to make that choice free from state interference....

. . .

Mr. Justice Marshall, dissenting.

It is all too obvious that the governmental actions in these cases, ostensibly taken to "encourage" women to carry pregnancies to term, are in reality intended to impose a moral viewpoint that no State may constitutionally enforce. Roe v Wade, Doe v Bolton. Since efforts to overturn those decisions have been unsuccessful, the opponents of abortion have attempted every imaginable means to circumvent the commands of the Constitution and impose their moral choices upon the rest of society... The present cases involve the most vicious attacks yet devised. The impact of the regulations here falls tragically upon those among us least able to help or defend themselves. As the Court well knows, these regulations inevitably will have the practical effect of preventing nearly all poor women from obtaining safe and legal abortions....

. . .

I am appalled at the ethical bankruptcy of those who preach a "right to life" that means, under present social policies, a bare existence in utter misery for so many poor women and their children. . . .

.　.　.

It is no less disturbing that the effect of the challenged regulations will fall with great disparity upon women of minority races. Nonwhite women now obtain abortions at nearly twice the rate of whites, and it appears that almost 40 percent of minority women—more than five times the proportion of whites—are dependent upon medicaid for their health care. Even if this strongly disparate racial impact does not alone violate the Equal Protection Clause, "at some point a showing that state action has a devastating impact on the lives of minority racial groups must be relevant.". . .

.　.　.

When this Court decided Roe v Wade and Doe v Bolton, it properly embarked on a course of constitutional adjudication no less controversial than that begun by Brown v Board of Education. The abortion decisions are sound law and undoubtedly good policy. They have never been questioned by the Court and we are told that today's cases "signal no retreat from Roe or the cases applying it." The logic of those cases inexorably requires invalidation of the present enactments. Yet I fear that the Court's decisions will be an invitation to public officials, already under extraordinary pressure from well financed and carefully orchestrated lobbying campaigns, to approve more such restrictions. The effect will be to relegate millions of people to lives of poverty and despair. When elected leaders cower before public pressure, this Court, more than ever, must not shirk its duty to enforce the Constitution for the benefit of the poor and powerless.

.　.　.

Mr. Justice Blackmun, with whom Mr. Justice Brennan and Mr. Justice Marshall join, dissenting.

The court today . . . allows the States, and such municipalities as choose to do so, to accomplish indirectly what the Court in Roe v Wade, and Doe v Bolton—by a substantial majority and with some emphasis, I had thought—said they could not do directly. The Court concedes the existence of a constitutional right but denies the realization and enjoyment of that right on the ground that existence and realization are separate and distinct. For the individual woman concerned, indigent and financially helpless, as the Court's opinions ... concede her to be, the result is punitive and tragic. Implicit in the Court's holdings is the condescension that she may go elsewhere for her abortion. I find that disingenuous and alarming, almost reminiscent of "let them eat cake." ...

.   .   .

There is another world "out there," the existence of which the Court, I suspect, either chooses to ignore or fears to recognize. And so the cancer of poverty will continue to grow. This is a sad day for those who regard the Constitution as a force that would serve justice to all evenhandedly and, in so doing, would better the lot of the poorest among us.

The Hyde Amendments

The Hyde Amendment (named for its original sponsor Henry Hyde of Illinois) was attached to Appropriation Acts for the Department of Health, Education and Welfare beginning in 1976.

Hyde Amendment 1976 [90 Stat 1418, 1434]: None of the funds contained in this Act shall be used to perform abortions except where the life of the mother would be endangered if the fetus were carried to term.

Hyde Amendment 1977 and 1978 [91 Stat. 1460, 92 Stat. 1567, 1586]: [N]one of the funds provided for in this paragraph may be used to perform abortions except where the life of the mother would be endangered if the fetus were carried to term; or except for such medical procedures necessary for the victims of rape or incest, when such rape or incest has been reported promptly to a law enforcement agency or public health service; or except in those instances where severe and long-lasting physical health damage to the mother could result if the pregnancy were carried to term when so determined by two physicians.

Hyde Amendment 1979 [93 Stat. 923, 926]: [N]one of the funds provided in this joint resolution shall be used to perform abortions except where the life of the mother would be endangered if the fetus were carried to term; or except for such medical procedures necessary for the victims of rape or incest when such rape or incest has been reported promptly to a law enforcement agency or public health service.

Harris v. McRae

448 U.S. 297, 65 L Ed 2d 784, 100 S Ct 2671 (1980)

The facts are contained in the opinion of the Court.

. . .

Mr. Justice Stewart delivered the opinion of the Court.

This case presents statutory and constitutional questions concerning the public funding of abortions under Title XIX of the Social Security Act, commonly known as the "Medicaid" Act, and recent annual appropriations acts containing the so-called "Hyde Amendment.". . .

. . .

Since September 1976, Congress has prohibited—either by an amendment to the annual appropriations bill for the Department of Health, Education, and Welfare or by a joint resolution—the use of any federal funds to reimburse the cost of abortions under the Medicaid program except under certain specified circumstances. . . .

. . .

[Respondents] alleged that the Hyde Amendment violated the First, Fourth, Fifth, and Ninth Amendments of the Constitution insofar as it limited the funding of abortions to those necessary to save the life of the mother, while permitting the funding of costs associated with childbirth. Although the sole named defendant was the Secretary of Health, Education, and Welfare, the District Court permitted Senators James L. Buckley and Jesse A. Helms and Representative Henry J. Hyde to intervene as defendants. . . .

. . .

After a lengthy trial, which inquired into the medical reasons for abortions and the diverse religious views on the subject, the District Court filed an opinion and entered a judgment invalidating all versions of the Hyde Amendment on constitutional grounds. . . . The Court concluded that the Hyde Amendment violates the equal protection guarantee because, in its view, the decision of Congress to fund medically necessary services generally but only certain medically necessary abortions serves no legitimate governmental interest. As to the Free Exercise Clause of the First Amendment, the Court held that insofar as a woman's decision to seek a medically necessary abortion may be a product of her religious beliefs under certain Protestant and Jewish tenets, the funding restrictions of the Hyde Amendment violate that constitutional guarantee as well. . . .

. . .

It is well settled that if a case may be decided on either statutory or constitutional grounds, this Court, for sound jurisprudential reasons, will inquire first into the statutory question. This practice reflects the deeply noted doctrine "that we ought not to pass on questions of constitutionality . . . unless such adjudication is unavoidable." Accordingly, we turn first to the question whether Title XIX requires a State that participates in the Medicaid program to continue to fund those medically necessary abortions for which federal reimbursement is unavailable under the Hyde Amendment. . . .

. . .

Since the Congress that enacted Title XIX did not intend a participating State to assume a unilateral funding obligation for any health service in an approved Medicaid plan, it follows that Title XIX does not require a participating State to include in its plan any services for which a subsequent Congress has withheld federal funding. Title XIX was designed as a cooperative program of shared financial responsibility, not as a device for the Federal Government to compel a State to provide services that Congress itself is unwilling to fund. Thus, if Congress chooses to withdraw federal funding for a particular service, a State is not obliged to continue to pay for that service as a condition of continued federal financial support of other services. This is not to say that Congress may not now depart from the original design of Title XIX under which the Federal Government shares the financial responsibility for expenses incurred under an approved Medicaid plan. It is only to say that, absent an indication of contrary legislative intent by a subsequent Congress, Title XIX does not obligate a participating State to pay for those medical services for which federal reimbursement is unavailable. . . .

. . .

Having determined that Title XIX does not obligate a participating State to pay for those medically necessary abortions for which Congress has withheld federal funding, we must consider the constitutional validity of the Hyde Amendment. . . .

. . .

We address first the appellees' argument that the Hyde Amendment, by restricting the availability of certain medically necessary abortions under Medicaid, impinges on the "liberty" protected by the Due Process Clause. . . .

. . .

The Hyde Amendment, like the Connecticut welfare regulation at issue in Maher, places no governmental obstacle in the path of a woman who chooses to terminate her pregnancy, but rather, by means of unequal subsidization of abortion and other medical services, encourages alternative activity deemed in the public interest. The present case does differ factually from Maher insofar as that case involved a failure to fund nontherapeutic abortions, whereas the Hyde Amendment withholds funding of certain medically necessary abortions. Accordingly, the appellees argue that because the Hyde Amendment affects a significant interest not present or asserted in Maher—the interest of a woman in protecting her health during pregnancy—and because that interest lies at the core of the personal constitutional freedom recognized in Wade, the present case is constitutionally different from Maher. It is the appellees' view that to the extent that the Hyde Amendment withholds funding for certain medically necessary abortions, it clearly impinges on the constitutional principle recognized in Wade.

It is evident that a woman's interest in protecting her health was an important theme in Wade. In concluding that the freedom of a woman to decide whether to terminate her pregnancy falls within the personal liberty protected by the Due Process Clause, the Court in Wade emphasized the fact that the woman's decision carries with it significant personal health implications—both physical and psychological. In fact although the Court in Wade recognized that the state interest in protecting potential life becomes sufficiently compelling in the period after fetal viability to justify an absolute criminal prohibition of nontherapeutic abortions, the Court held that even after fetal viability a State may not prohibit abortions "necessary to preserve the life or health of the mother." Because even the compelling interest of the State in protecting potential life after fetal viability was held to be insufficient to outweigh a woman's decision to protect her life or health, it could be argued that the freedom of a woman to decide whether to terminate her pregnancy for health reasons does in fact lie at the core of the constitutional liberty identified in Wade.

But, regardless of whether the freedom of a woman to choose to terminate her pregnancy for health reasons lies at the core or the periphery of the due process liberty recognized in Wade, it simply does not follow that a woman's freedom of choice carries with it a constitutional entitlement to the financial resources to avail herself of the full range of protected choices. The reason why was explained in Maher: although government may not place obstacles in the path of a woman's exercise of her freedom of choice, it need not remove those not of its own creation. Indigency falls in the latter category. The financial constraints that restrict an indigent woman's ability to enjoy the full range of constitutionally protected freedom of choice are the product not of governmental restrictions on access to abortions, but rather of her indigency. Although Congress has opted to subsidize medically necessary services generally, but not certain medically necessary abortions, the fact remains that the Hyde Amendment leaves an indigent woman with at least the same range of choice in deciding whether to obtain a medically necessary abortion as she would have had if Congress had chosen to subsidize no health care costs at all. We are thus not persuaded that the Hyde Amendment impinges on the constitutionally protected freedom of choice recognized in Wade.

Although the liberty protected by the Due Process Clause affords protection against unwarranted government interference with freedom of choice in the context of certain personal decisions, it does not confer an entitlement to such funds as may be necessary to realize all the advantages of that freedom. To hold otherwise would mark a drastic change in our understanding of the Constitution. It cannot be that because government may not prohibit the use of contraceptives, Griswold v Connecticut, or prevent parents from sending their child to a private school, Pierce v Society of Sisters, government, therefore, has an affirmative constitutional obligation to ensure that all persons have the financial resources to obtain contraceptives or send their children to private schools. To translate the limitation on governmental power implicit in the Due Process Clause into an affirmative funding obligation would require Congress to subsidize the medically necessary abortion of an indigent woman even if Congress had not enacted a Medicaid program to subsidize other medically necessary services. Nothing in the Due Process Clause supports such an extraordinary result. Whether freedom of choice that is constitutionally protected warrants federal subsidization is a question for Congress to answer, not a matter of constitutional entitlement. Accordingly, we conclude that the Hyde Amendment does not impinge on the due process liberty recognized in Wade.

The appellees also argue that the Hyde Amendment contravenes rights secured by the Religion Clauses of the First Amendment. . . .

.　.　.

[T]he District Court properly concluded that the Hyde Amendment does not run afoul of the Establishment Clause. Although neither a State nor the Federal Government can constitutionally "pass laws which aid one religion, aid all religions, or prefer one religion over another," it does not follow that a statute violates the Establishment Clause because it "happens to coincide or harmonize with the tenets of some or all religions." That the Judaeo-Christian religions oppose stealing does not mean that a State or the Federal Government may not, consistent with the Establishment Clause, enact laws prohibiting larceny. The Hyde Amendment, as the District Court noted, is as much a reflection of "traditionalist" values towards abortion, as it is an embodiment of the views of any particular religion. . . .

.　.　.

We need not address the merits of the appellees' arguments concerning the Free Exercise Clause, because the appellees lack standing to raise a free exercise challenge to the Hyde Amendment. . . .

.　.　.

It remains to be determined whether the Hyde Amendment violates the equal protection component of the Fifth Amendment. This challenge is premised on the fact that, although federal reimbursement is available under Medicaid for medically necessary services generally, the Hyde Amendment does not permit federal reimbursement of all medically necessary abortions. The District Court held, and the appellees argue here, that this selective subsidization violates the constitutional guarantee of equal protection.

The guarantee of equal protection under the Fifth Amendment is not a source of substantive rights or liberties, but rather a right to be free from invidious discrimination in statutory classifications and other governmental activity. It is well-settled that where a statutory classification does not itself impinge on a right or liberty protected by the Constitution, the validity of classification must be sustained unless "the classification rests on grounds wholly irrelevant to the achievement of [any legitimate governmental] objective." This presumption of constitutional validity, however, disappears if a statutory classification is predicated on criteria that are, in a constitutional sense, "suspect," the principal example of which is a classification based on race, . . .

. . .

For the reasons stated above, we have already concluded that the Hyde Amendment violates no constitutionally protected substantive rights. We now conclude as well that it is not predicated on a constitutionally suspect classification. . . .

. . .

Here, as in Maher, the principal impact of the Hyde amendment falls on the indigent. But that fact does not itself render the funding restriction constitutionally invalid, for this Court has held repeatedly that poverty, standing alone, is not a suspect classification. . . .

. . .

The remaining question then is whether the Hyde Amendment is rationally related to a legitimate governmental objective. It is the Government's position that the Hyde Amendment bears a rational relationship to its legitimate interest in protecting the potential life of the fetus. We agree. . . .

442

. . .

[T]he Hyde Amendment, by encouraging childbirth except in the most urgent circumstances, is rationally related to the legitimate governmental objective of protecting potential life. By subsidizing the medical expenses of indigent women who carry their pregnancies to term while not subsidizing the comparable expenses of women who undergo abortions (except those whose lives are threatened), Congress has established incentives that make childbirth a more attractive alternative than abortion for persons eligible for Medicaid. These incentives bear a direct relationship to the legitimate congressional interest in protecting potential life. Nor is it irrational that Congress has authorized federal reimbursement for medically necessary services generally, but not for certain medically necessary abortions. Abortion is inherently different from other medical procedures, because no other procedure involves the purposeful termination of a potential life. . . .

. . .

Where, as here, the Congress has neither invaded a substantive constitutional right or freedom, nor enacted legislation that purposefully operates to the detriment of a suspect class, the only requirement of equal protection is that congressional action be rationally related to a legitimate governmental interest. The Hyde Amendment satisfies that standard. It is not the mission of this Court or any other to decide whether the balance of competing interests reflected in the Hyde Amendment is wise social policy. If that were our mission, not every Justice who has subscribed to the judgment of the Court today could have done so. But we cannot, in the name of the Constitution, overturn duly enacted statutes simply "because they may be unwise, improvident, or out of harmony with a particular school of thought.". . .

. . .

Accordingly, the judgment of the District Court·is reversed, and the case is remanded to that court for further proceedings consistent with this opinion.

. . .

Mr. Justice White, concurring.
I join the Court's opinion and judgment with these additional remarks.

.　.　.

The constitutional right recognized in Roe v Wade was the right to choose to undergo an abortion without coercive interference by the government. As the Court points out, Roe v Wade did not purport to adjudicate a right to have abortions funded by the government, but only to be free from unreasonable official interference with private choice. At an appropriate stage in a pregnancy, for example, abortions could be prohibited to implement the governmental interest in potential life, but in no case to the damage of the health of the mother, whose choice to suffer an abortion rather than risk her health the government was forced to respect. . . .

.　.　.

The government does not seek to interfere with or to impose any coercive restraint on the choice of any woman to have an abortion. The woman's choice remains unfettered, the government is not attempting to use its interest in life to justify a coercive restraint, and hence in disbursing its Medicaid funds it is free to implement rationally what Roe v Wade recognized to be its legitimate interest in a potential life by covering the medical costs of childbirth but denying funds for abortions. . . .

.　.　.

Mr. Justice Brennan, with whom Mr. Justice Marshall and Mr. Justice Blackmun join, dissenting.

.　.　.

I write separately to express my continuing disagreement with the Court's mischaracterization of the nature of the fundamental right recognized in Roe v Wade, and its misconception of the manner in which that right is infringed by federal and state legislation withdrawing all funding for medically necessary abortions.

Roe v Wade held that the constitutional right to personal privacy encompasses a woman's decision whether or not to terminate her pregnancy. Roe and its progeny established that the pregnant woman has a right to be free from state interference with her choice to have an abortion — a right which, at least prior to the end of the first trimester, absolutely prohibits any governmental regulation of that highly personal decision. The proposition for which these cases stand thus is not that the

State is under an affirmative obligation to ensure access to abortions for all who may desire them; it is that the State must refrain from wielding its enormous power and influence in a manner that might burden the pregnant woman's freedom to choose whether to have an abortion. The Hyde Amendment's denial of public funds for medically necessary abortions plainly intrudes upon this constitutionally protected decision, for both by design and in effect it serves to coerce indigent pregnant women to bear children that they would otherwise elect not to have.

When viewed in the context of the Medicaid program to which it is appended, it is obvious that the Hyde Amendment is nothing less than an attempt by Congress to circumvent the dictates of the Constitution and achieve indirectly what Roe v Wade said it could not do directly. Under Title XIX of the Social Security Act, the Federal Government reimburses participating States for virtually all medically necessary services it provides to the categorically needy. The sole limitation of any significance is the Hyde Amendment's prohibition against the use of any federal funds to pay for the costs of abortions (except where the life of the mother would be endangered if the fetus were carried to term). . . . [T]he Hyde Amendment is a transparent attempt by the Legislative Branch to impose the political majority's judgment of the morally acceptable and socially desirable preference on a sensitive and intimate decision that the Constitution entrusts to the individual. Worse yet, the Hyde Amendment does not foist that majoritarian viewpoint with equal measure upon everyone in our Nation, rich and poor alike; rather, it imposes that viewpoint only upon that segment of our society which, because of its position of political powerlessness, is least able to defend its privacy rights from the encroachments of state-mandated morality. The instant legislation thus calls for more exacting judicial review than in most other cases. "When elected leaders cower before public pressure, this Court, more than ever, must not shirk its duty to enforce the Constitution for the benefit of the poor and powerless.". . .

· · ·

By thus injecting coercive financial incentives favoring childbirth into a decision that is constitutionally guaranteed to be free from governmental intrusion, the Hyde Amendment deprives the indigent woman of her freedom to choose abortion over maternity, thereby impinging on the due process liberty right recognized in Roe v Wade. . . .

445

. . .

A poor woman in the early stages of pregnancy confronts two alternatives: she may elect either to carry the fetus to term or to have an abortion. In the abstract, of course, this choice is hers alone, and the Court rightly observes that the Hyde Amendment "places no governmental obstacle in the path of a woman who chooses to terminate her pregnancy." But the reality of the situation is that the Hyde Amendment has effectively removed this choice from the indigent woman's hands. By funding all of the expenses associated with childbirth and none of the expenses incurred in terminating pregnancy, the government literally makes an offer that the indigent woman cannot afford to refuse. It matters not that in this instance the government has used the carrot rather than the stick. What is critical is the realization that as a practical matter, many poverty-stricken women will choose to carry their pregnancy to term simply because the government provides funds for the associated medical services, even though these same women would have chosen to have an abortion if the government had also paid for that option, or indeed if the government had stayed out of the picture altogether and had defrayed the costs of neither procedure.

The fundamental flaw in the Court's due process analysis, then, is its failure to acknowledge that the discriminatory distribution of the benefits of governmental largesse can discourage the exercise of fundamental liberties just as effectively as can an outright denial of those rights through criminal and regulatory sanctions. Implicit in the Court's reasoning is the notion that as long as the government is not obligated to provide its citizens with certain benefits or privileges, it may condition the grant of such benefits on the recipient's relinquishment of his constitutional rights. . . .

. . .

I respectfully dissent.

. . .

Mr. Justice Marshall, dissenting.

. . .

Under the Hyde Amendment, federal funding is denied for abortions that are medically necessary and that are necessary to avert severe and permanent damage to the health of the mother. The Court's opinion studiously avoids recognizing the undeniable fact that for women eligible for Medicaid—poor women—denial of a Medicaid-funded abortion is equivalent to denial of legal abortion altogether. By definition, these women do not have the money to pay for an abortion themselves. If abortion is medically necessary and a funded abortion is unavailable, they must resort to back-alley butchers, attempt to induce an abortion themselves by crude and dangerous methods, or suffer the serious medical consequences of attempting to carry the fetus to term. Because legal abortion is not a realistic option for such women, the predictable result of the Hyde Amendment will be a significant increase in the number of poor women who will die or suffer significant health damage because of an inability to procure necessary medical services. . . .

. . .

The Court's decision today marks a retreat from Roe v Wade and represents a cruel blow to the most powerless members of our society. I dissent. . . .

. . .

The impact of the Hyde Amendment on indigent women falls into four major categories. First, the Hyde Amendment prohibits federal funding for abortions that are necessary in order to protect the health and sometimes the life of the mother. . . .

. . .

Second, federal funding is denied in cases in which severe mental disturbances will be created by unwanted pregnancies. The result of such psychological disturbances may be suicide, attempts at self-abortion, or child abuse. The Hyde Amendment makes no provision for funding in such cases.

Third, the Hyde Amendment denies funding for the majority of women whose pregnancies have been caused by rape or incest. The prerequisite of a report within 60 days serves to exclude those who are afraid of recounting what has happened or are in fear of unsympathetic treatment by the authorities. . . .

. . .

Finally, federal funding is unavailable in cases in which it is known that the fetus itself will be unable to survive. . . .

. . .

An optimistic estimate indicates that as many as 100 excess deaths may occur each year as a result of the Hyde Amendment. The record contains no estimate of the health damage that may occur to poor women, but it shows that it will be considerable.

The Court resolves the equal protection issue in this case through a relentlessly formalistic catechism. Adhering to its "two-tiered" approach to equal protection, the Court first decides that so-called strict scrutiny is not required because the Hyde Amendment does not violate the Due Process Clause and is not predicated on a constitutionally suspect classification. Therefore, "the validity of classification must be sustained unless 'the classification rests on grounds wholly irrelevant to the achievement of [any legitimate governmental] objective.' ". . .

. . .

I continue to believe that the rigid "two-tiered" approach is inappropriate and that the Constitution requires a more exacting standard of review than mere rationality in cases such as this one. Further, in my judgment the Hyde Amendment cannot pass constitutional muster even under the rational-basis standard of review. . . .

. . .

[W]hile it is now clear that traditional "strict scrutiny" is unavailable to protect the poor against classifications that disfavor them, I do not believe that legislation that imposes a crushing burden on indigent women can be treated with the same deference given to legislation distinguishing among business interests. . . .

. . .

The Court treats this case as though it were controlled by Maher. To the contrary, this case is the mirror image of Maher. The result in Maher turned on the fact that the legislation there under consideration discouraged only nontherapeutic, or medically unnecessary, abortions. In the Court's view, denial of Medicaid funding for nontherapeutic abortions was not a denial of equal protection because Medicaid funds were available only for medically necessary procedures. Thus the plaintiffs were seeking benefits which were not available to others similarly situated. I continue to believe that Maher was wrongly decided. But it is apparent that while the plaintiffs in Maher were seeking a benefit not available to others similarly situated, respondents are protesting their exclusion from a benefit that is available to all others similarly situated. This, it need hardly be said, is a crucial difference for equal protection purposes.

Under Title XIX and the Hyde Amendment, funding is available for essentially all necessary medical treatment for the poor. Respondents have met the statutory requirements for eligibility, but they are excluded because the treatment that is medically necessary involves the exercise of a fundamental right, the right to choose an abortion. In short, respondents have been deprived of a governmental benefit for which they are otherwise eligible, solely because they have attempted to exercise a constitutional right. The interest asserted by the government, the protection of fetal life, has been declared constitutionally subordinate to respondents' interest in preserving their lives and health by obtaining medically necessary treatment. Roe v Wade. And finally, the purpose of the legislation was to discourage the exercise of the fundamental right. In such circumstances the Hyde Amendment must be invalidated because it does not meet even the rational-basis standard of review....

· · ·

In today's decision, as in Maher v. Roe, the Court suggests that a withholding of funding imposes no real obstacle to a woman deciding whether to exercise her constitutionally protected procreative choice, even though the government is prepared to fund all other medically necessary expenses, including the expenses of childbirth. The Court perceives this result as simply a distinction between a "limitation on governmental power" and "an affirmative funding obligation." For a poor person attempting to exercise her "right" to freedom of choice, the difference is imperceptible. As my Brother Brennan has shown, the differential distribution of incentives—which the Court concedes is present here—can have precisely the same effect as an outright prohibition. It is no more sufficient an answer here than it was in Roe v Wade to say that " 'the appropriate forum' " for the resolution of sensitive policy choices is the legislature....

· · ·

Mr. Justice Blackmun, dissenting.

I join the dissent of Mr. Justice Brennan and agree wholeheartedly with his and Mr. Justice Stevens' respective observations and descriptions of what the Court is doing in this latest round of "abortion cases.". . . There is "condescension" in the Court's holding "that she may go elsewhere for her abortion"; this is "disingenuous and alarming"; the Government "punitively impresses upon a needy minority its own concepts of the socially desirable, the publicly acceptable, and the morally sound"; the "financial argument, of course, is specious"; there truly is "another world 'out there,' the existence of which the Court, I suspect, either chooses to ignore or fears to recognize"; the "cancer of poverty will continue to grow"; and "the lot of the poorest among us," once again, and still, is not to be bettered.

. . .

Mr. Justice Stevens, dissenting.

. . .

This case involves the pool of benefits that Congress created by enacting Title XIX of the Social Security Act in 1965. Individuals who satisfy two neutral statutory criteria—financial need and medical need—are entitled to equal access to that pool. The question is whether certain persons who satisfy those criteria may be denied access to benefits solely because they must exercise the constitutional right to have an abortion in order to obtain the medical care they need. Our prior cases plainly dictate the answer to that question.

A fundamentally different question was decided in Maher v Roe. Unlike these plaintiffs, the plaintiffs in Maher did not satisfy the neutral criterion of medical need; they sought a subsidy for nontherapeutic abortions—medical procedures which by definition they did not need. In rejecting that claim, the Court held that their constitutional right to choose that procedure did not impose a duty on the State to subsidize the exercise of that right. Nor did the fact that the State had undertaken to pay for the necessary medical care associated with childbirth require the State also to pay for abortions that were not necessary; for only necessary medical procedures satisfied the neutral statutory criteria. Nontherapeutic abortions were simply outside the ambit of the medical benefits program. . . .

. . .

This case involves a special exclusion of women who, by definition, are confronted with a choice between two serious harms: serious health damage to themselves on the one hand and abortion on the other. The competing interests are the interest in maternal health and the interest in protecting potential human life. It is now part of our law that the pregnant woman's decision as to which of these conflicting interests shall prevail is entitled to constitutional protection. . . .

.   .   .

If a woman has a constitutional right to place a higher value on avoiding either serious harm to her own health or perhaps an abnormal childbirth than on protecting potential life, the exercise of that right cannot provide the basis for the denial of a benefit to which she would otherwise be entitled. The Court's sterile equal protection analysis evades this critical though simple point. The Court focuses exclusively on the "legitimate interest in protecting the potential life of the fetus." It concludes that since the Hyde amendments further that interest, the exclusion they create is rational and therefore constitutional. But it is misleading to speak of the Government's legitimate interest in the fetus without reference to the context in which that interest was held to be legitimate. For Roe v Wade squarely held that the States may not protect that interest when a conflict with the interest in a pregnant woman's health exists. It is thus perfectly clear that neither the Federal Government nor the States may exclude a woman from medical benefits to which she would otherwise be entitled solely to further an interest in potential life when a physician, "in appropriate medical judgment," certifies that an abortion is necessary "for the preservation of the life or health of the mother." Roe v Wade. The Court totally fails to explain why this reasoning is not dispositive here.

It cannot be denied that the harm inflicted upon women in the excluded class is grievous. As the Court's comparison of the differing forms of the Hyde Amendment that have been enacted since 1976 demonstrates, the Court expressly approves the exclusion of benefits in "instances where severe and long lasting physical health damage to the mother" is the predictable consequence of carrying the pregnancy to term. Indeed, as the Solicitor General acknowledged with commendable candor, the logic of the Court's position would justify a holding that it would be constitutional to deny funding to a medically and financially needy person

451

even if abortion were the only lifesaving medical procedure available. Because a denial of benefits for medically necessary abortions inevitably causes serious harm to the excluded women, it is tantamount to severe punishment. In my judgment, that denial cannot be justified unless Government may, in effect, punish women who want abortions. But as the Court unequivocally held in Roe v Wade, this the Government may not do. . . .

· · ·

Having decided to alleviate some of the hardships of poverty by providing necessary medical care, the Government must use neutral criteria in distributing benefits. It may not deny benefits to a financially and medically needy person simply because he is a Republican, a Catholic, or an Oriental—or because he has spoken against a program the Government has a legitimate interest in furthering. In sum, it may not create exceptions for the sole purpose of furthering a governmental interest that is constitutionally subordinate to the individual interest that the entire program was designed to protect. The Hyde amendments not only exclude financially and medically needy persons from the pool of benefits for a constitutionally insufficient reason; they also require the expenditure of millions and millions of dollars in order to thwart the exercise of a constitutional right, thereby effectively inflicting serious and long lasting harm on impoverished women who want and need abortions for valid medical reasons. In my judgment, these amendments constitute an unjustifiable, and indeed blatant, violation of the sovereign's duty to govern impartially.

I respectfully dissent.

Proposed Amendments to the Constitution

Three proposed amendments to the Constitution concerning abortion follow. The first is a "states' rights" type, the second the "human life" variety, and the third is an example of the most general type possible.

· · ·

Senate Joint Resolution 110, 97th Congress, 2nd Session: A right to abortion is not secured by this Constitution. The Congress and the several

States shall have the concurrent power to restrict and prohibit abortions: *Provided*, that a law of a State which is more restrictive than a law of Congress shall govern.

. . .

Senate Joint Resolution 17, 97th Congress, 2nd Session: Section 1. With respect to the right to life, the word 'person,' as used in this article and in the fifth and fourteenth articles of amendment to the Constitution of the United States, applies to all human beings, irrespective of age, health, function, or condition of dependency, including their unborn offspring at every stage of their biological development.

Section 2. No unborn person shall be deprived of life by any person; *Provided, however,* that nothing in this article shall prohibit a law permitting only those medical procedures required to prevent the death of the mother.

. . .

Senate Joint Resolution 19, 97th Congress, 2nd Session: The paramount right to life is vested in each human being from the moment of fertilization without regard to age, health, or condition of dependency.

Senate Bill 158 (Human Life Statute)

Section 1. The Congress finds that present day scientific evidence indicates a significant likelihood that actual human life exists from conception.

The Congress further finds that the fourteenth amendment to the Constitution of the United States was intended to protect all human beings.

Upon the basis of these findings, and in the exercise of the powers of Congress, including its power under section five of the fourteenth amendment to the Constitution of the United States, the Congress hereby declares that for the purpose of enforcing the obligation of the States under the fourteenth amendment not to deprive persons of life without due process of law, human life shall be deemed to exist from conception, without regard to race, sex, age, health, defect, or condition of dependency;

and for this purpose 'person' shall include all human life as defined herein.

Section 2. Notwithstanding any other provision of law, no inferior Federal court ordained and established by Congress under Article III of the Constitution of the United States shall have jurisdiction to issue any restraining order, temporary or permanent injunction, or declaratory judgment in any case involving or arising from any State law or municipal ordinance that (1) protects the rights of human persons between conception and birth, or (2) prohibits, limits, or regulates (a) the performance of abortions or (b) the provision at public expense of funds, facilities, personnel, or other assistance for the performance of abortions.

EPILOGUE

In these chapters, we have dealt with a dynamic institution that is only part of an equally dynamic political process. It is difficult to draw final conclusions about the issues discussed here. Decisions made in the upcoming Court term, statutes adopted by the next Congress, changes in the makeup of the Court, and a variety of other influences easily could change some of the generalizations made in earlier chapters. In addition, we have dealt with matters of constitutional interpretation; statutory interpretation cases in five other areas of the law could lead to different conclusions. Most importantly, social scientists know that conclusions based on a limited number of observations are no more than tentative and therefore subject to later modification.

Nevertheless, some propositions have a fair degree of validity. These decisions and the reactions to them give us an idea of conditions under which the Supreme Court is most effective in making policy or, at least, when the Court's efforts will draw a minimum of fire from other policymakers. The loser will be unhappy about any Supreme Court decision, and the Court's insistence on taking cases that have applicability beyond the immediate parties to the litigation ensures that others also will be threatened by a particular decision. If these affected persons are politically powerless or largely indifferent to the outcome, the Court will not encounter much opposition. Rarely, however, are those affected by a decision powerless, indifferent, or quiescent. Policy decisions by the Court almost always generate opposition; it may vary in intensity depending on the perceived immediacy of the threat, the number of persons who believe that they will be affected, the importance they place on their preferred policy, and the extent to which they already are organized or can organize to express their opposition. These four factors interact to such an extent that it is difficult to separate them even for analytical purposes; however, some illustrations can be offered.

A host of interest groups exist and maintain Washington offices to monitor governmental activity and to mobilize their memberships in the event of danger. None of these groups is monolithic, and a division among their memberships may make reaction to a court decision impossible.

455

Nonetheless, they are present, alert, and skilled in making their opinions known. Such a group does not even need to be in existence before the decision is made; the speed with which Right to Life groups sprang into being after *Roe* suggests that an immediate threat can rapidly propel an opposition organization into existence. Any group faced with a threat will mobilize as many allies as possible by first alerting them to threats that could spread to the ally's interests. An ally, in this context, includes the general public. The size of a group—even its very existence—is not an adequate indicator of the amount of opposition it can generate. For example, the media was moderately successful in its attempts to draw the entire public to its side by its reporting after the decision in *Gannett*. This discussion of groups does not mean that the general public cannot or will not express opposition to a decision without the benefit of a formal organization, but usually a group will focus that opposition.

A first set of generalizations emerges. The more immediate or direct the threat to the person's or group's interests, the more vigorous the response will be. The greater the value placed by the person or group on that interest, the more intense the reaction will be. The larger the group that feels threatened is, the stronger the opposition to the decision will be. The corollary of this last point is equally true; the larger the court's supporting constituency is, the more difficult it will be to attack it. The school desegregation cases illustrate these propositions. The initial *Brown* decision did not threaten values or practices except in a single region, and the negative reaction was largely confined to that same section of the country. The number of persons threatened was smaller than the number of persons who were indifferent or approving, and efforts to halt the Court's decision were localized. But *Swann, Keyes,* and their progeny began to threaten a greater number of people in other regions of the country and also began to challenge a highly prized value—neighborhood schools. Opposition to the Court's actions grew rapidly, and by 1972 Congress was at least thinking about corrective measures and thinking about them seriously.

These school cases are illustrative of another generalization. Some decisions, initially, are quite acceptable to a large segment of the population; but if the basic principle of the decision is expanded to cover more situations, the pool of opposition will grow and, perhaps, grow at a faster rate than the expansion of the principle. This is most likely true when the applicability of the basic decision is broadened rapidly. Groups and individuals have less chance to grow accustomed to and anticipate the possibility of change. Reapportionment is an example of a rapidly developing issue area where the Court may have been saved from a more successful opposition only because the electorate was divided, with the majority believing that benefits could be derived from supporting the Court. But as a general rule, rapid development and expansion of a doctrine breeds more resistance than does slow and incremental development.

The effects of these two different types of decisions are closely related. The "bomb-shell" decision that arises with no warning or buildup should generate more resistance than a new policy announced after careful preparation of the parties to be affected. People do not like to be surprised, and they react accordingly. *Engel* v. *Vitale*, 370 U.S. 421 (1962), struck down an officially prescribed school prayer in New York and paved the way for the *Schempp* decision a year later. So effective was the signal given in *Engel* that some church groups warned their members that the second decision would soon arrive. On the other hand, *Roe* v. *Wade* arrived without any national warning or opportunity to build up acceptance of the policy change. Despite the fact that the school prayer issue is still alive in Congress, the reaction to *Roe* must be considered the more vigorous of the two. The manner in which the decision was made is not the sole difference between the two, but it was a major contributory factor.

Most of these generalizations can be applied to other policymakers—national, state, and local officials—but in some ways these policymakers need to be considered separately. Interest groups and the general public make their displeasure over a court decision known, but it most often will be by way of the other actors in the political system. Officials may respond to the cries of persons outside the formal process, anticipate the reaction and try to lead it, or see their own interests challenged by a decision. Before deciding whether or at what level to respond, officials must consider the political importance of the constituents or clienteles that are hurt, the degree of unrest manifested, and the threat to the legislature, administrative agency, or executive branch. In general, the more aggrieved clients or constituents are, the more likely officials are to react to a decision. Alternatively, the more value placed on the threatened program by the officials themselves, the more likely they are to move to obtain a modification of the decision—even if public outcry is rather muted. It is worth noting that a single unit of the bureaucracy, because of its narrower range of concerns, is more likely than the president or Congress to react to a decision either in self-defense or in response to the concerns of clients. This is true even though that reaction may be less noticeable to the public than one from the White House or Capitol Hill.

One major distinction between government officials and the public is that officials have the means to make the Court concretely aware of their displeasure over a particular decision. The public can make a lot of noise, but members of Congress can introduce legislation or constitutional amendments, bureaucrats can frustrate implementation of the Court's policy, and the president can appoint persons to the Court to bring about changes. These are not the only means available to officials, but they are more substantive than what the public can do. Officials must keep in mind, however, that they, interest groups, and the general public will need the Court at some future date to legitimize a policy, and they cannot afford to destroy, seriously weaken, or permanently alienate it on a single issue. The political process is a system of perpetually shifting alliances and today's opponent may be tomorrow's ally.

All five issue areas examined in this book illustrate the importance of societal values as a determinant of the reaction to the Court's decisions. The American people say that they believe in majority rule and in fair trials for the criminally accused. The reapportionment and free press-fair trial decisions came under less fire by implementing these values than the desegregation, abortion, and death penalty decisions, where public consensus was almost completely lacking. Marshall's assertions in *Marbury* may have been saved from reversal because they appeared to be no more than a simple restatement of the accepted constitutional values of separation of powers and checks and balances. Court decisions based on widely shared values are more acceptable than decisions that run counter to those values or that take sides between hotly contested value positions.

The general values prevalent in society can be used by the courts in their policymaking, but the Constitution is an even better beginning point. The public feels that judges are supposed to understand and apply the Constitution as a part of their ordinary behavior. Running public opinion polls is not thought of as a standard judicial practice. The free press-fair trial decisions suggest that judicial policymakers will be in a stronger position if the language of the part of the Constitution they rely upon is precise and clear. Constitutional imprecision weakens the Court's position. Criticism of the Court's ability to find in the Constitution a right to privacy comprehensive and clear enough to support the abortion decisions is a case in point. It also may be that when the Court is implementing relatively clear constitutional provisions, fewer of its members will find it necessary to dissent and proclaim that the majority is making law. Unanimity is a great assist to effectiveness in Court decisions; a decision by a divided Court leaves room for doubt, confusion, argument, and evasion. *Brown* would not have been as effective as it was had the Court not been unanimous in its decision.

A broader question about values and beliefs still needs to be presented. Can the courts create values or build a consensus for a particular set of them? The materials herein are not conclusive, but the answer appears to be "no." Courts, like other makers of public policy, are better *reflectors* of values and attitudes than *creators* of them. This is not to say that courts are impotent—they are not—but it is to say that they are not very effective when they try to change attitudes too rapidly, or try to resist changes in values for too long. "The secret root from which the law draws all the juices of life," Justice Holmes reminds us, is "consideration of what is expedient for the community concerned." [1] Indeed, it is possible to argue that the Court should remove itself from disputes in which values are in sharp conflict and allow them to be settled in another forum. This prudent argument is answered by the contention that while the Court may not be able to resolve an issue, it can help to crystallize it and contribute to, or even lead, the public discussion of the problem. History suggests that a more activist Court runs the risk of becoming engaged in serious combat on too many fronts at once and may suffer a diminution in its ability to participate in the policy process; the overly prudent Court may allow its powers to atrophy until they become unusable. Each judge and student of the Court will balance these considerations in different ways and come to different conclusions about the Court's proper role.

Some narrower generalizations also may be drawn from these materials. When the Court is prescribing procedures to be followed, as in the fair trial decisions, it is on stronger ground than when it is telling some other policymaker the substantive policy that must be followed (as in the abortion cases) or when it is setting down substantive remedies (as in the desegregation cases). This proposition also may apply to reapportionment, for there the Court merely was giving legislators the one-person, one-vote, formula and letting them apply it. The implied threat was that the courts would do the reapportioning by the formula if the legislators would or could not. Of course, prescribing procedure for other courts to follow is even easier than prescribing it for other actors in the process. This generalization cannot be pushed too far. Donald L. Horowitz of the Smithsonian Institution's Research Institute on Immigration and Ethnic Studies has concluded that extension to state criminal proceedings of the rule banning introduction of improperly seized evidence (*Mapp* v. *Ohio,* 367 U.S. 643, 1960) was to a degree ineffective because the justices misconceived the nature of the criminal justice system in the states. Horowitz found that the nature of the plea bargaining process changed, making the exclusion of illegally seized evidence unnecessary. [2] Using court procedure to affect police behavior did not work effectively in this instance, but in the fair trial cases prescribing court procedure to affect court behavior did. We can hypothesize, then, that the Court will be more effective when its instructions are directed to the participating actor rather than to some third party who, in turn, must deal

459

with the primary actor or change the environment in which he or she operates.

The equal protection cases point up one of the greatest weaknesses of judicial policymaking: it is slow and incremental. The lapse in time between *Brown* II (1955) and the demand for desegregation plans that "promise realistically to work now" in *Green* (1968) was 13 years. The reaction time is painfully slow because the Court lacks a "self-starter," a means of systematic oversight once a decision is made, and a way to solve the issue without generating new litigation in each separate jurisdiction. This inability to follow through quickly is a serious, and perhaps desirable, hindrance to the effectiveness of judicial policymaking.

The equal protection record since *Swann* also illustrates the incremental nature of the judicial process. A legislature could have handled the same situation much more expeditiously once it had decided that school integration was appropriate public policy. The legislature could have required by statute that each school board apply some sort of racial balance formula in every school. The problem would have been solved, except for enforcement in the courts by civil and criminal sanctions for noncompliance. But the Court has had to look at each district individually, determine whether segregative intent was present *(Keyes)*, worry over whether the amount of busing was excessive either in time or in burden placed on one of the groups involved, and decline to adopt cross-district remedies that could be mandated by a legislature *(Millikin)*. The courts also needed to maintain a legal principle in the face of concern over "white flight" and its effect on quality education. In short, the courts are not well suited to making policy requiring widespread and long-term managment. Case by case determinations, characteristic of the common law, are the courts' only available tool, but whether they are the best of all possible tools is doubtful. This, in turn, raises the question of whether courts should even try to be primary policymakers in areas where their methods are not the best suited to a resolution of the problem.

A tentative, nonjudicial generalization also emerges from these materials. Congress may have the means to overturn or alter Supreme Court rulings, but that power is not exercised except in a small number of instances. The political reasons for this are fairly obvious. It is difficult to get a majority together in each house of Congress for a simple statutory assault on the Court, and it is even harder to collect the extraordinary majority required for a constitutional amendment. In addition to the political factors, it must be remembered that the symbolic role of the Court still affects the attitudes of both the public and the policymakers in other branches. The relative lack of regular conflict between the Court and Congress is also partially explained by the short attention spans both Congress and the public have on most issues. [3]

A recapitulation to this point might be useful. On occasion, the lack of public consensus on values ensures that the courts' effectiveness will be limited because no agreement exists on the direction public policy should take. Other instances exist where the tools available to all judges are inadequate or inappropriate to resolve the problems presented. Under these circumstances, a prudent court might wish to consider remaining on the fringe of the policymaking process, but these same circumstances also are those under which persons ask the court to intervene and solve the issue. The judges are thus firmly impaled on the horns of a dilemma.

One final observation. The materials in this casebook, with the exception of those in Chapter I, are drawn from the Warren and Burger eras. It would have been possible to use earlier material, but modernity seemed preferable to historical sweep. Had the older materials been included, another generalization would have emerged: the style of judicial policymaking has changed since 1937 along with the Court's oversight of economic policy. John Marshall's nationalizing decisions and the Court's *laissez-faire* holdings from 1890 to 1937 marked the Court's effort to stem the tide of legislative action by saying "no" to new departures. The Court's "no's" came too frequently and got the justices into trouble in 1937. Nonetheless, the Court was able to deal systematically with threats to the established order and demonstrated clearly that the case-by-case approach works well as a defense mechanism against change.

In sharp contrast, the Warren and Burger Courts have become activist by doing more than merely reacting to primary decisions made elsewhere in the system. This role change—with the courts having greater involvement in the day-to-day operation of other institutions of society—has placed strains on and exposed weaknesses in the judicial policymaking process. Those strains have led to greater criticism of the Court, to more efforts to curb or circumvent its decisions, and to potentially less effective judicial involvement in the policymaking process.

It must be added, however, that some of the Court's troubles are not of its own making. Legislators and executives, by adopting policies that are not fully thought out or that contain contradictory premises, "pass the buck" to courts with some regularity. The affirmative action decisions may be the result of congressional unwillingness to specify the means to be used to accomplish a desired result. Legislators and executives also tend to ignore problems in the hope that they will go away; this was surely the case with those states that had not reapportioned their legislatures since the turn of the century. The sex discrimination cases are another illustration of legislative refusal to recognize a problem. When legislative ambiguity or legislative inaction exist, individuals or groups are practically forced to turn to the courts for a determination of their status under the law. Obviously, the loser in one part of the political process will try to prevail in another forum. Added to these considerations is a tendency that must never be forgotten—Americans are a litigious people who often equate wisdom with legality. As Toqueville observed, "Scarcely any political question arises in the United States that is not resolved, sooner or later, into a judicial question." [4] The wonder is, therefore, not that courts are activist from time to time, but that they are not more activist all of the time.

When all is said and done, judges, for the most part, understand and recognize the limitations on judicial policymaking; they only occasionally have to be reminded, as Justice Harlan F. Stone did in *United States* v. *Butler,* that "courts are not the only agency of government that must be assumed to have capacity to govern." [5] The fact that the basic political power of the courts asserted in *Marbury* is still intact, despite regular assaults on it, indicates a long-term approval of the courts' role in policymaking that is punctuated by short-term disagreement with certain decisions. Whether that state of affairs will continue depends upon the degree to which judges continue to heed Justice Stone's admonition.

NOTES

1. Oliver Wendell Holmes, *The Common Law* (Boston: Little, Brown & Co., 1881), p. 35.
2. *The Courts and Social Policy* (Washington, D.C.: Brookings Institution, 1977), Chap. 6.
3. See Walter F. Murphy, *Congress and the Court* (Chicago: University of Chicago Press, 1962).
4. Alexis de Tocqueville, *Democracy in America,* Phillips Bradley trans. (New York: Vintage, 1960), Vol. 1, p. 290.
5. Justice Harlan F. Stone dissenting in *United States* v. *Butler,* 297 U.S. 1 (1936), at 87.